Social History &
African Environments

Edited by

WILLIAM BEINART

Professor of Race Relations, University of Oxford

&

JoANN McGREGOR

Lecturer in Human Geography, University of Reading

James Currey
OXFORD

Ohio University Press
ATHENS

David Philip
CAPE TOWN

PUBLISHED IN COLLABORATION WITH
THE OHIO UNIVERSITY PRESS ECOLOGY AND HISTORY SERIES

James Currey Ltd
73 Botley Road
Oxford OX2 0BS
www.jamescurrey.co.uk

Ohio University Press
Scott Quadrangle
Athens
Ohio 45701

David Philip Publisher
An imprint of New Africa Books (Pty) Ltd
99 Garfield Rd
Claremont 7700, Cape Town

© James Currey Ltd, 2003
First published 2003

1 2 3 4 5 07 06 05 04 03

ISBN 0-85255-951-8 (James Currey cloth)
ISBN 0-85255-950-X (James Currey paper)
ISBN 0-8214-1537-9 (Ohio University Press cloth)
ISBN 0-8214-1538-7 (Ohio University Press paper)

British Library Cataloguing in Publication Data
Social history & African environments. - (The Ohio University Press ecology and
history series)
1. Human ecology - Africa - History 2. Environmental policy -
Africa - History 3. Africa - Environmental aspects - History
4. Africa - Social conditions
I. Beinart, William   II. McGregor, JoAnn
333.7'096

Library of Congress Cataloging-in-Publication Data
available on request

Typeset in 10/11 pt Times by Long House, Cumbria, UK
Printed and bound in Great Britain by
Woolnough, Irthingborough

Contents

Notes on Contributors

William Beinart is Professor of Race Relations at the University of Oxford. He has published widely on South Africa and is completing a book provisionally entitled the *Rise of Conservation in South Africa*.

David Bunn is Director of Arts at the University of Witwatersrand. He has published widely on southern African landscapes.

Jane Carruthers is Senior Lecturer in the Department of History at the University of South Africa. She has published widely on South African environmental history. Her books include *The Kruger National Park: A Social and Political History* (Pietermaritzburg, University of Natal Press, 1995) and *Wildlife and Warfare: The Life of James Stevenson-Hamilton* (Pietermaritzburg, University of Natal Press, 2001).

Grace Carswell is Leverhulme Special Research Fellow at the University of Sussex. Her doctoral research was on the agricultural history of Kigezi, southwestern Uganda and she is currently undertaking further work on livelihood change in the area. Her interests include rural livelihoods in eastern Africa, population environment interactions and agricultural change under the influence of colonialism.

Robert Gordon teaches anthropology at the University of Vermont. He has published widely on Namibia and is currently developing a comparative perspective on the former mandates of New Guinea and South-West Africa, to be published as a book.

Emmanuel Kreike is Assistant Professor of African and Environmental History and Director of the African Studies Program at Princeton University. His revised Yale University PhD thesis on socio-environmental destruction and reconstruction in Ovamboland will be published by Heinemann.

John McCracken is Honorary Senior Research Fellow, University of Sterling. He has published extensively on Central Africa and is currently completing a history of Malawi under the British.

JoAnn McGregor is Lecturer in Human Geography, University of Reading. She is co-author (with Jocelyn Alexander and Terence Ranger) of *Violence and Memory: One hundred years in the 'dark forests' of Matabeleland* (James Currey, 2000) and is currently working on the politics of landscape ideas in the Zambezi Valley.

Karen Middleton holds a Nuffield Foundation fellowship at Oxford University. She has carried out extensive fieldwork in southern Madagascar. She is the author of a number of articles on kinship, gender, and ritual, and is the editor of *Ancestors, Power, and History in Madagascar* (Brill, 1999). She is currently researching the environmental history of southern Madagascar.

Innocent Pikirayi is Senior Lecturer in Archaeology in the Department of History at the University of Zimbabwe. He has published widely on Zimbabwean archaeology, including studies of the historical archaeology of the Mutapa State, and the Zimbabwe culture from the early second millennium to the late nineteenth century. His current research also includes projects on the dynamics of state formation and human responses and contributions to environmental change.

Terence Ranger is Emeritus Professor at St Antony's College, Oxford, and until recently Visiting Professor at the University of Zimbabwe. He has written extensively on Zimbabwean history, especially on religion and landscape.

Sandra Swart is a hybrid of environmental historian and social historian. She received both a DPhil in history and MSc in Environmental Change from the University of Oxford. She is currently lecturing at the University of Stellenbosch, where she is researching the history of the horse and horse-based society in southern Africa.

Helen Tilley is Assistant Professor in the History Department at Princeton University where she is affiliated with the History of Science and African Studies programs. Her research concentrates on the history of environmental, medical, and anthropological scientists active in colonial Africa. She has recently completed an introduction to a new edition of W. Allan, *The African Husbandman*.

Ingrid Yngstrom is currently a research consultant and previously held a junior research fellowship in Oxford. Her doctoral research was a study of the social dynamics of landholding and related policy issues in Tanzania with a gender focus.

Preface

This book arises from a conference entitled 'African Environments: Past and Present', convened by William Beinart, Richard Grove and JoAnn McGregor and held at St Antony's College, University of Oxford in July 1999. It was sponsored largely by the *Journal of Southern African Studies* (*JSAS*), with additional assistance from St Antony's College, the University of Oxford and the Department of Geography, University of Reading. Over 90 papers were presented at the conference; a majority focused on southern Africa but other parts of the continent, especially East Africa, were also well represented. The focus of this volume is on southern, central and eastern Africa.

African environmental history, as the conference demonstrated, has become a thriving field of study closely linked with other branches of African studies. Such a large gathering, with participants from many different countries and disciplinary backgrounds, provided a fascinating cross-section of current work. Important dialogues developed between historians, social scientists, geographers and – to a limited extent – natural scientists. The conference also provided an ideal opportunity for reflection on how topics, approaches and interpretations had changed since interest in the history of the African environment began to flourish in the early 1980s. Continuities, changes and conflicts in the field are reflected in this volume.

This collection should be read in conjunction with a special issue of *JSAS*, vol. 26, no. 4 (2000), which also arose out of the conference.[1] The *JSAS* collection is primarily focused on the southern African region, whereas here we cover a broader geographical range. The *JSAS* collection also has greater interdisciplinary representation, and includes some papers more centrally concerned with policy debates. In this book, the papers reflect broad-ranging historical and cultural perspectives discussed at the conference. Our aim has been to include chapters that cover most of the major historical themes addressed. However, material from some of the panels is largely absent from both this volume and the *JSAS* issue because the papers are included in other collections: one on long-term environmental change and archaeological methods,

[1] Edited jointly by members of the *JSAS* Board who participated in the conference: Jo Beall, William Beinart, JoAnn McGregor, Debby Potts and David Simon (eds), 'African Environments: Past and Present', *Journal of Southern African Studies*, 26, 4 (2000).

with particular focus on East Africa;[2] another on contemporary debates over environmental justice, focusing on South Africa.[3] Taken together, these publications reflect the diversity of African environmental studies and also chart important new directions. We hope they will stimulate further research in this exciting new field.

[2] See Mats Widgren and John Sutton (eds), *Islands of Intensive Agriculture in the East African Rift and Highlands: A 500 year perspective*. Working Paper No. 43. Environment and Development Studies Unit, University of Stockholm, 1999.

[3] David Macdonald (ed.), *Environmental Justice in South Africa*, (Athens OH, Ohio University Press, 2002).

Introduction

WILLIAM BEINART & JoANN McGREGOR

The explosion of interest in African environmental history has resulted in a rich new literature. In part this reflects an urgent need to revisit debates over the historical transformation of African landscapes in the light of mounting economic, political and moral argument about the fate of the continent's wildlife, forest, pasture and water resources. Not only has 'the environment' become one of the most contentious topics in current African and global politics, but historical arguments have also been central to the different strands in this debate.

Starkly different views of African environmental history have been canvassed. On the one hand, it has been widely asserted in scientific, popular and historical literature that negative environmental trends characterise the recent African past. Images of retreating forests, eroding soils, dessicating water resources and species extinctions abound. Such 'declinist' arguments have sometimes been reinforced by a powerful representation of Africa's past as a pristine or barely exploited wilderness.

On the other hand, a new paradigm has been developed recently which profoundly questions judgments made about environmental degradation.[1] It suggests that much environmental damage has been caused by colonial intervention, but that, even when under considerable stress, African rural societies have managed their interaction with nature constructively and often beneficially.[2] In this context, both sympathetic social scientists and local African leaders have called upon history in a different way. They emphasise the salience and validity of local knowledge and indigenous peoples' rights over their resources. Some claim a continuous tradition of living close to the land and, to a degree, in harmony with nature.

While exploration of local knowledge has largely been pursued by social scientists and historians, those within scientific disciplines have also been deeply divided about how to judge and measure environmental change. One example can be found in range ecology, a field of particular importance in African environmental history because so much of the continent has been, and remains, open pasture. Old orthodoxies saw heavy

---

[1] See, for example, M. Leach and R. Mearns (eds), *The Lie of the Land: Challenging received wisdom on the African environment* (Oxford, James Currey, 1996).

[2] For a recent review, William Beinart, 'African History and Environmental History', *African Affairs* 99, 395 (2000), pp. 269–302.

grazing pressure by livestock as inevitably causing unidirectional and undesirable degradation – or deviation from an optimum balance of plant species.[3] Radical range ecologists have fundamentally questioned this view. They suggest that scientists will seek in vain for a stable ecological balance in any particular context and see disequilibrium as central to ecological history.

Similarly, they suggest that it is difficult to regulate successfully the use of pastures by livestock because outcomes are unpredictable: climate and rainfall, as much as human intervention, tend to shape the richness and value of pastures. Rapid changes in the numbers of livestock, as well as movement, so characteristic of stock-keeping practices in Africa, facilitate the recovery of rangelands, though they do not necessarily restore them to earlier balances. Whereas older views provided the intellectual justification for interventionist policies to regulate the human use of rangelands, the new range ecology advocates great caution and provides an analytical template for a minimalist approach by the state. This approach, in turn, has been criticised for giving unjustified legitimacy to overstocking and for its 'negative impact on conservation science in Africa'.[4]

Many contributors to these debates have sought not only to explain environmental change, but also to attribute historical responsibility for it. They have made implicit and explicit claims about who best understands African environments, and who should have the right to control them – whether scientists, national governments or local people. Such arguments have become centrally important as bases for intervention, conservation and regulation. Environmentalists sometimes emphasise, especially in more popular discussions, responsibility to future generations for the well-being of the planet and its plant and animal resources.[5] Africanists, by contrast, sometimes see access to resources as the critical issue for communities and suggest that the very dependence of poor people on natural resources is likely to result in cautious usage.

All such approaches imply both historical investigation and historical judgment. These contested ideas also increasingly demand that we stand back from today's perceptions and debates about degradation. They call for an examination of the moral and cultural filters though which concepts about the natural world have been passed in different times and places. In this book, we consider new work that approaches these relationships in different ways. While all chapters are informed by recent environmental debates, this is not a book about policy. By tailoring historical narratives too closely to current ideological and policy debates, the specificity and contexts of past ideas about African environments and their management can be eclipsed. Our argument is not against scientific methods or policy prescriptions. On the contrary, the integration of scientific, historical and social science approaches is essential for an understanding of environmental change, and for strategies of regulation. Rather, the essays

---

[3] R. Behnke, I. Scoones and C. Kerven (eds), *Range Ecology at Disequilibrium* (London, ODI, 1993); I. Scoones (ed.), *Living with Uncertainty: New directions in pastoral development in Africa* (London, Intermediate Technology Publications, 1994). Recent responses, which challenge the new approaches, include A. W. Illius and T.G. O'Connor, 'On the Relevance of Nonequilibrium Concepts to Arid and Semiarid Grazing Systems', *Ecological Applications* 9, 3 (1999), pp. 798–813; C.A.M. Attwell and F.D.P. Cotterill, 'Postmodernism and African Conservation Science', *Biodiversity and Conservation* 9 (2000), pp. 559–77.

[4] Attwell and Cotterill, 'Postmodernism', p. 559.

[5] For example, Lloyd Timberlake, *Africa in Crisis: The causes, the cures of environmental bankruptcy* (London, Earthscan, 1985); Paul Harrison, *The Greening of Africa* (Harmondsworth, Penguin, 1987).

illuminate ideas about nature, about environmental interventions, and about past practices which remain key elements in building towards a more comprehensive analysis of the relationship between people and nature. We need to know about these ideas and practices in order to discuss historical legacies, to evaluate past regulation, and to grasp the fervour with which present positions are held.

The purpose of this volume is to capture some of the diversity of themes and approaches to the current study of African environments. We have divided the book's chapters into thematic sections: i) African environmental ideas and practices; ii) colonial science, state policy and African responses; and iii) settler culture and ideas about landscape and nature. We believe that the essays in each section present challenging new directions of investigation. Before spelling out how the essays contribute to debate in each of these three areas, let us first tease out some of the volume's overarching themes and emphases.

Firstly, *Social History and African Environments* brings together new work that develops the social and cultural dimensions of environmental history. The contributions reflect the way the field has expanded and diversified in recent years; recent volumes on Tanzania and on African landscapes have been especially valuable in this respect.[6] As we elaborate further below, the surge of interest in African environmental history since the 1970s was situated firmly within Africanist social history. Some of the essays here revisit themes which have been well developed in the literature since that time, such as African strategies of environmental management, the politics of colonial conservationism and African resistance to intervention. Others address new topics and suggest new directions of enquiry. Even those chapters revisiting old themes do so in the light of intellectual changes since the 1970s. They bring new perspectives and sources to bear on familiar topics.

Secondly, the chapters in the collection offer new perspectives on the relationship between Africans, colonial officials, settlers and scientists. In so doing they modify some of the interpretive conventions of Africanist scholarship. We have decided to include several chapters on settlers, scientists and colonial policy not only because the research on these topics has cut new ground, but because their impact on African lives, livelihoods and landscapes has been enormous, particularly in the former settler colonies of southern and eastern Africa. It is a weakness of past writings that indigenous and scientific, African and settler ideas are often considered separately. John Iliffe, in his overview *Africans*, argues that one of the major contributions of Africans to global history was to inhabit, and make usable, some of the most difficult environments in the world.[7] White settlers, assisted by colonial scientists, continued that process, greatly intensifying production in some intractable areas such as the Karoo and Namibian semi-arid zones, as well as through the irrigation schemes that have transformed lowveld and other environments throughout the continent. The environments of the South African, Zimbabwean and Kenyan highveld were changed

---

[6] Gregory Maddox, James Giblin and Isaria N. Kimambo (eds), *Custodians of the Land: Ecology and culture in the history of Tanzania* (London, James Currey, 1996); Ute Luig and Achim von Oppen (eds), *The Making of African Landscapes*, special issue of *Paideuma: Mitteilungen zur Kulturkunde,* 43 (1997). With respect to southern African, Terence Ranger, *Voices from the Rocks: Nature, culture and history in the Matopos Hills of Zimbabwe* (Oxford, James Currey, 1999); Jocelyn Alexander, JoAnn McGregor and Terence Ranger, *Violence and Memory: One hundred years in the 'Dark Forests' of Matabeleland* (James Currey, Oxford, 2000).

[7] John Iliffe, *Africans: The history of a continent* (Cambridge, CUP, 1995).

profoundly in the course of settler occupation and the development of capitalist production regimes. There were costs to such dominance, in both social and environmental terms. But these have been central processes in African environmental history that required a rapid accretion of knowledge and technique, as well as substantial financial and intellectual investment. Whilst the labour regimes and dispossession that accompanied white settlement have quite rightly attracted much attention, the essays collected here suggest that there are new questions to be asked about environmental change and environmental knowledge in the colonial period.

Some chapters suggest a more open approach to scientific discoveries. They show evidence of a retreat from the blanket condemnations of colonial science sometimes made in Africanist literature in the past. The new environmental knowledge acquired in colonial contexts was not developed and applied in settler contexts alone; it also contributed to the transformation of African agriculture and environmental practice, and sometimes built on African practices. Although each body of knowledge and practice may have its own distinctive historical and cultural memories on which to draw, all have developed in mutual interaction. At different historical moments they have borrowed from, incorporated or rejected elements drawn from one another. Although the chapters on settler ideas are grouped separately in the text, these interactions are addressed in a number of papers in this volume.

Thirdly, the volume includes significant contributions on landscape history and ideas about nature, particularly regarding the relationship between landscape and identity. Notwithstanding a long tradition of studying landscape within the discipline of geography, it is only recently that this topic has been explicitly addressed in African social and environmental history. In the past, many historians of Africa were reluctant to use the term 'landscape' because they felt it to be too firmly associated with a particular European tradition of seeing, related to the emergence of specific property relations and artistic expression, and therefore inappropriate for other contexts. Yet by defining 'landscape' broadly, as an imaginative construction of the environment, new areas of investigation have opened up for Africanists. The notion of landscape has provided a valuable means of bringing together discussion of material changes in the environment, with imaginative interpretations – a combination that should stand at the heart of environmental history.

Several chapters in the volume explore how ideas about landscape have provided a source of social unity in different times and places, and have been instrumental in the forging of new notions of nation and identity. Africans categorised themselves, and were categorised by others (whether neighbouring African groups or colonial officials) as river people, mountain people, plains people, cattle people and so on. The importance of such categorisations, and their relationship to other ethnic designations, has not been fully discussed in the rich Africanist literature on constructions of ethnicity, and deserves further attention.[8] Such identities and their relationship to landscape are not fixed. They may lose their importance as conditions change, linked to processes of urbanisation and modernisation. Or they can become more important; as they cease to be statements about actual relations with the environment, so they can take on a new life as powerful symbols in collective memory, or as a commercialised understanding of rural 'heritage'.

[8] See, however, T. Spear and R. Waller, *Being Maasai: Ethnicity and identity in East Africa* (London, James Currey, 1993); M. Wagner, '"Nature in the Mind": in Early Twentieth Century Buha, W. Tanzania', in Maddox et al., *Custodians of the Land*.

Landscape ideas were also important in constructions of settler identity. For example, settlers from diverse backgrounds could be invited to unite around a love of 'wilderness' or an idealised rural background. Politicians could invoke landscape as the foundation for an inclusive South African settler identity that would unite both British and Afrikaner settlers. But although landscape ideas could help present organic unifying visions, they have often hidden divided realities, or helped to create new boundaries between groups defined by origin, or race, or ethnicity, or gender. Claims to land, or identification by people with a particular region, typically have had such divisive potential. They may begin with an apparent rhetorical inclusiveness, but frequently also exclude. In the current southern African context such ideas about relations with the land have been newly politicised and increasingly moralised – revealing both their unifying and divisive potential.

In Zimbabwe, Robert Mugabe has reasserted the authenticity of African relations with the land to justify his programme of forcible occupation and redistribution, but in so doing has excluded whites from any legitimate place in the landscape, along with a much larger population of farmworkers of Mozambican and Malawian extraction, as well as other 'enemies of the revolution'. The chaotic and hasty process of redistributing the land has reinvigorated debate about imaginative links to particular pieces of land, mountains, rivers and ancestral graves. While some have gained enhanced access to land, new tensions and conflicts have been produced, which are now reverberating throughout southern and eastern Africa. Although the land restitution process in South Africa has, thus far, been very different, it has also, in some contexts, lent power to collective definitions by self-defined 'communities' of ties to the land. Intellectuals involved in such ideological assertions can also, in some contexts, construct environmentally deterministic interpretations of history. In the light of these political processes and the debates surrounding them, it has become increasingly relevant to explore the historical links between environment, landscape ideas and collective identities.

Fourth, this volume brings together writing based on a novel range of sources. Environmental history has a long tradition of interdisciplinary connections and has built on interactions between history, geography, anthropology, archaeology and the natural sciences. Recently, however, environmental historians have also begun to engage with ideas and approaches developed in cultural studies and literary criticism. In the past, a collection of essays on environmental history would have drawn on archival research, oral history and detailed field investigations of environmental practices. In this volume, such sources and methods are combined with explorations of African concepts, myths and legends, literary narratives and other texts, landscape perceptions, as well as colonial and wildlife photography. Such sources bring the fields of social or cultural history and African environmental history together in new ways.

Fifth, this diversification of sources has been accompanied by the elaboration of new social and cultural perspectives on environmental change. Such perspectives have pulled in different directions. Old tensions between the methods and assumptions of the natural sciences, social sciences and the humanities are now compounded by divisions within the social sciences. One set of approaches to environmental history, for example, is concerned with actual processes of environmental change. Within this body of work, authors are prepared to make evaluations as to whether or not environmental changes occurred, and whether such shifts were beneficial or detrimental. Some evaluate change in terms of human welfare, while others do so by measurements and valuations of biodiversity, vegetation cover, soil erosion and the like. But other writers draw back from any possibility of judging processes of environmental change. They discuss historical debates about degradation as contradictory narratives, reflecting different perspectives. Some authors refuse to arbitrate between these narratives, in recognition that historical evidence is inextricably culturally and politically embedded. Megan Vaughan and Henrietta Moore's *Cutting Down Trees*, for example, deliberately works against 'narrative closure' and endeavours to allow multiple interpretations of the agricultural history of Zambia's Northern Province.[9] Such differences of interpretation are reflected in this volume, as some authors make judgments about ecological change and others do not. Notwithstanding these tensions both within the volume and the field, it is fair to say that all chapters reflect a sensitivity to the social production of textual and oral historical sources and a new caution relating to assessments of environmental change.

Sixth, in keeping with the volume's focus on understanding the cultural context of environmental ideas, most contributing authors recognize that the sources with which they work are at once evidence and representation. Thus they handle their material with caution. With regard to archival material produced by officials, for example, contributors approach these sources not only with the aim of understanding a generalised colonial ideology or Western scientific approaches, but also in relation to the background, attitudes and experience of individual officials. Chapters using visual sources discuss these as the products of particular technologies and frames of vision. David Bunn's exploration of the early conventions of wildlife photography and wildlife viewing is particularly revealing in this respect.[10]

Contributors have tried to remain sensitive to the limits of their sources. Thus the environmental 'evidence' produced by Nyasaland officials with a military ethos, which is discussed by John McCracken, is very different from the rigorous field investigations made by the Ugandan officials considered by Grace Carswell, or the range of scientific opinion discussed by Helen Tilley. McCracken cannot trust his official sources enough to pass judgment on actual environmental change, whilst Carswell feels the evidence her officials produced does enable such assessments. The environmental opinions expressed by the Tanzanian officials in Ingrid Yngstrom's chapter were so fully entwined with (strongly gendered) assumptions about pastoralism and the 'cattle complex' as to be inextricable from these cultural preconceptions. The focus of her investigation is the way in which environmental assessments were bound up with colonial judgments of African society. Similarly, the scientific writings of Eugene Marais are read by Sandra Swart for the light they shed on the politics of Afrikaner identity rather than their contributions to environmental understanding.

The treatments of oral evidence are no less sensitive to a variety of contexts and judgments. On the one hand, the landscape ideas and river mythologies discussed by JoAnn McGregor, in connection with societies bordering the Zambezi, do have a good deal to say about past imaginations of communities along this great waterway. On the other hand, like many oral narratives, they are told in such a way that they demand attention to the present. McGregor interprets the ideas and metaphors they incorporate in the context of current political processes, particularly the politics of a defensive

---

[9] H. Moore and M. Vaughan, *Cutting Down Trees: Gender, nutrition and agricultural change in the Northern Province of Zambia, 1890–1990* (London, James Currey, 1994).

[10] See also, Patricia Hayes and Andrew Bank (eds), 'Special Issue: Visual History', *Kronos: Journal of Cape History* 27 (2001).

assertion of cultural difference on the part of marginalised minorities. Terence Ranger looks back at myth and folklore recorded by colonial officials in the 1960s for the light it sheds on past religious ideas, but also reads these texts with a new sensitivity to gender. Carruthers' approach to her sources – which include newly articulated claims by San (Bushmen) communities about their authentic connection, as first people, to the land – underlines the importance of the contemporary context. She discusses San claims not in relation to their historical validity, but as part of the current politics of land in South Africa, and as influenced by a globalised concern with culture and 'the indigenous'. In contrast, Kreike uses his interviews not so much to explore imaginative constructions of landscape and their relationship to identity politics, but with the primary aim of understanding physical changes in the landscape. He is, however, also aware that his sources tell of the cultural background of Ovambo migrants who have moved into new areas and altered their environment.

These are some of the broad aims and themes of the collection. In further discussing the three main sections of the book, we will attempt to spell out in more detail the contribution of various chapters to a range of academic debates within African environmental history. Before doing so, however, we first look back at the field from its emergence in the 1970s.

African environmental history: continuity and change

Environmental history has always stretched the boundaries of historians' conventional field of inquiry, reaching out into domains formerly considered the realm of other academic disciplines. Drawing on geography and the natural sciences, environmental historians have insisted that trees, rocks, diseases and climate had dynamics of their own, and are important not just as a backdrop for social history, but as an intrinsic part of it. Environmental history has drawn attention back to the material and cultural significance of the natural world.

Some historians have felt uncomfortable with this idea, particularly in the context of African studies, because they desired to maintain a distance from discredited environmental determinist views of a previous era, especially those associated with the rise of scientific racism, colonial domination and ideas of white superiority. In such analyses, Africans could be interpreted as creatures of nature, exhibiting the indolence induced by the tropics, or subject to 'primitive' impulses born of a non-technological society. As Fanon argued, and as Gordon illustrates in this volume, everyday settler racism could metaphorically attribute animal characteristics to colonised people.[11]

If an environmental approach to African history was to flourish, it required new informing ideas which were more in tune with post-colonial intellectual trends. The environmental concerns that emerged in the 1970s were situated within Africanist historical writing as it developed in the highly politicised context of the University of Dar es Salaam in Tanzania. Helge Kjekhus's pioneering and controversial study *Ecology Control and Economic Development in East African History*, first published in 1977, was a product of this reorientation.[12] His own reflections on the influences that informed his work are revealing of the key arguments formulated about African

---

[11] Frantz Fanon, *The Wretched of the Earth* (Harmondsworth, Penguin, 1971).
[12] H. Kjekhus, *Ecology Control and Economic Development in East African History* (London, Heinemann, 1977), second edition, 1996.

environmental history twenty years ago. *Ecology Control*, Kjekhus elaborates, was stimulated by Terence Ranger's influential plea for a reinsertion of African agency and initiative into history, partly as a reaction against colonial histories that had written them out. Kjekhus' was concerned to 'portray ... the East Africans as doers: as people living close to their environments, but as masters and shapers of them, not as their prisoners'.[13] He was also strongly influenced by Walter Rodney's thesis on the under-development of Africa, which explored ideas of dependency and unequal exchange in the international system. Kjekhus acknowledges in particular the influence of debates among demographers and historians of technological change, reflected in the work of Rudolf Kuczynski and Ester Boserup. Equally important were the ecological insights of John Ford's study of the tsetse fly.[14] Ford was critical of colonial attempts to control this scourge which had inhibited development in substantial parts of Africa; he advocated research into the strategies adopted by African societies that lived with the fly. Kjekshus was not alone in developing these themes. John Iliffe's *History of Tanganyika*, published in the same year, wound environmental arguments into a broader historical narrative, although he placed less emphasis on pre-colonial control.[15]

    Interest in environmental history dovetailed with that in agricultural history. Most of the latter enterprise, especially in southern African studies, focused on social relations of production, rather than interaction between people and the natural world.[16] Scholars tried to unravel the complex transitions involved in the making of colonial peasantries, and in the relations between settler landowners and their African tenants. Such analyses provided one means of addressing fundamental issues in an African history that was seen to concentrate too much on states and trade, on leaders and nationalists, on missions and religion. These new approaches provided insight into the means by which basic livelihoods were secured as well as the key lines of social exploitation. There was inevitably some discussion of the state of natural resources transformed through agricultural intensification, although this was often marginal to the main lines of enquiry in agrarian history. The devastating series of droughts and famines that affected East and West Africa in the 1970s and 1980s undoubtedly contributed to the growing focus on environmental issues by compelling academics, who might not otherwise have been interested, to reflect and write about ecological change, about coping strategies and adaptation to environmental stress.[17]

    Analyses produced in the 1970s and early 1980s on the theme of African environmental control were criticised from various viewpoints. Some highlighted a tendency to over-romanticise the precolonial African past, or an anti-science bias.[18] Others felt that environmental histories, despite bringing in ecological factors, saw change simply as a response to capitalist penetration rather than casting the environment as dynamic in itself.[19] It was difficult to steer the delicate course, in Elias

---

[13] Kjekhus, *Ecology Control*, introduction to 1996 edition, p.xxx.

[14] See, for example, discussion of John Ford's work in Paul Richard's *Indigenous Agricultural Revolution: Ecology and food production in West Africa* (London, Unwin Hyman, 1985).

[15] John Iliffe, *A Modern History of Tanganyika* (Cambridge, CUP, 1979).

[16] For example, R. Palmer and N. Parsons (eds), *The Roots of Rural Poverty in Central and Southern Africa* (London, Heinemann, 1977).

[17] See the discussion in D. Anderson and D. Johnson (eds), *The Ecology of Survival: Case studies from Northeast African history* (Boulder, CO and London, Westview Press, 1988), p. 23.

[18] See discussion in Paul Richard's review of Anderson and Grove (eds), *Conservation in Africa*, JSAS, 15, 2 (1989).

[19] See Mandala's own critique of the field of 'agricultural history' in *Work and Control*.

Mandala's words, between 'environmental determinism' and 'social relations determinism'.[20] However, these early studies drew on, and opened up, enduring and central debates within African history. To enumerate a few: What was the influence of the relative underpopulation of the African continent on its environmental and social history? Did colonialism depopulate parts of Africa, and how sharp was the discontinuity in the environmental and demographic characteristics of precolonial and colonial eras? What were the central ideas through which Africans perceived and regulated their environments; were these essentially part of religious cosmologies, and if so how did they relate to ecological practice and politics? Should we see the intruding colonial and capitalist systems as essentially destructive in environmental terms, and how can we evaluate colonial and settler conservationist concerns? Were colonial conservation interventions themselves, and the scientific suppositions which often underpinned them, misconstrued and ineffective? To what extent can environmental change be attributed to initiatives within African communities or to external forces? And to what extent are African environments still degrading?

As the field has developed, so regional strengths and weaknesses in scholarship have emerged. Historians of East Africa have paid particular attention to demography and disease histories, partly because evidence of population decline in the late nineteenth and early twentieth centuries seems to be strongest there; the uniquely African disease, trypanosomiasis, played a particularly important historical role in east and central Africa. West African literatures were at the forefront in investigations of indigenous knowledge and practices, and in historicising strategies for coping with drought and famine; again this is unsurprising as the region was least affected by settler colonialism. Although the Southern African literature lagged behind in both these respects, it had its own, rather diverse, strengths which reflected both the interests of key groups of scholars and of central historical processes in the region. With respect to South Africa, colonial hunting and wildlife conservation, as well as the highly intrusive reorganisation of African land use, called 'betterment', centralisation or rehabilitation, have been widely investigated. Those focusing on Zimbabwe and Malawi gave early attention to the environmental dimensions of African religion and the moralities of environmental control; Zimbabwe has also been a major focus of studies on community involvement in wildlife management. Research is perhaps richest on the environmental policies pursued by southern African colonial and settler states. What the historiographies of all regions have in common is a shared emphasis on African resistance to a range of unpopular state environmental interventions. Many such studies were conceived within a framework of what is now called 'political ecology'.[21]

In some respects, continuities in the central issues addressed by environmental historians over the last twenty years are more striking than the changes. Many Africanists have often continued to take a political economy approach that emphasises Africa's long-term external 'extraversion' and marginalisation in the international sphere.[22] Many still lay great stress on the disruptive impact of colonisation. The huge body of careful research that is needed to make meaningful judgments about longer-term environmental change in different places over a diverse continent is taking time to accumulate. But in other respects the field has moved on. As contributions to this

[20] E. Mandala, *Work and Control in a Peasant Economy: A history of the Lower Tchiri Valley in Malawi, 1840–1960* (Madison, WI, University of Wisconsin Press, 1990).

[21] Raymond L. Bryant and Sinead Bailey, *Third World Political Ecology* (London, Routledge, 1997).

[22] See J.-F. Bayart, 'Africa in the World: A history of extraversion', *African Affairs* 99, 395 (2000), pp. 217–68.

volume attest, intellectual history and cultural perspectives have become increasingly important. And it may be possible to argue that environmental concerns have become of greater relative importance to academics working on Africa than they have to those studying most other parts of the world, and that Africanists, lacking in documentary records, have been particularly innovative in the strategies of research deployed. It is already very difficult, probably impossible, for any one individual to command the material in so diverse a field and to make fully informed generalisations and effective, balanced comparisons between regions. We believe, however, that the material in this book is suggestive of new directions, and points to modifications in some of the orthodoxies recently established in a rapidly expanding field of enquiry.

African environmental ideas and practices

African mastery of nature has been a condition of survival and expansion in a difficult continent. The first generation of Africanist writing on environmental history, as noted above, reacted strongly against ideas of Africans as passive victims of their environments. More recent studies – such as those by Vansina and Schoenbrun – have also seen the long history of environmental control by African communities as essentially benign rather than 'degrading'.[23] Advocates of indigenous ecological knowledge have continued to stress its depth in Africa. This does not imply a static 'tradition', or a separation between scientific and local forms of knowledge: Paul Richards' portrayal of West African agricultural practice as a 'performance', for example, emphasises that shifting cultivation was a collection of techniques, chosen in response to changing social and environmental circumstances. Farmers pick and mix from a range of options, including experimentation with introduced species and ideas. Richards has illustrated the latter point vividly by describing how local farmers incorporated hybrid crop species discarded from an agricultural research station into their own farming systems without scientists' knowledge.[24]

In developing earlier work on indigenous knowledge, recent studies have linked traditional African management practices to readings of the landscape, and narratives of environmental change. James Fairhead and Melissa Leach's influential study of the forest/savanna zone of West Africa has shown how farmers transformed their landscape by creating 'islands' of forest vegetation around their settlements. Previous interpretations had cast these forests as relics threatened by farmers and were used to justify state intervention and control.[25] Careful historical research combined with detailed field investigation allowed Fairhead and Leach to deconstruct these 'colonial' narratives and tell a different historical story that also lent support to advocates of local environmental management.

[23] Jan Vansina, *Paths in the Rainforest: Toward a history of political tradition in Equatorial Africa* (Madison, WI, University of Wisconsin Press, 1990); David Lee Schoenbrun, *A Green Place, a Good Place: Agrarian, gender and social identity in the Great Lakes Region to the 15th century* (Portsmouth, NH, Heinemann, 1998).

[24] Paul Richards, 'Agriculture as Performance' in R. Chambers, A. Pacey and L.A. Thrupp (eds), *Farmer First: Farmer innovation and agricultural research* (London, Intermediate Technology Publications, 1989); Richards, *Indigenous Agricultural Revolution*.

[25] J. Fairhead and M. Leach, *Misreading the African Landscape* (Cambridge, CUP, 1987) and *Reframing Deforestation: Global analysis and local realities – studies in West Africa* (London, Routledge, 1998).

Two papers in this volume use illustrations of plant transfers to develop such arguments. Plant transfers have arguably been one of the most important processes in human history, facilitating population movements, demographic expansion, the growth of empires and intensification of production. The expanding use of new cultivars is an old-established theme in African history: early introductions such as plantain/banana from the east have been considered important in the process of Bantu expansion eastwards and southwards, and especially in the settlement of forested zones. Africa's staples have been fundamentally changed by American cultivars, particularly maize.

Kreike's focus here, on the management of indigenous species, is a less frequently rehearsed argument. His chapter discusses how Africans in Ovamboland (southern Angola and northern Namibia) expanded the range of favoured indigenous fruit trees, notably the marula (*Schlerocarya birrea*) because they were important in subsistence and central to their cultural life, especially for brewing. African colonisers of new frontiers preserved some established trees, thinned them out where necessary to produce sturdier specimens with heavier fruit, or planted new indigenous fruit trees. In some cases, informants suggested that trees seeded themselves, probably from the detritus of fruit consumption, and were simply protected. Kreike's findings support a body of research in the expansive miombo woodlands of central and southern Africa, which has documented how some of the most deforested landscapes in heavily populated rural areas are enriched with fruit trees. Less heavily used woodlands, by contrast, have far fewer. As a result rapid increases in population have not reduced the availability of many favoured fruit trees and other valued species.[26] Kreike argues that his material supports the conclusions of Fairhead and Leach, but also extends them in clarifying the modes by which specific indigenous fruit trees have been spread and their significance in social and cultural conceptions of what constituted inhabited, tamed land – rather than wilderness. In contrast to the situation discussed by Fairhead and Leach, 'islands' of forest were not created, but useful trees multiplied in homeyards, fields and commonages. This is not necessarily an argument for the absence of deforestation, but suggests that African management can increase the density and quality of vegetation in these parts of the landscape.[27]

Karen Middleton discusses a less well-known introduction from America – the prickly pear (*Opuntia* species) – to southern Madagascar. Her chapter illustrates further both the close interconnection between colonial and local initiatives, and the way in which African people could transform their own environments. Introduced in order to improve fortifications in an unsuccessful colonial intrusion in the eighteenth century, the plant soon spread throughout this region. Far from being regarded by Androy people as an unwanted invader, they adopted it wholeheartedly for fences, fruit and cattle fodder. Like indigenous fruits in Ovamboland, it was spread partly by self-reproduction (seeding and clones from the cladodes or leaves), and partly by human

---

[26] B. Campbell (ed.), *The Miombo in Transition: Woodlands and welfare in Africa* (Malasia, Centre for International Forestry Research, CIFOR, 1996); B. Campbell, 'The Use of Wild Fruits In Zimbabwe', *Economic Botany* 43, 3 (1987), pp. 375–85; Ken Wilson, 'Trees in Fields in Southern Zimbabwe', *JSAS* (1989); J. McGregor, 'Gathered Produce in Zimbabwe's Communal Lands: Changing Resource Availability and Use', *Ecology of Food and Nutrition*, 33 (1995), pp. 163–93.

[27] East African studies have also argued that increasing population has seen an intensification of environmental management. See Mary Tiffen, Michael Mortimore and Francis Gichuki, *More People Less Erosion: Environmental recovery in Kenya* (Chichester, John Wiley, 1993); P. de Wees, *Farms, Trees and Farmers* (London, Earthscan, 1997).

management. Prickly pear became naturalised, central both to subsistence and social life in the area. It facilitated far larger herds of cattle, and denser populations, than had been possible in this semi-arid area, and later was a major asset in resisting colonial control and settlers. In this case, however, the pear almost certainly stifled considerable areas of indigenous vegetation, and Middleton notes that the environmental consequences of prickly pear were distinctly ambivalent. Moreover, such dependence on a single species had disastrous consequences in the 1930s when introduced cochineal insects destroyed the pear.[28]

Studies of such interactions strongly suggest the centrality of environmental change in social history. More recent processes, which are better documented, or – as in Kreike's case – open to investigation by systematic interviews, also help to raise questions about longer-term changes and the more distant past. They illustrate how quickly new plants, or new resources, can be mastered and how important these can be in both social and environmental transformations. Analysis of more recent plant transfers may assist in raising questions about older introductions, such as bananas. The longer view has been a particular strength in the East African literature, which has paid detailed attention to regional environmental characteristics, and their links to social organisation, as well as exchanges between communities in different areas, and subtle changes of techniques.[29] Consideration of 'broader ecological continuities, as well as long-term environmental changes' has allowed for new interpretations of shifts in the centres of Ethiopian and Nubian state power.[30] Concentrations of population and power – for example, around irrigation centres – could fall as well as rise, possibly in part because of environmental factors.[31]

Precolonial regional patterns of land use are perhaps less well understood in southern Africa – a result partly of the impact of settler colonialism on both natural environments and subsequent historiography. Important debates have focused, however, on environmental factors in the rise and fall of precolonial kingdoms, notably the Zimbabwe and Zulu states. In the case of the Zulu state, conflict resulting from scarcity, rather than scarcity itself, has been offered as one explanation of social and political change. An emerging consensus seemed to attribute the decline of Great Zimbabwe in the fifteenth century to environmental factors such as overgrazing, deforestation and drought.[32] In this volume, Innocent Pikirayi revisits these issues, and cautions against the environmental determinism evident in some archaeological writing. Rather, he suggests that political authority may have crumbled as a result of famine related to war. He explores evidence for environmental change in Portuguese texts over a long period of time in order to reconsider their utility to historians interested in relating political and environmental change. His conclusions are not hopeful in this regard; it is difficult to tell whether texts are describing regular and

---

[28] Karen Middleton, 'Who Killed "Malagasy Cactus"? Science, Environment and Colonialism in Southern Madagascar (1924–1930)', *Journal of Southern African Studies* (*JSAS*), 25, 2 (1999).

[29] Mats Widgren and John Sutton (eds), *Islands of Intensive Agriculture in the East African Rift and Highlands: A 500 year perspective*. Working Paper No. 43. Environment and Development Studies Unit, University of Stockholm, 1999..

[30] Anderson and Johnson, *The Ecology of Survival*, pp. 19–21.

[31] James C. McCann, *Green Land, Brown Land, Black Land: An environmental history of Africa, 1800–1990* (Oxford, James Currey, 1999), pp. 36–48 on Aksum; J.E.G. Sutton, 'Irrigation and Soil Conservation in African Agricultural History', *Journal of African History* 25, 1 (1984).

[32] Graham Connah, *African Civilisations: Precolonial cities and states in tropical Africa, an archaeological perspective* (Cambridge, CUP, 1987).

cyclical events or referring to more dramatic changes that may have helped to transform society. The subsequent spread of Zimbabwe-culture states to new centres of power, largely further north, are also susceptible to environmental and non-environmental interpretations.

The dilemma faced by Pikirayi concerning the salience of environmental explanations is not limited to the deep precolonial period. Drought, for example, is widely invoked in southern African history, often in passing, as a self-evident explanatory tool of analysis: it is held partly responsible for the decline of African peasantries; for labour migration and proletarianisation; for the rise of poor whiteism; and for particular rebellions. Yet drought is a frequent and recurring phenomenon and its impact, as recent analyses of famine suggest, depends greatly upon changing forms of production and distribution.[33] The same reservations should apply to more recent debates about environmental scarcity. Environmental scarcity, such as the shortage of water, or of some other natural resource, or general degradation, is frequently offered as an explanation of conflict, or as a likely cause of future conflict.[34] There is a strong tradition of environmental explanation in Western historiography, which has recently been revived by increasingly sophisticated understandings of El Niño climatic cycles, as well as claims – especially in popular history – about its impact.[35] Such linkages cannot be ignored; undoubtedly environmental factors are of central importance in explaining long-term social change, and this literature provides exciting examples of how and when they can be effectively introduced to explain specific crises and conflicts. But popular history can also exaggerate the immediate impact of environmental events. Pikirayi's point is that we need also to understand social and political decisions, in relation to environmental events, if we are to link environmental to political change.

If past southern African systems of land use are still inadequately researched, parts of the region have served as a focus for a rich body of literature on the links between religion and environmental control, and on historical changes in African religious ideas and institutions. Schoffeleers' discussion of central African cults provided extensive evidence of their function as *Guardians of the Land*.[36] Terence Ranger's work on the history of the regional Matopos rainshrine and David Maxwell's analysis of mhondoro cults

[33] Amartya Sen, *Poverty and Famines: An essay on entitlement and deprivation* (Clarendon Press, Oxford, 1982); Megan Vaughan, *The Story of an African Famine: Gender and famine in twentieth century Malawi* (Cambridge, CUP, 1987).

[34] See Marq de Villiers, *Water Wars: Is the world's water running out ?* (London, Weidenfeld and Nicolson, 1999); T. Homer-Dixon, *Environment, Scarcity and Violence* (Princeton, NJ, Princeton University Press, 1999) and for critiques see N.P. Gleditsch, 'Armed Conflict and the Environment – a Critique of the Literature', *Journal of Peace Research* 35, 3 (1998) and E. Hartmann, 'Population, Environment and Security': a New Trinity', *Environment and Urbanization* 10, 2 (1998).

[35] See Richard H. Grove, 'Environmental History' in Peter Burke (ed.), *New Perspectives on Historical Writing* (Cambridge, Polity, 2001) for a review of these themes in environmental history and historical geography; H.H. Lamb, *Climate, History and the Modern World* (London, Routledge, 1997) and E. Le Roy Ladurie, *Times of Feast, Times of Famine: A history of climate since the year 1000* (London, 1972) for a more academic example of environmental impact over different time-scales; Mike Davis, *Late Victorian Holocausts: El Nino famines and the making of the Third World* (London, Verso, 2001) and Ross Couper-Johnston, *El Nino: The weather phenomenon that changed the world* (London, Hodder and Stoughton, 2001), for two recent and challenging popular books.

[36] M. Schoffeleers (ed.), *Guardians of the Land: Essays on Central African territorial cults* (Gweru, Zimbabwe, 1979).

in Eastern Zimbabwe are recent cases in point.[37] Both argue that environmental issues became,, if anything, more rather than less significant in the colonial period; local eco-religious cults developed as a means of coping with agroecological stress, or resisting colonial intrusions.[38] Mhondoro mediums elaborated territorial aspects of their control over land, and emphasised their responsibility for rain and the 'cooling of the earth'.

Ranger's paper in this volume extends discussion of precolonial African religion and change in the colonial era by focusing on the place of women in African environmental cosmologies – hitherto a neglected topic. He does so by exploring the diverse roles of women in ritual, myth and narrative associated with traditional religious practice. He argues that previous studies underestimated the number of women mediums, priestesses and prophets, and downplayed women's public roles. He is cautious, however, in applying any lessons from recent ecofeminist approaches which might picture women in particular as in harmony with the natural world.[39] He suggests that there was no clear gender division in African religious thinking that established women as protectors of nature, and men as bearers of culture or nature's destroyers.

Ranger raises important questions of how women's roles, as well as traditional religion, are conceptualised in environmental history. Women were most certainly bearers of culture, and there has been a wide-ranging academic effort to understand their role as producers who could impact upon nature in different African contexts. For example, women's gathering or 'foraging' has been emphasised as a source of subsistence in San society, as much as men's hunting; pastoral societies are also being reconceptualised in a less gender-specific way.[40] Nevertheless, we need to be sensitive to traditions of thought in both Western and African contexts which conjure women as linked to the earth, to nature or elemental forces. These precede ecofeminism and have had negative as well as, more recently, positive connotations. African variants were sometimes expressed in taboos or disabilities of long standing which might exclude women from access to productive and natural resources or particular activities (such as iron-making) and spaces (such as cattle kraals). Men and women were differentiated by gender and age in respect of such relationships. Historical analysis must explore such deeply set cultural understandings because they provide organising ideas which have had an important material impact.

Debates over African religious ideas in relation to the environment have also contributed to the surge of interest in African landscapes that explores aesthetic and imaginative appropriations of the land.[41] This strain of environmental history has been particularly well developed in metropolitan contexts. Simon Schama's *Landscape and*

---

[37] Terence Ranger, 'Religious Studies and Political Economy: The Mwari cult and peasant experience in Southern Rhodesia' in W.M.J. van Binsbergen and M. Schoffeleers (eds), *Theoretical Explorations in African Religion, Politics and Patriarchy* (London, Kegan Paul International, 1985); David Maxwell, *Christians and Chiefs in Zimbabwe: A social history of the Hwesa people c. 1870–1990s* (Edinburgh, Edinburgh University Press, 1999).

[38] W. van Binsbergen, *Religious Change in Zambia: Exploratory studies* (London, Routledge, 1981).

[39] For the classic extra-European statement, see Vandana Shiva, *Staying Alive: Women, ecology and development* (London, Zed Books, 1988).

[40] R. Lee, *The !Kung San* (Cambridge University Press, New York, 1979); Dorothy L. Hodgson (ed.), *Rethinking Pastoralism in Africa* (Oxford, James Currey, 2000).

[41] Luig and von Oppen, *The Making of African Landscapes*. African landscapes, with particular reference to Zimbabwe, were the subject of a follow-up to the 1999 conference, also sponsored by *JSAS*, and held in Bulawayo, July 2000.

Memory, for example, underlined the centrality of particular landscape traditions for European and American national identities, arguing that these nationalisms, as well as a range of other ideas such as empire and freedom, 'invoked topography' and derived power from implied natural forms.[42] British romantics recreated both real and imaginary landscapes. In nineteenth-century France, the 'spectacle of nature', and a proliferation of images of a bucolic countryside, was an essential element in bourgeois and nationalist culture.[43] In the African context, Terence Ranger's *Voices from the Rocks* focused on the landscape of the Matopos hills in Zimbabwe, which became a central symbol for both white and black nationalisms. Jane Carruthers' study of the Kruger National Park emphasised the Park's relationship to white South African identity, as well as Afrikaner nationalism;[44] David Bunn's chapter in this collection focuses more systematically on ways of seeing in the Park and how its landscape was recorded both in photography and in its visitors' minds.

It is certainly possible to begin reconstructing changing material landscapes in Africa, 'what Africa looked like, when, and why'.[45] It is possible to write about the formation of landscapes as a result of the daily activities of people in their myriad tasks of building, farming, clearing and planting. Notwithstanding Ranger's recent work, however, research on landscape has been less fully developed in relation to African ideas. This is partly because it has proved difficult to historicise indigenous ideas on the basis of oral traditions, or to elaborate specifically aesthetic components within them. Luig and von Oppen have struggled to find systematic evidence of concepts of landscape within African traditions of thought. Historians have, however, tried with some success to periodise ideas about 'the wild' and 'the tame' in African cosmologies – concepts of long-standing concern to anthropologists.[46] New work examines categories of thought and metaphors that express environmental loss.[47] Nevertheless, African environmental ideas have perhaps been most sensitively discussed not through deploying the notion of landscape, but through studies of resource use and traditional religious environmental controls. Such practices are also filled with cultural meaning. Moore and Vaughan have discussed the relationship between Bemba masculinity and 'cutting down trees'; Thomas Spear has explored Maasai herders' settlement of Mount Meru in nineteenth-century Tanzania and their cultural adaptation to what they at first saw as the 'debased toil' of agricultural life.[48]

In this volume, JoAnn McGregor contributes to such debates by excavating ideas about the Zambezi river in oral histories of Tonga-speaking people in Northwestern

[42] Simon Schama, *Landscape and Memory* (London, Fontana Press, 1996).

[43] Nicholas Green, *The Spectacle of Nature: Landscape and bourgeois culture in nineteenth-century France* (Manchester, Manchester University Press, 1990).

[44] Jane Carruthers, 'Creating a National Park, 1910–1926', *JSAS* 15, 2 (1989): 188–216; Ranger, *Voices from the Rocks*.

[45] McCann, *Green Land*, p. 48.

[46] Emmanuel Kreike, 'Recreating Eden: Agro-ecological change and environmental diversity in southern Angola and northern Namibia, 1890–1960', PhD thesis, Yale University, 1996. Such distinctions are also implied in Robert Harms, *Games Against Nature: An eco-cultural history of the Nunu of Equatorial Africa* (Cambridge, CUP, 1987).

[47] Tamara Giles-Vernick, '*Doli*: Translating an African Environmental History of Loss in the Sangha River Basin of Equatorial Africa', *Journal of African History* 41, 3 (2000).

[48] Moore and Vaughan, *Cutting Down Trees*. Thomas Spear, *Mountain Farmers: Moral economies of land and agricultural development in Arusha and Meru* (Oxford, James Currey, 1997).

Zimbabwe. She argues that rich mythologies of the river are revealing of its role as a central focus of social, political and religious life in the nineteenth century. Narratives of the twentieth century, on the other hand, convey an image of the river's desacralisation. Local people lost access to the river during the colonial period as a result of tourist developments around the Victoria Falls, displacement from the Kariba dam and new networks of state control over the resources of the Valley. Far from becoming irrelevant when life ceased to be focused on the river, memories of past relations with it, including the idea of being a 'river people', have had a persistent importance. Memories were not only an expression of nostalgia, but were also mobilised in conflicts over access to resources and in a defensive cultural assertion of Tonga rights in the context of a profound sense of economic and political marginalisation.

McGregor's chapter shows the potential for using a distinctive geographic region as a focus for environmental history which combines social, economic and ecological analysis. Like Carruthers' chapter in this volume, it underlines the way in which minorities have mobilized a strongly territorialised identity politics in efforts to reverse an unjust partition of resources. In both cases, they have been encouraged by global movements valuing indigeneity, as well as the growth of cultural tourism and related markets for what are seen as traditional crafts and commodities. As in Kreike's research on Ovamboland, McGregor's chapter illustrates the potential for recording and unravelling African ideas about landscape and memory through systematic interviewing. While the riverine environment clearly at one time provided a focus for religious shrines, some of which still exist, invocations of past relations with the landscape were not primarily religious. They have been absorbed in the making of a distinctive ethnic identity and in ideas of heritage. In this respect there are also parallels with European writing on marginalised communities associated with swamps, or forests. Marginalised by progress during the industrial revolution, they can now be invoked as part of the national or regional heritage, valued for tourism, and their identities are sometimes unproblematically linked to their former remoteness.[49]

The chapters in this section collectively enhance understanding of the reciprocal interaction between people and their environments, between nature and culture in the making of landscapes. They elaborate in particular on the symbolic and imaginative dimensions in African perceptions of landscape and natural resources. They suggest both distinctive features of the African experience and also many commonalities with analyses in other contexts. Contributors explore how natural resources, plants, landscapes, have been appropriated in the construction of local cultures and identities. This is not simply because African societies have in the past been close to nature, or deeply dependent upon direct access to natural resources in order to survive. Similar patterns are identifiable in European and American history. These chapters also hint at interactions between African and colonial approaches to the same landscapes: illustrating not merely contrasts and conflicts, but also mutual influences. The next section on colonial science and policy shows further linkages – whether in the form of violent confrontations or subtle incorporations of particular ideas and practices.

---

[49] David Blackbourn, '"Conquests from Barbarism": Interpreting Land Reclamation in Eighteenth-century Prussia', unpublished paper delivered to the 19th International Congress of Historical Sciences, University of Oslo (2000), summarised in Anders Jolstad and Marianne Lunde (eds), *Proceedings of the 19th International Congress of Historical Sciences* (Oslo, 2000), p. 396; Schama, *Landscape and Memory*.

Colonial science, the state and African responses

One of the most persistent themes and significant achievements in African environmental history has been its systematic examination of state conservation policies across a wide range of countries, particularly those in the former British Empire.[50] Discussions of colonial environmental regulation have commonly dwelt on the arrogance of rationalising science and official policies that were insensitive to local ecological realities. They have often contrasted colonial intrusions with holistic and technically appropriate African ideas and practices. Concurrently, and often as part of the same exercise, scholars have investigated the significance of environmental regulation in provoking anti-colonial resistance.[51] Studies of conservation and resistance have been an integral part of the reassessment of anti-colonial protest, helping to inform a critique of nationalist historiography and of a linear trajectory in the development of resistance. They have shown that rural resistance movements at different times and places were not necessarily nationalist, or that local leaders could develop their own versions of ethnicity and nationalism to give wider meaning to environmental conflicts. As Stephen Feierman discusses, 'peasant intellectuals' in Tanzania moulded 'traditional' or customary ideas about the land, and resistance to state intervention, with ideas taken from independent Christianity and new African nationalist rhetoric.[52]

The chapters in this section of the book include papers which affirm the importance of these themes, but also begin to offer a critique of what are becoming accepted orthodoxies. While much recent environmental literature has focused on the intrusive and coercive aspects of the colonial state, older themes in African history, which emphasise the limits of colonial control, are again being raised.[53] 'Colonial science' has been the subject of a rather condemnatory and ideological judgment in recent literature; more nuanced approaches to the history of science in Africa are now being canvassed. These chapters suggest further that history has sometimes been used too instrumentally in debates over current environmental policy, and that simply highlighting continuities in policy has given too little attention to the contexts in which particular ideas were initially shaped and thereafter reproduced. In addition, the contributions emphasise the degree to which some aspects of colonial science, especially in the interwar years, could be sensitive to local knowledge, and that the gains made in scientific ecological understanding could be impressive, even if they were often not acted upon effectively or sensitively. Finally, examples are discussed of situations where colonial intervention was accepted.

This revisiting of colonial science, policy and African response builds on studies which have looked at the exchange of ideas within the British Empire and the

---

[50] William Beinart, 'Soil Erosion, Conservationism and Ideas about Development: A Southern African Exploration 1900–1960', *JSAS* 11 (1984); Anderson and Grove, *Conservation in Africa*.

[51] For key recent texts, see A. Fiona D. Mackenzie, *Land, Ecology and Resistance in Kenya 1880–1952* (Edinburgh, Edinburgh University Press, 1998), Ranger, *Voices from the Rocks*.

[52] S. Feierman, *Peasant Intellectuals: History and anthropology in Tanzania* (Madison, WI, University of Wisconsin Press, 1990). See also William Beinart and Colin Bundy, *Hidden Struggles in Rural South Africa* (London, James Currey, 1987) which similarly investigates individual rural activists, and Peter Delius, *A Lion Amongst the Cattle: Reconstruction and resistance in the Northern Transvaal* (Oxford, James Currey, 1997).

[53] Beinart, 'African History and Environmental History'; Monica M. van Beusekom and Dorothy L. Hodgson (eds), 'Lessons Learned? Development Experiences in the Late Colonial Period', special section of the *Journal of African History* 41, 1 (2000).

incorporation of ideas from the periphery.[54] The role of 'science' in a colonial context, and of particular colonial scientists, has been the object of increasingly fine-grained study. While scientific discourse could often be used to justify segregationist policies or colonial economic agendas, not all science or all scientists could fit comfortably in this stereotype. Scientific research strategies were shaped by a multitude of institutional contexts that extended well beyond particular colonies. 'Counternarratives' were often evident, even when eclipsed as a result of the rise of technical bureaucracies after the Second World War.[55] Helen Tilley's chapter in this volume makes such points by reconstructing the scientific networks and ideas that were drawn on in the compilation of Lord Hailey's *African Survey* (1938) – a major research effort that was designed to inform and shape British colonial rule. The *Survey* reflected rapidly increasing knowledge about African environments resulting from new approaches to ecology and a new emphasis on fieldwork. While many scientists worked in association with colonial states, their ideas and priorities were often framed by broader scientific debates. Tilley asks whether 'colonial science' is a useful category of analysis. She examines a range of inquisitive scientists and officials whose minds were not simply fixed on standard regulatory policies. Certainly, they sounded the alarm about degradation in some areas, but they could also draw upon and even sometimes advocate the wisdom of local approaches. They provided studies that could be taken as a baseline of recorded knowledge and developed a language for discussing African environmental problems.

Just as some scientists could be sensitive to local knowledge, so it has also become apparent that further investigation is needed of how Africans embraced colonial interventions in different contexts. Those who co-operated with state conservation policies – for example some chiefs – had diverse motivations. As Mandala illustrates in the lower Tchiri valley of Malawi, chiefs themselves could advocate the need for environmental regulation and work discipline.[56] They could use the profound reorganisation of land management and landscape proposed by colonial officials to enhance their control and authority over people. Ordered rows of houses and separated arable and grazing lands could also become a source of modernist pride for a wider segment of African society, and a deforested landscape sometimes came to be associated with 'emerging' from the forests and a primitive life.[57] People living in a context of tenure insecurity could demand land-use planning, not because they wanted it in its own right, but as a means of securing land rights.[58] Social and economic transformation could be the harbinger of radically different rural demands for planning and services, and women in particular found village settlements, with greater access to education, water and healthcare, attractive.[59] This volume includes studies of both

---

[54] T. Griffiths and L. Robin (eds), *Ecology and Empire: Environmental history of settler societies* (Edinburgh, Keele University Press, 1997); R. Grove, *Green Imperialism: Colonial expansion, tropical island edens and the origins of environmentalism, 1600–1800* (Cambridge, CUP, 1995).

[55] A. Fiona D. Mackenzie, 'Contested Ground: Colonial Narratives and the Kenyan Environment, 1920–1945', *JSAS* 26, 4, (2000).

[56] Mandala, *Work and Control*.

[57] J. McGregor, 'Conservation, Control and Ecological Change: The politics and ecology of colonial conservation in Shurugwi, Zimbabwe', *Environment and History* 1, 3, (1995), pp. 257–80; Alexander *et al.*, *Violence and Memory*.

[58] J. Alexander, 'The State, Agrarian Policy and Rural Politics in Zimbabwe: Case Studies of Insiza and Chimanimani Districts, 1940–1990', unpublished D.Phil. thesis, University of Oxford (1993).

[59] Anne Kelger Mager, *Gender and the Making of a South African Bantustan: A social history of the Ciskei, 1945–1959* (Oxford, James Currey, 1999).

resistance to and 'successful' implementation of state conservation regulations. They explore the local circumstances and cultural context of different responses, investigating the influence of officials, specific local chiefly politics, and particular histories of local nationalism and anti-state protest.

Grace Carswell's chapter on soil conservation policy in Kigezi, southwest Uganda, shows how terracing was successfully implemented in this area in the 1930s and 1940s. Agricultural officials observed and worked with existing Bakiga practice and were prepared to adapt their conservation techniques and strategies to local circumstances, responding flexibly to technical problems and political opposition. The political and cultural context was important in other respects too. Chiefly authority was relatively secure and nationalist mobilisation largely absent. Moreover, land was available elsewhere for voluntary resettlement. This chapter raises broader questions about the relative balance in historical writing, between discussion of resistance and acquiescence to conservationist interventions.

Although many colonial projects were highly ambitious on paper, their 'technical imagination' was often only partially realised on the ground, and this too affected African responses.[60] Thackwray Driver has argued that the ambitious schemes for the management of extensive highland grazing areas in colonial Lesotho, seen to be ecologically vulnerable, were never realised, although a great deal was written about them.[61] Harder questions need to be asked about which types of intervention remained inoperative, which were accepted, sometimes after initial opposition, and how and why attitudes towards interventions changed. We know little about the extent to which Africans developed their own conservationist discourses. In addition to the terracing discussed by Carswell, other examples such as contour ploughing, ridging in fields, and the adoption of new crops and techniques were all practices introduced in the colonial era, with official backing, that have become established in some areas. By contrast, fencing of pasturelands, while it has had some African supporters, has more often cut across local practices and has been difficult and expensive to maintain.

In contrast to the Kigezi case, John McCracken's chapter points to more familiar patterns of heavy-handed intervention and angry resistance. His contribution on conservation policy in the 'dead north' of Malawi starts by questioning the characterisation of that area as devastated by nineteenth-century Ngoni invasion, slaving, and twentieth-century colonial neglect. Certainly it was on the peripheries of colonial state concern, but agriculturally, religiously, and politically, this was a region of innovation and significance in the colonial period. In part his chapter is a corrective to the focus in much Malawian historiography on the more densely settled and heavily colonised south of the country. Eventually, in the 1930s, the state caught up with the region, in the shape of Major Smalley and the Misuku land usage scheme.

Environmental conflicts were produced in a context where chiefs were weak, where a part of the country regarded as marginal in colonial eyes was subjected to policies devised elsewhere and poorly tailored to local contexts. Official readings of the landscape, drawing on older missionary interpretations, were embedded in derogatory

---

[60] W. Beinart, 'Agricultural Planning and the Late Colonial Technical Imagination' in J. McCracken (ed.), *Malawi: An alternative pattern of development* (Edinburgh, Centre for African Studies, 1985).

[61] Thackwray Driver, 'The Theory and Politics of Mountain Rangeland Conservation and Pastoral Development in Colonial Lesotho', unpublished Ph.D. thesis, University of London (1997) and 'Anti-erosion policies in the Mountain Areas of Lesotho: the South African connection', *Environment and History* 5, 1 (1999).

stereotypes of ethnic groups and assumptions about the detrimental impact of shifting cultivation. They were rooted in caricatures rather than detailed investigation. Major Smalley, who co-ordinated the initial interventions, was highly ambitious, with a military background, and his very commitment helped to trigger local grievances which nationalists were able to exploit. In McCracken's analysis of these processes, strongly held colonial cultural and social ideas helped to give conservationist policy its notorious reputation amongst Africans. These persisted into the late colonial period when more widespread interventions triggered resistance on a scale not experienced in other parts of Malawi, and which were a major element in the insurrection of 1959, and the central African emergency that helped to precipitate the demise of Federation.

The imbrication of colonial ideas about the environment with notions of tribe and custom is further pursued by Ingrid Yngstrom. In her case study of the Gogo in central Tanzania, she demonstrates how official concerns about the state of the land were enmeshed with their view of the Gogo as culturally unadaptive and trapped within a cattle complex. They failed fully to grasp the systems of cattle management which involved transhumance and exchange to meet environmental contingencies. Nor did they appreciate the dynamics of accumulation and impoverishment in Gogo society. Yngstrom reveals the deeply gendered nature of official understandings of Gogo society as well as their explicitly and restrictively male vision of progress. Policies for agricultural improvement and conservation paid inadequate attention to the division of labour and the role of women in agricultural decision-making. The 'script of Gogo identity', with which the colonial officers approached their task, made misapprehension of their subjects almost inevitable. Yngstrom balances a critique of colonial perceptions and interventions with an attempt to illustrate some of the dynamics of Gogo society during a period of significant agricultural and social change, as this area near Dodoma became a focus for transport and trade routes. Like McCracken, she explores why local African people understood their environment differently.

The chapters in this section offer a carefully contextualised analysis of colonial policy at various periods, which does not simply oppose 'science' and 'modernity', on the one hand, and local practice and traditionalism, on the other. Together with other material, they reveal the need to include the regulation of white farmers in southern Africa as well as African peasants in colonial territories as part of the same analytical framework. Measures were sometimes pursued first in respect of white farmers, and some projects, such as the eradication of livestock diseases, weeds or locusts, were applied across racial and territorial lines.[62] Colonial intervention could be careless and brutal. But an understanding of this broader context may help to modify some of the moral certainties that have attended critiques of the state in Africa.

These chapters suggest the need for a careful periodisation of scientific research and state policy, as well as different approaches by scientists and officials in different places during the period from the 1920s to 1950s. To some extent they affirm the distinctions that have been made in historical literature between scientists concentrating on research, and agricultural officials who had to implement major schemes. These chapters also tend to support a distinction between the interwar years, when colonial intervention was more cautious, and post-war 'high-modernist' projects. However, this periodisation may be less relevant to white farmers in South Africa. And evidence is also beginning to emerge of new community-oriented thinking – for example in connection with wildlife – during the late colonial period in Botswana and

---

[62] Beinart, 'Soil Erosion, Conservationism'.

Kenya.[63] An understanding of the limits of state power even in post-war British colonial territories might also open the way to a reassessment of that period. Collectively these chapters suggest that the colonial state should not be seen simply as an instrument of intervention, but also as a bearer of complex and conflicting values, with internal tensions and disputes about the most appropriate way in which to rule. They raise questions about the context of interventions, about the new orthodoxies concerning environmental conflicts, and about the possibility of other outcomes.

Settlers, culture and nature

The final section of the book focuses on the link between identity and nature. Most of the papers are primarily about white settler ideas, but they draw in African subjects to illustrate a range of different conflicts and interactions. Research on settler societies in southern Africa has demonstrated both the scale of environmental destruction attendant on conquest, and the linked rise of conservation. Mackenzie's work on hunting and the decimation of wildlife is a case in point.[64] Both he and Carruthers have explored the transition towards a conservationist approach in respect of wildlife, especially amongst imperial hunters and anglophone South Africans.[65] Some officials and white farmers, who explicitly saw themselves as progressive, became committed supporters of veld conservation. The chapters in this section develop the analysis of settler ideas into other spheres such as landscape, literature, tourism, pets, and the natural sciences. Images and symbols drawn from the natural world were significant in various strands of white southern African nationalisms and racial identities. An exploration of the range of natural metaphors and landscape imagery used in different times and places, and their relationships to intellectual and cultural traditions, brings a new richness to our under-standing of white culture in southern Africa, and also its metropolitan connections.

In his paper to the conference, Peter Merrington explored the way in which white Capetonians began to imagine themselves in a 'mediterranean' environment by the second half of the nineteenth century.[66] But identification with local rather than metropolitan landscape images proved to be more significant, and South African settlers were not unique in this respect.[67] Colonial space was an attractive asset, which could be contrasted with the cramped and crowded landscape of Europe. The dry inland plain called the Karoo, which could be crossed by train in a day by the early twentieth century, and was no longer a dangerous barrier, was one source of symbolic

---

[63] Material based on theses in progress by Maitseo Bolaane, on the history of the Moremi reserve, northern Botswana, and by Dawn Nell, on the history of wildlife utilisation in South Africa and Kenya, both at the University of Oxford.

[64] John Mackenzie, *The Empire of Nature: Hunting, conservation and British imperialism* (Manchester, Manchester University Press, 1988).

[65] J. Carruthers, *The Kruger National Park: A social and political history* (Pietermaritzburg, Natal University Press, 1995).

[66] Peter Merrington, 'Conservation, Heritage, Character: Colonial Environments in South Africa c. 1910', unpublished paper presented to the conference on 'African Environments: Past and Present', St Antony's College, University of Oxford, 1999.

[67] For a comparative discussion that excludes South Africa, see Thomas R. Dunlap, *Nature and the English Diaspora: Environment and history in the United States, Canada, Australia, and New Zealand* (Cambridge, CUP, 1999); for literary representations, see Kate Darian-Smith, Liz Gunner and Sarah Nuttall (eds), *Text, Theory and Space: Land, literature and history in South Africa and Australia* (London, Routledge, 1996).

materials. Life on the road, the open campfire, the 'wild' terrain of the Transvaal lowveld – celebrated in the bestselling dog story *Jock of the Bushveld* – provided other attractive images.[68] In particular, South Africa's rich indigenous wildlife fuelled the settler imagination.

In the existing literature, Afrikaner approaches to nature have been seen as particularly destructive. Carruthers argues that even the Kruger National Park, named after an Afrikaner icon, was essentially the invention of an anglophone South African who invoked Kruger's name in order to win broad support for the Park as an expression of a more unified white South African identity. One critic of Carruthers feels that she neglects the significant shift in Afrikaner, or at least Kruger's own ideas, at the close of the nineteenth century.[69] Swart's paper, focusing on the Afrikaner nationalist poet and naturalist Eugene Marais, indirectly sheds light on this issue. It is not Marais' landscape poetry which she analyses, although that flourishing early twentieth-century literary expression would surely add to the picture, but his work on natural history which included widely read books on ants and baboons.[70]

Marais' writing proved popular, Swart argues, not only because of Afrikaner familiarity with the natural world from their farm backgrounds, but also because natural history was identified with a specifically Afrikaner modernity. His work on the organic organisation of ant colonies was attractive to Afrikaners seeking to emphasise similar characteristics in their ideas about the volk. Marais' accusations against a Belgian scientist for plagiarising his ideas became of public importance because he seemed to carry the flag for an assertion of Afrikaner intellectual prowess and organic knowledge about nature. In this and other respects, nature was being appropriated into the nationalist project. It should be noted parenthetically that settlers could draw positive as well as negative images and metaphors from the animal and insect world, just as Africans also drew on their understanding of animal behaviour to create narratives and folklore about human society. Many cultures have had a tendency both to anthropomorphise animal behaviour, and zoomorphise human. This is a measure of how closely the great majority of humans interacted with animals on a regular basis, until recent times.

Writing on white identity and national parks is expanded in a different direction by David Bunn who analyses not how the Kruger National Park came into being, but how animals came to be viewed in the park. He explores the work of photographers and publicists as well as the experiences of visitors. The demand for visual images of wildlife from both South African and international publications produced an active, sometimes competitive group of photographers. Photographs in turn publicised the park and helped to shape ways of viewing its animals; here knowledge of waterholes proved critical for photographers because these proved to be their best sites. Visitors were compelled to stay in their cars and were instructed by the media in how to focus on animals. They were to take their pleasure from spotting and identifying species, and

---

[68] Percy Fitzpatrick, *Jock of the Bushveld* (London, Longmans, Green, 1907); John Buchan, *Prester John* (1907), an equally important colonial novel of the time also featured a dog as a central character. See also chapters by Gordon and Bunn.

[69] Jane Carruthers, 'Dissecting the Myth: Paul Kruger and the Kruger National Park', *JSAS* 20, 2, (1994) and 'Defending Kruger's Honour? A Reply to Professor Hennie Grobler', *JSAS* 22, 3, (1996); Hennie Grobler, 'Dissecting the Kruger Myth with Blunt Instruments: A rebuttal of Jane Carruthers' view', *JSAS* 22, 3 (1996), pp. 455–72.

[70] Eugene N. Marais, *The Soul of the White Ant* (Harmondsworth, Penguin, 1973), first published 1937.

from nature rather than human company in the wilderness; to some degree their object of vision initially included African people as well as wildlife.

Afrikaner natural scientists and politicians increasingly took control in the 1950s. They projected themselves as scientific conservationists displacing amateur English military men. This had complex effects on the evolving formula of management: it affirmed the exclusion of black people from the park; it undermined privileged access by English-speaking photographers; and it helped to broaden the range of white visitors. Wildlife entered more generally into the white South African consciousness, and became a significant feature of the way Afrikaners projected their identity: as guardians of nature, as people who knew how to appreciate nature and to look at, as well as look after, wild animals. Africans were not completely absent from this protectionist project. They served as guards, guides and, in the case of Magqubu Ntombela in Natal, a source of local wisdom and lore about animal behaviour. Popularisation of African wildlife in South African perceptions was to some extent contemporaneous with that in British and American society, where film and especially television gave African animals, and their presenters, a particularly high profile in the 1950s and 1960s.[71] In the region, most African governments continued to protect wildlife reserves or National Parks after independence – an increasingly international project.

Robert Gordon's discussion of dogs in Namibia provides an alternative route into discussion of settlers and animals. Like Lichtenstein, the early nineteenth-century German traveller to the Cape, Gordon suggests that dogs have been underestimated in the colonising process.[72] They had certainly been important for Africans in precolonial times for hunting and guarding livestock; they were even more so for rural white landowners in pursuing these activities, in the control of predators and as guards. Gordon's arguments also go beyond an analysis of utility. He wishes to penetrate the social and cultural significance of dogs for settlers. They were admitted to human households, showered with favourable emotions (at least in texts) and were ubiquitous in photographs. Moreover, dogs and dog ownership were racialised. African-owned dogs were seen as neglected, while whites claimed that they cared for their dogs properly. Attempts were made to control the number of African dogs, which was a major reason for an African rebellion in 1922. Legislation and voluntary associations enshrined this racialisation in colonial society. Even more than wild animals, dogs and their treatment became an element in the formation of settler identity, as an essential feature of the settler domestic sphere.

Southern African landscape, wildlife, nature and domestic animals were all appropriated in the framing of settler identity, and sometimes in more explicit nationalist projects. Such ideas about nature in turn deeply influenced policies towards natural resources, especially as protectionist impulses began to evolve alongside the imperatives of exploitation. These, in turn, affected African access to natural resources throughout the region, but they also set down markers in the landscape, such as national parks, which have largely been defended by new African ruling elites. Global interests,

[71] Greg Mitman, *Reel Nature: America's romance with wildlife on film* (Cambridge, MA, Harvard University Press, 1999); W. Beinart, 'The Renaturing of African Animals: Film and Literature in the 1950s and 1960s' in P. Slack (ed.), *Environments and Historical Change* (Oxford, Oxford University Press, 1999); Derek Bouse, *Wildlife Films* (Philadelphia, University of Pennsylvania Press, 2000).
[72] W.H.C. Lichtenstein, *Travels in Southern Africa in the Years 1803, 1804, 1805 and 1806*, 2 vols (van Riebeeck Society, 1928), first published 1812, 1815, vol. 2, p. 18.

from the World Wildlife Fund to media networks and tourist companies, have reinforced and developed such processes in African countries. Draper and Mare have begun to analyse such relationships in contemporary Kwazulu/Natal, as they were developed through networks that included the eccentric English millionaire, casino-owner, and zoo-keeper John Aspinall, the KwaZulu/Natal National Parks Board, Chief Mangosutu Buthelezi and the Inkatha Freedom Party, and NGOs fostering eco-tourism.[73]

The fluidity of relationships between landscape and identity, and the way in which nature can be taken up by opposing groups in conflicts, is further illustrated by Jane Carruthers' chapter on the politics of claims by indigenous San communities over the Kalahari Gemsbok National Park in South Africa. Marginalised San communities are beginning to reassert themselves or be reasserted as 'original conservationists', even if they have by no means the ideological or political purchase achieved by Australian Aboriginal people. Many have been deeply impoverished, and absorbed as farmworkers or unemployed in small towns and camps in the northern Cape, Namibia or Botswana. Those who have attempted to rediscover and articulate their roots find themselves doing so in a world of international heritage sites, interested and sympathetic NGOs, lawyers and claims, and commercial demand for their skills as guides or craftspeople.

Using an Australian comparison, Carruthers notes that the context for their reassertion of community rights, and traditional knowledge, is a newly global and increasingly commodified context. To survive and prosper they may need to turn such opportunities to their advantage. Here community management of natural resources implies economic skills, not least the engagement with tourism and agencies that promote it. As Ben Page argued in his paper to the conference, community management of natural resources in Africa, which is now a major factor in both research and international funding programmes, does not always result in keeping commercial forces at bay. On the contrary, his example of village water projects in Cameroon suggests that community (rather than state) management can be a vehicle for increased commodification and more systematic involvement of international companies and organisations such as NGOs.[74]

These chapters should prompt caution in focusing only on continuities between colonial conservationism and contemporary environmental approaches and interventions. Western environmentalism has evolved in many directions since the 1960s and all of these have influenced African debates. Environmentalists certainly remain protagonists for the natural world, and draw on scientific, ecological advances, but some have been influenced by concerns about equity and social justice, and some green philosophies have championed local knowledge and community control.[75] The effects of these ideas have been varied in both environmental and social terms. Just as the varieties of 'colonial science' require further investigation, so too do the multi-faceted nature of scientific enquiry, environmental advocacy and their effects in the post-colonial world.

---

[73] M. Draper and G. Mare, 'Going in: The Garden of Eden's Gaming Zookeeper and Zululand' *JSAS*, forthcoming; Malcolm Draper, 'Zen and the Art of Garden Province Maintenance: the Soft Intimacy of Hard men in the Wilderness of KwaZulu-Natal, South Africa, 1952–1997', *JSAS* 24, 4 (1998).

[74] Ben Page, '"A priceless commodity": Resisting the Commodification of Water in Modern Cameroon', unpublished paper presented to the Conference on 'African Environments: Past and Present', St Antony's College, University of Oxford, 1999.

[75] David Pepper, *Ecosocialism: From deep ecology to social justice* (London, Routledge, 1993); Ramachandra Guha and J. Martinez Alier, *Varieties of Environmentalism: Essays North and South* (London, Earthscan, 1997).

Part I

African Environmental Ideas & Practices

1

Hidden Fruits

A Social Ecology of Fruit Trees in Namibia & Angola
1880s–1990s[1]

EMMANUEL KREIKE

[During the late 1910s] I picked jackalberry and birdplum fruit.... I sold it and bought goats with the proceeds ... the fruit trees were many in Angola. Marula trees also abounded but ... the alcoholic drink made from it was not sold.... You could collect jackalberry and birdplum fruit freely. If the trees were within someone's garden I first asked permission. Nowadays you cannot climb into someone's birdplum and pick its fruit, because people are very fond of making *ombike* liquor and selling it. This is very different from the old days.[2]

The early twentieth-century kingdoms in the northern Ovambo floodplain, namely Oukwanyama and the Ombadjas, abounded with such indigenous fruit trees as, for example, marula and birdplum. In contrast, these fruit trees were rare south of the *oshilongo* (sing.), i.e., south of the settled zone. War and famine during the 1910s, however, caused thousands to flee their villages and seek safety in the middle floodplain *ofuka* or 'wilderness'. As they slowly created a new *oshilongo*, replete with farms and fields, they also propagated fruit trees. Later, as new migrants from Angola joined their numbers and settlement expanded south and eastwards, a fruit tree frontier followed in their wake. This resulting process of afforestation in Ovamboland appears to sharply contradict studies that have argued that north-central Namibia's twentieth-century history is marked by dramatic deforestation. Fairhead and Leach's criticism of the declinist paradigm is highly relevant to an understanding of environmental change in this part of southern Africa.[3] While the seminal articles on the same fruit tree species

[1] The author gratefully acknowledges the generous support of a Social Science Research Council International Doctoral Thesis Research Grant, Yale University, the Namibian Directorate of Forestry, Wageningen Agricultural University, and Princeton University.
[2] Helena Nailonga, interview by author, Ekoka, 23 February 1993.
[3] On deforestation, see A. Erkkilä and H. Siiskonen, *Forestry in Namibia* (Joensuu, University of Joensuu, 1992) and M. Seely and A. Marsh (eds.), *Oshanas: Sustaining People, Environment, and Development in Central Ovambo* ([Windhoek], 1992). J. Fairhead and M. Leach, *Misreading the African Landscape: Society and ecology in a forest-savanna mosaic* (Cambridge, CUP, 1996). O*shilongo* (settled zone) and *ofuka* (wilderness) approximate the English translations, but they are not identical. See E. Kreike, 'Recreating Eden: Agro-Ecological Change, Food Security and Environmental Diversity in Southern Angola and Northern Namibia, 1890–1960', unpublished Ph.D. thesis, Yale University (1996).

in Zimbabwe by Wilson and Campbell suggest that some fruit trees were 'wild', and were spared when original vegetation cover was removed for settlement, both also note that some had been planted.[4]

The marula, birdplum, and palm trees that dot Ovamboland's fields are not the relic vegetation of an earlier extensive forest cover; neither are they 'wild' trees from a former wilderness. Rather, they were propagated through human agency both passively and actively from seeds and cuttings, and they were rare in the uninhabited 'wilderness' areas throughout the period under consideration. The study of the southern African environment is dominated by a political ecology approach, which focuses on the power struggles between the colonial state and local populations.[5] Less is known about subtle changes in land-use strategies or plant transfers within areas of African settlement. Although fruit trees certainly became a hotly contested resource, and state actions affected the use and management of tree resources in Ovamboland, the spread of fruit trees must also be located in the social, economic, and cultural domains of households and villages.

Fruit trees in the late nineteenth-century Ovambo floodplain

The earliest Europeans travellers to the Ovambo floodplain were struck by the abundance of fruit trees. In the early 1890s, upon entering the southern floodplain from the south, the missionary Wulfhorst noted Ondonga's fertile fields, which were 'here and there interspersed with groves of dark leaved trees or tall palm trees and through the leaves [were] large numbers of huts'.[6] The 'dark leaved trees' were most likely fig trees, which grew to gigantic dimensions reaching a height of 80 feet. The baobab grew to the same height and its trunk could be up to 40 feet in circumference, but it was confined to the drier western half of the floodplain and the far northern districts of Oukwanyama and adjacent Evale.[7]

The northern floodplain was dominated by deciduous fruit trees that shed their leaves during the dry season. The most important of these were jackalberry (*omwandi* or *Diospyros mespiliformis*), birdplum (*omuvelomuye* or *Berchemia discolor*); and marula (*omwongolomugongo* or *Sclerocarya birrea*). Jackalberry lined the banks of the seasonal watercourses in the central and middle floodplain. During the 1880s and

---

[4] For Ovamboland, see Seely and Marsh, *Oshanas* and R.J. Rodin, *The Ethnobotany of the Kwanyama Ovambos* (Missouri Botanical Gardens, 1985), p. 34. K.B. Wilson, 'Trees in Fields in Southern Zimbabwe', *Journal of Southern African Studies (JSAS)*, 15, 2 (1989): 369–83 and B.M. Campbell, 'The Use of Wild Fruits in Zimbabwe', *Economic Botany* 41, 3 (1987): 375–85.

[5] See, for example, W. Beinart and C. Bundy, *Hidden Struggles in Rural South Africa: Politics and popular movements in the Transkei and Eastern Cape, 1890-1930* (Berkeley and Los Angeles, University of California Press, 1987) and *JSAS* 15, 2 (1989) special issue on 'The Politics of Conservation in Southern Africa'. Wilson's contribution to the latter also highlighted the religious-cultural roles of fruit trees, 'Trees in Fields', pp. 378–80.

[6] A. Wulfhorst, *Aus den Anfangstagen der Ovambo-Mission* (Barmen, Rheinisches Missionshaus, 1904), p. 4. See also, B. Lau (ed.), *Carl Hugo Hahn Tagebücher/Diaries, 1837–1860*, part iv 1856–1860 (Windhoek, Archives Services Division, 1985), p. 1039; National Archives of Namibia (NAN), NAO 104, Anderson to Hahn, extract diary Jordan, *Cape Quarterly Review* vol II (1882), pp. 519–39.

[7] Interviews by author: Johannes Shipunda, Omundaunghilo, 14 July 1993; Kulaumoni Haifeke, Oshomukwiyu , 11 May 1993; Elisabeth Ndemutela, Okongo, 16 February 1993; Helemiah Hamutenya, Omuulu Weembaxu, 17 July 1993.

1890s, missionaries waxed enthusiastic about the 'wild' birdplum and marula trees and interviewees recalled their abundance throughout pre-1915 Oukwanyama and Ombadja.[8] During the last decades of the nineteenth century, palm wine was a major alcoholic beverage in the southern floodplain, while in the northern floodplain the fruit of marula trees and raisin bush (*Grewia*) fruit were also made into wines. In Oukwanyama, when the marula fruit ripened during the months of February and March, men and women engaged in celebrations at which marula wine flowed freely for weeks on end. Not even recent mission converts could resist participating and a despairing missionary wrote: '[u]nfortunately [marula] trees are too abundant and everyone has them on their fields'.[9] Despite their distaste for marula and its wine, however, the missionaries understood that tree fruit proved to be invaluable during the seasonal period of shortages early in the rainy season (before the main field crops ripened) and during famine years.[10]

Fruit trees were not simply 'communally' owned. During the early 1900s, on-farm baobab trees in Omukwa (Angola) were the property of the farm owners. When the fruit was ripe, the owners presented some of it to other households.[11] In 1916–17, British-South African troops who entered the floodplain to quell Oukwanyama resistance received strict orders to '[s]pare all fruittrees viz : Palm, Wild Fig, Marula etc. and all trees in inhabited areas [of Ovamboland]' after the local colonial officials concluded that '[p]ractically all trees in such areas are wild fruit trees bearing and native owned'.[12] The marula tree was subject to complicated overlapping rights. Part of the marula wine had to be brought to the king of Oukwanyama. The remainder was consumed by the households on whose land the trees grew.[13]

Refugees and the fruit tree frontier

The situation described above changed dramatically in 1915, when famine and violence

[8] Archives of the United Evangelical Missions at Wuppertal (AVEM), RMG 2599 C/i 19, Bernsmann, Omburo, 6 January 1892; Archives of the Holy Ghost Congregation (AGCSSp) 466-A-VII, Duparquet, Carnets de Notes-Voyages # 3, entries August-September 1879 and info. Mr. Leen, 29 April 1879; *ibid.* Duparquet, 1880 journal, July 10–11, 14, 1880. Interviews by author: Elisabeth Ndemutela, Okongo, 16 February 1993; Helemiah Hamutenya, Omuulu Weembaxu, 17 July 1993; Johannes Shipunda, Omudaunghilo, 14 July 1993 and Julius Abraham, Olupito, 16 June 1993. Cf. P. Möller, *Journey in Africa through Angola, Ovampoland and Damaraland* (Cape Town, Struik, 1974), pp. 125–6.

[9] NAN, NAO 104, Anderson to Hahn, diary Jordan; Möller, *Journey* , p. 125. AGCSSp Duparquet, 1879 journal, August 17, September 10, 12, 14, 21, 23; C. Estermann, *Etnografia do Sudoeste de Angola: Vol. 1, Os Povos não-Bantos e o Grupo Étnico dos Ambós* (Lisbon, 1960), p. 134; Wulfhorst, *Anfangstagen*, p. 28; and quarterly reports in AVEM RMG 2518 C/h 34, Ondjiva, 10 April 1911, 12 April 1912, 1 April 1913, and 30 June 1914; RMG 2517 C/h 33 folio 10, Omupanda, 1 April 1914; RMG 2515 C/h 31, Omatemba, 30 March 1916.

[10] AVEM, RMG 2599 C/i 19, Bernsmann, Omburo, 6 January 1892. On famines and fruit trees, see, for example, RMG 2518 C/h 34, Ondjiva, 1 April 1913; Helena Nailonga, interview by author, Big Ekoka, 23 February 1993.

[11] Johannes Shipunda, interview by author, Omundaunghilo, 14 July 1993.

[12] NAN, RCO 10, f. 15/1916/1, 'Notes for Officer Commanding Military Detachments Ovamboland, October 1916' and 'Preliminary Memorandum for Expeditionary Force by Resident Commissioner C.N. Manning and Lt. Hahn [1916]'.

[13] AVEM, quarterly reports RMG 2517 C/h 33, Omupanda, 1 April 1914 and RMG 2518 C/h 34, Ondjiva, 1 April 1913.

caused by the Portuguese conquest of the northern floodplain cast tens of thousands adrift. Many refugees eventually settled south of the modern Angolan-Namibian border in the middle floodplain that was almost entirely devoid of farms, fields, dams, waterholes, and the abundant fruit trees that marked the *oshilongo* settled zones of Oukwanyama and Ombadja.[14] When observing large numbers of abandoned farms and crop fields in 1927, an official commented: '[m]uch of it was a perfect Paradise for natives abounding as it did in fruit trees and grazing.'[15]

Most of the middle floodplain and the entire region east of the floodplain were considered *ofuka* 'wilderness'. Monika Hidengwa was born in Ombuwa (Angola) in what at the time was not really part of the *oshilongo* or settled zone of Oukwanyama. Although trees and bush abounded, the area was devoid of birdplum, marula, and palm trees. During the 1920s, Monika Hidengwa moved with her family to Ombwabwa near Omulunga (also in Angola). The only fruit trees in this village were manghetti (*omungete* or *Riciondendron rautanenii*).[16] An official who travelled east of Omafo into what was then considered *ofuka* wilderness was struck by a 'singular absence of fruit trees which attract the natives in selecting settlement places'.[17] Marula, birdplum, and palm trees made their appearance as refugees from the north colonised the middle floodplain *ofuka* wilderness, clearing land, constructing farms, fences, and waterholes and laying out fields. While these fruit trees were not entirely absent in the middle floodplain before 1915, their occurrence was often associated with settlements that had been abandoned in the nineteenth century.

For example, in the 1920s, when settlers from the northern floodplain arrived in Okalongo, they found palm and jackalberry trees that were associated with the early nineteenth-century kingdom of Haudanu: a cluster of palm trees at Onandjaba was known as *Omilunga yaHaudanu*, or the palm trees of Haudanu. Despite these signs of past settlement, however, the region was considered *ofuka* wilderness and most fruit trees in the area's villages appeared after the colonists established their farms and fields.[18]

Only the southernmost district of the pre-1915 Oukwanyama kingdom, which included such villages as, for example, Namakunde, stretched into the middle flood-plain. In 1879, the missionary Duparquet had noted clusters of fruit trees and signs of previous settlement at pans in this area, although at the time it was entirely abandoned. In 1915 it was regarded as *ofuka* wilderness.[19] Following the influx of refugees, the area changed dramatically. A 1928 description of the Angolan-South West African border between border markers 16 and 23 stressed the abundant signs of recent colonization: '[t]he first Ukuanyama werft [homestead] is at Point 16. The country

[14] Kreike, 'Recreating Eden', chapters 3–4; NAN, NAO 11, f.6/1/1 (I), Native Affairs Ovamboland (NAO) to Finnish Missionary Society (FMS), Ondangwa 25 November 1928; NAO 18 f. 11/1 (i), Hahn, 'Notes on Ovamboland for His Honour the Administrator', Windhoek, 15 May 1924; Julius Abraham, interview by author, Olupito, 16 June 1993.

[15] NAN, KAB 1 (vi), Draft Report Kunene Water Commission, Olusandja, July [1927], to Secretary SWA.

[16] Monika Hidengwa, interview by author, Eenhana Refugee Camp, 16 July 1993. Ombuwa was probably a cattle post where her family sought refuge during the 1915 war.

[17] NAN, KAB 1 (ii), Submission to Administrator, Secretary and Attorney-General of SWA, 1927.

[18] Interviews by author: Julius Abraham, Olupito, 15–16 June 1993; Mathias Walaula, Onandjaba, 15 June 1993; Kanime Hamyela, Omutwewondjaba, 15 June 1993; Personal observations, 15 July 1993; NAN, KAB 1 (iii), Volkmann, 30 October 1928, 'Report on the Agricultural and Political Conditions at the Angola Boundary'.

[19] AGCSSp Duparquet, 1879 journal, August-September 1879; Malita Kalomo, interview by author, Omutwewondjaba, 15 July 1993.

becomes more open.... The werfts are on the dune-like banks; the bush has been destroyed. Everywhere one sees the beautiful Onjandi [jackalberry] trees or wild figs.'[20] Marula and birdplum trees (and to a lesser extent palm trees) – with the exceptions noted above – by and large only made their appearance in the middle flood-plain *ofuka* wilderness after the area was colonised during the 1920s and 1930s. Oral histories confirm this for such villages as, for example, Omupanda (Namibia) and Oshomukwiyu. In the early 1930s, marula trees were confined to only two of the eight existing farms in Omupanda, one of which was the farm of the first person to settle there around 1900.[21]

Fruit trees were not only associated with human settlement; human action also caused their southward expansion, although the extent to which people intervened in 'natural' processes varied. Born in 1930, Kulaumoni Haifeke, a daughter of the first pioneers to settle Oshomukwiyu, saw her village change from *ofuka* wilderness into an *oshilongo* rich in full-grown marula, birdplum, and palm trees. Her assessment was that they grew naturally: 'only God makes them grow.'[22]

Paulus Nadenga, however, emphasised that human management facilitated the self-propagation of fruit trees. In his view, the rains caused the stones of the fruit to germinate. But human intervention was essential during the rainy season: '[seedlings] only survived because during the dry season [they] lose their leaves and animals cannot eat them. During the rainy season, if they are located in the fields, people will till the soil and prevent the goats from entering.'[23] Kanime Hamyela proudly recounted how he had shaped the dense bush into a fertile garden with stately trees: '[t]he plants are like grains. If you thin millet it will grow fast and properly. It is the same with the bushes – if you cut out some then the remainder will grow fast and healthy.'[24] Mathias Walaula stressed that in Onandjaba, fire was used to thin out the palm bushes because only a free standing palm bush could grow into a tree.[25]

Similarly, Paulus Wanakashimba attributed the introduction of marula and birdplum trees in his village to the agency of women who collected fruit in older villages further north. The pits were discarded and some developed into seedlings. His village had few marula trees when he was a young boy during the early 1920s. By the mid-1930s, however, both his and a neighbouring village boasted many marula and birdplum trees. After he cleared his own farm in 1947, he fenced new seedlings with thornbush to protect them from livestock and, by the early 1990s, his farm had birdplum, marula, and palm trees.[26] In 1993, Julius Abraham's large and shady marula tree on his Olupito farm produced enough fruit to brew a 30 litre pot of marula wine with which to entertain his friends and guests. His father – one of the pioneers to settle the Okalongo area – discovered the tree when it was a mere bush hemmed in by huge trees. His father felled the trees around the bush and kept its surroundings free of weeds. In addition,

[20] NAN, KAB 1 (iii), Volkmann, 30 October 1928, 'Report on the Agricultural and Political Conditions'. 'Points' were boundary markers.

[21] Interviews by author: Mateus Nangobe, Omupanda, 24 May 1993; Paulus Wanakashimba, Odimbo, 10 and 11 February 1993; Paulus Nandenga, Oshomukwiyu, 28 April 1993; Kulaumoni Haifeke, Oshomukwiyu, 11 May 1993.

[22] Kulaumoni Haifeke, interview by author, Oshomukwiyu, 11 May 1993.

[23] Paulus Nandenga, interview by author, Oshomukwiyu, 28 April 1993.

[24] Kanime Hamyela, interview by author, Omutwewondjaba, 15 June 1993.

[25] Interviews by author: Mathias Walaula, Onandjaba, 15 June 1993 and Paulus Wanakashimba, Odimbo, 10–11 February 1993.

[26] Paulus Wanakashimba, interview by author, Odimbo, 10–11 February 1993.

one of the older villagers, Joseph Kashinghola, watered his birdplum seedlings and they developed into large trees.[27]

'Traditional' fruit tree tenure

Colonial officials were baffled by fruit tree tenure arrangements which, in addition to being extremely dynamic, seemed contradictory because different interpretations of 'traditional tenure' were used to support competing claims. The colonial officer in charge of Ovamboland, C.H.L. Hahn, attempted to codify local resource tenure as a means of consolidating colonial rule. His main sources were missionaries, chiefs and headmen, and his Ovambo assistants. One of his sources, probably a Finnish missionary stationed in Ondonga, noted that '[i]n some districts the fruit trees in the field do not follow the ownership of field, but must be purchased separately'.[28]

Hahn's codification of customary Ovambo law tended to favour claims by chiefs and headmen. His rough personal notes based on information he gathered during the 1920s attest to the enormous variation in tree tenure. In Ongandjera, '[the] [o]ccupier [of a farm] has not always got the right to all the fruit trees in the area allotted him as in many areas fruit trees are reserved for chiefs (fruit for beer making) and occupiers understand this condition'. In Onkolonkathi and Eunda in the southwestern edge of the floodplain '[f]ruit trees are general(ly) shared particular marala [marula] tree by the headman who has right to collect fruit from certain trees reserved for himself. Owner of kraal may not use fruit from reserved trees unless he receives headman's permission.' In Ombalantu, Hahn was persuaded that control of the headmen over land and trees had collapsed.[29] During the early 1930s, in South West African Oukwanyama, Hahn concluded:

> Omuongo (marula) trees and fruit belong to the chief [king] but the headman of the omukunda [village] owns the fruit which remains after the chief had his share collected; it is the duty of the headmen to collect it and to send it to the Chief. If a chief does not require the fruit from a particular area the headman owns it. Today, in the absence of a chief, the eight principal headmen exercise the rights of the chief in this respect; each in his own district.... The right of use of indigenous fruit trees other than omuongo … depends upon the situation of such trees. If a tree stands in a cornfield the fruit belongs to the cornfield and the possessor or occupier for the time being becomes the owner of such fruit. If the tree is outside the cornfield or kraal its fruit is public property.[30]

Fruit tree tenure, however, was even less structured than Hahn's notes suggested. Petrus Mbubi claimed that his parents owned all of the 39 fruit trees that grew on their farm in Oikokola (Ondonga) during the 1920s.[31] He did not qualify his parents' claim to ownership, even in respect to marula trees, although Hahn had been told that the Ondonga king had claims to the fruit. Paulus Wanakashimba recalled that fruit trees were not owned by 'the household' as a collective or 'the head of the household', but

---

[27] Julius Abraham, interview by author, Olupito, 16 June 1993.
[28] Kreike, 'Recreating Eden'. On the missionary: NAN, A450, vol. 9, f. 2/35, 'Ovambo Customs (1926)'.
[29] NAN, A450, vol. 23, D6, Land Tenure.
[30] NAN, A450, vol. 9, file 2/38, 'Property Rights'.
[31] Petrus Mbubi, interview by author, Onanime, 26 February 1993.

by the owners of individual fields. Until the 1950s, in Oukwanyama, it was common that all members of the household (except small children) received an individual plot (*oshikokola*) and the millet (the staple crop) produced there belonged to the person to whom the plot had been allocated. Paulus Wanakashimba thought the same applied to fruit trees: 'a palm tree belongs to the owner of the particular piece of land. If it is in a woman's piece of land then it is the wife's palm tree. All trees within a garden when they are taken care of – if in a woman's garden then [they] are her birdplum trees.'[32]

A broad interpretation of the concept of the 'moral economy' sheds light not only on the contested claims to fruit tree ownership but also on some of the contradictions.[33] Gifts of fruit and fruit products assured chiefly patronage, and reciprocal access to fruit trees between neighbouring households permitted marginalised households (especially elderly single women) access to either 'private' or 'communal' fruit trees. For example, Shangeshapwako Hauladi's family lived in Onelombo (Angola) until the late 1920s. Her family had no fruit trees on their farm but jackalberry and fig were abundant throughout the village and 'anybody could come and gather the fruit from any tree'. In 1920s Omundaunghilo in eastern Ovamboland, birdplum trees similarly abounded and every household had fruit trees. Children could go anywhere to pick the birdplum tree fruit. The neighbours of Paulus Nadenga's parents gathered fruit from their birdplum and marula trees; the neighbours in turn allowed his family to gather fruit from their marula tree which bore fruit later in the season.[34]

Guns and stills

A series of drought years that culminated in the 1930–31 Famine of the Dams served yet again to highlight the importance of fruit trees. During the famine, tree fruit and palm wine were critical alternative sources of food. In fact, palm wine was tapped on such a scale that it contributed to the destruction of large numbers of palm trees in the southern floodplain during the late 1920s and early 1930s.[35]

Missionaries and colonial officials alike abhorred the consumption of alcoholic beverages produced from the fruit of indigenous trees. While the Finnish missionaries in the 1920s were less perturbed by the marula 'wines' that had worried their predecessors, they urged the administration to act against the increasing production and sale of 'distilled spirits, called Olambice, from the different fruits of trees'. Missionaries attributed increased violence, immorality, and decreased crop yields to alcohol abuse. They pointed out that, by distilling it, people 'are wasting the necessary fruit which until now has been a considerable part of their foodstuff'.[36] By 1930, the most popular fruits used for distilling *ombike* or *olambika* were birdplum and

---

[32] Paulus Wanakashimba, interview by author, Odimbo, 10–11 February 1993. For the *oshikokola*-plot, see Kreike, 'Recreating Eden', ch. 7.

[33] On the concept of 'moral economy', see J. Scott, *The Moral Economy of the Peasant: Rebellion and subsistence in Southeast Asia.* (New Haven, CT and London, Yale University Press, 1976).

[34] Interviews by author: Shangeshapwako Hauladi, Omundaunghilo, 14 July 1993; Paulus Nandenga, Oshomukwiyu, 28 April 1993; see also Helena Nailonga, Ekoka, 23 February 1993 and Mateus Nangobe, Omupanda, 24 May 1993.

[35] NAN, NAO 18-19 f. 11/1 (I-v), Monthly Reports, November-December 1928, January–February 1929, April 1930, March 1931, and July–August 1932.

[36] NAN, NAO 11, f. 6/1/1 (I), FMS to NAO, Olukonda, 12 November 1928.

jackalberry. The quantities produced were reportedly 'large', and during a single month in 1928 35 stills were located and destroyed. Hahn explained that 'it is generally reported that the art of making this drink [*olambike*] was introduced to Ovamboland by Portuguese natives. In the old neutral zone particularly it was fairly extensively practised because of the number of suitable indigenous fruit trees growing in that area.' Oukwanyama was singled out as the centre of *olambike* production and both '[t]he people from Uukuanyama [Oukwanyama] and from North-Ondonga are openly selling bottles of "olambica" in the other districts of Ondonga'.[37] Missionaries and officials stressed that the effects of the consumption of *olambike* and other alcoholic beverages spread at an alarming rate, undermining order and stability in Ovamboland.[38]

Home distilling of *olambike* in the floodplain was introduced around the turn of the century. Helena Hailonga was born in the Oukwanyama kingdom during the reign of King Nande (who died in 1911) and as a young girl gathered the fruit of the birdplum and jackalberry trees to sell it to women who distilled *olambike*.[39] The refugees from the north brought not only the fruit trees but also the practice of distilling *olambike*. One reason why so much of the fruit was distilled into liquor was that the Famine of the Dams caused shortfalls in household food production. A second factor was a sharp drop in wage labour recruitment and thus in the inflow of money and goods as a result of the worldwide economic recession of the early 1930s.[40] Sharing alcoholic beverages renewed social networks, and patrons and friends could offer needy households some food; the sale of *olambike* and palm wine also offered alternative sources of income for the purchase of food and other goods. That the sale of *olambike* was highly profitable is attested to by interviewees but also by the fact that, in 1928, inferior Portuguese wine smuggled into Ovamboland was sold in 'large quantities' for five shillings per bottle, roughly half the monthly wage of a migrant labourer.[41]

Distilling *olambike* remained an important source of income, especially for single women without a wage-earning male partner (or son or other close male relative), even when migrant labour recruitment picked up during the mid-1930s and reached new heights during the 1940s. Indeed, although the number and percentage of men who engaged in wage labour increased, the number of households without a male wage-earner may actually have risen. During this era, the divorce rate seems to have soared as a result of intra-household strife over resources, the increase in male absenteeism and the dissolution of polygamous marriages as Christianity spread rapidly. Distilling *olambike*, tapping palm wine, or brewing beer for sale under such conditions seemed an attractive way to supplement household production.[42]

For example, during the 1930s, Philippus Haidima's unmarried aunts who owned a farm in Onamunama distilled *olambike* from birdplum and fig tree fruit and sold it for money, grain and other necessities. The remaining fruit was eaten fresh or dried and stored.[43] After the death of her husband in 1930, Mwulifundja Haiyaka moved in with

[37] NAN, NAO 18 f. 11/1 (I), Monthly Report December 1928. NAO 11, f. 6/1/1 (I), FMS to NAO, Olukonda, 12 November 1928 and NAO to FMS, Ondangwa 25 November 1928.

[38] NAN, NAO 11, f. 6/1/1 (I), FMS to NAO, Olukonda, 12 November 1928; NAO to FMS, Ondangwa 25 November 1928; A450, 12 f. 3/21/5, SWA Commission: Minutes of Evidence, vol. 12, pp. 671–2.

[39] Helena Nailonga, interview by author, Ekoka laKula , 23 February 1993.

[40] Kreike, 'Recreating Eden', ch. 6, pp. 189-98.

[41] NAN, NAO 18 f. 11/1 (I), Monthly Report December 1928 and Helena Nailonga, interview with author, Ekoka laKula, 23 February 1993. On wages, see Kreike, 'Recreating Eden', p. 206.

[42] Kreike, 'Recreating Eden', chs. 6–7.

[43] Philippus Haidima, interview by author, Odibo, 9 December 1992.

her mother and grandmother. The women's farm did not yield enough millet and they owned no cattle. She turned to distilling: '[i]n those days when I was still strong I would go and gather fruit and make *ombike* and sell it. With the money I could buy food.'[44]

Native Commissioner Hahn played down the extent of alcohol use and home distilling before a 1935 commission of inquiry. He maintained that the Ovambo 'is a pretty sober man in his habits' and rejected any new regulations to control alcohol use as superfluous. Hahn, however, may in fact have wanted to head off any possible interference by the central colonial administration: at the time he had himself mounted an active campaign to suppress the production and sale of alcoholic beverages. During the same inquiry, Hahn conceded that the headmen in Oukwanyama and Uukwambi had requested that he 'give them authority to destroy any little distilling plants that they may find'.[45] An Anglican Mission lay worker observed five smiths next to Hahn's Ondangwa headquarters feverishly forging confiscated gun barrels into hoes: '[t]hese old muzzle loader barrels were being used as the condenser to distil a vile spirit which was very potent so that the commissioner [Hahn] thought that if he got rid of the gun barrels it would at least slow down the distilling'.[46] *Olambike* also continued to be produced in Angolan Oukwanyama, for example by Franscina Herman's parents, and was smuggled south across the border.[47]

As the fruit tree frontier advanced into the middle floodplain, so the production of fermented marula wines spread, although Ovamboland's administrators showed little interest in its production. During the February–March 'marula season' in Oukwanyama – which in the 1930s along with northeastern Ondonga was the marula wine country *par excellence* – the carrying of weapons was prohibited. Marula wine consumption in western Ovamboland, where it was a much more precious drink, was largely confined to the highest notables. For example, King Iipumbu of Uukwambi was a great fan of marula wine.[48]

Marula fruit was considered to be so valuable that communal marula trees were frequently fenced with thornbush to protect the fruit from animals and to establish claims to the fruit. In 1939, the fencing of a communal marula tree in an Oukwanyama village caused a conflict between two neighbouring households and resulted in a murder.[49] Philippus Haidima recalled that, in addition to large fruit-bearing marula trees, birdplum and jackalberry in the village commons were also sometimes fenced. In contrast, the fig tree was never fenced because its fruit was for everybody.[50]

While marula wine production only rarely attracted the attention of colonial

[44] Interviews by author: Mwulifundja Haiyaka, Omhedi, 8 March 1993 and Franscina Herman, Odibo, 12 December 1992.

[45] NAN, A450, 12 f. 3/21/5, SWA Commission, vol. 12, pp. 671–2.

[46] MacDonald Diary (courtesy Nancy MacDonald), p. 9.

[47] NAN, NAO 9 f. 2/12, Assistant Native Affairs Commissioner Ovamboland (ANC) Oshikango, 30 October 1942, 'Comments on Statement made by Makili Haimbudu to the Native Commissioner, Runtu' and NAO 60, f. 12/1 (I), Quarterly Report January–March 1949; Franscina Herman, interview by author, Odibo, 12 December 1992.

[48] NAN, NAO 19 f. 11/1 (iv), Monthly Report January-February 1931 and March 1932.

[49] NAN, NAO 46 f. 45/1/1, Native Commmissioner Ovamboland (NCO) to Registrar High Court, Ondangwa, 8 June 1939, Statements by Muvayi Kangolo, Haimbodi Hanalua, Ndeshiyala Hafingo, Nanapo Kaidhanapela, Ondangwa, 8 March 1939 and ANC, 9 March 1939.

[50] Philippus Haidima, interview by author, Odibo, 9 December 1992. Cf. interviews by author: Joseph Nghudika, Onamahoka, 3 February 1993 and Nahandjo Hailonga, Onamahoka, 4 February 1993.

officials, the opposite continued to be true for home distilling. In 1947, Eedes succeeded Hahn as Native Commissioner and immediately launched a campaign to eradicate home distilling once and for all. He ordered his deputy in Oukwanyama to have all the stills destroyed and to have 'the persons guilty of distilling ... severely punished. The Headman in charge of the area in which stills are found in future must be warned that action will be taken against him also.' As a result, from May 1947 to 14 September 1947, 352 stills were destroyed in Oukwanyama alone. The metal pipes of stills were flattened and buried at the Oshikango office and the senior headmen of Oukwanyama received a 'final warning' against illegal distilling in November 1947.[51] But these measures failed to stamp out home distilling. In December 1948, four more stills were located and destroyed in Oukwanyama. One of those implicated was a village headman.[52]

Distilling was not confined to Oukwanyama. The head of the Finnish Mission conceded that in Uukwambi even

> [s]ome of our Christians are also cooking whiskey [from fruits], in spite of our severe warnings... the Headmen are especially drinking whisky [sic], and therefore they are protecting the makers of the drink, 'Olambika'or 'Ombike'. The Headmen are fond of putting into 'Omalovu' [*omalodu*: millet or sorghum beer] also 'Ombike', and many people are following this custom. We hear from Natives that in Uukwanyama the cooking of 'Ombike' is strictly forbidden, and the making of it is a punishable thing.[53]

Nevertheless in early 1949, at least 38 stills were dismantled in Ondonga and 12 stills were located and destroyed in Ombalantu.[54] Ironically, the colonial administration at the same time in effect 'protected' the home brewing industry by preventing the trading stores in Ovamboland from selling alcoholic beverages and prohibiting the import of alcohol from across the border, although alcohol smuggling from Angola was never effectively stopped.[55]

From the 1930s to the 1950s, the fruit tree frontier advanced into a radically new environment: eastern Ovamboland beyond the confines of the Ovambo floodplain. Omundaunghilo east of the floodplain was already a fully fledged village with birdplum, marula and palm trees by 1923. But in most of the region, mature floodplain fruit trees appeared later because settlement only really took off during the early 1920s. Kalolina Naholo observed settlers in the east seeding marula, birdplum, and jackalberry. Marula and manghetti could also be propagated by cutting off a green branch and planting it in moist soil.[56]

Whereas interviewees from eastern Ovamboland in general emphasised human agency in the propagation of fruit trees, interviewees from the floodplain and from the

[51] NAN, NAO 71 f. 32/3, NCO to ANC, Ondangwa, 12 May 1947; NCO, [Ondangwa], 29 August 1947; NCO to Chief Native Commissioner (CNC), Ondangwa, 14 September 1947; ANC to NCO, Oshikango, 13 November 1947.

[52] NAN, NAO 71 f. 32/3, ANC to NCO, Oshikango, 15 December 1948 and Rodin, *Ethnobotany*, pp. 36–7.

[53] NAN, NAO 71 f. 32/3, Victor Alho (FMS) to NCO, Onajena, 6 November 1948.

[54] NAN, NAO 71 f. 32/3, NCO to Chief Kambonde, Ondangwa, 28 December 1948 and to CNC, Ondangwa, 20 February 1949.

[55] NAN, NAO 60–61, f. 12/1 (I-ii), Quarterly Reports January–March 1949 and April–June 1954.

[56] Interviews by author: Kalolina Naholo, Ohamwaala, 26–27 January 1993; Paulus Nandenga, Oshomukwiyu, 28 April 1993; Franscina Herman, Odibo, 12 December 1992; cf. Helemiah Hamutenya, Omuulu Weembaxu, 17 July 1993. On eastern Ovamboland, see Kreike, 'Recreating Eden', ch. 9.

westernmost part of eastern Ovamboland tended to stress that the fruit trees that appeared in their new villages and farms grew 'naturally' or were 'gifts of God' even if seedlings were carefully nurtured. Pauline commented that during her childhood: '[a]ll people took care of these trees.... Young men of today don't take care of plants (trees); they cut them down or plough them under.... Because they were not abundant we took care of every birdplum, jackalberry, and fig [tree].'[57]

Colonial officials were blind to the advancing fruit tree frontier, which they presumed to be part of the original 'wild' vegetation cover, but not to the deforestation that resulted from the creation of entire new villages and districts. Except for selected fruit-bearing species and individual non-fruit trees (to serve as shade trees, for example), most trees and bush on a new farm were cut down and the materials used to construct huts, palisades, and fences. The impact of settlement on vegetation cover was especially dramatic in the eastern half of the middle floodplain where a new Oukwanyama had been carved out of the *ofuka* wilderness in less than 15 years. In 1931, the Assistant Native Commissioner for Oukwanyama, newly arrived at his post, was shocked by the '[m]any cases of wilful [sic] destruction of large, often fruit, trees ... to quote the words of Mr. Hahn in one particular case, "The area had altered so much, due to destruction of trees, that it was hard to believe it was the same area".' He immediately issued a 'tribal order' to re-establish 'the old tribal law' that protected 'all fruit trees, palm trees and trees, the trunk of which is thicker than the thigh of a man'. His superior, Hahn, however, surmised that tree clearing for new farms was unavoidable and pointed out that fruit trees were 'generally speaking' protected in all the 'tribal areas' of Ovamboland. He added that '[i]n fact certain species are very jealously guarded and many species have special names and there are definite laws in regard to their ownership'. Yet he acknowledged that outside of the inhabited area, in the *ofuka* wilderness, the protection of fruit trees was insufficient.[58] Beyond attempts to limit tapping palm wine from adult trees (which could kill the tree) and championing customary preservation regulations to prevent fruit trees from being cut down in the inhabited areas of the floodplain, little was done in terms of conservation. In fact, most conservation regulations were either ignored or not enforced by the local colonial officials themselves.[59]

Whose wild trees?

In a 1953 letter to Petrus Kuferi, Native Commissioner Eedes challenged local con-cepts of fruit tree ownership: 'I notice that you are concerned about what you call YOUR marula trees [emphasis in original]. The trees are not yours – they belong to the Government. You are really worried about them because they produce a form of

---

[57] Interviews by author: Pauline, Onenghali, 15 December 1992; Alpheus Hamundja, Ohamwaala, 26 January 1993; Joseph Nghudika, Onamahoka, 3 February 1993; Nahandjo Hailonga, Onamahoka, 4 February 1993; Kaulikalelwa Oshitina Muhonghwo, Ondaanya, 2 February 1993.

[58] NAN, NAO 44 f. 37/1, Officer Oshikango to NCO, Oshikango, 17 March 1931 and NCO to Secretary SWA, Ondangwa, 20 April 1931.

[59] NAN, NAO 101 f. 43/7, NCO to CNC, Ondangwa, 17 April 1948; NAO 44 f. 37/1, NCO to CNC, Ondangwa, 2 June 1941; NAO 43 f. 35/1 (iv), NCO to CNC, Ondangwa, 26 August 1946 and telegram NCO to Secretary SWA, Ondangwa 26 August 1946; NAO 60-61 f. 12/1 (I–II), Quarterly Reports, October-December 1952 and April–June 1954.

liquor.'[60] He did not, however, in any way effectively follow up on this statement and it is unlikely to have had much, if any, effect. But after Eedes retired and the Native Affairs Department of the Union of South Africa took control of the reserves of South West Africa in 1954, South African conservation policies were introduced in Ovamboland. Ovamboland was assigned an agricultural officer who included creating forest reserves and conserving indigenous trees amongst his many priorities. Although the agricultural officer in 1957 concluded that fruit trees were already being protected by the local population, he nevertheless recommended that a list of 'valuable trees' that could not be cut down be compiled. The list was to be distributed to all the district and village headmen. In 1978, the new forester for Ovamboland, apparently unaware of these earlier attempts, compiled a separate list of protected trees that included all the principal indigenous fruit trees. He, too, acknowledged that most were already protected under 'Owambo tradition'. However, he stressed that while most of the trees on his list were already protected in South West Africa, there was no formal legislation to that effect in the Ovambo homeland.[61]

Colonial conservation regulations had an impact. Interviewees recalled that fully grown indigenous fruit trees could not be cut down without the permission of the village and the district headmen, even if they were located on a household's farmlands. The restriction also applied to the non-fruit-bearing male trees, which previously had enjoyed little protection, and it was also extended to lopping branches of indigenous fruit trees. Philippus Haidima mentioned that cutting down a marula tree could even get one arrested. Permission to cut was granted only when, for example, a fruit tree contained a hole that could house snakes.[62]

To colonial officials, the location of fruit trees in the landscape appeared random. Yet the opposite was true. The actual homestead consisting of living quarters, kitchens, and storage huts and surrounded by a palisade (*omiti*) was the perfect nursery for the active and passive propagation of fruit trees. Fruit was prepared and eaten within the *omiti*; pits and used water were discarded around the huts or on household middens next to the *omiti*, and under favourable conditions pits sprouted and developed into saplings. Moreover, the *omiti* offered saplings protection from the burning sun, merciless winds, frost, and livestock. The entire palisade-enclosed homestead was relocated within the farm every 3–5 years or so; by then, seedlings were much better prepared to face the elements and livestock. Full-grown fruit trees therefore often marked former locations of the enclosed homestead.[63]

The apparent randomness in the location of indigenous fruit trees reinforced colonial officials' misperception that indigenous fruit trees were 'wild trees'. In his

[60] NAN, NAO 63 f.17/1 (I), NCO to Petrus Kuferi, Ondangwa, 10 December 1953.

[61] NAN, NAO 61 f. 12/1 (ii), Quarterly Reports, April–June and July–September 1954; BAC 133 f. HN 8/21/4/1, Agricultural Officer to CNC, Ondangwa, 19 November 1956 and to NCO, Ondangwa, 4 July 1956; BAC 131 f. HN 8/17/4, Agricultural Officer to Bantu Commissioners Ondangwa and Oshikango, [Ondangwa], 28 January 1957; OVJ 19 f. 23/20/2, Forester Owambo to Secretary, [Ondangwa], 18 August 1978.

[62] Interviews by author: Kaulikalelwa Oshitina Muhonghwo, Ondaanya, 2 February 1993; Philippus Haidima, Odibo, 9 December 1992; Joseph Nghudika, Onamahoka, 3 February 1993.

[63] Interviews by author: Kaulikalelwa Oshitina Muhonghwo, Ondaanya, 2 February 1993; Moses Kakoto, Okongo, 17 February 1993; Timotheus Nakale, Ekoka laKula, 21 February 1993; Helemiah Hamutenya, Omuulu Weebaxu, 17 July 1993; Philippus Haidima, Odibo, 9 December 1992; Paulus Wanakashimba, Odimbo, 10–11 February 1993.

report for 1956–57, the agricultural officer stated that the abundant indigenous 'natural fruit tree species ... grow without any care and succeed well in meeting the needs of the population.... they really occur everywhere in the forested areas of the region'.[64] But the forested areas to which he referred were not in the wilderness; rather, they were in the inhabited zone (*oshilongo*) where villages and farms were located.

Indeed, colonial officials' observations inadvertently confirm that the most important fruit trees, such as palm, marula, birdplum, fig, and baobab, were located in the inhabited parts of Ovamboland, as they were often explicitly described as being associated with habitation and homesteads. In 1942, the Native Commissioner emphasised that 'wild fruits' were part of the diet but that these sources of food were located near the homesteads and '[were], however, not available when working in the bush'. In 1953, elephants damaged a large number of '*home-trees* [emphasis added] especially ... marura [marula] and palm trees – necessary trees which supply people with nutritive food'. In 1961, the Deputy Secretary for Forestry of the Union of South Africa followed the border road from Kavango in the east to Oshikango in the west and noted that the landscape changed from a more or less closed forest to a much more open landscape with beautiful marula, jackalberry, and fig trees scattered in the fields.[65] The 1963 Odendaal Commission reported: 'Westwards towards the oshana region of Ovamboland [the Ovambo floodplain] the bush becomes sparser and the ana tree (*Acacia albida*), mopane and palm ... make their appearance. Marula and manketi [manghetti], as well as wild fig and other kinds of trees such as omwaandi [jackalberry] also occur here.... In the southern region of Ovamboland the palm belt merges into extensive grassy plains.'[66]

Despite this awareness that the bulk of the fruit trees occurred in the villages and not in the wilderness, it proved beyond the colonial officials to revisit their assumption that these fruit trees could be more than 'wild' trees that were the sole relics of a previous 'natural' forest cover. In 1957, the agricultural officer for Ovamboland wrote that '[t]ree species that carry fruit such as Maroela [marula], Wildevy [fig], Jakkalvrug [jackalberry] ... usually are not eradicated because of their economic and food value. The Makalanie palm is also protected because of its fruits.'[67]

Contestation about the ownership of fruit trees on private farms and rights to their fruits that emerged during the early 1970s underscores the value of tree fruit and its products. A committee of the new Ovambo homeland legislative council undertook to evaluate land tenure in Ovamboland. It held closed meetings with a limited number of notables in all the 'tribal areas'. One of the objections raised against the existing land tenure arrangements was that if a person 'bought' a piece of land with fruit trees, the fruit would not belong to the buyer. The committee concluded that 'people' demanded that '[f]ruit trees belong to the owner of the parcel of land and if a headman wanted, for

---

[64] NAN, BAC 133 f. HN 8/21/4/1, Agricultural Report Ovamboland 1956/1957; NAO 17 f. 10/3 (ii), ANC to NCO, Oshikango, 25 January 1942; BAC 123 f. HN 7/8/2/2, Famine Relief Schemes Oshikango vol. 2, Bantu Affairs Commissioner Oshikango to Chief Bantu Affairs Commissioner, Oshikango, 15 November 1961.

[65] NAN, NAO 17 f. 10/3 (ii) ANC to NCO, Oshikango, 25 January 1942; NAO 67 f. 24/14, Tribal Secretary Uukwaluthi to NCO, Uukwaluuthi, 22 September 1953; BAC 131 f. HN 8/17/2, Deputy Secretary of Forestry, 'Report of a visit by the Deputy Secretary of Forestry to South West Africa: 17–29 April 1961', Pretoria, 10 May 1961.

[66] Report of the Commission of Enquiry into SWA Affairs 1962-1963, 12 December 1963, p. 9.

[67] NAN, BAC 131 f. HN 8/17/4), Agricultural Officer Ovamboland to Bantu Commissioners Ondangwa and Oshikango, 28 January 1957.

example, marula drink, he should receive this as a percentage and indeed in a friendly way'.[68]

Yet barely a decade earlier in the southern Ondonga area, fruit trees (including the marula) were owned by the king and headman even if they were on people's farms. Those who picked the forbidden fruits for their own use were punished with heavy fines. In contemporary Oukwanyama, where royal authority had been destroyed during the 1910s, the owner of a farm had full rights to the use of all fruit trees on the parcel of land except in the case of the marula tree: part of the marula wine had to be presented to the village headman who in turn gave a share to his district headman. For other fruit trees, however, the owner of the farm could even sub-allocate rights to the use of fruit trees on his land to a third party.[69]

The floodplain filled with farms, fields, and fruit trees during the 1950s-1990s, and the fruit tree frontier pushed into the far eastern part of Ovamboland, towards the border with Kavango.[70] Moses Kakoto settled in Okongo on an existing farm during the late 1960s. Birdplum trees on his farm grew 'naturally' but he planted palm seeds from the floodplain in his first homestead.[71] Timotheus Nakale stressed that fruit trees were more numerous in fields in the west, on the floodplain, because they grew naturally and people did not need to plant the seeds as was the case in the east. Some of the fruit trees, notably jackalberry, did not grow at all in the far east. During the 1960s and 1980s he planted marula and birdplum seeds gathered from further west and these grew into large trees. In 1992, when he moved his homestead to a new location he successfully seeded more birdplum in addition to palm seeds, the latter from Uukwambi.[72] In 1993, small birdplum trees could be found as far east as Olukula; beyond Olukula, however, birdplum, marula, and palm trees were rare.[73]

Seeing the fruit trees through the forest

The most important fruit trees in Ovamboland were not wild trees, and they did not occur in the wilderness. Rather, they were associated with human settlement in the floodplain, and refugees and migrants introduced fruit trees to new areas. In 1890, marula and birdplum were largely confined to the northern floodplain. By 1990, these fruit trees had spread not only throughout the middle floodplain but also beyond it, hundreds of miles into eastern Ovamboland. The very advance of a fruit tree frontier in north-central Namibia supports Fairhead and Leach's conclusion that a declinist paradigm clouds the study of Africa's changing environment.

[68] NAN, OVJ 15, f. 12/1 'Minutes of the elected Committee on land ownership and use', Oshakati, 4 December 1970, appendix to Secretary of the Interior to Secretary Justice and Labor, Ondangwa, 9 November 1973 and 'Kommentaar op konsepverslag van gekose komitee van die Owambo wetgevende raad' (1974?).

[69] NAN, BOS, N.A. to Omuhona [Bantu Commissioner Ondangwa], Oranjemund, 27 March 1961 and Native Commissioner Oshikango to CNC, Oshikango, 24 June 1958 and 8 October 1961.

[70] Tree propagation in the older villages continued. See, for example, Philippus Haidima, interview by author, Odibo, 9 December 1992

[71] Interviews by author: Kalolina Naholo, Ohamwaala, 26 and 27 January 1993; Kaulikalelwa Oshitina Muhonghwo, Ondaanya, 2 February 1993; Moses Kakoto, Okongo, 17 February 1993.

[72] Timotheus Nakale, interview by author, Ekoka laKula, 21 February 1993.

[73] Werner Nghionanye, interview by author, Olukula laKula, 18 February 1993 and personal observations, 20 February 1993.

The Ovamboland case also highlights some of the limitations of the political ecology framework of analysis. In the first place, the framework tends to over-emphasise the role of the state and state policies. Yet the colonial state has proved to be much less of a monolith and much weaker than has been assumed. The impact of the colonial state is often assessed by looking at formal laws and regulations. Gordon, however, has pointed out that much legislation in early colonial Namibia was simply not implemented or enforced.[74] These considerations certainly played a role in colonial Ovamboland where conservation regulations were simply ignored or not enforced by the local colonial officials themselves, in part for fear of triggering resistance. Moreover, in the case of fruit trees ignorance and lack of interest were writ larger than any weakness of the colonial state *per se*. Fruit trees were simply not a priority for the colonial officials in Ovamboland.

This also draws attention to a second weakness of the political ecology framework: its overriding attention to the political domain. Fruit trees were a contested resource. In the eyes of colonial officials, however, compared to such issues as labour recruitment, cattle production, and grain crop cultivation, fruit trees were – at most – of marginal importance, since they were perceived to have no real market value. As Wilson pointed out in southern Zimbabwe, officials regarded trees in fields merely as obstacles to modern crop production. Fruit trees were invisible to officials in much of early colonial Namibia. Similar comments have been made in the literature about women, and this is more than a coincidence.[75] Women were key in the propagation of fruit trees and their use and management, as well as in processing and distributing fruit tree products. Outside the control (and mostly even outside the purview) of colonial officials, tree fruit liquor became an increasingly important source of income for many women, since only men had access to money wages through migrant labour.

In general, on-farm fruit trees became less of a 'communal' resource as households with fruit trees became less willing to share their valuable fruit with third parties, including headmen. Yet, in sharp contrast to, for example, birdplum fruit and especially *olambike* liquor, marula fruit and marula wine were not commercialised. Marula wine remained a social drink par excellence. Although palm wine to a certain extent played the same role, by the 1990s palm wine was being offered for sale. Marula wine served exclusively to establish and maintain social relations and social networks. The latter were critical – especially for single women – to gain access to land, labour, livestock, and food especially during times of drought and famine.[76] But these networks became less exclusively centred around kings and headmen. People who harvested marula fruit preferred to share their marula wine with invited friends, relatives, patrons (who could include headmen), and guests, rather than giving all or a portion of it to headmen as a form of tribute.

Consequently, despite a trend towards 'privatisation', or perhaps in reaction to it, tree fruit became a hotly contested resource. For example, during a 1968 'tribal' meeting at Ohangwena in Oukwanyama, Haihambo Hangola lamented the demise of traditional rules: '[l]ong ago ... [n]obody was allowed to pick unripe fruit.... Now since the country is under the Europeans people are doing these things and the country

[74] P. Hayes et al. (eds), *Namibia under South African Rule: Mobility and containment, 1915–46* (Oxford, James Currey, 1998).

[75] See chapters by Gordon and Hayes in P. Hayes et al; Wilson, 'Trees in Fields' pp. 272–7. Campbell, 'The Use of Wild Fruits', p. 34, pointed out that wild fruit trees were given little attention.

[76] Kreike, 'Recreating Eden', ch. 7.

is getting mixed up.'[77] Elderly single women like Kaulikalelwa Muhonghwo had difficulty preventing children from picking their fruit. In the past, small children who did not understand the concept of ownership were always allowed to take some fruit, but older children and adults were expected to ask the owner's permission.[78] Thus, as the history of fruit trees in the Ovambo floodplain shows, questions of control and access to fruit trees and their products were intimately intertwined with economic, ecological, cultural, and last but not least, social considerations.

[77] NAN, AHE 1/15 f. (16)N1/15/4 minutes of a meeting at Ohangwena, 13 January 1968.
[78] Kaulikalelwa Muhonghwo, interview by author, Ondaanya, 2 February 1993.

2

The Ironies
of Plant Transfer

The Case of the Prickly Pear in Madagascar

KAREN MIDDLETON

Between the sixteenth and nineteenth centuries, Europeans made a number of attempts to colonise the island of Madagascar. Yet the most successful coloniser of Madagascar's Deep South during this era was probably a prickly pear. This plant, a type of Opuntia cactus,[1] was introduced into the southeast of the island by the Comte de Maudave [Modave] who between 1768 and 1771 tried to create a French colony at Fort Dauphin. Within two years the colony had been abandoned, while prickly pear, by contrast, spread so quickly that when French colonial troops next appeared here at the turn of the twentieth century it had become one of the region's most characteristic plants.[2] On maps dating from the time of the French conquest, the territory between the Menarandra and Manambovo rivers, roughly south of Latitude 25°, is designated 'cactus region' (*région cactée*) or 'cactus bush' (*brousse cactée*). This chapter explores the history of this plant transfer from two angles, the interplay between European expansionism and local response, and its consequences for the economies of the Deep South.

Like almost all *Cactaceae*, this prickly pear had originated in the Americas. Thus, in its broadest sense, the introduction belonged in the extraordinary movement of biological species between continents that accompanied expanding European political and economic systems over the last half millennium. In a pioneering study of this phenomenon, Alfred Crosby insisted upon its pronounced asymmetry. He contrasts 'the tiny number' of Neo-European weeds and pathogens that naturalised in the Old World with the outstanding success of European portmanteau biota – his 'collective name for the Europeans and all the organisms they brought with them' – in the 'Neo-Europes', which he defines as places outside Europe where Europeans now compose the great

---

[1] The literature gives at least seven different botanical names for this prickly pear; see K. Middleton, 'Who Killed "Malagasy Cactus"? Science, Environment, and Colonialism in Southern Madagascar (1924-1930)', *Journal of Southern African Studies (JSAS)* 25 (1999), p. 219. Pending reliable taxonomic identification, I shall use the term 'Malagasy cactus' (*raketa gasy*), which is how this particular Opuntia is remembered in much of southern Madagascar today.

[2] See for example, R. Decary, *L'Androy (Extrême Sud de Madagascar): Essai de Monographie Régionale*, 1 (Paris, Societé d'Editions Géographiques, Maritimes et Coloniales, 1930), pp. 79, 81–2, 128; G. Grandidier, 'Une mission dans la région australe de Madagascar en 1901', *La Géographie* 6, 7 (1902) 4.

majority in the population.[3] European imperialism, Crosby argues, had ecological allies, including European plants which rapidly acclimatised and often spread aggressively in the new environments. 'Dandelion imperialism', he suggests, became particularly important once the symbiosis between native mammals and native flora had been destroyed. 'The exotic plants saved newly bared topsoil from erosion and baking in the sun. And the weeds often became essential feed for exotic livestock, as these in turn were for their masters.'[4]

Many historians profess to finding Crosby's thesis seductive, while nonetheless complaining of its oversimple correlations and its reductionism. Some question the evolutionary advantage Crosby attributes to Eurasian biota by pointing to reverse processes of ecological imperialism,[5] and to instances where introduced or indigenous plants have hindered European settlers rather than abetted them.[6] Others criticise Crosby's ecological history for ignoring the key issue of how culture, power, and socio-economic relations mediated interactions between 'nature' and imperialism.[7] 'The aboriginal biotas of the neo-Europes', writes Drayton, 'confronted the European portmanteau on terms which for non-biological reasons were extremely unequal.'[8] Others take issue with Crosby for failing to explore complex and changing inter-dependencies that existed between settler imperialism in the 'Neo-Europes' and the 'tropical face' of European plantation, tributary and commercial imperialism in Africa, Asia and the Caribbean.[9] But if Crosby's critics all call for more complex under-standings of plant transfer and empire, there are also significant differences of emphasis between them. While some accept the generalising thesis of European imperialism but want to situate it primarily in political and cultural frameworks, others appear to be attracted to more localising, multi-linear or non-linear, eco-political histories that envisage plant transfers as having a range of possible outcomes.

In so far as Crosby focuses on the one-way movement of European biota to the 'Neo-Europes', his frame of reference precludes any consideration of the inter-continental journeys made by a Meso-American species such as prickly pear. This is a pity since prickly pears in many respects embody Crosby's idea of the plant 'as pioneer and conquistador'.[10] Inextricably linked with European mercantile expansion – ships

[3] A. Crosby, *Ecological Imperialism: The biological expansion of Europe 900–1900* (Cambridge, Canto, 1993 [1986]), 270.

[4] Crosby, *Ecological Imperialism*, p. 170.

[5] T. Griffiths, 'Ecology and Empire: Towards an Australian History of the World', in T. Griffiths and L. Robin (eds), *Ecology and Empire. Environmental history of settler societies* (Edniburgh, Keele University Press, 1997), pp. 1–16; J. MacKenzie, 'Empire and the Ecological Apocalypse: the Historiography of the Imperial Environment', in Griffiths and Robin, *Ecology and Empire*, p. 219.

[6] L. van Sittert, '"The Seed Blows About in Every Breeze": Noxious Weed Eradication in the Cape Colony, 1860–1909', *JSAS* 26 (2000), pp. 655–74; W. Frost, 'European Farming, Australian Pests: Agricultural Settlement and Environmental Disruption in Australia, 1800–1920', *Environment and History* 4 (1998), pp. 129-43; but see D. Freeman, 'Prickly Pear Menace in Eastern Australia 1880–1940', *Geographical Review* 82, 4 (1992), pp. 413–29.

[7] W. Cronon, *Changes in the Land* (New York, Hill and Wang, 1983), p. 14; see also Cronon, 'Review of Ecological Imperialism', *Journal of American History* 74 (1987), p. 150.

[8] R. Drayton, 'Ecological History as a Just-So Story: A Critique of Alfred Crosby's Ecological Imperialism', Paper presented at Ecology, Politics, and Imperialism Symposium, Nuffield College, Oxford, March 1990.

[9] B. Tomlinson, 'Empire of the Dandelion: Ecological Imperialism and Economic Expansion, 1860–1914', *Journal of Imperial and Commonwealth History* 26, 2 (1998), pp. 90–1.

[10] Crosby, *Ecological Imperialism*, p. 155.

are reported to have carried barrels filled with Opuntia cladodes as a precaution against scurvy[11] – prickly pear was the original post-Columbian traveller, often by nature a superb coloniser. In the wake of Columbus' voyage to the New World, Opuntia species were carried to many other parts of the globe, generally, though not always, in the context of colonising projects, where they often naturalised to become a feature of the landscape (notably, Australia, the Canary Islands, the Mediterranean region, India, South Africa, Sri Lanka, and Madagascar). These contrastive trajectories offer some useful perspectives on the relationship between European expansionism, ecological parameters, and local response.

In the case of Madagascar, we appear to have an instance in which a non-European people subverted an incipient link between plant transfer and empire. Not only did the prickly pear introduced by the Comte de Modave 'outlive' his colony by 150 years; but all the evidence suggests that it became a key resource in local agro-pastoral economies in Madagascar's Deep South.[12] Montagnac, for example, speaks of 'robust tribes, numbering more than 300,000 souls, numerous herds ... living almost exclusively on Opuntia'.[13] By the 1920s, the plant had become so entwined with everyday life in Androy that, according to Raymond Decary, a colonial administrator, a local saying declared that 'the Tandroy and prickly pear are kin'.[14] And when French colonial troops attempted to seize control of this semi-arid region in the early 1900s, dense prickly pear thickets, 4–5m high and 7–8m thick, constituted, as they saw it, the most formidable obstacle they faced. For the next three decades, the plant became entangled in intense power struggles between southern Malagasy and the French colonial state.[15]

Crosby does not consider the possibility that biota introduced by Europeans might offer a means of resistance and evasion to local communities. Although he allows indigenous peoples some part in creating the 'degraded' landscapes that allowed European weeds to triumph in the 'Neo-Europes', he otherwise offers a fairly minimal account of local response.[16] In this respect, his narrative follows conventional 'diffusionist' or Eurocentric historiography. Over the past twenty years, however, historians and anthropologists have demonstrated the poverty of such accounts in understanding colonial encounters whose political, economic and cultural dimensions were often both more diverse and more complex. Similarly, it can be argued that, while many botanical transfers were certainly made in the context of European mercantile expansion, and some indeed proved vital to colonial systems of production,[17] their outcomes were by no means either predictable or uniform. For example, coffee imposed as a cash crop on to East Coast Madagascar by French colonial policy was soon appropriated by Malagasy farmers, enabling them to

[11] H. Le Houérou, 'The Role of Cacti (*Opuntia* spp.) in Erosion Control, Land Reclamation, Rehabilitation and Agricultural Development in the Mediterranean Basin', *Journal of Arid Environments* 33 (1996), p. 136.

[12] See, for example, Decary, *L'Androy*, pp. 1, 123, 127–8, 181; R. Decary, 'L'utilisation des Opuntias en Androy (Extrême-Sud de Madagascar)', *Revue Botanique Appliquée* 5, 50 (1925), pp. 769–71; Grandidier, 'Une mission', p. 4.

[13] P. Montagnac, 'Cactacées alimentaires dans le Sud de Madagascar', *Bulletin de Madagascar* 11, 182 (1961), p. 610.

[14] Decary, *L'Androy*, pp. 1, 127.

[15] K. Middleton, 'Who Killed "Malagasy Cactus"?'

[16] Crosby, *Ecological Imperialism*, p. 295.

[17] See, for example, L. Brockway, *Science and Colonial Expansion: The role of the British Royal Botanic Gardens* (New York, Academic Press, 1979).

escape wage labour on European concessions.[18] And of course many of the very African transfers such as plantain, bananas or sugar cane came from the east and predated Western intrusion.

A rather different approach to African farmers and species transfer is taken by John Iliffe in his book *Africans*. Iliffe's aim is to refocus 'African history on the peopling of an environmentally hostile continent', and he draws on the long history Africans have of appropriating American domesticates, such as maize, cassava, beans, sweet potatoes, brought to their shores by Portuguese and other sailors, to support his thesis that Africans are 'the frontiersmen [sic] of mankind [sic] who have colonised an especially hostile region of the world on behalf of the entire human race'.[19] Iliffe's narrative contrasts with Crosby's not only because it emphasises the agency of Africans in accepting or rejecting plant transfers during the era of European expansion, but also because it implies that Africans consciously and deliberately mastered new germoplasm and new technologies in order to increase agro-pastoral productivity. For Iliffe, the adoption of diverse exotics to supplement known staples such as sorghum and millet was among the elaborate precautions Africans took as successful frontiers-people to minimise risk.[20] In contrast, by stressing the *ecological* dimension of European expansion, Crosby explicitly downplays those human elements, such as intent, agency, and knowledge, that have dominated conventional historiography. Unintentional and accidental introductions of European biota, he argues, were almost as crucial to the prosperity of 'Neo-Europeans' as were the food crops that they deliberately introduced or adapted from native plants.

The analysis presented in this chapter weaves a course between these various texts. On the one hand, the Madagascar data clearly call for elements of Iliffe's heroic African planter welcoming exotic species that seem to facilitate optimal exploitation of multiple environments and to meet a range of local needs in risk-prone drylands. 'Malagasy cactus' spread with exceptional rapidity, and human agency was clearly an important factor here. Indeed, historical sources indicate close associations between prickly pears and social processes of human settlement that in many respects echo the peri-village forest islands that have been described for the savanna regions of Guinea by Fairhead and Leach. In their influential book *Misreading the African Landscape*, they argue that such islands, which were generally assumed by Europeans to be the 'relics' of a vast forest, have in fact resulted from deliberate management by local farmers.[21]

Yet this chapter also argues that, in the case of 'Malagasy cactus', there is some truth in Crosby's 'ecological history'. The plant's distribution in southern Madagascar at the turn of the twentieth century cannot be understood wholly in terms of settlement history and social life. While the balance between human agency and other factors is difficult, perhaps even impossible, to determine precisely, and probably differed in time and space, it seems important to acknowledge that 'Malagasy cactus' had many of the characteristics of an invasive plant. In this respect, the chapter takes issue with Jeffrey Kaufmann, who seeks to place the landscapes of early twentieth-century

---

[18] J. Fremigacci, 'Les difficultés d'une politique coloniale: le café de Madagascar à la conquête du marché français (1930-9)', *Omaly sy Anio* (1985), pp. 21–2.

[19] J. Iliffe, *Africans. The history of a continent* (Cambridge, CUP, 1995), preface, pp. 1, 110.

[20] *Ibid.*, pp. 5, 113.

[21] J. Fairhead and M. Leach, *Misreading the African Landscape. Society and ecology in a forest-savanna mosaic* (Cambridge, CUP, 1996).

southern Madagascar totally in the cultural domain.[22] Influenced by works such as *Misreading the Landscape*, which seek to uncover the hidden human hand in vegetation history, he is also reacting to a tendency in some of the French colonial literature that de-emphasises the role of local people in spreading prickly pear.

Failed colony, successful plant

In 1767, Modave had persuaded the Duc de Praslin, Secretary of State for the [French] Navy, of the pressing need to 'lay the foundations of a powerful establishment in Madagascar'.[23] At that time the plantation economies of the Isle de France (Mauritius) and Bourbon (Réunion) in the southwest Indian Ocean depended heavily upon Madagascar for cattle, rice, and slave labour.[24] But while the Mascarenes, formerly administered by the Compagnie des Indes, had been ceded to the French Crown in 1765, Madagascar was still an independent island with a veritable kaleidoscope of polities. Attempts to found a French colony in Fort Dauphin in the mid-seventeenth century had culminated in a massacre.[25] Frustrated in the desire to bend Malagasy peoples to his purpose, Flacourt, its administrator, inscribed a warning upon a marble stele: *cave ab incolis* (beware the locals). Modave, however, was hopeful of making Fort Dauphin 'the source and seed nursery' of French influence in Madagascar; he intended to extend his hold north along the east coast, and then into the interior, until a single administration embraced the whole island.[26]

Authorised to take repossession of Fort Dauphin as the 'King's Commander in the island of Madagascar', Modave landed there on 5 September 1768. His papers reveal him to have been a man obsessed with fortifications.[27] In December 1768, dissatisfied with the fort's appearance, which at the time was 'scarcely [...] more than a sheep pen, surrounded on three sides by a ten feet high wall', Modave had requested 'two or three barrels full of prickly pear leaves [from the Isle de France] to arm the part of the fort that faces the sea and by this means to render it impenetrable on all sides'.[28]

Describing the flora of the Isle de France in September 1768, Bernadin de Saint-Pierre had listed 'The *Raquettes*, of which they here make very dangerous hedges.... This plant is stuck full of very sharp prickles, that grow upon the leaves; and also upon the fruit.'[29]

---

[22] J. Kaufmann, 'La question des raketa: colonial struggles with prickly pear cactus in southern Madagascar, 1900–1923', *Ethnohistory* 48, 1–2 (2001), pp. 87–121.

[23] Centre des Archives d'Outre-Mer, Aix-en-Provence (hereafter CAOM) C⁴. sous-série Correspondance à l'arrivée en provenance de Madagascar. Modave to Duc de Praslin. Projet d'Etablissement 21 November 1767.

[24] For the history of economic relations between Madagascar and the Mascarenes see A. Toussaint, *Histoire des iles Mascareignes* (Paris, 1972), pp. 66–9; J. Filliot, *La traité des esclaves vers les Mascareignes au XVIIIᵉ siècle* (Paris, 1974).

[25] Étienne de Flacourt, *Histoire de la Grande Isle Madagascar* (Paris, Karthala 1995 [1658]).

[26] CAOM C ⁵ᴬ 2 No. 62. Modave to Duc de Praslin, 7 August 1768.

[27] See, for example, CAOM C⁵ᴬ 2 No. 67. Modave to Duc de Praslin, 11 December 1768.

[28] Bibliothèque centrale du Muséum national d'histoire naturelle, Paris (hereafter BCMNHN) MS. 888 Commerson, 'Mémoires pour servir à l'histoire Naturelle et Politique de la grande ile de Madagascar, anciennement appellée isle de St. Laurent par les Portugais qui la découvrirent les premiers l'an I. Journal de ce qui s'est passé au Fort-Dauphin dans l'isle de Madagascar depuis le lundi 5 septembre 1768 jusqu'au 11 décembre suivant', p. 63.

[29] Bernardin de Saint-Pierre, *Voyage to the Island of Mauritius (or the Isle of Bounbon)* (London, W. Griffin, 1775).

The following year, in the interests of forest conservation, Poivre had secured an Ordinance permitting 'only live hedges of bamboo, "acacia", "mourouc" or other spiny plants, apart from "raquettes" which should be destroyed with all necessary precautions'.[30] Bernadin de Saint-Pierre, however, expounds at length on the role 'raquettes' might play in defending the Isle de France against attack from the English navy. Not only 'will [they] grow in the driest places. They have besides, this advantage, they cost but little; and time, the destroyer of every other fortification, increases and strengthens [them].'[31]

It is difficult to reconstruct the early days of the introduction – how many cladodes were dispatched to Madagascar, when they were received, and where the first plantings were made – because the pertinent sections of Modave's Journal have disappeared. But we can be certain that Modave's request was met because, when the naturalist Philibert Commerson visited Fort Dauphin two years later, he listed 'Opuntia of the Isle de France' in the notebook he kept of 'plants common to both Madagascar and the Isle de France'.[32] Fifty years later, the plant appears to have been in common use by Malagasy farmers, for when the *L'Amaranthe* visited the Fort Dauphin region in 1819, Frappaz, the ship's lieutenant, reported that: 'A great number of prickly pears are to be found all over. This plant was imported by M. de Maudave and is used to good effect to enclose fields and gardens and to prevent thieves and animals entering.'[33] The geographical range at which the plant was found had also extended: oral traditions which Georges Heurtebize collected among the Afomarolahy, and calibrated with genealogies, suggest that when the ancestors of this Tandroy clan settled near Lahabe (some 150 km west of Fort Dauphin) *circa* 1800, prickly pear was so dense around a nearby pond that the incomers remained oblivious to its existence for fifty years.[34]

This has led Heurtebize to doubt that Modave was responsible for the introduction. Even acknowledging the plant's exceptional capacity to proliferate, he writes, it is difficult to believe that prickly pear had first appeared in Androy only thirty years before.[35] Decary, on the other hand, thought it 'not at all surprising. The exceptional ease with which it can be propagated, its speed of growth in arid lands, the range of possible uses, its use as food for the natives and the cattle are all factors which explain how, with people's help, this plant had multiplied in an extraordinary way in the space of one century and a half.'[36] In fact, the literature on prickly pears in Australia is full of 'statistics' that, assuming comparable conditions, would make it possible for an Opuntia to have transformed 'a territory roughly equal to a third of France into a barely

---

[30] Cited by E. Brouard, *A History of Woods and Forests* (Port Louis, J.E. Felix ISO Government Printer, 1963), p. 16.

[31] de Saint-Pierre, *Journey to the Isle of France*, pp. 178–9.

[32] BCMNHN MS 887 n, 223 XXIV Labor botanicus Hicce in Madagascaria australi exantlatus, October to November 1770, Commerson. 'Note de quelques végétaux communs aux Iles de France et de Madagascar'. As far as I have been able to establish, this is the earliest reference to prickly pear in Madagascar.

[33] BCMNHN, Fonds Decary 3014, 4, 'Rapport de la campagne de la goëlette de Sa Majesté *L'Amaranthe* à la côte orientale de l'île de Madagascar, adressé par Mr Tle Frappaz, enseigne de Vau aide de camp, capitaine de ce bâtiment, à Monsieur Milius, commandant et administrateur pour le roi a l'île de Bourbon', 1819. Typed copy, 58 p.

[34] G. Heurtebize, *Histoire des Afomarolahy (Clan Tandroy- Extrême-Sud de Madagascar)* (Paris, Editions du Centre National de la Recherche Scientifique, 1986), p. 295.

[35] *Ibid.*

[36] Decary, 'Sur l'époque de l'introduction de l'*Opuntia Dillenii* Haw. ou *Raiketa* de Madagascar', *Bulletin Académie Malgache* 17 (1934), p. 49.

penetrable maze' in just over 100 years.[37] According to Osmond and Munro, for instance, some hundred years after its introduction, a prickly pear 'had restricted human access to 25 million ha […] of Eastern Australia and was continuing its advance at approximately 100 ha per hour'.[38] Some of these calculations, I suspect, invite closer scrutiny. Talk of prickly pear 'devouring' land at rates of 100 hectares per hour – sometimes the figure quoted is represented as an average; at other times the maximum – is more than a little reminiscent of the racy language which has been used to describe advancing 'desertification' in parts of Africa. Upon re-examination, such seemingly quantitative language has been shown in many contexts to be both exaggerated and imprecise.[39] Nonetheless, the evidence from Australia and South Africa is compelling, that certain Opuntia species can become 'invaders' and escape human control.

Is it possible to assess how invasive prickly pear had become in southern Madagascar from currently available data sets? European travellers, from the first English LMS missionaries in the early nineteenth century to French colonial troops arriving in the early twentieth century, invariably testify to impenetrable prickly pear thickets around villages. But this does not mean that there were similar densities beyond these deliberate plantings. Descriptions of landscape beyond the village are often highly ambiguous because they use terms such as 'thorny bush' (*brousse épineuse, la brousse à épines*) inconsistently and variably of both prickly pear and the native xerophytic flora, much of which has evolved 'cactus'-like features on account of the aridity.[40] Observers seldom make any attempt to quantify the balance of species.

Landscape histories gathered from Malagasy people may be thought to prove more reliable in reconstructing the past composition of local flora, since people living and working with plant material are less likely to confuse species. Those I collected among elderly people in the Karembola certainly remember a time when they lived amongst dense prickly pear infestations. Local toponymy also records this 'density': Anjedava, for instance, refers to the long, narrow paths that snaked between the prickly pears around the village 'in the days before the foreigners came'. Such material tends to lack specificity and it is also possible that local memories of the landscapes of the early colonial era have been partly shaped by colonial discourses on prickly pear.

Many writers attribute the spread of 'Malagasy cactus' to non-human influences such as climate. Thus, Montagnac writes: '[it] spread little in the rainy climate of Fort Dauphin but once over the "collar" of Tranopiso, 60 kilometres to the west, it found its favoured habitat and invaded the low-lying, arid regions inhabited by the Tandroy, Karembola and Mahafale tribes'.[41] With its low, irregular rainfall, the Deep South would appear to present ideal environmental conditions for cacti, although cacti are not native plants. Yet soil type also appears to have been significant. Comparing the distribution of 'Malagasy cactus' with the geological constitution of Tsihombe district, Decary noted that 'only scattered, weak populations were to be found on the crystalline

[37] Montagnac, 'Cactacées alimentaires', p. 610.

[38] C. Osmond and J. Munro, 'Prickly Pear', in D. Carr and S. Carr (eds), *Plants and Man in Australia* (Academic Press, Sydney, 1981), p.194.

[39] U. Helldén, 'Desertification: Time for Assessment?', *Ambio* 20 (1991): 372–83; J. Swift, 'Desertification: Narratives, Winners and Losers', in M. Leach and R. Mearns (eds), *The Lie of the Land: Challenging received wisdom on the African environment* (Oxford, James Currey, 1996), pp. 73–90.

[40] See R. Rabesandratana, 'Flora of the Malagasy Southwest', in A. Jolly, P. Oberlé, R. Albignac (eds), *Key Environments: Madagascar* (Oxford, Pergamon Press, 1984), pp. 55–74.

[41] Montagnac, 'Cactacées alimentaires'.

soils of the north'. By contrast, the plants were extremely abundant along the Menaran-dra river from the point where it entered the sedimentary soils of its vast alluvial plain. However, prickly pear was 'truly at home' (*chez elle*) on the red calcareous sands of the southern band of the Plateau. *Raketa* was so hardy that it would establish almost anywhere - Decary had even seen it growing in old baobab trunks - but to grow and fruit perfectly it needed plenty of heat and sun, and a silico-calcareous soil.[42]

But other factors probably also made a difference. The plant had been introduced into Madagascar without the predators and diseases that control prickly pear varieties in their native American habitats. It is also very likely, though as yet unproven, that both introduced and native fauna, including lemurs and giant radiated tortoises (*Geochelone radiata*),[43] helped disperse the seeds by eating the fleshy fruit. Prickly pears are endowed with two modes of reproduction: sexual and vegetative. By all accounts, clonal propagation was extremely effective in the case of 'Malagasy cactus'. 'If one plants a leaf or a fruit, at the end of fortnight, some rootlets emerging from the "eyes" of the buried part; it is enough simply to place the cutting on the ground, and young roots soon emerge.' [44] Colonial botanist Perrier de la Bâthie alleged that this was the plant's only mode of reproduction in the region. Opuntia, he wrote, had not fully naturalised because 'it never reproduces there by seed and its fruits never ripen even in the driest parts of the Southwest'.[45] While Decary agreed that fruits that grew in shade by the Menarandra river tended to wither before ripening, he insisted that mature fruits were extremely abundant to the east. Even so, he too thought sexual reproduction 'far rarer and almost abnormal [...] because the fruit simply falls on the ground, grows roots, then "leaves"'. Germination tended to occur only when cattle ate the fruits and excreted the seeds. This, he argued, explained the isolated clumps of *raketa* occasionally found growing in 'unfavourable' places, such as in deep shade or on crystalline soils.[46] Decary's account is rather puzzling. Since cattle were both numerous in southern Madagascar, and constantly on the move over both short and longer distances, one would expect their effect as seed dispersers to have supplemented the efficacy of vegetative reproduction rather than be rendered redundant by it. On the other hand, I have as yet found nothing in the archival sources to match the sight recorded for South Africa of prickly pear seedlings growing 'like miniature forests on cow dung, a natural fertilizer pack'.[47]

But is it possible that local people were the greatest influence upon the relative abundance and habitat colonisation of prickly pears? Certainly, all the evidence suggests that Malagasy farmers and herders appreciated its many advantages very early, and actively propagated the plant. Its potential for fortifying settlements, penning animals, and securing crops against marauders and wandering stock was obvious, and

---

[42] Decary, 'Monographie du district de Tsihombe', *Bulletin Économique de Madagascar* 18, 1 (1921), p. 16.

[43] Decary, *L'Androy*, pp. 1, 77.

[44] BCMNHN Fonds Decary Ms 3075. Rapports Administratifs de Lieutenant Decary, chef du poste de Beloha, 'Rapport sur la "Raketa" et son exploitation industrielle'. Beloha 29 June 1918.

[45] Perrier de la Bâthie, 'Les pestes végétales à Madagascar', *Revue de Botanique Appliqué et d'Agriculture Coloniale* 8, 77 (1978): 36–43.

[46] Decary, 'La dissémination des graines chez quelques plantes de Madagascar', *La Feuille des Naturalistes* 19 (1925), p. 135.

[47] W. Beinart, 'Colonialism and Species Suppression: Prickly Pear in South Africa', paper presented to conference on 'African Environments: Past and Present', St Antony's College, Oxford, 1999 and Seminario Internacional Historia e Meio Ambiente, Funchal, 1999.

thick defensive prickly pear hedges around hamlets, cattle-pens and fields soon became commonplace.[48] In the case of chiefly and royal residences, nineteenth and early twentieth-century authors appear to be describing something akin to the 'peri-village forest islands' described for Guinea by Fairhead and Leach. Prickly pears here form enormous 'belts', 'rings' or 'copses', between 3 and 5 metres high and up to 50 metres thick, woven through with labyrinthine paths, so that the settlement 'takes on the aspect of a small fortress'.[49]

There were many good reasons for planting 'Malagasy cactus'. Its fruits could be consumed by people, providing an important source of food and water, especially at times of drought. The height of the *raketa* season between early August and February corresponded to the period of shortage before the main field crops (manioc, maize, millet, and sweet potatoes) ripened. From October to late January, the fruits reputedly 'constituted one of the main foods for the natives of the Deep South'.[50] During true famines, people also ate the cladodes (*ravenbaketa*, the fleshy 'leaves'). A sweet if tasteless drink (*kidrasy*) could be extracted by grating the fruit on rough bark before boiling, and water was also obtained by pounding the cladodes or even the plant's fleshy trunk. This made the plant especially valuable in the arid land between Cap St Marie and the Menarandra (the Karembola) where water-points are few and far between. People of this region otherwise depended on temporary ponds and *ranovato*, rain-water reservoirs created by excavating natural crevices in the limestone rock, and covered with branches and stones to prevent evaporation in the hot sun. This exotic plant soon found its place alongside the native roots and aqueous tubers that people drew upon in times of drought.

'Malagasy cactus' also became an important forage crop and standing buffer feed for cattle. Most animals are reluctant to graze spiny forms of cactus which therefore grow unhindered when rain falls. When drought ensues and other greenstuffs become scarce or non-existent, the spines are burned off and the cladodes fed to the stock. In 1930 Decary published a photograph purporting to show a five-year-old steer that had taken no water other than that contained in prickly pear. 'In the dry season', he adds, 'columns of smoke are to be seen everywhere as men lightly grill the cladodes in order to destroy the thorns.'[51]

At the same time, accounts of precolonial southern Madagascar indicate highly mobile societies whose members were constantly warring, trading, driving cattle to pasture, searching for missing stock, or visiting kin. More particularly, the fifty or so years after Modave's colony saw extensive migrations in all parts of the Deep South but especially from the Manambovo basin and around Faux Cap.[52] Prickly pear was inextricably bound up with these human movements. The cuttings travel well. 'A

[48] Decary, 'L'utilisation des Opuntias', p. 771.

[49] Decary, *L'Androy*, pp. 1, 144; cf. Grandidier, 'Une mission', p. 4; E. Bastard, 'Mission chez les Mahafaly en 1899', *Revue de Madagascar* 2 (1900), pp. 778 –85; A. and G. Grandidier, *Histoire Physique, Naturelle et Politique de Madagascar. Ethnographie de Madagascar* IV, 3 (Paris, Societé d'Editions Géographiques Maritimes et Coloniales, 1917), p. 238 n. 1(a).

[50] Decary, 'Rapport sur la "Raketa"'.

[51] Decary, *L'Androy*, pp. 1, 181.

[52] E. Defoort, 'L'Androy', *Bulletin Economique de Madagascar* 2 (1913): 157–74; M. Esoavelomandroso, 'Milieu naturel et peuplement de l'Androy du XVIe au XIXe S.' in C. Kottak, J.-A. Rakotoarisoa, A. Southall and P. Vérin (eds), *Madagascar: Society and history* (Durham NC, Academic Press, 1986); Heurtebize, *Histoire des Afomarolahy*; K. Middleton, 'Power and Meaning on the Periphery of a Malagasy Kingdom', *Ethnohistory* 48, 1 (2001), pp. 171–204.

detached segment can remain alive, and even produce new growth, for months without contact with the soil.'[53] Everywhere the migrants went, they carried 'Malagasy cactus' with them, planting it as hedging around settlements, in clearings and around newly created fields. In effect, it served a triple purpose: not only of providing defences and food and water, but also of socialising newly acquired lands.

It is also possible that the activities of people and their livestock contributed indirectly to prickly pear colonisation by creating opportunities of open surface in which the plant could establish and thrive. Perrier de la Bâthie thought that 'none of the alien species now naturalised in Madagascar could ever have penetrated absolutely intact autochthonous formations'. *Raketa* 'had grabbed hold of the alluvial soils of the rivers [...] where it competes with the native flora for terrain modified by floods or by very old fields'.[54] Another writer supposed 'that the Opuntia had developed with such intensity precisely on land the Antandroys had cleared'.[55] In addition, the grazing of cattle and small ruminants may have facilitated prickly pear colonisation. Domesticated sheep had been present in the Androy since at least the eleventh century[56], as were zebu cattle, although these were rare at first. By the early seventeenth century, zebu cattle and goats were herded in large numbers throughout the Deep South.[57] Thus, the spread of 'Malagasy cactus' may well have involved a kind of 'dandelion imperialism', in other words, this exotic plant may have spread rapidly in southern Madagascar partly because it was well-adapted to colonising bare soil and to dispersal by equally exotic livestock. However, the impact of people and their domesticates upon the ecosystems of Madagascar during the precolonial era is controversial,[58] and putative links between the spread of 'Malagasy cactus' and pasture history require closer examination than I have the space to undertake here.

I have identified a number of factors, both social and ecological, that may have favoured the spread of 'Malagasy cactus'. To determine their relative importance in shaping the landscapes of southern Madagascar over the nineteenth century, we need to know rather more than we do at present about the physiology and population biology of this particular Opuntia and about how local peoples managed their environments at the time. Data I collected in the Anjedava region in the late twentieth century show that the decisions people took about planting prickly pears and managing their growth were embedded in a broader set of management decisions around labour and land use. For example, one villager who was short of labour elected to plant an 'exhausted' field with prickly pears rather than leave the land fallow, while others created clearings in the forest specifically in order to plant *raketa,* believing that the fired 'virgin' soils would promote faster growth. Another planted prickly pears in the forest to establish rights in disputed land.

Thus, in this community, the ecology of prickly pears was highly socialised,

---

[53] A. Dodd, *The Biological Campaign against Prickly Pear* (Brisbane, Commonwealth Prickly Pear Board, 1940), p. 14.

[54] Perrier de la Bâthie, 'La Végétation Malgache', *Annales du Musée Colonial de Marseille* 9 (1921), pp. 48–9.

[55] G. Petit, 'Introduction à Madagascar de la cochenille du figuier d'Inde (*Dactylopius Coccus* Costa) et ses conséquences inattendues', *Revue d'histoire naturelle appliquée* 10, 5 (1929), p. 162 n. 1.

[56] D. Rasamuel, 'Alimentation et techniques anciennes dans le sud Malgache à travers une fosse à ordure du XIème siècle', *Etudes de l'Océan Indien* 4 (1984), p. 83.

[57] See for example, Flacourt, *Histoire de la Grande Isle*, pp. 140–1.

[58] See, for example, essays in S. Goodman and B. Patterson (eds), *Natural Change and Human Impact in Madagascar* (Washington, DC: Smithsonian Institute Press, 1997).

inextricably bound up with pastoral strategies, cultural understandings of soil fertility in swidden fallow cycles, and socio-economic relations that determine access to labour and land. But it would be mistaken to try to reconstruct precolonial farming practices from the ethnography of one particular late twentieth-century community. First, there is important local variation in agro-pastoral systems and vegetation composition in southern Madagascar, partly in response to varying patterns of precipitation and humidity. Second, land use and resource management almost certainly underwent changes during 150 years. Third, and most importantly, the people I studied in the 1990s were growing a different and (in their opinion) far less invasive species of prickly pear. Indeed, some of my informants stressed the difference between past and present, insisting that, in contrast to contemporary practice, 'Malagasy cactus was *never* planted but simply grew'. This 'memory' of a time when prickly pear was only *hatsa* (gathered, 'wild' produce) is contradicted by a number of historical accounts, however, indicating that 'Malagasy cactus' was planted as hedging *and* cultivated in fields. Visiting Cap Sainte Marie in 1866, Grandidier recorded how '[e]ach family has its plantation of nopals, of Barbary figs just as our peasants have their field of wheat'. 'The nopals are not left to their own devices; one cultivates them, one takes cuttings, and one looks to increase the harvest each year.'[59] This underscores the difficulties of depending uncritically on oral sources – what Fairhead and Leach term 'local, more experience-grounded landscape histories'[60] – to reconstruct past environments. Like all landscape readings,[61] Malagasy 'memories' of 'Malagasy cactus' are socially constructed, and carry powerful political and moral symbolism about the articulation of the present and the past.[62]

The extent to which the landscapes described in the early twentieth century had been created by men and women is therefore difficult to determine from currently available data sets. Decary indicated that in 1917 many apparently 'wild' populations of prickly pear were actually the sites of abandoned fields and homesteads; but substantiating this today through oral recollections is problematic because the rich body of settlement histories that was once sedimented in the landscape in the shape of prickly pear stands of different densities and ages was eradicated in the 1920s by cochineal insects.[63] The essential point, however, is this. Whereas Fairhead and Leach argue that, since it is normally everyday life activities which promote the growth of a forest island, village abandonment can precipitate forest island loss,[64] abandoned prickly pear peri-village islands continued to thrive and expand. With spines that deterred grazing, stands of 'Malagasy cactus' rapidly recruited new members as stem joints and fruit became detached from parent plants. Thus, while prickly pear was associated with human settlement and the social dynamics of land use, it almost certainly also grew wild. Indeed, the ambiguities in local cultural representations partly reflect the fact that

[59] P. Vérin, 'Une vision de l'extrême sud de Madagascar en 1866 d'après le témoignage d'Alfred Grandidier', in C. Allibert (ed.), *Autour d'Étienne de Flacourt* (Paris, Institut National de Langues et Civilisations Orientales, 1996), pp. 226–7.

[60] Fairhead and Leach, *Misreading the African Landscape,* pp. 21, 23.

[61] D. Cosgrove, *Social Formation and Symbolic Landscape* (London, Croom Helm, 1984); B. Bender (ed.), *Landscape: Politics and perspectives* (Oxford, OUP, 1993).

[62] K. Middleton,'Circumcision, Death, and Strangers', in K. Middleton (ed.), *Ancestors, Power and History in Madagascar* (Leiden, Brill, 1999).

[63] K. Middleton, 'Who Killed "Malagasy Cactus"?'

[64] Fairhead and Leach, *Misreading the African Landscape*, p. 88.

'Malagasy cactus' moved constantly on the rather indistinct boundary between the 'cultivated' (*amboleañe*) and the 'wild' (*hatsa*). In accounting for the uneven 'naturalisation' of 'Malagasy cactus', we probably therefore need to move beyond explanations that invoke one or two macroscopic factors –climate, plant physiology, geology or human agency – to seeing its dynamics as shaped by multiple, interacting factors, both social and ecological.

'Tandroy and prickly pear are kin'

Colonial administrator Raymond Decary argued that prickly pear had not only made human settlement of Madagascar's Deep South possible but had profoundly shaped local identity. 'The climate and the difficulty of finding food and water', he wrote, 'have given the natives of the Deep South, despite their diverse origins, a common identity..., a family likeness.., so that today a true Antandroy tribe exists.' In the development of this 'race' or people, 'an imported plant, the *raiketa*, has played a primordial role'.[65] Of course, Decary's argument was overstated because Androy had been inhabited long before the introduction of 'Malagasy cactus', and domestic stock had been a primary element of economic activity since at least the eleventh century. Moreover, a range of food plants, many equally of American origin, had been imported; in fact, almost all cultivated food plants in this region are exotics (millets, manioc, pumpkins, sweet potatoes, groundnuts, and maize).

To a large extent, Decary's 'botanico-human association' has to be read as a contribution to colonial ethnology, which helped to construct the 'Tandroy' at a time when, in Madagascar as in Africa, ethnicity acquired a particular significance for colonial regimes. Whether prickly pear was as central to indigenous self-identification in the nineteenth century as it later became in the colonial imagination is open to dispute. Decary quoted a local saying to the effect that 'Tandroy and cactus are kin' (*longo Tandroy sy raiketa*), remarking that this showed in a striking way 'what intimate union can exist between plants and men'.[66] But the ethnonym 'Anterndroe' first appears in *Madagascar; or Robert Drury's Journal*, published in 1729, that is, fifty years before the introduction was made. Moreover, there were many 'Tandroy' to the north where, by Decary's own account, prickly pear was relatively scarce. Nonetheless, even when Decary's text has been deconstructed, it seems likely that widespread use of 'Malagasy cactus' as a fodder intensified local pastoral production. There is also some evidence that it led to human population growth in some parts.[67]

On Decary's evidence, the lives of the Karembola people in Tsihombe District were even more closely entwined with prickly pear. He claimed that in 1917 approximately 40,000 cattle in this region fed 'almost exclusively' on singed cladodes for six months of the year, and that around 15 tonnes of the fruit were harvested for human consumption daily from August to February.[68] Yet 'Karembola' as a regional identity

[65] Decary, *L'Androy,* pp. 1, 205; 'L'utilisation des Opuntias', p. 771.

[66] Decary, *L'Androy*, pp. 1, 127.

[67] K. Middleton, 'Opportunities and Risks: A Cactus Pear in Madagascar', in A. Nefzaouli and P. Inglese (eds), Proceedings of the Fourth International Congress on Cactus Pear and Cochineal, *Acta Horticulturae*, 581 (ISHS, 2002), pp. 63–73.

[68] Decary, 'Rapport sur la "Raketa".'

has a history dating to at least the seventeenth century.[69] Nonetheless, there is some substance to Decary's thesis, because from the late eighteenth century onwards the Karembola was a 'frontier' society in which incomers from the east gradually displaced earlier settlers from the land.[70] Prickly pear may have been among the politico-economic innovations that drove this westward expansion, while the prickly pear frontier in turn moved west as incomers used the plant to demarcate boundaries and lay claim to conquered land. Karembola today remember Modave's prickly pear as 'Malagasy Cactus' (*raketa gasy*), and speak of 'the time of Malagasy cactus' (*tamy raketa gasy*) as 'the time of the ancestors' (*tamy razañe*).[71] This appears to place 'Malagasy cactus' centrally in their ethnohistory. But it is possible that this exotic plant became 'vernacularised' and 'ancestralised' only *after* its eradication in the 1920s, within the context of a retrospective symbolic reconstitution of 'tradition' during the colonial era.

Be that as it may, it is clear that the relationship between plant transfer and empire in this instance differs significantly from the pattern hypothesised by Crosby. Where Crosby talks of successful 'Europeanisation' of New World landscapes with European biota, we need to talk of successful 'Malagasisation' of a New World plant. Socially and culturally, if not in a strictly botanical sense, prickly pear had become a 'native' plant. One reason why Crosby does not consider this possibility is because he restricts the scope of his book to 'Neo-Europes', environments which were successfully 'Europeanised';[72] in this sense, his narrative is *not* intended to encompass arid and semi-arid zones such as southern Madagascar where European settler colonisation failed and land remained largely in local hands. But, precisely because it precludes consideration of the many important biota transfers that were made to Africa during the era under study, Crosby's narrative fails to capture the diverse and complex exchanges that actually characterised this period of world history.

It is tempting to trace out multiple ironies in the fact that a plant transfer, so closely associated with European expansionism, was turned by local peoples to their own ends. For instance, while Modave's proposal for the settlement at Fort Dauphin had incorporated the typical Physiocratic vision of colonial agriculture based on wheat and oats grain production, the economies that actually developed in southern Madagascar in the wake of the colony's failure were reportedly based on prickly pear. And when French colonial troops next arrived in southern Madagascar in the early years of the twentieth century, the very plant Modave had introduced in order to fortify his establishment proved to be the primary obstacle to their occupation. Subsequently, 'Malagasy cactus' was perceived in certain colonial factions as fostering resistance to colonial systems of production by preventing the rational and profitable exploitation of local resources of cattle, labour, and land because it enabled the peoples of the Deep South to satisfy their primitive wants without work or trade.[73]

The idea that an exotic plant enabled a non-European people to oppose expanding global systems is certainly seductive. We should be wary, however, of analyses that reproduce without question or modification the stark dichotomies of colonial discourses on prickly pear. While precolonial local economies of southern Madagascar *appear* to have been orientated to production for exchange and use value, they had in fact been

[69] See, for example, Flacourt, *Histoire de la Grande Isle*, pp. 137, 140.
[70] L.H.G. Middleton, 'Power and Meaning'.
[71] K. Middleton, 'Circumcision, Death, and Strangers'.
[72] Crosby, *Ecological Imperialism*, p. 291.
[73] K. Middleton, 'Who Killed "Malagasy Cactus"?'

inextricably entangled with expanding trading systems in the Southwestern Indian Ocean from well before Flacourt's time. Nor did this engagement diminish in the nineteenth century. On the contrary, for several reasons, the number of Creole traders calling at the smaller, less favoured bays of the Deep South probably increased.[74] Local products such as rubber and orchil, newly in demand and deeply implicated in the expansion of Western industrial capitalism, were exchanged for cloth, guns and powder, while cattle, the perennial export, found new markets in southern Africa, where great losses had resulted from epidemics and the South African war. In short, the interplay between evolving Malagasy agrarian societies and processes of Western expansion was far from straightforward. Prickly pear became essential to local Malagasy 'subsistence' economies, yet these 'subsistence' economies were inextricably entangled with a global economy. 'These immense herds of the Androy whose cattle leave Fort Dauphin for Lourenco Marques in their hundreds by each boat', Lyautey wondered in 1901, 'On what do they live? What do they drink?'[75] The answer surely was that many of them had been raised on prickly pear. At the same time, prickly pear may also have facilitated the gathering of wild rubber and orchil by reducing the labour input required by annual crop production and by providing gatherers with 'wild foods' to eat on the way.

The social history of prickly pear in southern Madagascar thus discloses a curious 'double movement' between insularity and accessibility, between globalisation and relocalisation, between 'opening' and 'closure'. Decary failed to grasp this 'double movement' when he drew on prickly pear to construct imagery of a primitive people not yet ready for the impact of the modern world. More recently, archaeologist Parker Pearson so emphasises the precolonial insularity of southern Malagasy peoples that he finds himself unable to explain the 12,000 imported guns that were confiscated in the Androy during the first few years of French colonial rule.[76] In fact, 'Malagasy cactus' was part of a broader social dynamic whereby southern Malagasy engaged in Indian Ocean trading systems, actively incorporating foreign elements into local cultural practice, hoping to canalise the power of *vazaha* ('strangers'), even as they sought to maintain their political and economic autonomy. Southern Madagascar neither experienced 'biotic meltdown'[77] during this period, nor was it reshaped into preferred patterns of a mercantilist ecology. Yet the scale of its exports to European colonies on the African mainland, and to markets elsewhere, underscores the complex links that sometimes existed between European expansion and seemingly 'local' systems of production based, in fact, on introduced alien plants.

'Knowing the land'

This paper has followed recent work in African history in stressing the skill, ingenuity, and tenacity shown by southern Malagasy in colonising 'on the hostile frontiers' of a

[74] M. Esoavelomandroso, 'Note sur les espaces économiques du Mahafale occidental à la fin du XIXe siècle', *Histoire et organisation de l'espace à Madagascar*, Cahiers du CRA 7 (Paris, 1989), pp. 147–52; Middleton, 'Power and Meaning'.
[75] L.H.G. Lyautey, *Lettres du Sud de Madagascar 1900–1902* (Édition Colin, Paris, 1935), p. 134.
[76] M. Parker Pearson, 'Close Encounters of the Worst Kind: Malagasy Resistance and Colonial Disasters in Southern Madagascar', *World Archaeology* 28 (1997), pp. 393–417.
[77] S. Pyne, *Vestal Fire. An environmental history, told through fire, of Europe and Europe's Encounter with the World* (London and Seattle, WA, University of Washington Press, 1997), p. 416.

small continent. As my Karembola informants remarked, people must be resourceful, energetic and optimistic if they are to 'know a thirsty land, withstand its trials, and still prosper and increase' (*mahay tane marandrano, mahatante ty hasarotse, mahavelone teña*). For Karembola, 'knowing the land' meant drawing on a wide range of skills and knowledge, from the wisdom of earlier settlers who had excavated the first *ranovato*, through the political acumen and military prowess that enabled them to obtain territorial dominion, to respecting ancient territorial taboos and experimenting with unfamiliar or exotic species such as prickly pear.

As a planter in the Isle de France, Modave had been impressed by the flair for adaptability his Malagasy slaves had shown.[78] In Madagascar, he observed how Madecasse were drawn to inspect each ongoing and newly completed work of construction at the Fort. Noting 'the cries of admiration and astonishment that escape them upon first inspecting the armoury', he was certain of 'subjugating [them] by the superiority of our arts'.[79] Curiosity almost certainly drew Malagasy to examine the prickly pears that established at Fort Dauphin, and they were probably fascinated by the the plant's unusual appearance: its flat, broad cladodes, bearing exceptionally long spines, and in time its flowers, its fruits, and its ease of growth. We can imagine a prickly pear revolution moving silently over the landscapes of southern Madagascar as peoples took cladodes from the deserted colony and began to propagate the plant and to experiment with methods of preparation and use.

The value of prickly pear as defensive hedging had been demonstrated by Modave; but other uses were discovered independently. It is unlikely that Modave and his men ever saw the need to press prickly pear trunks for water or burn spines from cladodes to feed cattle in the relatively well-watered environment of Fort Dauphin. I have found no evidence in Modave's Journal or his letters to indicate that he was aware of prickly pear's potential as a dry season fodder, although raising cattle for export figured prominently in his plans for the colony. Some of the uses southern Malagasy devised for 'Malagasy cactus' elaborated on existing local practices: for example, in Androy, it was planted according to a vernacular tradition of palisade settlement.[80] It is also possible that local farmers may have selected clones for fruit quality and vegetative vigour. Decary describes considerable morphological variation among prickly pears in Tsihombe district, although he explains this as an adaptative response to local environmental conditions.[81]

But while acknowledging the skills, energy and agency Malagasy deployed in colonising a hostile frontier, and in shaping vegetation histories, we also need to recognise that in certain environments some varieties of prickly pear can be very difficult for people with low input technologies and limited resources to control. Managing 'Malagasy cactus' by mechanical measures such as cutting, felling, and fire proved time-consuming and expensive for twentieth-century European colonisers. To eradicate it was almost impossible since it regenerated from small 'almost indestructible'

---

[78] Cited by B. Foury, *Maudave et la Colonisation de Madagascar* (Paris, Société de L'histoire des Colonies Francaises et Libraire Larose, 1956), p. 23.

[79] CAOM C[5A] 2 No 66. Extrait du journal relatant les événements qui se sont déroulés à Madagascar. Entry for 10 November 1768.

[80] *Madagascar; or Robert Drury's Journal, During Fifteen Years' Captivity On That Island* (London, 1890 [1729]), pp. 125, 59; CAOM C[5A] 2 No. 66. Entry for 9 October 1768.

[81] Decary, 'Rapport sur la "Raketa"'.

fragments of stem or root.[82] For Malagasy hoe/spade cultivators, this vigour proved paradoxical. The plant's ease of cultivation and high biomass productivity, effectively locked in against predation by thorns, made it immensely attractive to households that for want of labour were hard-pressed to meet their subsistence needs. But considerable investment of labour was required if the plant was not to become invasive. Among both Karembola and Hazohandatse, taboos forbade women either to cut down prickly pears or to 'grill' the cladodes for stock. Wherever taboos of this kind existed, they restricted the labour available to control infestations of prickly pear.

It can be argued that 'Malagasy cactus' was crucially important to Malagasy prosperity during the nineteenth century, as both cultivar and weed. It probably increased agro-pastoral productivity in both the subsistence and export commodity sectors, and may also have sustained population growth. But 'Malagasy cactus' differed in an important way from those weeds that Crosby dubs 'the Red Cross of the plant world', which 'deal with ecological emergencies [subsequently giving] way to plants that may grow more slowly but grow taller and sturdier'.[83] 'Malagasy cactus' was not a colonising plant that enabled vegetation succession, thereby laying the basis for fertility in swidden-fallow cycles. It was a shrubby invader that once established became difficult to remove.[84] It is this profile that distinguished it from other plant introductions into southern Madagascar, such as manioc, sweet potatoes, and maize.

In his portrayal of 'Malagasy cactus' as 'very much a cultivated plant', Kaufmann states that Malagasy people did not ascribe 'agency' to the plant.[85] This thesis, which appears to be based on the author's experience of less invasive Opuntia varieties in the Androka region in 1996/97, appears difficult to sustain. First, the historical record suggests that the plant grew freely outside of cultivation. Second, we do not, in fact, know how peoples in late precolonial southern Madagascar viewed 'Malagasy cactus' and its spread. One cannot assume that local opinions were positive or homogenous.[86] Among the Karembola in the drylands south of Beloha, 'Malagasy cactus' appears to have been highly valued when the 'iron belt clamped upon the belly'. But peoples living on the banks of the Menarandra river may well have preferred to cultivate its rich alluvial soils – soils that not only 'nourish' greedy crops like sugar cane and maize but also crop twice a year – rather than see them infested by prickly pears that grew immensely tall but rarely produced ripe fruit. And even among the Karembola it is possible that the plant was sometimes experienced as a nuisance in bush-fallowing systems. Today, Karembola memories of 'Malagasy cactus' are certainly ambivalent. Women in particular emphasise the threat the dense infestations posed to their security, suggesting that preferences may have differed within farming communities according to gender and socio-economic status.

[82] Perrier de la Bâthie, 'Les pestes végétales', p. 37.

[83] Crosby, *Ecological Imperialism*, p. 169

[84] Some scientists today argue that prickly pears can be used in soil erosion control in arid and sub-arid lands (see, for example, Le Houérou, 'The Role of Cacti'). But this is a controversial proposition, which needs to be tested in a range of farming environments under swidden-fallow cycles of varying lengths (see Middleton, 'Benefits and Risks').

[85] Kaufmann, 'La question des raketa', pp. 111, 109.

[86] For a careful exploration of how perceptions of two common weeds vary among Indonesian peasants, see M. Dove, 'The Practical Reason of Weeds in Indonesia: Peasant Vs. State Views of *Imperata* and *Chromolaena*', *Human Ecology* 14, 2 (1986), pp. 163–90. On the importance of taking account of local socio-ecological variation, see J. Koponen, *People and Production in Late Precolonial Tanzania, History and structures* (Jyväsklyä, Finland, 1988).

I began writing this chapter with every intention of creating a relatively simple, easily graspable narrative in imperial history. In playing the failure of Modave's colony against the success of 'Malagasy cactus', I sought to highlight the irony that an introduction made in the context of an imperial project had been turned against imperialism itself. I hoped thereby also to contrast local people's knowledge, skill and agency in managing Madagascar's drylands with Modave's evident shortcomings in this respect. In the course of researching and writing the chapter, however, a rather more equivocal picture of the intertwined histories of prickly pear, colonial projects, and local responses has emerged. It now seems to me that prickly pear's trajectory in southern Madagascar from 1770 to 1924 can sustain multiple narratives: narratives both of Malagasy resistance to and entanglement with European expansion, narratives of both local people's role in creating and shaping landscapes and of their impotence before an invasive plant. Indeed, the legacy of a failed colonising project, while boosting productivity in the short term, may have circumscribed local peoples' ability to manage their environments even before the imposition of colonial rule.

Thus, over and against Crosby's biologistic thesis, the case study certainly points to the need to develop understandings of plant transfer which include local responses to and appropriation of plants. People introduced prickly pear to Madagascar, and other people - Malagasy herders and farmers - directly and indirectly helped it to spread. But we also need to be careful not to overestimate the latitude of human actions. While any assessment of the ecological potential of particular species has to take full account of human agency, operating within highly specific political and cultural frameworks including access to and control of land, in the case of 'Malagasy cactus' at least, it would be mistaken to assume that landscapes are nothing other than cultural and political artefacts.

3

Environmental Data & Historical Process

Historical Climatic Reconstruction & the Mutapa State
1450–1862

INNOCENT PIKIRAYI[1]

This chapter discusses the potential for using Portuguese texts to assess the role of environmental change in the rise and fall of precolonial states. It focuses in particular on documentation relating to the disasters affecting the Mutapa state from the sixteenth to nineteenth centuries. [2] The Mutapa state was part of the Zimbabwe Culture – a system of states that dominated the area between the Zambezi and Limpopo rivers, the Mozambican coastal plains and the Kalahari Desert margins during the entire second millennium AD. The states were characterised by urban centres, mostly built in stone and whose people exploited the varied Zimbabwe plateau and adjacent lowland environments.[3] Based on the Mutapa case, I suggest that environmental degradation was not primarily responsible for the decline or collapse of Zimbabwe Culture states. Rather, emphasis must be placed on society's response to environmental change; famine must be explained in relation to conflict and war. Thus, the paper provides a critique of environmental determinism as applied to the decline of Great Zimbabwe in

[1] Since 1994, the Archaeology Unit at the University of Zimbabwe has been involved in a regional project entitled Human Responses and Contributions to Environmental Change which seeks an archaeological understanding of how humans reacted and contributed towards environmental change during the past two thousand years. The project examines the relationship between culture, bio-geography and climate in the southern and eastern Africa regions from late Holocene times, especially the last 2000 years. Specifically the projects aims at (i) identifying those periods in the late Holocene where environmental change is most apparent, (ii) conducting spatial and temporal analysis of the development of settlement systems on inland plateau and drainage systems, rivers and coastal areas in relation to environmental change, and (iii) understanding patterns of resource utilisation adopted by foraging farming and urban communities and the long-term effects these have upon the various landscapes. Research in the Mwenezi and Mateke Hills aims at gaining a better insight into the development and decline of Mapungubwe and the rise of the Zimbabwe states. Archaeological sites in different environments have been documented and the data will then be used to conduct spatial and temporal analysis of the development of settlement systems in relation to environmental change. Field surveys have been used to define parameters of settlement location as well as determining long-term shifts in the utilisation of available resources.

[2] See, for example, I. Pikirayi, 'Portuguese encounters with the landscape of the Mutapa State, northern Zimbabwe, 1500–700 AD' (Unpublished paper, History Department, University of Zimbabwe, 1996).

[3] See, for example, P.S. Garlake, *Great Zimbabwe* (London, Thames and Hudson, 1972); Martin Hall, *The Changing Past: Farmers, kings and traders in southern Africa 200–1860* (Cape Town, David Philip, 1987).

some archaeological literature, and argues that archaeologists have often ignored historical evidence.[4]

The Zimbabwe culture and environmental explanations

The term 'Zimbabwe Culture' subsumes a number of state societies, which originated on the Zimbabwean Plateau and the adjacent lowlands at the beginning of the second millennium AD. These include Mapungubwe (1050–1270) in the Shashe-Limpopo basin, Great Zimbabwe (1290–1450) in the south-central plateau, Torwa-Changamire (1450–1830) in the south-west and Mutapa (1450–1900) in the north, including the Zambezi lowlands of Dande and Chidima. The rise and fall of these states was associated with a shift in settlement between the plateau and the lowlands. These were highly differentiated societies, which commanded a range of resources including valuable minerals, wildlife, livestock and fertile soils.[5] The wealth generated by the exploitation of these resources and through long-distance trade with the Indian Ocean, was channelled into monumental architecture. The neatly constructed stone buildings represent major centres in the form of state capitals, as well as regional or local centres. Exotic goods elevated the status and power of the local rulers. The Zimbabwe Culture lasted some eight or nine centuries, from the foundation of the Mapungubwe and Great Zimbabwe states in the eleventh and thirteenth centuries respectively to the decline of the Mutapa and Rozvi states in the nineteenth.

The middle Shashe-Limpopo area, once occupied by the state centred at Mapungubwe, is currently dry and prone to severe droughts. Its hot climate makes it largely unattractive for human settlement. It is therefore puzzling that the area was once host to a settlement system synonymous with a state from the eleventh to the thirteenth century.[6] Perhaps environmental conditions at that time were more attractive to large human and animal populations than at present. Explanations must, however, remain speculative, as the reasons for the demise of the Mapungubwe state are unknown. Periodic droughts and environmental degradation may have decreased human settlement in the area, but direct evidence for this is very scanty.[7] Perhaps a northward shift in the character of long distance trading networks eventually robbed Mapungubwe of its influence and prestige.[8] The rise of Great Zimbabwe in the thirteenth century as a

---

[4] D. N. Beach, *The Shona and Zimbabwe, 900–1850: an outline of Shona history* (Gweru, Mambo Press, 1980); P. J. J. Sinclair, *Space, Time and Social Formation: a territorial approach to the archaeology and anthropology of Zimbabwe and Mozambique, c. 0–1700AD* (Uppsala, Societas Archaeologica Upsaliensis, 1987); T. N. Huffman, 'Archaeological evidence for climatic change during the last 2000 years in Southern Africa', *Quaternary International* 33 (1996), pp. 53–60.

[5] See, for example, P.J.J. Sinclair, *Spatial Analysis of Archaeological Sites from Zimbabwe*. Working Papers in African Studies 7, African Studies Programme (Uppsala, Department of Cultural Anthropology, 1984).

[6] L. Fouche (ed.), *Mapungubwe: Ancient Bantu civilisation on the Limpopo* (Cambridge, CUP, 1937); G. A. Gardner, *Mapungubwe* (vol. II) (Pretoria, J.L. van Scalk, 1963); E. A. Voigt, *Mapungubwe: An archaeozoological interpretation of an Iron Age community* (Pretoria, Transvaal Museum, 1983); see also J. F. Eloff and A. Meyer, 'The Greefswald sites', in E. A. Voigt (ed.), *Guide to Archaeological Sites in the Northern Transvaal* (Pretoria, Southern African Association of Archaeologists, 1981) and T. N. Huffman, 'Iron Age settlement patterns and the origins of class distinction in Southern Africa', *Advances in World Archaeology* (1986).

[7] Huffman, 'Archaeological evidence'.

[8] Hall, *The Changing Past*.

major regional centre with considerable political and economic influence followed the decline of Mapungubwe, which lost contact with Indian Ocean traders. Great Zimbabwe's architectural and material cultural traits seem to derive from Mapungubwe, strongly suggesting some cultural links between the two.

Great Zimbabwe flourished as a major centre until the mid-fifteenth century. It probably controlled a hierarchy of settlements (*zimbabwe*) stretching westwards to the Suwa Pan in present-day Botswana and eastwards to the Save Valley.[9] The Great Zimbabwe state, like Mapungubwe, traded gold and ivory to centres on the western Indian Ocean coast such as Kilwa. The reasons for its decline sometime in the fifteenth century remain unclear, but some interpretations of present-day land use and population pressure in the southern plateau suggest that increased human settlement has seriously undermined its agricultural and grazing potential. Such commentators also stress that land suitable for agriculture around Great Zimbabwe is severely limited. During the late 1970s and early 1980s, Bannerman proposed that ecological degeneration or collapse around the site was the main reason for the polity's decline. His interpretation was challenged by Peter Garlake, who gave a social determinist explanation for the state's failure, and argued that politics and war could explain why Great Zimbabwe could not cope with drought.[10] We shall see below, that such explanations may be more plausible in explaining the decline of later states as well. The major limitation with these explanations was the absence of written sources. Tim Huffman has further questioned the environmental degradation hypothesis recently: he suggests that the fields around the site are not vulnerable to degradation and that the state relied not only on local agricultural production but on tribute drawn from a large area. Furthermore, the site was abandoned between 1420 and 1450, when the climate was becoming warmer and wetter, making it possible to feed larger populations. Environmental degradation would have forced an earlier abandonment of the site.[11]

The subsequent simultaneous rise of two state systems in the northern and southwestern plateau regions must be examined within the context of the decline of Great Zimbabwe as a political power. Portuguese texts suggest that, by the late fifteenth century, northern Zimbabwe was offering better agricultural and commercial opportunities than the south-central plateau regions, while in the south-west the Torwa state was more attractive environmentally, and more able to support a viable pastoral economy.[12]

Researchers of these questions have often ignored northern Shona oral traditions. One such tradition, recorded in the late 1950s from a spirit medium, suggests that Great Zimbabwe was abandoned because of a shortage of salt.[13] This shortage is given as a reason for the migration north towards the Zambezi. This particular tradition is itself

[9] Garlake, *Great Zimbabwe*; T.N. Huffman, *Snakes and Crocodiles: Power and symbolism in ancient Zimbabwe* (Johannesburg, Witwatersrand University Press, 1996).

[10] P. S. Garlake, 'Pastoralism and Zimbabwe', *Journal of African History* 19, 4 (1978), pp. 479–93; Sinclair, *Space Time and Social Formation*.

[11] Huffman, 'Archaeological evidence'.

[12] I. Pikirayi, *The Archaeological Identity of the Historical Mutapa State: towards an historical archaeology of northern Zimbabwe*. Studies in African Archaeological 6 (Uppsala, Societies Archaeologica Upsaliensis, 1993); P.J.J. Sinclair, *Space, Time and Social Formation*.

[13] D. P. Abraham, 'The early political history of the kingdom of Mwene Mutapa (850-1589)', in E. Stokes (ed.) *Historians in Tropical Africa: Proceedings of the Leverhulme Inter-Collegiate Conference, September 1960* (Salisbury, University College of Rhodesia and Nyasaland, 1962), pp. 61–92; D. N. Beach, *A Zimbabwean Past: Shona dynastic histories and oral traditions* (Gweru, Mambo Press, 1991).

infused with environmental information, and suggests ways in which humans responded to shortage of certain resources such as pasture and fertile land. It must, however, be treated with caution. It seems highly unlikely that a shortage of salt could have been the main reason for the abandonment of the area around Great Zimbabwe: a massive investment such as Great Zimbabwe surely could not have been deserted solely from the shortage of one such community. Rather, the appeal of the gold and the ivory trade with the western Indian Ocean zone, the good rainfall and the fertile soils North of the central watershed seem to be the main factors luring settlement and state formation to this area. It has been established more definitively that the later Mutapa capitals shifted from one area to another in response to the demands of security, water supply and trade, further suggesting that the environment alone was not the prime reason for the abandonment of major centres.[14]

As I shall explore further below, an analysis of documents relating to the Mutapa state indicates that environmental factors alone were not responsible for its decline. Useful insight into the dynamics of the Zimbabwe Culture states can be gained from combining study of past accounts of drought and famine with information on climate. My approach is guided by Sharon Nicholson's methodology of historical climate reconstruction.[15]

Historical climate reconstruction and its applications to the Zimbabwe Plateau

In her study of the Sahel region, Sharon Nicholson lists three types of data useful for historical climatic reconstruction. These are descriptions in historical texts of landscape and of drought, which she considers in association with climatic and meteorological information, derived from assessments of temperature, rainfall and other related variables.[16] From such data, Nicholson was able to construct a database that allowed her to cross-check different sources of information about conditions in the past. Her first category of data, landscape descriptions, is derived from past observers' comments on relief and vegetation, which can be compared to present-day conditions. In the Sahel, it was also crucial to collect data relating to lakes and rivers: the height of the annual flood could be measured, months of maximum flood recorded, and the position of lake shores determined. The navigability of rivers was also important, together with measures of how this changed seasonally. Information on the desiccation of present-day lakes and evidence of former lakes constituted another valuable source, as did data relating to flooding and the flow of desert wadis. Some travel journals give information about the height of lake surfaces or on other physical features including wells, oases and bogs.

Nicholson's second category relates to drought and information on poor harvests and famine. It is necessary to document information on when and where they occurred and who reported them. It is also important to determine the severity of the drought and/or famine, the causes of the latter, and whether it was widespread or a localised phenomenon. Agricultural prosperity is linked to drought, and can be assessed by

[14] Beach, *The Shona and Zimbabwe*; Pikirayi, *The Archaeological Identity*.
[15] S. Nicholson, 'The methodology of historical climate reconstruction and its application to Africa', *Journal of African History* 20, 1 (1979), pp. 31–49.
[16] *Ibid.*, p.34.

information relating to the condition of the harvest, the months of harvest, the crops grown, pests and many other things. Data on the cultivation of crops suited to relatively wet climates in regions that are arid today, for example, would be useful in assessments of past climates. Information on El Nino cycles is not yet available, but would certainly help to define past climatic trends over a longer period.

Information on climate and meteorology is diverse, and can include measurements of temperature and rainfall, weather diaries, descriptions of rainfall patterns and seasonal variations, as well as prevailing winds. There are some references to rains, storms, tornadoes, their seasonality and frequency, snowfalls, freezing temperatures, frost and hail. Some historical sources make simple references to dry and wet years, while others refer to severe and mild winters. References to wind are useful in that some winds are associated with dry periods, while others are associated with rain.

The Zimbabwe Plateau is considerably smaller in territorial extent than the Sahel considered by Nicholson, and the historical sources are more limited. Although northern Zimbabwe and the lower Zambezi have been in contact with the Portuguese since the early sixteenth century, there is very little meteorological information of the nature and range to which Nicholson refers. There are some references to rainfall, flooded rivers, dry and wet periods but they are too sporadic spatially and diachronically to be really useful for long-term comparative purposes. The most useful type of data relate to drought and famines, which, although vague, sparse and scanty, can inform us about how the inhabitants of the Mutapa state contributed to or responded to such phenomena.

Famine, often accompanied by epidemic disease, was probably responsible for population stagnation during the precolonial period in Zimbabwe. The Zimbabwe Plateau experiences drought about once in every five years, and famines were recurrent phenomena, often in association with drought.[17] Precolonial Zimbabweans devised methods of preventing famine from crop failure, through techniques of food storage, and also supplemented their food sources by hunting, gathering wild resources and trading gold they had mined. Families also practised mutual aid. Clientage ties between commoners and powerful people could also ease suffering, as the latter were expected to provide relief food. In this way the effects of famine were minimised. Seventeenth-century and later Mutapa kings tried to check famine by stabilising the food supply and establishing grain stores.[18] During politically unstable periods, however, depopulation, violence and destruction often resulted in famine. Mutapa Mukombwe's resettlement scheme in the seventeenth century was probably designed to stabilise population in the Mutapa state. It was organised at a time when the state was experiencing depopulation related to Portuguese mining in the heartland of the state, which impoverished the people, drained the state's wealth and destroyed its local economic base.[19] The ability of the Portuguese to dominate foreign trade sidelined the Mutapa rulers, who were increasingly regarded as subservient.

The Portuguese chroniclers and traders never described the landscape of the Mutapa state in geographic detail, except for the lands along the Zambezi River. Published cartographic specimens are based on descriptions provided by individuals who had traversed parts of the state. However, some of the information they contain is largely imaginary, especially that related to the distant interior, which very few Portuguese

[17] See, for example, John Iliffe, *Famine in Zimbabwe, 1890–1960* (Gweru, Mambo Press, 1987).

[18] S. I. G. Mudenge, *A Political History of Munhumutapa* (Harare, Zimbabwe Publishing House, 1988).

[19] Pikirayi, *The Archaeological Identity.*

reached.[20] These maps are of limited use in the exercise of environmental reconstruction on the Zimbabwe Plateau. The cartographers responsible were using the same
documents available to us, and they lacked knowledge of the exact location of rivers,
mountains, and other terrain and incorporated details based on preconceived ideas
about inland lakes, longitude and the magnetic north. Moreover, their use of different
documents to produce a specimen is confusing. The belief that the Zambezi River
emerged from a large inland lake was still strong, having been popularised by the
sixteenth-century editions of Ptolemy, and originally borrowed from the Swahili
traders who were acquainted with the Plateau.[21] The one exception is de Barros, who
cites six tributaries of the Zambezi: the Panhame (Manyame), the Luamguo
(Luangwa), the Arruya (Ruya), the Manjouo (Mazowe), the Inadira (Nyadiri) and the
Ruenia (Ruenya). He provides the documentary evidence that, by the middle of the
sixteenth century, the Portuguese had explored the Plateau well inside the present
borders of Zimbabwe. As their travels appear to have been restricted to the courses of
the major rivers, however, their information on landscape could not provide information on the scale available to Nicholson, working on the Sahel.

These limitations notwithstanding, the historical documents that do exist for the
Mutapa state contain valuable information on landscape and climate, which it is
important to reconsider.[22] It is also important, however, to reflect on how such evidence
relates to human decision-making processes.

Portuguese documents
and the environment of the northern Zimbabwe Plateau

Seventeenth-century Portuguese accounts about the northern Zimbabwe Plateau, the
adjacent Zambezi Lowlands, as well as Manyika and distant territories such as 'Butua'
(the south-western Plateau) clearly suggest that climatic conditions were similar to those
of today. The Plateau, homeland of the Mutapa state, is described as cool, with plenty of
food, good water and cattle.[23] There were clearly noticeable temperature variations
between the higher altitude regions of Mukaranga, which the Portuguese described as
cold with 'pure and better air', and the Kingdom of Botonga (the Tonga-speaking Sena
area of the Lower Zambezi) which they regarded as very hot and humid.[24] Although it

---

[20] *Ibid.*, Ch, 6; Pikirayi, 'Portuguese encounters'.

[21] W. G. L. Randles, 'South east Africa and the empire of the Monomotapa as shown on selected printed
maps of the sixteenth century', *Studia* 2 (1958), pp. 103–63; D. N. Beach, *A Zimbabwean Past: Shona
dynastic histories and oral traditions* (Gweru, Mambo Press, 1991).

[22] See, for example, Huffman, 'Archaeological evidence'.

[23] Bras de Figueirado writing on behalf of the clerk Alvaro Nunes, in Sena, on 23 July 1633 cited Jacome de
Carvallo a resident of Mozambaique for 40 years, who visited the Mutapa State as envoy. Similar
information was echoed by Custodio Lopez d'Alamo, a resident of Sena, who had lived in the region for
about twenty years, as well as Father Antonio Gomes. See D.N. Beach and C. de Noronha, *The Shona and
the Portuguese* (Vol. 1), unpublished (History Department, University of Zimbabwe, n.d.), pp. 21, 22, 23,
and 112.

[24] This information was gleaned from a document compiled in Lisbon in March 1683, reporting on the
importance of the Rivers of Cuama (Lower Zambezi region) as well as from a chapter by Francisco de
Sousa, writing in 1697, discussing the climate of the same region. Beach and Noronha, *The Shona and the
Portuguese* (Vol. 1), pp. 159, 237.

is arguable that their accounts of the Mutapa state were primarily concerned with conflict and with Portuguese attempts to control gold mining, it seems safe to conclude that they did not witness negative climatic extremes (if they did, they did not consider them worth recording). This conclusion is supported by the fact that sixteenth- and eighteenth-century accounts *do* record such information, as well as documenting their devastating effects. Comments relating to droughts and lengthy dry spells are particularly notable.

Early sixteenth-century Portuguese accounts do not inform us about droughts and dry spells in the Mutapa state. This is understandable because the primary concern of their authors was to find the source of the gold traded from the interior to the coast. Thus they focused on civil wars in the interior, as well as on attempts by rulers in the immediate hinterland to control the terms of coast-interior trade.[25] Francisco de Sousa (in an account dated 1697), however, reports a serious drought during the 1560s, which followed the death of Father Goncalo da Silveira, who was a Portuguese missionary to the Mutapa court. This drought was apparently accompanied by a plague of locusts.[26] Written 136 years after the event, the entire account seems infused with Biblical myths, which is to be expected in accounts of the death of a missionary. It seems that much of the factual basis of the story had been distorted, and Francisco de Sousa notes that he heard it from the people of 'Mocaranga as ... handed down to them by their ancestors'. It is, however, possible that there was a drought: prolonged dry spells in the Mutapa state just after the middle of the sixteenth century, which could have contributed to heightened resentment at the Mutapa court. Combined with the arrival of the Portuguese, who attempted to convert the people to Christianity, traditionalists may have found a scapegoat in Father Goncalo da Silveira. Some academic commentators have suggested that the priest was killed during times of severe drought, and that, after his death, conditions returned to normal.[27]

Late sixteenth-century Portuguese accounts do not describe conditions in the Lower Zambezi or adjacent highland territories as normal. There had been a disastrous campaign during the 1570s, and the cannibalistic Zimba people, who had emerged from Maravi, were regarded as a serious 'menace' by the Portuguese.[28] The result was a conflict lasting nearly thirty years, which the Portuguese accounts detail with considerable exaggeration. Although the accounts fall short of describing the environmental conditions at the time, it is clear that the last three decades of the sixteenth century were times of hardship for the inhabitants of the Lower Zambezi and adjacent regions. Serious droughts or long dry spells could have disrupted the availability of food resources, forcing some communities to resort to cannibalism.

The worst drought recorded in Portuguese accounts occurred in 1714. The drought seems to have been widespread and its effects were quite severe. At that time, two powerful houses that were vying for the throne were fighting a bitter civil war.

---

[25] Oral traditions collected by Donald Abraham in the late 1950s seem to suggest there was a drought between 1450 and 1482 in northern Zimbabwe. It is now clear that these traditions are unreliable, according to Beach, *A Zimbabwean Past*. A prolonged dry spell could have increased the competition for gold mining and trade during the late fifteenth century, as reported by the Portuguese documents.

[26] Beach and Noronha, *The Shona and the Portuguese* (Vol. 1), pp. 260-1.

[27] See Hoyini K. K. Bhila, *Trade and Politics in a Shona Kingdom: The Manyika and their Portuguese and African neighbours, 1575-1902* (Harare, Longman, 1982)

[28] Beach, *The Shona and Zimbabwe*; de Couto, in G. M. Theal, *Records* (Vol. 6), p. 409; Pikirayi, *The Archaeological Identity*, Ch. 8.

According to Mudenge,[29] more than 200,000 people died from a devastating smallpox epidemic and a terrible drought. The figure is probably exaggerated, but clearly points to the worst catastrophe to befall south-east central Africa since the Portuguese came into the region. The on-going civil wars of the first half of the eighteenth century could have worsened the effects of drought and epidemic. Whatever the precise causes of the catastrophe, it seems clear that the early eighteenth century in northern Zimbabwe as well as the adjacent Lower Zambezi was 'abnormal' in climate or environmental terms.

In the eighteenth century, a much greater number of Portuguese accounts were produced, especially with regard to the Lower Zambezi. Hence more information is available about the environment, as well as other disasters. Between 1736 and 1745 for example, there was a serious locust plague, at the time of the November and January rains. Wild animals, especially elephants and hippos, destroyed agriculture, most notably in the 1760s. In addition, there were droughts and lengthy dry spells.[30]

The most detailed landscape descriptions are found in post-1850 documents, especially in the writing of Albino Manoel Pacheco. His descriptions contain information relating to the rains, the flooding and silting of rivers, and descriptions of other relevant physical features of the land. The data can be compared with current norms. A more interesting question, however, arises from the fact that the Mutapa state had moved from the higher altitude cooler and well watered plateau, to the hotter and drier Zambezi lowlands of Chidima. This is a territory between the Zambezi, Mukumbura, Ruya and other southern tributaries of the Zambezi.

The Musengezi area borders Chidima, and is described by Pacheco as 'stretching over a great length (about seventy Portuguese leagues) and has a width not inferior to its length but which I cannot [describe] for lack of reliable data ... starting at the south, on the left bank of Rusenha ... by the Mussenguese ... on the west, the Zambezi on the north and the Tete territory on the east....'[31] This particular territory was 'generally mountainous and the mountains, although they are covered with trees, are formed of very fragile, red clay ... criss-crossed with rivers, little streams and brooks, some of them periodic and others not navigable because of obstacles that block them and because they are shallow, it therefore suffers from a shortage of water in the dry season....'[32]

When Pacheco arrived in Chidima on 19 December 1861, he described the territory as 'enormous' but was disappointed by its ruler, whom he cast as weak. He passed through Chidima on his way to Zumbo, noting the physical features, such as rivers, mountains and forests. Most of the Dima people lived close to the Inhamnoya mountains. The Machekampanga range is described as high, massive and covered with woodlands. He crossed it with extreme difficulty. In less than two years of his visit to the Lower Zambezi, Pacheco had observed much about the physical environment and its dynamics, as well as the way people used it. The agricultural lands were well cultivated but had to await the rains, which by December, had not arrived. He reported rains in early January 1862, but even then, some of the rivers were still dry and heavily silted. Particularly notable was the Musengezi River, which he found dry. Rains eventually arrived in the middle of February, filling the rivers. Like any visitor before him, it was

---

[29] Mudenge, *A Political History of Munhumutapa*. The ruling Mutapa was Samutomba Nyanhanda (1712–1723).

[30] Beach and Noronha, *The Shona and the Portuguese* (Vol. 2), pp. 91–3.

[31] *Ibid.*

[32] *Ibid.*

hard for him to link some of these phenomena with the political and economic crises experienced by some of the peoples he encountered. Yet, some of these political and economic events appear to have impacted on the environment in a significant way.

Responses to political and economic crises, 1570s–1750s

In order to understand how the various Mutapa and their subjects responded and contributed to environmental change between the mid-sixteenth and mid-eighteenth centuries, it is necessary to examine some of the political and economic crises that the state experienced. From these, one can deduce the effects of turmoil and instability on scarcity and droughts. The period 1570–1750 can be divided into five broad periods characterised by certain important events. These are: the Zimba menace, already mentioned above, during the last thirty years of the sixteenth century; the Matuzianhe revolt and the wars of Mutapa Gatsi Rusere, which dominated the first two decades of the seventeenth century; the Portuguese conquest, up to the 1660s; the revival of the state under king Mukombwe; and the subsequent loss of the plateau lands and the shift towards the Zambezi during the first half of the eighteenth century.

The Matuzianhe revolt and the wars of Mutapa Gatsi Rusere, 1600–24

The Zimba phenomenon had ripple effects on the Mutapa state that can be seen in the form of the Chunzo-Matuzianhe revolt. During this time, the Mutapa state experienced one of the greatest challenges to its existence. This is archeologically represented by fortified settlements in the mountain regions of the Ruya and Mazoe valleys. The Portuguese tried to interfere with Mutapa court politics, supporting rebel groups or manipulating weak Mutapa. Beach[33] and Mudenge[34] have given full historical accounts of this period, while Pikirayi[35] presents a summary which also examines the archaeological evidence for fortified settlements.

The Portuguese conquest and aftermath, 1624–50s

After 1624 the Portuguese interfered directly in Mutapa court politics. This resulted in civil war between 1624 and 1629. The number of Portuguese within the state increased and some of them began to grab large areas of land (*prazos*), especially in the lower Zambezi.[36] There was a treaty in 1629 between the Portuguese *prazo* holders and Mutapa Mavura, whom they had assisted against a rival, Mutapa Kapararidze. But the new system of land ownership was parasitic in character and became a major source of violence and conflict in the Zambezi Valley and adjacent regions. It probably affected agricultural production and resulted in hunger and periodic famines in environmentally sensitive areas of the state. Depopulation of these areas probably started around this time.

The Portuguese clearly undermined the authority of the ruling Mutapa. The 1629 treaty unleashed a wave of violence and unrest in which the main actors were the *prazo* holders and their slave armies, the Chikunda. Local people were attacked, deprived of their property, and enslaved in the process. The situation was so terrible that many people fled the gold mining areas and the heart of the state. Some *prazo* holders seized

---

[33] Beach, *The Shona and Zimbabwe.*
[34] Mudenge, *A Political History of Munhumutapa.*
[35] Pikirayi, *The Archaeological Identity.*

land that belonged to the Mutapa, while some local rulers joined them in order to occupy certain areas of the state.[37]

One of the key problems was the weakness of the ruling Mutapas who were unable to resist the Portuguese invaders. It is arguable whether or not the Mutapas who ruled up to the 1650s or 1660s should be called puppets, but all had insecure reigns as they depended on the Portuguese. All gave unlimited concessions to the Portuguese, apart from Mavura who tried to control their behaviour by alerting the authorities in Portugal of the situation, and by confining the traders to the newly established *feiras* (trading centres). By 1667 there was widespread depopulation, partly due to a plague of locusts and partly due to the violence. The mining economy was depressed and people were reluctant to mine gold for the Portuguese. The seriousness of this crisis is emphasised by Mudenge who describes how smallpox, measles and plague had decimated the population of the regions south of the Zambezi. Many villages and settlements were abandoned and fields were left unharvested. Very few people remained to work in the gold mines.[38]

Mutapa Mukombwe, 1660s–1700s

Mukombwe features in the Portuguese sources from the 1660s to the 1690s. It is not clear whether Mukombwe was a single figurehead or the name represented a number of rulers stemming from the one ruling dynasty.[39] It was during this time that the Mutapa state lost Mukaranga, its heartland on the plateau area. Mukaranga territory was extremely valuable to the state for centuries: it was well watered, had good arable land and grazing and gold resources that provided wealth to the state. By this time most of these resources appear depleted or could not be exploited.

Mukombwe revived the seriously weakened state by adopting an anti-Portuguese stance. The state had to recover from the excesses of the *prazo* holders, and seemingly went through a rebuilding phase. The numbers of Portuguese in the state had decreased considerably as it was no longer profitable for them to stay there; disease also took its toll. Both Beach and Mudenge indicate that, during the late 1680s, the Mutapas staged a comeback by reoccupying the trading centres.[40]

In the 1660s and 1680s, the Tonga of the Zambezi rose against the Portuguese. In the 1670s, the Manyika joined Mukombwe to fight the *prazo* holders, eventually defeating them in the 1680s. Changamire Dombo organised an army and expelled them between 1693 and 1695, ending the Portuguese 'menace' on the Zimbabwe Plateau.

Shift towards the Zambezi, 1700s–1750

After the wars of the seventeenth century, the Mutapa state finally lost its plateau base and shifted its capital into the Dande and Chidima areas of the lower Zambezi. As I shall argue below, one of the factors compelling the move seems to have been the security of the state in relation to Portuguese economic activities and attack. In addition, the eighteenth-century Mutapa state was characterised by fighting among

---

[36] A. F. Isaacman, *Mozambique, The Africanisation of a European Institution: the Zambezi prazos, 1780-1902* (Madison, WI and London, University of Wisconsin Press, 1972).

[37] Beach, *The Shona and Zimbabwe*, p.130.

[38] Mudenge, *A Political History of Munhumutapa*, p.132.

[39] Beach, *The Shona and Zimbabwe*, p. 132.

[40] *Ibid.*; Mudenge, *A Political History of Munhumutapa*.

rival ruling houses, especially those of Boroma and Nyamhandu. The drought of 1714 was certainly worsened by such conflict and the resulting violence.[41]

Summary and conclusions

The history of the Mutapa state during the sixteenth and seventeenth centuries, which I have briefly outlined, seems to support Iliffe's argument that catastrophic droughts and famine occurred when violence intensified scarcity. The Portuguese attempts to conquer the state in the 1570s, the Zimba 'menace', the revolts affecting the state during the early seventeenth century and the wars between the Mutapa and the Portuguese ending in the 1630s, all seem to point in this direction. Written sources suggest a state of degradation and negative change in the physical environment. Droughts were evident through increased or lengthy periods of aridity, reduced river flow, crop failure and livestock deaths. There were also drought-related catastrophes such as locust plagues and disease (though these were sometimes a product of increased wetness).

The crises of the late sixteenth and early seventeenth centuries affected the peripheral areas of the state, especially the environmentally sensitive lower Zambezi. The Zimba moved towards the Indian Ocean following the turmoil of the 1570s onwards. Revolts occurred near the core, but this did not destroy the state. Portuguese invasion during the first half of the seventeenth century affected the state in that the violence connected with it intensified resource scarcity and was associated with the significant undermining of the authority of the Mutapa state. The violence connected with the movement of the Mutapa state from the plateau is reflected archaeologically by fortified settlements sited mostly on hilltops, especially in the Ruya Mazoe basin. Their construction clearly had an impact on the immediate physical environment in terms of stone clearance/quarrying, utilisation of vegetation resources and mining of gold in the rivers. This development should certainly be linked with the emergence of *prazos* in the lower Zambezi and their negative influence on local food production.

Poor governance, arising out of a weak response to the Portuguese presence and the highly divisive succession system, could have forced the ruling Mutapa rulers to scale down their levels of control. The decision to relinquish command of certain territories was probably taken during this time. Conditions conducive to depopulation, plague and disease probably resulted in the loss of the Plateau segment of the state during the later part of the seventeenth or the early eighteenth century.

The decision to shift the state towards the Chidima and Dande areas of the Zambezi seems rather puzzling, given the fact that the area is generally hot and dry. Portuguese sources suggest otherwise, however. The climate here was warm and hospitable. Environmentally, the territory of the Dima is well drained; a radial drainage emanates from a plateau surface. Mountains were probably used for defensive needs, as written sources suggest. The state was also close to the Zambezi, which never runs dry, and this allowed cultivation near the river banks and its creeks. The devastating drought of 1714 could have reinforced the decision to re-locate to Chidima, but this aspect is not clear from the written accounts.

In short, I hope to have shown the value of approaching historical texts in new ways, and exploring in detail the information they contain relating to landscape and climate,

[41] Mudenge, *A Political History of Munhumutapa*.

however scanty. However, this information cannot be considered on its own, and must be related to political processes, particularly conflict and war. I have argued against environmental determinist arguments in explaining the rise and fall of precolonial Zimbabwean states, underlining the necessity of situating information relating to environmental change in its political and economic context.

4

Women & Environment in African Religion

The Case of Zimbabwe*

TERENCE RANGER

In precolonial Zimbabwe – as in the communal areas to the present day – women had few rights to land.[1] In the ideal model of the patrilineal system of Shona and Ndebele society, wives moved into their husband's home area. They were regarded as intrinsically strangers to that environment. The right of the community to land was vested in the spirits of male patrilineal ancestors; the ancestors of wives, whether male or female, did not exercise any influence. Yet women carried out most agricultural tasks. The result was a situation in which those who worked the land seemed to have the least interest in maintaining its fertility. As the Zimbabwean novelist, Chenjerai Hove, expressed it in *Bones*, 'most women are just "one big scar" which has blighted the earth which has systematically denied them their rights for ages'.[2]

In the terms of some European feminist literature, this sounds like a classic context for the secret nurturing by women of the beliefs and rites of 'witchcraft', maintaining underground an old female fertility religion which had been displaced by the rise of patriarchy. In fact, in Zimbabwe witchcraft belief and practice did not work in this way. There were plenty of other positive rites of fertility; both men and women regarded witchcraft as the evil opposite of social religion; the witch damaged the environment by blighting crops or withholding rain. Female participation in positive rituals of the environment did not work in hidden opposition to patriarchy. Instead women occupied public religious roles either within the patriarchal system, or in the cult of the Creator God, Mwali, which operated above patriarchy. These roles profoundly modified the idea of women as a scar upon the land.

Women's environmental roles within patriarchal religion

Environmental religion typically operated in Zimbabwean patriarchal society in the form of a hierarchy of male ancestor spirits. The founders of a chieftainship and their

---

[1] A differently focused discussion of the same issues is Bella Mukonyora, 'Women and Ecology in Shona Religion' in *Word and World* (St Paul, MN, Luther Seminary, 1999).

[2] Hove is cited in Abel Mutsakani, 'Mumbengegwi fights for women's land rights', *The Financial Gazette*, 24 September 1998, p. 6.

immediate successors were known as *mhondoro*, lion spirits. Such spirits possessed human mediums. Through these mediums, the *mhondoro* spirits legitimated chiefs of the same ancestral line, cleansed the land from the stain of incest, made rain, and gave out ritually treated seed. The graves of dead senior ancestors were surrounded by sacred groves, which were never to be cut. Such graves were usually on mountains, and these spiritually powerful high places marked out the territory of the chief. Environmental catastrophes such as drought were explained as the result of one or other infraction of the spiritual order – witchcraft, incest, disrespect to the ancestors, disobedience of the *mhondoro*. In some chiefdoms every medium of a *mhondoro* spirit was male; so too were the acolytes, messengers, drummers and mbira (thumb-piano) players who attended them. David Lan, who has written the most sophisticated account of the *mhondoro* system for any part of Zimbabwe, insists that very few Korekore *mhondoro* mediums in the Zimbabwean north-east are women and that when they are it is always an indication that their possessing spirit is not a significant one but 'a low-level ancestor'.[3]

This archetypal structure allowed for many exceptions, however, which taken together compel a considerable modification of Lan's generalisation. There were many powerful women mediums and important female rainmakers. In some exceptional chiefdoms every *mhondoro* medium was female, no matter whether the possessing spirit was thought of as a man or as a woman. In 1974 the Rhodesian Front administration commissioned an Index of Spirits, which listed and described every significant medium throughout the country. The result is very much an official overview rather than an anthropologically sensitive study.[4] But some large contrasts emerge. In Mount Darwin district in northern Zimbabwe, for instance, chief Makoni and chief Rusambo had only female mediums, even for male spirits; neighbouring chieftaincies had only male mediums, even for female spirits. In Chipinge district, in

[3] The classic account of the way this system operates is David Lan, *Guns and Rain. Guerrillas and spirit mediums in Zimbabwe* (London, James Currey,1985), pp. 70,88.

[4] The 'Spirit Index' was the second of two overviews of Zimbabwean African religion compiled in the mid-1970s as a contribution to 'pyschological operations'. It was drawn up partly as a result of the experience of guerrilla intrusions into north-east Zimbabwe, where some spirit mediums had worked with the ZANLA fighters, and partly as a result of historical and anthropological literature which stressed the importance of African religion. It was compiled on the basis of reports by District Commissioners under the overall direction of C.J.K.Latham of Internal Affairs. The result gave a very fragmented picture of African religion. Latham therefore also produced what was known as 'The Shamanism Book', which gave detailed historical and anthropological accounts of the five major rain-shrine systems in Zimbabwe. Latham called these five systems 'commonwealths' and believed that in combination they gave 'national' spiritual direction. The 'Shamanism Book' is not available in the National Archives in Harare, but portions of it are still held in district administrative offices. The 'Spirit Index', for all areas of the country except Matabeleland, was donated to the National Archives by an ex-administrative officer and is available for consultation under the general reference S 3276. Both documents have 'top secret' printed in green capital letters at the top and bottom of every page. Between them the 'Spirit Index' and the 'Shamanism Book' constitute a unique colonial record of African religious institutions. Latham later wrote up his experiences as an MA thesis: C.J.K.Latham, 'Mwari and the Divine Heroes: Guardians of the Shona. Pan-Shona Religion as an Inspiration for Nationality', Rhodes University, Grahamstown (December 1986). He describes how he was 'in a sort of personal race' with guerrillas 'to identify [mediums] of importance'. (p. 156). There have been a number of studies of Zimbabwean African religion by anthropologists but these have focused on particular areas. For all its flaws, the 'Spirit Index' is the only record available which seeks to document every district in the country.

eastern Zimbabwe, similarly, chief Mutema had female mediums, while neighbouring chiefs had male ones.[5]

There were similar contrasts in the operation of chiefship. In most chieftaincies a single male office-holder reigned. But in the northeastern Mtoko district Chief Mtoko was obliged to nominate a female chieftainess, Charewa, who ruled over half the territory of the chiefship. Moreover, Charewa cared in her village for the female medium of Nehoreka, the chieftaincy's apical ancestor:

> Nehoreka, son-in-law of Dzivaguru, is the founding ancestor. He settled the area between the Nyadiri and Chitora rivers, which now forms the Chieftancy of Charewa..., He set himself up as the tribal High Priest and convinced the elders that, after death, he would possess a woman and she was to be immediately installed as his svikiro [medium]. Thereafter he would speak through this woman. Nehoreka further strengthened his position ... by introducing various reciprocal obligations of a religious nature, including ... Chief Mtoko's obligation to nominate a woman to fill the post of Chieftainess Charewa.... The svikiro lives in Charewa's Dzimbahewe [sacred area] where she is cared for by Wa-Dziva – a woman who can be characterised as the Chieftainess's handmaiden.... Rain-making ceremonies are also held under the auspices of the Chieftainess and Nehoreka.

The District Commissioner, Mtoko emphasised that the Nehoreka spirit had 'built up a reputation as a rain-god of no mean ability'. But women made the rain.[6] In the Mutema Chieftancy of eastern Zimbabwe a chief of the spirits, chosen by a woman medium, has long balanced the 'administrative' chief.[7]

In yet other areas a female medium, not incarnating a chiefly ancestor, nevertheless wielded great political as well as spiritual power. This was true for the Nemakonde chiefship of colonial Lomagundi district in west central Zimbabwe. Here and elsewhere in this paper I draw upon the community delineation reports composed in the mid-1960s.[8] These, too, were not careful anthropological studies but hastily compiled records of local history, political structure and religious belief. Nevertheless, they offer evidence of the major prevailing ecological myths at the time they were drawn up. The report for Nemakonde, drawn up in 1966, records an interview carried out ten years earlier:

> Droughts had fallen upon the country and these had a disturbing effect on Mzilikazi [the first Ndebele King]. He had, therefore, consulted the svikiro of the Magondi people. She

---

[5] File S 3276/2, National Archives of Zimbabwe [hereafter NAZ].'Spirit Index', Mount Darwin; Chipinge.

[6] 'Spirit Index', Mtoko District, S 3276/2. During the month of September 1998 the current Chief Mtoko faced a unanimous call from his headmen to resign because he had not given Chieftainess Charewa due respect. The current Chief is a Christian and the Charewa office-holder stands for 'traditional' religion and environmental practices.

[7] C. Vijfhuizen and L. Makora, 'More than one paramount chief in one chieftancy? The gender of maintaining worlds', *Zambezia* 25, 1 (1998).

[8] The Rhodesia Front regime pursued a policy of 'Community Development' in the African Reserves. This was intended to revive 'traditional' institutions as a bulwark against nationalism, and to decentralise spending on education and health. The 'delineation' exercise, carried out in the mid-1960s, was intended to identify traditional 'communities' on the basis of history, culture and judicial practice. The reports contain a wealth of 'traditional' historical information. But they are patchy in their coverage of African religion: hence the need for the inquiries of the mid-1970s. See NAZ S 2929.

was Va Chibanya. Chibanya told Mzilikazi that if he came to these parts with his evil ways, his killing of people, and so forth, he would be driven out by the wind. And so Mzilikazi left us alone, and thereafter he used to send four cattle every year, three for Chibanya.... Lobengula [the second Ndebele King] continued with this custom after Mzilikazi's death ... I was a goatherd when the Europeans came to this country ... Chibanya told Lobengula that what she had told him had come to pass. His killing of people had brought retribution.[9]

For once we have an archival confirmation of an oral historical account of female power and of its basis in spiritual control of nature. The Methodist missionary, Isaac Shimmin, seeking to establish a station in Nemakonde's country in 1892, was told that he must approach

a great prophetess ... Salokazana [old woman]. The mother of the present occupant of the office was also a prophetess ... and as such was acknowledged by the mighty Moselikatse .... The reigning Salokazana came into power after his death and Lobengula has always been largely governed by her prophecies and advice.... The natives clothe her with authority almost divine. They say she can make rain, govern harvests, avert sickness or bring punishment.[10]

These exceptions and many others seem to have arisen in four main ways. The first is that early rain and environmental shrines in Zimbabwe had taken the form of sacred pools tended by the wives of the High God. This pattern was disrupted by the rise of patriarchal chiefship but it could not be entirely obliterated. It left a legacy of belief in female power over the forces of nature. Secondly, in the conquest of earlier polities, the patriarchal chiefships often transformed defeated – and murdered – predecessors, both male and female, into powerful spirits of the land. Thirdly, in some patriarchal chiefdoms themselves myths spoke of the immigrant founding figure as a woman who had spiritual power over the animals and the soil. Finally, in some kingdoms and chiefdoms in the historical period the male ruler drew upon female relatives in order to balance male rivals; characteristically such 'chieftainesses' and 'princesses' had a special responsibility for the environment. In all these ways important female sub-texts were constructed to the main text of patriarchal authority and religion.

Early female-operated environmental shrines

The Malawian feminist theologian, Isabel Phiri, has written on the religious experience of Chewa women in Malawi in general and in particular on 'African Traditional Women and Ecofeminism'. [11] She demonstrates that in early Chewa religion between 900 and 1600 AD 'the religious roles of women were very clear and accepted at the territorial rain shrines. Women, known as spirit wives, *Mbona*, were the controllers of

[9] NAZ S 2929/4/1.

[10] Box 333, WMMS, School of Oriental and African Studies, London. Shimmin thought that Nemakonde's people possessed a strongly feminised religion. They believed in the Creator, Mwali, but used as their intercessor the 'mother of God, Banamarambe'.

[11] Isabel Phiri, 'African Traditional Women and Ecofeminism: The Role of Women at the Chisumphi Cult in Preserving the Environment', *Religion in Malawi*, 5 (1995); *Women, Presbyterianism and Patriarchy. Religious experience of Chewa women in central Malawi* (Blantyre, Claim, 1997).

these shrines. The women received messages from God to the community when in a state of ecstasy.' Some of these female religious leaders exercised ritual political control as well, as in the case of the *Mwali* priestess who ruled over the Banda clan. One of the rain-shrine priestesses bore the title, Chiuta, which was a name for God among the Chewa. Phiri maintains that the 'Chewa recognised the feminine nature of God', stressing the woman as mother of all people and as nurturer of the environment.[12] At a later date, Phiri argues, 'the role of spirit medium passed over from women to men due to changes in traditional religion brought about by external factors such as conquest and the pre-dominance of a new cult ideology'. In one striking case, Mbona, a male martyr, replaced the Mbona spirit wife.[13]

It seems likely that similar patterns and processes operated in Zimbabwe. Before the sixteenth century the main rain shrine in northeastern Zimbabwe took the form of a sacred pool set among white trees. Here a manifestation of the High God, *Dzivaguru* or Great Pool, was venerated. The shrine was tended by the *Karuva/Chikara* priestess who guarded the spirit wives of God. Requests came in from a wide area for rain and for divinely treated seeds. The shrine monitored the environment drawing on symbols of female fecundity.[14] Further to the south the main rain shrine in this early period was established and operated by a brother and sister who belonged to the *Dziva* [Pool] people. The *Dziva* culture was strongly feminised; its totem was the pool; its ritual experts were recognised as great rainmakers. The central figure of what later came to be called the *Musikavanhu* cult was, in these early days, the virgin priestess Chapo, possessor of the rain charms.[15]

Conquest and the ritual power of the conquered

Just as in Malawi, therefore, women controlled the central shrines of original Zimbabwean eco-religion. Just as in Malawi the shrines were conquered by incoming rulers, who were legitimated by male ancestor spirits. The result was a masculinisation of eco-religion. So far as the Dzivaguru cult was concerned, this process was commemorated in a myth first recorded by the Portuguese, Pacheco, in 1862. Matope, the conquering founder of the Munhumutapa Empire, found himself cut off by the powerful princess Chikara with a large army. He learnt the secret of her magic power, protected his men against it and she vanished into the Nyamakate pool at the Dzivaguru shrine.[16]

Thereafter, in the Mutapa Empire, state religion balanced the influence of the *mhondoro* mediums of the founding kings – and particularly of Matope – with the ritual power of the officials of the Dzivaguru cult. Two male representatives of the cult, the *Netondo* and *Bushu* priests, attended on the Mutapa at all times and officiated at his coronation and burial. Karuva/Chikara, now usually thought of as male, was said by

---

[12] *Ibid.*, pp. 21–32.

[13] Matthew Schoffeleers, *River of Blood: The genesis of a martyr cult in Southern Malawi, c.AD 1600*, (Madison, WI, Wisconsin University Press, 1992).

[14] I have here extended the argument in S. I. G. Mudenge, *A Political History of Munhumutapa, 1400–1902* (Harare, Zimbabwe Publishing House, 1988) especially pp. 42, 84, 87, 95, 121, 122,127, 130,131.

[15] J.K.Rennie, 'From Zimbabwe to a Colonial Chieftancy. Four Transformations of the Musikavanhu Territorial Cult in Rhodesia', in M. Schoffeleers (ed.) *Guardians of the Land*, (Gwelo, Mambo, 1978).

[16] S.I.G. Mudenge, *A Political History of Munhumutapa* (Harare, Zimbabwe Publishing House, 1988), p. 42.

Portuguese observers to be the chief priest of the Empire; royal messengers went every season to the Dzivaguru shrine and pool which Chikara controlled to ask for rain and good crops. But even if Chikara was now a male priest, there were still virgin wives at the pool, controlled by the *Mushongavudzi*, a woman past childbearing age who after assuming office was recognised as a chief.[17]

In late colonial times Dzivaguru and Karuva were thought of merely as male spirits connected to a rain shrine under Chief Chiswiti.[18] The Musikavanhu cult underwent something of the same transformation, passing from a cult celebrating female environmental power, to a series of male mediums, to a colonially recognised male chieftainship![19]

In both cases, however, myths survive into the late twentieth century which still stress the divine character of Dzivaguru and Musikavanhu, their authority over territory and environment, and the centrality of their female incarnations. Thus David Maxwell tells us that the most influential spirit medium of the Katerere chieftaincy of north-east Nyanga, Diki Rukadza, recites a myth of how '*ambuya* (grandmother) Karuva/Chikara reconciled the warring dynasties of Mutasa, Saunyama, Katerere and Mutoko; nominated leaders; and gave them totems and land to live on. She sat at the apex of a spiritual pyramid and the *mhondoro* could approach her on matters of great importance. She would judge each *mhondoro* by making them jump over fire.' The Katerere people use Chikara as their name for the Creator.[20] The name Musikavanhu is still used in Masvingo Province in southern Zimbabwe not as the name of a mere chief but as the title of the Creator God. 'Musikavanhu, the ultimate regulator of the cosmos', writes Ezra Chitando, 'is the most appropriate recipient of animal sacrifice.'[21]

These historical processes seem to account for some of the exceptional female rainmaking and environmental power recorded in the 1974 survey. The Charewa chieftainess, guarding the female spirit medium of Nehoreka, and balancing the political power of Chief Mtoko, is probably a legacy of this sort of history. The chieftainess and the medium may be survivors of an old Dzivaguru shrine which was partially brought into the patriarchal system by the device of making the chiefly ancestor, Nehoreka, a son-in- law of Dzivaguru.

We may conjecture that the chieftaincies where every medium was female, or where the dominant spirit was female, often looked back to similar transitions from female shrines to male *mhondoro* spirits. I would hypothesise, for example, that the powerful women mediums of the Mutema chieftaincy, now thought to incarnate male chiefly ancestors, were originally linked to the Musikavanhu shrine and to the environmental powers of princess Chapo. The 'Spirit Index' tells us that even in the 1970s Chief Mutema was held to be the senior intermediary between the other chiefs and the Musikavanhu shrine and linked to Musikavanhu as 'husband' to 'wife':

[17] Mudenge, *A Political History*; M.F.C.Bourdillon, 'The Cults of Dzivaguru and Karuva amongst the North-Eastern Shona peoples', in Schoffeleers, *Guardians of the Land*.

[18] 'Spirit Index', Mount Darwin, NAZ S 3276/2.

[19] L.C.Meredith, 'The Rain Spirit of Mabota Murangwadza, Melsetter District', *Native Affairs Department Annual [NADA]* (1925), describes how the virgin Chapo held the rain charms; how there followed a succession of rain-making chiefs; how these chiefs came to be possessed by the spirits; and how Meredith himself deposed the medium, Munotswa, recognising his brother, Neseni, as official chief.

[20] David Maxwell, *Christians and Chiefs in Zimbabwe. A social history of the Hwesa people.c.1870s–1990s* (Edinburgh, Edinburgh University Press for the International Africa Institute, 1999), p. 19.

[21] Ezra Chitando, 'Sacrifice as a Type. An Application to Karanga Religion', MA thesis, University of Zimbabwe (1993), pp. 93, 94.

Musikavanhhu and his associates claim relationship with Dzivaguru in Darwin. By tradition the Musikavanhu spirit is the guardian spirit of all the tribes in the area. Approach to him [sic] is through traditionally laid down channels, i.e the people of Maranke go through Zimunya, thence to Mutambara, thence through Muusha, then to Mutema and finally to Musikavanhu. It is said in Melsetter that Mutema is the senior chief and father of all the tribes. By tradition Chief Musikavanhu is the wife of Mutema and guardian of the tribal spirits.[22]

The 1974 survey gives a less common example from Mutoko district in which aboriginal female power has survived without masculinisation. In Chief Chimoyo's area, there are male mediums of *mhondoro* ancestors. But by far the 'most important spirit of all in the Chimoyo area' is incarnated by a woman medium who is not related to the chief at all. She represents the original rainmakers who owned the area before Chimoyo moved into it. She 'holds major rainmaking rituals [and] plays an important part in testing other mediums in Chimoyo's area'.[23]

In addition to cases in which the conquered indigenes became spiritually powerful, thus preserving some elements of the older female eco-religion, and cases of the co-option and masculinisation of female rain shrines, there were also cases where the incoming conquerors tried to co-opt more free-ranging female nature spirits by inserting them into their genealogies. Thus under the Mutapa kings the female mediums of the Nehanda spirit, now influential in central Zimbabwe, were crucial in 'ensuring the fertility of the nation and the crops'. Official Mutapa ideology insisted that Nehanda was the sister and consort of Matope. But it is much more likely that the Nehanda spirit long predates the Mutapa Empire, operating as the major rainmaker in the areas to the west of the Dzivaguru and Musikavanhu cults. The Nehanda spirit's medium has always been a woman; it has two distinct manifestations – 'the Head' and 'the Foot', in the north and south respectively; it has always been superior to chiefly *mhondoros*; it owns sacred pools which are death to whites who see them. It controls wild animals as well as water and the soil.[24] David Lan's structuralist reading of the Mutapa myths of origin sees Nehanda as standing for the procreative power of the vagina, a 'wet and fertile mother', from whom flowed the rivers.[25]

---

[22] 'Spirit Index', Melsetter and Chipinge, NAZ S 2376/1. L.C.Meredith tells us that when he installed Neseni as chief in 1896, Mutema came 'with a small army' to depose him, to re-install the medium, Munotswa, and to hand to him 'all the Musikavanhu wives and cattle'. *NADA* (1925).

[23] 'Index of Spirits', Chimoyo area, Mtoko, NAZ S 2376/2.

[24] The delineation report on Chief Sipolilo records that the Chingowo *mhondoro* told the original Sipolilo settlers that if they sent a cup of water to Nehanda 'they would receive no more troubles from wild animals, and this was so'. 14 October 1965, NAZ S 2929/2/7.

[25] David Lan, *Guns and Rain*, Chapter 5. The delineation report for chief Makope in Chiweshe records a myth which brings out the full ambiguity of Nehanda. It recounts a long migration through central and western Zimbabwe until their ancestors reached a great river: 'We could see the water of the Zambesi reflecting like a looking glass. Then we went down ... to the Zambesi River. That is where Nehanda struck the river with her staff.... The water upstream stopped and downstream the water stopped and we crossed on the bed of the river.' Still led by Nehanda, they went far north 'beyond Nyasaland and suffered from sores, tsetse fly and wounds and deaths'. Then they returned 'and there at the Zambesi Nehanda struck the water again and we crossed once more'. Then, suddenly, this female force of nature changes into the daughter of Mutapa Mutota. In this form she is Princess Nyamita, ruler of Handa, and hence Nehanda. Her father dies and his body could not be lifted for burial. Before his death the old king had said that one of his sons must have ritual intercourse with their sister. Matope undertook to do so. 'A reed mat enclosure was

Women as mistresses of nature and founders of chiefdoms

Nehanda and other 'regional' female spirits date from a period before the establishment of the present chieftaincies. But I have been very struck that the myths of origin of many of these patriarchal chiefdoms themselves stress an immigrant female foundress. Here and elsewhere in this paper I cite such myths not, of course, as evidence of historical events but as demonstrating ideas about female environmental power.

Some of these stories of how an immigrant woman became owner of the land are banal enough, though still emphasising female control of the elements:

> Chief Masana, Gumbo, Bindura. Traditional history says they originated from Mazumba, Mount Darwin, and migrated to the area around Shamva where they met people under one Tande. Tande was overcome by magical means – mashiri- piripiti (miracles). One story is that Tande and Nyarambe (the ambuya [grandmother] of the Gumbo clan) held beer parties: the most successful party would show who should own the land. Tande had his party spoilt by rain whereas Nyarambe, not many yards away, held a successful beer party, untroubled by the storm. Tande left the district and Nyarambe became the Muridzi we Nyika.

Nyarambe also became the senior spirit of the Masana chieftaincy. [26]

More dramatic is the story of Anemasvu, a niece of the great male spirit, Chingowo, in Concession district. When the forebears of Chief Nyachuru arrived in his now country, 'it was Anemasvu who ruled that the country should be divided between them':

> Anemasvu died and was buried at Tsungubve. Her spirit entered wild dogs and they became like domestic dogs and chased buck into the houses of her people, and she caused bees to enter into holes in the ground and into anthills so her people might have the honey, and to this day when bees swarm or the cry of the wild dog is heard. the people believe that the spirit of Anemasvu is about and that she is providing for her people.[27]

Most dramatic of all is the story of Nyemba. In Chiota chieftaincy the myth was told to the delineating officer in 1964 that the founding ancestor first entered the area as a

---

25 (cont.) prepared and Nyamita, Matope's half sister, was persuaded to enter therein with her eyes bandaged, in ignorance, it is said, of what was wanted of her. Once they had committed *kupinga pasi* Mutota's corpse was lifted.... The ruware (rock) was split open by Nyamita with a special knife.... Nehanda was childless and after the *kupinga pasi* ceremony she was appalled at what she had done. She therefore returned to her dunhu and vanished into a small hill.... Later it is said that her feet, 'Makambo a Nehanda', went to Guruuswa ... [and] finally settled near Domboshowa.... She later died in this country and is thus venerated by many of the Vazezuru as their *Ambuya* and great Mhdondo and rain-petitioning spirit.' NAZ S 2929/2/3/1. In her incarnation as Nyamita, Nehanda attracts further cultic veneration. In the Teveteve stream in Chief Mangwende's country, so the 'Spirit Index' tells us, 'there is a pool called Nyamita. Many years ago a woman by that name ... committed suicide in this pool'; sacrifices of cattle are made there.

26 Delineation report, Masana, Bindura, NAZ S 2929/2/1. An even more banal story comes from the Seke chiefship whose founder is said to be 'a female ancestor ... who went to Zimbabwe (where the Rozwi king was resident at the time) to get approval for the Seke Chieftainship. She was required to stand on one leg along with other competitors, and having "outstood" them all, without falling over, won the competition.' Delineation report, Seke, July 1965, NAZ S 2929/3/1.

27 Delineation Report, Nyachuru chiefdom, Concession, NAZ S 2829/2/3/1.

hunter. With him came his sister, Nyemba, 'who was a virgin and a person capable of performing magic (which helped make the elephant easy prey)'. She was raped; killed herself; and her spirit was still propitiated to ensure rain and fertility. [28]

Forty years earlier Native Commissioner F.W.T.Posselt had recorded his version of Nyemba's life and death, and of the ritual which subsequently grew up around the story:

> On these hunting expeditions they were accompanied by Banyemba, who, by means of her magic, was able to restrict the roving elephants, thus permitting the hunters to come up to them and hamstring them ... On one occasion, while the brothers were absent hunting, Banyemba was left in the camp with her slaves. Gungowo, the chief of the country, who had heard of her, suddenly appeared and told the defenceless princess that he wished to take her to wife. She was seized by his servants, and carried off and then ravished by him.

Shamed and stripped of her powers, Nyemba had a platform built in a tall tree; she took refuge there, with her slaves and her dog, Muroro. The ladder to the platform was thrown down and one by one the slaves died of hunger and thirst and were thrown to the ground. Eventually her brothers found her and begged her to come down but, instead of climbing down the rope they threw her, she hanged herself and her dog. Her brothers then killed Gungowo and all his people, saying 'This land is ours; we have purchased it with the blood of our sister'. Posselt went on to describe the Banyemba ritual:

> It was the practice to hold periodically, generally about every fourth year, a certain ceremony at the time of planting their fields. Beer was brewed by young maidens and a young heifer killed by boys who were sexually pure. In addition an ox and a dog (called Muroro) were sacrificed ... After the feasting, with drums beating, the votaries danced and the males ran after the females and pretended to use violence towards them, dragging them along. Then with shouts of '*Imwe! imwe ya Banyemba*' [You! You of Banyemba] each male had intercourse with a female ... The ceremony was a propitiation of the spirits, the chief being those of Muroro and Banyemba and it was undertaken to ensure the welfare of the people, abundant rain, that the fields might yield a good harvest and the crops of wild fruit be plentiful.[29]

Female power deployed by male chiefs and kings

There were other manifestations of female ecological authority within the patriarchal system. 'It was the custom of the Monomatapa (and the Varozwi Mambos) to place princesses (*vadzi mambokadzi*) in authority over some of their principalities', the delineation report for Mount Darwin tells us. It goes on to recount stories of how these princesses established themselves in new fiefs of the Mutapa Empire and of how these fiefs eventually became male chieftaincies.

A particularly vivid narrative is that of Princess Koswa, 'the *ambuya* and principal Mhondoro' of the Nyakusenga chiefdom. In the mid-1960s 'Chief Nyakusenga was installed in office by the Mhondoro Koswa, the female ancestor of the tribe.

[28] Delineation report, Chiota, 19 August 1964, NAZ S 2929/3/4.
[29] F.W.T.Posselt, 'The Banyemba Legend and Ceremony', *NADA* (1924).

Rainmaking and harvesting ceremonies are ... regarded as serious business. The Chief plays no significant part.... The actual spiritual function is in the hands of the Svikoro [medium]'.

Koswa is remembered in myth as typical of the female ruler – exempt from the normal taboos surrounding her sex; sensual and rapacious. The titillated delineation officer took up her story:

> Of Koswa herself very little is remembered today. She was, apparently, quite notorious at the court of the Monomatapa, and gave birth to an illegitimate child..... Historians date Koswa's migration with Princess Nyahuwi at about 1680. She is said to have been very comely (her affairs at court indicate this) and must have been in the prime of life when she set out for Chirudya. Near Usirisiri, near Gungwa hill, she and Nyahuwi came into country occupied by one Ganganyama, said to have been a giant of a man, and very hairy. Since fighting seemed dangerous, the two women seduced the rustic gentleman and persuaded him to take them both to his couch. Such was their loyalty to each other and their passion for him that they could not easily be parted even in the intimacies of the bridal bed. Ganganyama readily acceded to their request and after being fortified for the event with liberal quantities of beer, he ventured forth to do justice to the situation. However, he had reckoned without the cunning of the two girls, who complained that their hirsute lover's rank growth of hair so tickled them that they could not enjoy themselves. He granted them permission to shave him and so the poor man's fate was sealed. With one quick cut of the knife as he lay under the ministrations of his two 'amorous barbers' he was slain. [30]

Thus Koswa gained the territory of the Nyakusenga chiefdom. Nyahuwi went on to other areas. She is remembered as the foundress of what is now the Rusambo chieftaincy, giving the area to a woman, Chiwadi. She also became 'founding ancestor' to the Makuni chieftaincy and is still its senior spirit. [31]

But the use of princesses does not only lie in the mythical past. In some nineteenth century chiefdoms, particularly among the Manyika-speakers of eastern Zimbabwe, ruling chiefs made use of female relatives to control sensitive areas and to perform eco-rituals. At the end of the nineteenth century, the then Chief Mutasa recognised several 'princesses' to whom he gave chiefdoms:

> Certain of the women of Mutasa's family are placed out in various district [wrote an Anglican missionary] as princesses (*washe we wakadzi*); their names, or rather official titles are Chikanga, Mupotedzi, Nyakuwanika, Nemhanda, Manunhure, Nyambvu, Jana, Muredza, Sherekuru and Resinauta. There may be others. [32]

---

[30] Delineation report for Nyakusengwa chiefdom, 1965, NAZ S 2929/2/1. The 'Spirit Index' for Mount Darwin district, compiled in 1975, records Koswa as the second most important spirit for Chief Nyakusenga, the first being the apical male ancestor, Nhemuro.

[31] Delineation reports, Rusambo and Makuni chieftaincies, Mount Darwin, December 1964. The delineation officer explained the transition from a princess to a chief by writing unconvincingly: 'Unable to rule herself, the princess appointed her brother Dombo Makuni as chief to act for her in all matters ... It is quite possible that he and his sister engaged in ritual intercourse.' One of Makuni's headmen, Chipara, lived in an 'area first settled by Anadondo, a princess', and now his senior spirit. NAZ S 2929/2/1. The 1975 'Spirit Index' for Mount Darwin records that Nyahuwe is the senior spirit of Chief Makuni. All the mediums in the chieftaincy are female.

[32] R.H.Baker, 'The Mutopo among the Wamanyika', *NADA* (1925), pp. 48-54.

Muredzwa was so famous as a rainmaker that it was said that rain filled her footsteps as she passed. In the 1980s a later Mutasa, told the traditions as a child at Muredzwa's knee, revived the system of women chiefs.[33]

More recently, the current Chief Makoni, who lacks the support of the *mhondoro* mediums of the chieftaincy, has revived the ancient institution of the princesses.[34] These are women drawn from each of the Makoni chiefly houses. They report to the Chief on events in their area; they sit with him to hear domestic cases; and they enforce traditional ecological laws. In 1998 they have prohibited the sale of caterpillars and locusts – which God sent for food not as a marketable commodity; they have rebuked men for fencing in pools which ought to be public resources; they have tried to stop the cutting down of sacred groves. These princesses are certainly not 'a scar on the land'.[35]

Matrilineality beneath patrilineality

Some scholars have suggested that all early African societies in Zimbabwe were matrilineal before the rise of the patrilineal chieftaincy. However this may be, a fact not given adequate attention in the historiography of Zimbabwean religion is that matrilineal peoples penetrated deep onto the patrilineal plateau in historical times. Most people imagine that Tonga speakers barely moved further south than the Zambezi escarpment. But the delineation reports for plateau districts reveal many chieftaincies of valley Tonga origin. Thus reports for what were then called Buhera, Gatooma, Hartley, Shabani and Belingwe districts in central Zimbabwe all record Tonga in-migrations. The Tonga chief Ngezi once 'controlled a vast territory virtually from the Umniati River to where Gatooma now stands'. Among the Hartley Tonga of Chief Mupawose there was still clear evidence in the mid-1960s of repressed matrilineality: 'Their tribal system, whenever a new chief was about to be appointed, was to first kill the son of the late Chief's sister.'[36] Some of these Tonga groups are reported to have spirit mediums; others sent to the Mwali shrines in the Matopos. But the delineators did not bother to probe deeply into their eco-religion.

In the Lundi Tribal Trust Land in Shabani, however, the legendary history of the Masunda chiefdom was recorded: 'When people were few and animals were many, a small group of the Batonga crossed the Zambezi from an area between the Kafue and Chongwe rivers.' They went as far south as Gutu and scattered through Chibi and Ndanga; then some of them moved north and Northwest into Lundi:

---

[33] Heike Schmidt, 'Muredzwa: Superwoman', unpublished paper, Oxford.

[34] The delineation reports for Makoni chiefdom, NAZ S 2929/1/4, refer to two areas controlled in the 1960s by male headmen, one of which had been ruled in the past by Princess Nedope and the other by Princess Nyamotsi. It describes the 'hill Chitsotso where the Makoni princesses were traditionally buried' and 'the belief, still held, that the spirits of the princesses bring good luck to the rulers of the Makoni house'. Every year the ruling Chief Makoni went to Chitsotso hill, cleansed the ground around the graves of the princesses, brewed beer and slaughtered cattle on 1 October for rain and on 1 February for the first fruits ceremony.

[35] I owe this information to Mercy Wachtmeister, who is carrying out doctoral research in Makoni District on women and water.

[36] NAZ S 2929/1/1; S 2929/4/1; S 2929/4/2; S 2929/7/1.

It is believed that at the time the Vaera-Shiri were still imbued with Batonga customs and way of life.... Doubtless they assimilated the customs of those whom they met in their travels – first the Makaranga, the Rozvi, and ultimately the Ndebele – but even today there is a tendency to refer to a house of a wife as opposed to a son.

Masunda, the first chief, was imposed by the Ndebele. But when he died his eldest daughter, Vavusavi 'acted as Regent'.[37] In ways which I cannot yet document, this Tonga substratum undoubtedly affected ideas about female eco-religion.[38]

Above patriarchy: the oracular cult of the High God

So far I have been writing about chiefly or royal religion. But in the south-west of Zimbabwe there still operates a system of ecological religion which is autonomous of any African king or chief and is not part of the patriarchal system; which draws pilgrims from hundreds of miles and from many different language zones; which seeks ritually to control the environment and its use. This is the cult of Mwali, the High God, whose Voice can be heard in the cave shrines of the Matopos. These shrines control the environment, determining which areas can be cultivated and which not; where trees can be cut and where not; where streams and pools can be used and where not. They also control the agricultural year, providing seeds soaked in the water of the caves and laying it down when planting can start; when fire can be used for clearing the land; what the rest days shall be and when harvesting can commence. Here one might expect to find female eco-religion operating as it has not done anywhere else in Zimbabwe since the sixteenth century.[39]

Indeed, female spiritual and environmental principles are much more regularly apparent in the Mwali cult than in the *mhondoro* system. Yet here too there is conflict between male and female, not now between male conquerors and female priestesses, but between men and women for the control of the main Mwali shrines. Successful male assertions have often obscured the female dimensions of the cult.[40]

For its adepts, the Mwali cult is not about lineage and succession, even though the shrines endorse candidates for the chiefships of southern Zimbabwe. The cult is essentially about creation; human and natural fertility; rain; the environment. Hence

---

[37] Delineation report for Lundi TTL, March 1965, NAZ S 2929/7/7.

[38] Further north, the valley Tonga believed that rainmakers were hermaphrodite figures, half man and half woman. The *Sunday Mail* of 7 March 1999 carried a remarkable letter on female dimensions of Tonga belief. Entitled 'Nyaminyami is female', it read: 'My husband died on Lake Kariba ... All along I was virtually pummelled into believing that Nyaminyami was a heathen god and as a Christian I was not to acknowledge the existence of this evil being. It was a very difficult time all these years wondering why my husband had to die just after my son was born. Now, 20 years down the line, I believe that Nyaminyami is a female. Why? Because her victims are mostly males. But their wives and children more often than not, accompany them ... Now that I believe in Nyaminyami and I acknowledge her existence I have found peace in my soul at last. She is real and she survives on male souls ... Well, isn't it the male species that built the dam wall and separated her from her mate for ever?'

[39] I have discussed the Mwali cult extensively in Terence Ranger, *Voices From the Rocks. Nature, culture and history in the Matopos* (Oxford, James Currey, 1999). The environmental role of the cult is discussed on pp. 23–5.

[40] Thus Martinus Daneel, in his reconstruction of the priestly succession at Wirirani/Dzilo, showed it as a sequence of males. In fact the succession is one of matrilineally inheriting priestesses.

there is no barrier to full emphasis being placed on both the male and the female attributes of God.[41]

At the shrines priests present praises to each of the triple manifestations of Mwali – *Shologulu*, the father; *Banyachaba*, the mother; and *Lunji*, the needle or shooting star, who runs errands between the father and the mother. At Njelele, the senior shrine of the cult, priests praise *Shologulu* for the might of the thunder and *Lunji* for the penetration of the lightening; they praise *Banyachaba*, the female manifestation of God, as the protector of helpless animals, and as 'the pool that supplies the whole world with water'.[42] A myth which describes Mwali's return to earth, after a period of withdrawal and punishment, combines all three manifestations: 'the sky became pregnant by the clouds and God's Voice came like a needle which sewed up the earth, and a stone began to speak.'[43]

The shrines are called 'the rocks of the pool'; each oracular cave contains within itself a perennial pool, which myth compares to the amniotic fluid.[44] Chenjerai Hove's marvellous book, *Guardians of the Soil*, quotes an old woman from eastern Zimbabwe: 'Ambuya Manditsera is the memory of the landscape, of the people of the living and the dead. She talks about the womb of a woman as shrine, like those caves in the hills.'[45]

In the Matopos it is the other way around – the shrine caves and their pools are compared to the womb of a woman. In these pools there live female water spirits, *Njuzu*; Mwali adepts are said to go down into the pools for years on end, there to be taught by the *Njuzu*, learning among other things how the environment should be managed and protected. All the rivers and streams of Zimbabwe are said to be peopled with *Njuzu*, who originate from the shrines of the Matopos. They constitute an 'underwater' – rather than an underground – female ecological army.

Among the shrines themselves, some are thought of as male and some as female. In the eastern Matopos the Dula shrine is 'male' (and connected with war) and the Dzilo shrine is 'female' (and connected with fertility); the male manifestation of God travels between them to be with the female and rests on the way at a grove still regarded as sacred. Dzilo is supposed to be controlled by a succession of matrilineally inheriting priestesses, though in the twentieth century this sequence has been blurred by the claims of husbands and brothers.[46] Recent research at Dzilo has revealed, however, the persistence of the myths of female origin. Dzilo, the elders say, is merely the name of the place at which the shrine is now situated. The real name of the shrine is Zame, an

---

[41] I have myself speculated that the cult was originally more exclusively female. The word *Mwali* is a widely dispersed Bantu term connected with female puberty, female initiation, and female ecological power. Isabel Phiri reminds us that the Chewa initiation ceremony for girls is called *chinaMwali* ; that the *Mwali* priestess presided over the Mankhamba rain shrine; and that the Banda clan assert that they were once ruled over by a female ritual leader called *Mwali*. Terence Ranger, 'The Meaning of Mwari', *Rhodesian History*, 5 (1974). I focus here on the current condition of the cult in which male and female power are complementary without either being dominant.

[42] Leslie Nthoi, 'Social Perspective of Religion: A Study of the Mwali Cult of Southern Africa', Ph.D thesis, Manchester University (1995).

[43] Herbert Aschwanden, *Karanga Mythology* (Gweru, Mambo, 1990), p. 217.

[44] Aschwanden, *Karanga Mythology*, thoroughly explores the sexual symbolism of the shrines.

[45] Chenjerai Hove and Ilija Trojanow, *Guardians of the Soil. Meeting Zimbabwe's elders* (Harare, Baobab, 1996), p. 30.

[46] The matrilineal succession at Dzilo, established by District Commissioner I.G.Cockcroft, is recorded in the 'Shamanism Book'.

Ndebele rendering of a Kalanga word meaning 'breast'. At the breast the people drink for rain. In the original shrine cave at Shashe, the body of a remote ancestress is said to lie buried. In times of severe drought post-menopausal women carry water into the cave to 'wash' the ancestress and to give her to 'drink'.[47]

This long-standing duality between Dula and Dzilo has been complicated in more recent times by frustrated priestesses breaking away and founding new shrines. One of these is Bembe. Minye Ncube lived at Dzilo, that female shrine all too often controlled by men. In 1961 she was herself possessed by a rain spirit:

> Minye had to set up her own kraal. The site of this had been indicated to her in a dream when she was a child. In the dream she saw a boulder falling down the side of a hill and she knew that when this happened the time would have come for her to take up her duties. In 1963 a huge rock rolled down the side of Bembe Hill and Minye set up home at the base of a shrine 'where the boulder fell down'.[48]

The Voice of God was heard from the overhang; the fall of the rock seemed to portend a major symbolic and cosmological upheaval; Bembe became a place of mass pilgrimage and especially renowned for rainmaking. When the District Commissioner came to test her powers Minye made so much rain that he had to beg her to stop![49]

At other shrines, where men have long been in charge, there are nevertheless significant exercises of female spiritual power. It has been suggested that the Voice of Mwali is everywhere articulated by a series of women, inheriting matrilineally.[50] Moreover, there are gender-neutral shrines which may be controlled by either men or women, whichever reveals the greatest ecological power. One of these is Ntunjambili shrine, seventy kilometres northeast of Njelele. It was once controlled by a male priest, Daba, who figures largely in early colonial records. But when he died it was his daughter, Nhlangiso Mmeke Ncube, who became priestess, because her mother was the only one of Daba's wives who could germinate sorghum in her clenched fist. Her half-brothers were furious and bewitched her.[51] In her extreme old age she remains the priestess today.

Indeed in the 1990s the record of female priesthood in the Matopos is an impressive one. Minye controls Bembe; Nhlangiso controls Ntunjambili; even at the senior shrine, Njelele, a woman priestess, Ngcathu Ncube, was installed in the early 1990s. In the face of allegations by rival male claimants that no woman could be in charge of Njelele, Ngcathu told me that she had received a message from Queen Elizabeth II to say that women should rule! More seriously she talked with Jocelyn Alexander and JoAnn McGregor in 1996, when she claimed that 'Njelele's power covers the whole world. All these mountains – Dzilo – power comes from Njelele. Zimbabwe is very good in farming. You can go to Botswana, but we refer to Zimbabwe as Canaan, the

---

[47] This recent research has been done by a final year History student at the University of Zimbabwe, Lynette Nyathi, who is writing it up as an oral history project. Her family lives at Dzilo.

[48] 'The Making of a Rain Goddess', *Sunday News Magazine*, 26 October/8 November 1988.

[49] Interview with Minye Ncube, Bembe, 27 July 1989.

[50] Nthoi, 'Social Perspective of Religion', p. 373. Lynette Nyathi was told at Dzilo that the old woman who has been the medium for the Voice of Mwali has recently been replaced by a younger, pre-menopausal woman, a development which has greatly shocked the elders. Even at Dula, the shrine for war and for the male manifestation of Mwali, the male custodian has died and when I visited it in January 2001 it was controlled by the old woman who spoke as the Voice of God.

[51] Nthoi, 'Social Perspective of Religion', p. 384.

land of milk and honey and that's because of Njelele.' And she insisted that 'it is traditional in our [Kalanga] culture that women were in charge'.[52] Ngcathu became the accepted interpreter of the current ecological woes of southern Matabeleland, where there is perennial drought, and is cited as such even in the *Financial Gazette*! [53]

Finally, the Matopos shrines, and especially the female shrine of Dzilo, have long been associated with prophetic ecological movements, led by women adepts.[54] The latest of these swept across southern Zimbabwe in the 1990s. It is led by the prophetess, *Mbuya* Juliana, whose professed aim is to restore the balance between humanity and nature. Juliana claims to have been empowered by the *njuzu* in the pool at Dzilo shrine, where she lived under water for four years. 'The Njuzu said: "Go and teach the people, so they will live again according to law and order, so the rains will come again".' Juliana blames drought on government development plans, imposed from above, and on dynamiting for dams. A holy silence needs to be restored in which the *njuzu* can again operate.

Juliana attracts a huge following. She holds meetings on the mountaintops sacred to the chiefs and displaces the *mhondoro* spirits of the patriarchal system. Her authority is at once female and a-sexual: she says that if any man looks at her with desire he will explode![55]

Conclusion

It can be seen, then, that despite the dominance of patriarchy in Zimbabwean land ownership, inheritance, politics and ritual, women mediums, priestesses and prophets still play a major role in ecological religion. I have not dwelt adequately on the environmental role of men – and many chiefs, Mwali priests and male *mhondoro* mediums have rainmaking powers and are passionate about the right relationship of humanity, animals and the environment.[56] My argument has not been that women represent Nature and men Politics. Creation myths celebrate male potency as well as female fecundity. I have been concerned to show here that, despite the constraints of patriarchy, men and women play complementary roles in Zimbabwe's eco-religious ideology and practice.

[52] Interview between Jocelyn Alexander, JoAnn McGregor and Ngcathu Ncube, Njelele, 2 September 1996.

[53] Ncgathu fled from Njelele when her hut was struck by lightening in 1999 and has since died.

[54] For an account of earlier movements see Terence Ranger, 'Religious Studies and Political Economy: the Mwari Cult and the Peasant Experience in Southern Rhodesia', in W. van Binsbergen and M. Schoffeleers (eds), *Theoretical Explorations in African Religion* (London, RKP, 1986).

[55] Gurli Hansson interview with Mbuya Juliana, Mudavanhu, 3 November 1993; Abraham Mawere and Ken Wilson, 'Socio-religious Movements, the State and Community Change: Some reflections on the Ambuya Juliana Cult of Southern Zimbabwe', Paper at a Seminar, Britain Zimbabwe Society Research Day, Oxford, 23 April 1994.

[56] Chenjerai Hove and Ilija Trojanow in their *Guardians of the Soil. Meeting Zimbabwe's Elders* interview 9 men and 2 women.

* A shorter version of this chapter appeared in Alaine Low and Soraya Tremayne (eds), *Sacred Custodians of the Earth?* (New York, Berghahn Books, 2001), pp. 95–106.

5

Living with the River
Landscape & Memory in the Zambezi Valley
Northwest Zimbabwe[1]

JoANN McGREGOR

Introduction

This paper contributes to debates about landscape and memory, by exploring African ideas about past interactions with an evocative feature of the Central African environment – the Zambezi river. It also investigates the ways in which these ideas about landscape and nature are used today in conflicts over resources and the politics of identity. In doing so, it extends the existing literature on African landscape perceptions in various ways.[2] Much of the previous body of work has focused on religious sites and the accompanying moral economies of resource use, but here my focus is on a feature that was not straightforwardly a religious site, though it was essential to life for those who lived along it and has sacred 'places of power' within it.[3] It also breaks down the distinction that some authors have tried to draw between sites of 'positive' correspondence that invoke emotions of belonging and sites of 'negative' correspondence that invoke exclusion and threat, as the Zambezi river was both a positive source of, and a dangerous threat to, life.[4] The paper contributes in particular to a growing body of literature on the politics of landscape ideas, and how minority groups can use them to assert (often exclusive) claims to resources and to mark out a physical and cultural

[1] This research was funded by the University of Reading Research Endowment Trust Fund and the British Academy. I would like to thank my research assistants and translators Alexius Chipembere and Andrew Chiumu Mudimba, as well as Elizabeth Colson and Mark Leopold for constructive comments.
[2] For an overview, see Ute Luig and A.von Oppen, 'Landscape in Africa: Process and Vision. An Introductory Essay', *Paideuma: Mitteilungen zur Kulturkunde*, 43 (1997), pp. 7–45. Here I draw on ideas in S. Schama, *Landscape and Memory* (London, Fontana, 1995), but explore them in an African context.
[3] See the discussion in E. Colson, 'Places of Power and Shrines of the Land', special issue on 'The Making of African Landscapes', *Paideuma: Mitteilungen zur Kulturkunde*, 43 (1997), pp. 47–59. On moral economies, see G. Maddox, J.Giblin and I. Kimambo, *Custodians of the Land: Ecology and culture in the history of Tanzania* (Oxford, James Currey, 1996), particularly section four on 'Environment and Morality'; T. Ranger, *Voices from the Rocks: Nature, culture and history in the Matopos Hills, Zimbabwe* (Oxford, James Currey, 1999) includes such discussion in a much broader study of the politics of a sacred landscape.
[4] Luig and Van Oppen, 'Landscape in Africa' frame part of their discussion around this dichotomy, as developed initially in Martin Seel, *Eine Asthetik der Natur* (Frankfurt, Suhrkamp, 1996).

place for themselves in states from which they feel marginalised.[5] Their expressions of connections with the landscape are more than statements about idealised cultural norms and have become important as matters of nostalgia, and in the politics of heritage and identity.

I focus on a section of the Middle Zambezi Valley that stretches from the Victoria Falls downstream through a series of gorges and rapids into the upper reaches of Lake Kariba, where the river and lake now form the international boundary between Zimbabwe and Zambia.[6] It is a region that has been developed primarily for tourism and conservation, through the industry that grew up around Africa's most famous 'natural wonder' and the picturesque exclusionary wildernesses along the river and dam. European ways of seeing the river valley were centrally important in the appropriation of the landscape to these ends and the marginalisation of those who once lived along the river. Although my focus here is on African traditions of seeing the same environment, I do not want to suggest that these have developed in isolation: they are the product of historical dialogues and contestations among various African groups as well as with Europeans, all of whom mythologised the river and 'river people', and all of whom interacted with the river in different ways at different times. Nor can oral histories of today be seen as preserving past ways of seeing the landscape, un- contaminated by recent influences: some of the African ideas I discuss have strong resonances with biblical stories; some make assertions of 'ownership' of the river which probably developed in the course of colonial era conflicts;[7] others romanticise past traditions in ways not dissimilar to Western quests for authentic, pre-modern connections with nature. My aim here is not to disentangle in detail the historical interactions that produced these ideas (which I hope to do elsewhere), but to explore these historical representations in relation to their use today.

The paper is based on interviews with people who are marginal to the main centres of power in Zimbabwe today, just as they were marginal to the main centres of power in the nineteenth century. They identify themselves variously as Tonga, Leya, Dombe and Nambya and live in Hwange and Binga Districts of Northwest Zimbabwe, where together they form the vast bulk of the local population. Memories of past interactions with the river and of being 'river people' retain a significance today for some, even though economic, political and religious life has long since ceased to be focused on the river, much of which is inaccessible as a result of state restrictions, landmines and the waters of the Kariba dam. Such memories can play an important part not only as expressions of loss on the part of the older generation, but also provide a critique of the appropriation of the river and lake to tourist and conservationist priorities. They are used in on-going conflicts over access to resources, particularly in conjunction with demands for greater fishing rights and privileged access to river resources for locals. Invocactions of past ways of life with the river have also been deployed in arguments for compensation for the displacement from Lake Kariba, as well as in assertions of

---

[5] See Jane Carruthers' paper in this volume.

[6] Appropriations of the Victoria Falls itself are explored more thoroughly in J. McGregor, 'The Victoria Falls 1900–1940: Landscape, tourism and the geographical imagination', *Journal of Southern Africa Studies* (*JSAS*) 29, 3 (2003).

[7] See D. Maxwell, *Christians and Chiefs in Zimbabwe: A social history of the Hwesa peopl c.1870–1990s* (Edinburgh, Edinburgh University Press for the International African Institute, 1999), for a discussion of how early colonial era pressures produced enhanced territorial emphases in myth and environmental religion.

Tonga identity and heritage. The context is one of anger and disaffection on the part of old and young alike, in which a profound and deepening sense of political and economic marginalisation from the Zimbabwean nation is being expressed through a defensive assertion of cultural difference and an embrace of opposition politics.

River and society in the nineteenth century

The people who lived along this part of the Zambezi and who referred to themselves as 'river people'(*bamulwizi*) have a long history of interacting with the river, and distinguished themselves from the people of the hills or plateau.[8] Those who use the names Tonga, Leya or Dombe are generally regarded by themselves and others as the earliest settlers of this section of the river valley.[9] They all lack strong traditions of centralised political authority and all speak variations on the Tonga language. Riverine society was not tightly bounded: those who lived along the river shared broader identities with Tonga and Leya communities extending far away from the river onto the southern and northern plateau, and also interacted with other groups.

Those along the river occupied the unstable margins of larger nineteenth-century polities who regarded this part of the Zambezi as a boundary – the Lozi/Kololo state was located to the north, while the Nambya and Ndebele states were to the south. The Nambya were Karanga speakers from south-eastern Zimbabwe: their leaders set up capitals built in stone and dominated what is now Northwest Zimbabwe from the late eighteenth to the mid-nineteenth century, incorporating many Tonga and Leya communities, including those along the river. They often respected Tonga rainmaking powers and did not eliminate the Tonga language. In the mid-nineteenth century, however, their state was destroyed by the Ndebele and the Nambya fled to the Zambezi and lived on its northern bank under Lozi protection, mingling with the river people, until the Ndebele were themselves defeated in 1893.[10] At times some of the river people were incorporated within or allied with one or other of these more centralised polities, but often they managed to retain a degree of independence. As I shall explore below, this was largely because of their intimate knowledge of the river and how to cross it.

These larger polities looked down on the people of the river.[11] The meanings given to the name Dombe reflect such derogatory views, but also underline the importance of the river to the identity of those who lived closely with it.[12] The term is only used as an

---

[8] Elizabeth Colson notes that people living in villages on the Zambezi in Gwembe similarly termed themselves *bantu bamulonga* or *bantu balwizi*. E. Colson, *The Social Organization of the Gwembe Tonga* (Manchester, Manchester University Press, 1960).

[9] All three terms are used in Hwange District; in Binga only the term Tonga is used.

[10] These events can be dated from contemporary European texts: the capital was destroyed in 1853, after which the Nambya lived in hiding until their leader established himself on the North bank in 1862. See G. Ncube, 'A History of North-western Zimbabwe 1850–1950s: Comparative Change in Three Worlds' MPhil. thesis, University of Zimbabwe (1994).

[11] Traces of Kololo attitudes appear in Livingstone's diaries and other writings, as his closest guides, interpreters and companions were Kololo. On Ndebele stereotypes of the Tonga, see J. Alexander and J. McGregor, 'Modernity and Ethnicity in a Frontier Society: Understanding Difference in Northwestern Zimbabwe', *JSAS*, 23, 2 (1997), pp. 187–203.

[12] Although there is no consensus over the original meaning of 'Tonga', J. Moreau suggests that it derives from 'BaLonga' , the people of the river, or 'BaDonga', the people of the big river, 'Bakule Menyo', *Native Affairs Department Annual*, 1950. It is more frequently said to mean 'those who judge themselves'

identity by those Tonga and Leya communities incorporated into the Nambya state and appears to have originated as an insult from the Nambya, meaning 'the dirty ones' – a reference to the river people's practice of smearing themselves with ochre. But the Dombe themselves invested the term with new meanings that emphasised their relationship with the river (even though some of their communities spread away from the river valley): it is most commonly said to mean 'the strong ones' and to refer to the bravery of the young men who carved the canoes that carried them across the river to the hunting grounds south of the river.[13]

The people who lived with the river invoked their identites in a very fluid manner. The terms Dombe, Leya and Tonga, in particular, were used instrumentally, switching being a means of hiding. One man explained:

> We are the real Leya, the Munkuni from around the Falls on both sides of the river.... We were hunters of elephant and people of the river. What happened, because of war, after crossing the river, you'd sink the canoes, tying them under water. Then when the enemy comes, you say, 'No, we're not the ones you're looking for, we've no canoes'. But then when the danger is past, someone can dive in and fetch them. Dombe was a type of camouflage – those who followed us, they'd be told, 'No we're not Leyas here, we don't know them, we're the Dombes'. It was a security measure.[14]

If group names themselves, and the way they were used, can invoke a relationship with the river, so too can myths of origin. The Tonga have no common myth of origin, and few tell of originating outside the valley.[15] However, many tell of symbolic and magical crossings of the river by founding figures. Nelukoba's Leya, for example, claim to originate north of the river around the Victoria Falls but were led to the South bank by a certain Simbalane who made the crossing by walking under the river on the river bed holding a lighted torch that the waters did not extinguish.[16] Downstream, a Dombe group tell of how their leader Monga Mapeta led them to safety across the river to escape wars on the North bank between the Kololo and Lozi, first to the south bank and subsequently to the security of Mapeta island.[17] Elizabeth Colson recounts a myth in which Namansa Mutonga led his people across the river in the opposite direction: when he reached the Zambezi, the waters parted and his people walked across on the river bed. His wife had forgotten her pipe, but when she tried to cross back, the waters flowed together to prevent her doing so and she turned into a crocodile, which haunted

---

12 (cont.) or 'chiefless', derived from 'kutonga', to judge. See discusssions in Colson, *The Gwembe Tonga*; E. Colson, *The Plateau Tonga of Northern Rhodesia: Social and religious studies* (Manchester: Manchester University Press, 1962) and D. N. Beach, *The Shona and Zimbabwe, 900–1850* (Gweru, Mambo Press, 1980), p.158.

13 Less commonly, 'Dombe' is said to refer to the piles of detritus the river dumps on its banks or to be the name of a fish (*indombe*) which is unresponsive to bait and which people killed by throwing stones.

14 Interview, Peter Siatoma Musaka, Kanywambizi, 21 March 2000. Similarly, Josiah Siamwenda Chuma remembered 'When there was war on the Lozi side, we'd come here. Then when the Ndebeles made war on this side, we'd cross back again. This is our land. When we cross to the North, we are Leya, then when we come back we are Tonga. If anyone pursued us, we'd say, 'No, we're not the ones you're looking for, we're just Tongas', interview, 21 March 2000.

15 Colson, *The Gwembe Tonga*.

16 Interview, Mpala Siwela Dingane, Hwange, 2 April 2000.

17 Interview, Nelson Nengwa Munzabwa and Sungani George Munkuli,14 February 2000.

the river.[18] Such symbolic crossings appear in the myths of origin of others who are not intimately connected to the river, but they are perhaps exceptionally frequently heard in the Zambezi Valley.[19]

River crossings are also a feature of other historical stories. In these, knowledge of crossing or swimming often appears a symbolic marker of difference between river people and others. This section of the Zambezi has exceptionally strong currents and its flow is frequently interrupted by falls and rapids, making extended navigation up and downstream more or less impossible. It did not act as a 'highway of communication', either for those who lived along it or for outsiders.[20] For the river people themselves, who knew how to cross, the river was a link and strong connections were maintained between opposite banks, whereas connections up and down stream were much weaker. The nineteenth-century riverine political economy with its east-west linkages and trade in ivory, slaves, beads and other goods, appears to have operated overland rather than by boat in this section: Tim Matthews argues that Chikunda traders moved overland here, even if they often followed the course of the river. For the more powerful others who lived away from the river and were unfamiliar with it, the Zambezi was a fearful barrier, crossed at great risk and those who commanded its crossing points were seen as savage and theatening. (In this respect, European ideas dovetailed with, and reflected, those of the most important nineteenth-century powers to the north and south of the river, the Kololo and the Ndebele).[21]

The importance to the river people of their command of crossing is illustrated particularly clearly in the story of how the Nambya fled to the Zambezi after the Ndebele destroyed their capital in the mid-nineteenth century. At the river, they sought the assistance of the Dombe leader Mapeta, whose people lived on the banks of the river and islands of the Deka confluence. Mapeta, who controlled a fleet of canoes, instructed his ferryman to help the Nambya leader and his people cross the river to escape their pursuers, leaving the Ndebele stranded. In thanks, the Nambya leader gave Mapeta an honorary title and a daughter to marry. Living close to the river under the protection of the Lozi kings, Nambya and Dombe family histories became increasingly inextricably entwined. The following version is from a descendent of Mapeta:

> Now, when the Nambya ran from Bumbusi [their final stone-walled capital], the Ndebele were coming behind. They ran to the river where they … said 'please can you take us across'…. So Mapeta sent his man Sinechigani, giving him a canoe to take the Nambya across…. When the Ndebele arrived hot on their heels, Mapeta took his horn and blew it. The Ndebele heard it and all their weapons were thrown into disarray…. The Ndebele could see the Nambya chief on the island on top of a hill, and thought they could cross, as the river is narrow at this point, although its current is fierce and the water deep. They tied big logs together with fibre to make a raft, but the current swept it away and they fell into

---

[18] Colson, *The Gwembe Tonga*, p. 26.

[19] T. Ranger, this volume, describes such a myth told by a non-river people.

[20] Colson, *The Gwembe Tonga*, p. 17; T. Matthews, 'The Historical Tradition of the Peoples of the Gwembe Valley, Middle Zambezi', PhD. thesis, University of London (1976).

[21] European imperial ideas of the river as a commercial highway and route to the interior gradually faded as it became clear the river was unnavigable in this section. The river was increasingly represented as a barrier, in conjunction with the region's incorporation into the sphere of European influence focused on South Africa. Discussed in J. McGregor, 'The Great River: European and African Images of the Zambezi', seminar paper, 1999.

deep water, some dying in this way. Then they saw some Tonga men from the far bank swimming across, and they thought it must be easy to do so. But the Tonga knew the currents and where to cross. The Ndebele did not know this and more of them died trying.[22]

This history is remembered in the names of the islands and hills of the river valley. The idea of the river and its islands as places of refuge is reinforced by other aspects of the landscape: caves are pointed out to the visitor which were for hiding from the Ndebele; circular hollows in the rocky banks are said to have been used as mortars for stamping grain during this life of hiding, as the grain could be pounded less noisily than in a wooden pestle and mortar. Hills overlooking major paths to the river are named after the horn or trumpet blown on it for alerting others of forthcoming danger.

Up and downstream, similar stories are told. Descendants of the Leya who lived on islands around and above the Falls recount how the Ndebele would ask their assistance in crossing when they wanted to raid the Lozi on the North bank. The Leya would allow them into the canoes, but in the centre of the river the rowers would pull up to 'Ndebele island' and then jump into the water, leaving the Ndebele stranded on the island to die, as they did not know how to swim or manage the canoes.[23] Islands were always seen as 'places you could run to', associated with the memory of particular groups of people and their graves.[24] Most of the river's islands are associated with today's chiefs or important leaders. Sometimes, as in the case of (the now submerged) Tobwe island, different versions of the history of the island describe its occupants as slaves or chiefs. This underlines the role of islands as places of refuge and the insecurity of the era, but it also hints at the powerful assimilatory capacity of riverine society and the social importance of forgetting. (It also highlights current conflicts over the legitimacy of Tonga chiefly lineages, in ways I shall not elaborate.)[25]

In such a society of small, decentralised groups, people needed protection from each other as much as from more powerful outsiders. People talk of the nineteenth century as a time both of being raided by more powerful others and of raiding those less powerful. Oral histories do not tell of an overall shift from a period when people were being lost as slaves in a Zambezi-focused slave trade to a time when they were being bought back in the last decades of the nineteenth century, though this has been convincingly argued by academic historians.[26] Rather they tell of obscure local movements of people through raiding, in which some groups were more successful

---

[22] Interview, Mankonga Mapeta, Simangani, 24 March 2000.

[23] Interview, Maxon Musaka Ndlovu, Chidobe, 27 March 2000. A slightly different version has the rowers leaping into the water, capsizing the boat, swimming away and leaving the Ndebele to drown.

[24] Interview, chief Siansali, Kariangwe, 3 April 2001. Stories collected by E. Colson and Tim Matthews in Siameja and Mwemba describe how the Mwemba people had initially lived in Siameja before moving to an island in the Zambezi to escape raids from the Kololo/Lozi and the Ndebele. E. Colson pers. comm.

[25] For example, Tobwe island is now associated with the graves of chief Siansali's forbears, yet chief Siachilaba tells of how Siansali and his people came running as slaves (*vadzike*) from warriors, and he gave them Tobwe as a place to hide. Interviews, chiefs Siachilaba and Siansali,19 March 2001 and 3 April 2001. On assimilation, see E. Colson, 'The Assimilation of Aliens Among the Zambian Tonga', in R.Cohen and J. Middleton (eds), *From Tribe to Nation* (San Francisco, Chandler, 1970), pp. 35–54. On conflict over the legitimacy of Tonga chiefs, and the history of their creation, see Ncube, 'A History'.

[26] T. Matthews, 'Portuguese, Chikunda and Peoples of the Gwembe Valley: The Impact of the "Lower Zambezi Complex" on Southern Zambia', *Journal of African History* 22, 1 (1981), pp. 23–41. Ncube, 'A History'.

5.1 Fishing on the margins of the Zambezi before the dam   (Source: National Archives of Zimbabwe)

than others, and making your family grow – particularly through the accumulation of women – was the ultimate aim and mark of achievement. The more important families have stories of raiding women from those deemed 'low', attempting to buy them back again or using women to repay help and protection given to others: Mapeta, for example had to buy back a sister from a Leya group on the north bank after she had been taken in a raid, at the cost of a large box of beads.[27] People joke that one should not talk of those assimilated as slaves or one may find oneself insulting the chief's mother. The possession of a gun was particularly valuable for success in such local raids, and these were brought into the valley from the 1870s onwards, either through contact with Chikunda traders who acted as middlemen for the Portuguese on the East coast and whose networks expanded upstream to incorporate this part of the river after 1860, or as local men began to engage in migrant labour in South Africa and worked in various capacities for European hunters, traders and travellers in the Valley itself.[28]

[27] Interview, Koporo Chindelendele Mapeta, Simangani, 30 March 2000. The Dombe hunter Ngonzi accumulated his wives through raiding 'low' neighbours and in the form of gifts for killing elephant. Interview, Philip Ncube Ngonzi, Jambezi, 13 March 2000.
[28] See Matthews, 'The Historical Tradition' and 'Portuguese, Chikunda'. Before this time, the area appears to have been connected to the West coast though Mambari/Ovimbundu middlemen, as well as to the East

The river was central to all areas of life and not just to security. It was a provider in many ways; the retreating flood waters allowed the cultivation of riverine gardens and fish were plentiful.[29] Indeed, so important was the river that it did not need a name. Local people do not refer to the river as the Zambezi, which is said to be a foreign word, brought by the Portuguese from the coast: they explain that the term was perhaps derived from the phrase '*kasambabesi*', meaning only those who know can cross/swim, and underlining the symbolic importance of knowledge of the river.[30] But people refer to the Zambezi most commonly as 'the big river', 'the big one' or simply 'the river'.[31] They say this does not cause confusion: 'How could we confuse a river of such size with any other?'

One old woman elaborated: 'The river is so big it can never [run] dry: it is the only truth that will never end.'[32] People swore by the river, saying 'By the river', I never did that ('*nolukhulu*', or '*nolukhulu kasa*' in Nambya) or '*aleza upamanzi*' (by God who gives water) in Tonga. A court interpreter explained to me that such expressions would be commonly heard in court, and that old people regarded them as more meaningful than an oath on the Bible.[33] He elaborated:

> People would swear by the river because it is a great provider to them, which has never disappointed them, it is a holy, God-given river. People associated the good spirits with the river because it is a provider. People never lived far from it, they depended on its fish and flood waters.... God would come down and give them food through the river. It was a holy gift, something revered. It provided food like a mother.

The relationship between the river and the spirit world which this implies is very different from the River God imagined by Europeans.[34] People explain that the spirit of Leza (God) had no fixed location in the landscape: '[it] has no special place, it is on the tongues of people who give praises'. But 'People would go to their sacred places down by the river and say "If you are there, the spirit of our ancestors, please rise now from the water and help us"'.[35]

Tonga, Dombe, Leya and Nambya share a central concern for ancestral spirits in religious practice and not a river god. Many important shrines or sacred places are (or were) close to the river simply because people lived close to the river, not because proximity to the river was *per se* important. Thus, many *malende* shrines – on the basis

---

[28] (cont.) coast, perhaps through non-riverine routes to the North of the Zambezi.

[29] This system of agriculture has been detailed by Colson, *The Gwembe Tonga* and Thayer Scudder, *The Ecology of the Gwembe Tonga* (Manchester, Manchester University Press, 1973).

[30] M. Tremmel, *The People of the Great River: The Tonga hoped the water would follow them* (Gweru, Mambo, 1994) translates this phrase as only those who know can wash, though the implication is the same, as those who do not know the river cannot use it.

[31] *Lwizi, Mulonga mupati*, or *Lukhulu* in Tonga/Nambya. The latter term is less commonly heard in Binga.

[32] Interview, Alice Nduwo Ngwenya, Simangani, 11 March 2000.

[33] Interview, Mathias C. Munzabwa, Hwange, 3 April 2000.

[34] References to a River God in the Zambezi are frequent in nineteenth-century explorers' texts, in more recent European writing on the Kariba dam, and through the popularisation of the Nyaminyami myth in Zimbabwe. The latter is now a tourist icon on sale throughout the Zambezi Valley, including in areas where the myth did not originate, such as the region discussed in this paper. Elizabeth Colson notes that Nyaminyami is a foreign idea to the Gwembe Tonga she worked with, but was talked about in the 1990s by those returning from the South bank, and was incorporated into *masabe* possession cults.

[35] Interview, Peter Siatoma Musaka and Josiah Siameenda Chuma, Kanywambizi, 21 March 2000.

of which the colonial government defined Tonga neighbourhoods and chiefs – were along the river, marked by a baobab or small hut. So too were family shrines *(ntumba* in Tonga or *numba* in Nambya) which were in homeyards or riverbank gardens.[36] The most important ceremonies for Dombe, Leya and Nambya (including those for making rain) involve a tour of past leaders' graves. Such ritual often involved a crossing of the river and visit to islands because this is where the graves are located. The Nambya *miliya* ceremony, for example, held in times of drought, began on the North bank of the Zambezi (at Gambo, the former residence and grave of the mid- to late nineteenth-century Nambya leader), then involved crossing back to visit other important graves away from the river. Rainmaking for the Dombe leader Mapeta involved criss-crossing between islands and river banks touring former leaders' graves.

Although the river itself was not regarded as a shrine, it certainly evoked respect and awe, and some of its pools and waterfalls *were* seen as sacred places, associated with supernatural phenomena. Sometimes important religious rituals, such as those for rain, involved a trip specifically to the river to collect water or ask for rain, and some of the most senior mediums with rainmaking responsibilities (called *mpande* in Tonga or *mande* in Nambya) had particular biographical and spiritual connections with the river.[37]

Sacred places within the river were usually associated with vague former communities of unspecified ancestors rather than particular named, individual forebears (though a few were associated with the memory of the most powerful rainmakers, as detailed below). Most were pools – all of which had an individual name – where supernatural phenomena could be seen or heard, usually taking the form of the sound of invisible people, of grain being pounded, children playing, drums being beaten or cattle lowing.[38] Chief Saba's *malende* shrine, for example, was near the pool Fufu, located at the junction of the Mlibizi and Zambezi: 'it was a special place where we went for the *malende*, you would see young girls there or a whole village with women pounding and children crying, and you'd have to clap for permission to pass, and the girls and everything would disappear down into the pool. You couldn't fish there, the fish were fearful and strange.'[39] If fishing in some such pools was forbidden, in others it was possible only at certain times of year, under instruction from those responsible for the *malende* shrines.

The Victoria Falls itself was such a place: one sacred site was at the foot of the Falls 'at the very place where it thunders', another was in the second gorge 'where the water falls and swirls round as if it is boiling'. Both were places of appeasement for the Leya who lived in the vicinity. One old man remembered:

> On a special day, food would be prepared and carried down in clay pots. We'd creep down and down until we reached the water point. There we'd get water and all the food would remain behind untouched. So the spirits of the parents, if they should hear us, they'd take the food... When you go down the gorge for fishing, if you go at night, you can see lights. Then you would clap, persuading the spirit to be calm. The following morning you would return home with a good catch [of fish].[40]

---

[36] Dombe, Leya and Nambya often do not use this term, but speak of propiating spirits at graves *(magambo)*.
[37] This is not the case further downstream. E. Colson did not find that rain rituals were associated with the river; nor was immersion practised. See 'Places of Power'.
[38] Such sites are not only along the Zambezi, but also along its tributaries.
[39] Interview, Chief Saba, Sianzyundu, 12 March 2001.
[40] Interview, Maxon Musaka Ndlovu, Chidobe, 27 March 2000.

The two most important spirit mediums on the South bank – one a Dombe medium known as Siabumbe (or Jelekuja), the other a Tonga called Mawala (or Matenga) – had particular sacred places on the bank, particular pools, and a special spiritual relationship with the river itself. Siabumbe is said to have immersed himself in the river only to emerge with arms laden with agricultural produce. As some elders remembered: 'Siabumbe the great *mpande's* place was Kanokonoko, in the gorge below the Falls. He would jump into the water and stay under for seven days. After a week he'd emerge carrying all sorts of different kinds of seeds – millet, sorghum and nyemba [beans].'[41] The current medium of this spirit, a woman named Mambaita, explained how the life of Siabumbe and that of his descendants was intimately involved with the river, and how the spirit was passed on to his daughter Kasoso during an immersion in its waters:

> Siabumbe's daughter was Kasoso. Siabumbe's *mpande* spirit took her and threw her into the river two days after she was born. She stayed there in the river, until the community became concerned and asked Siabumbe what had happened. Siabumbe told the community she was fine, and that there was no need to worry. Kasoso was being bathed by the *mpande* spirit. After two days, Siabumbe marched to the river … he raised a stick, and struck the water with it. Immediately the baby was seen in the river and he commanded his wife to take the baby out of the water. This child was Kasoso. Kasoso came out of the river, close to Chekane. She used to go back to that place for rainmaking.[42]

Further down the river, the medium Mawala – one of the more important regional mediums, highly placed in a spiritual hierarchy and attracting visits from a number of different chiefs – was closely associated with the Binga hot springs, located only two hundred or so metres from the river and into which he would immerse himself. But he too had a special relationship with the Zambezi: 'he would sit on the boiling water [of Binga hot spring] with it coming up to his groin and then he'd go into the river, walking on top of the water like Jesus … he'd be standing on the water smoking his pipe'.[43] Others recalled how he would perform miracles, crossing the Zambezi on top of the water without a canoe, fetching water from pools on the north bank and bringing it back to the southern side.[44]

Not all ritual at the river was connected with rainmaking and other seasonal ritual. Fishing in the pools of the Zambezi often involved a ceremony; so too did important events, such as the launching of a canoe or the killing of an elephant or hippo. These often required an immersion in the river: a deep, still pool in the Zambezi called Chipito, near to Siachilaba's *malende* shrine, for example, was used for the community to immerse themselves after killing an elephant and before trading the ivory which was stored nearby,'each and every one had to immerse themselves, even the ladies who couldn't swim'.[45]

So far the river has appeared in my discussion of local memories of the nineteenth century in largely positive light, as a source of identity and place of refuge, as a source of fertility and life, and as a symbol of truth. These images are inscribed in the stone or held in the sand, detritus and vegetation of the river banks and its islands (where these

[41] Interview, Peter Siatoma Musaka and Josiah Siamwenda Chuma, Kanywambizi, 21 March 2000.
[42] Interview, Esinath Mambaita Kasoso, Milonga, 11 April 2000.
[43] Interviews, Siampiza Munsaka, Timothy Munsaka and chief Sigalenke, Manjolo, 2 April 2001.
[44] Interview, Joel Mudimba, Sigalenke, 24 March 2001
[45] Interview, chief Siachilaba, 19 March 2001.

have not been submerged), and are associated with the memory and actions of the leaders and spirit mediums who lived on them. But the river was also a place of danger; its waters themselves were dangerous, especially in unstable dugout canoes, and they harboured life-threatening crocodiles. People also remember the river as a fearful place, because it 'took people'.[46] The local imagery of the river includes a symbol of the river as a place of danger in the form of a river monster.[47] This is a great fish or snake that lived in the river, and could cause accidents on boats, or cause people to be taken and held down in the river's depths or carried away by the fast currents. It is said that the monster could spread its beard or tentacles out onto the river bank, and could sweep people down into the river. If signs of its presence were seen – such as the water turning red or becoming rough or 'heavy' – it was a bad omen, and one had to move away from the river. Nobody now talks about this monster in relation to everyday life, yet some people still remember stories about it, and its actions are sometimes interwoven in historical tales. Disappearances of women collecting water from the river banks, or of canoes capsizing, or of deaths by crocodiles could be explained through the monster's action. Children could be told stories of it to instil fear of the river in them, and warnings not to go alone too near to the banks at certain dangerous places. The monster could, however, never be seen; one only had signs of its presence. Nor could it be controlled; it was an intrinsic part of the river that had to be respected. It was also connected with rainbows, which are said to calm strong winds and to be a sign than the destructive rains and wind are over. Rainbows are said to reach the ground in deep pools in the river where the monster lived.

The fact that so powerful a symbol could not be seen is important for an understanding of local aesthetics of the river. I have described a rich and evocative riverine imagery in the history and mythology of the nineteenth century. It seems likely that at least some aspects of this imagery arose out of daily life with the river, though many of the stories also have biblical overtones, notions of ownership or a romantic nostalgia that may have been elaborated when such interactions had ceased. Although some particularly evocative parts of the landscape are the same features Europeans deemed worthy of admiration and awe (such as the 'smoke' of the falls, the pits where the waters boiled and the rainbows that formed in its mist), other locally significant places are unmentioned in European accounts, such as the different pools, the piles of detritus and the hollows of the river bank. Furthermore, oral histories, unlike European texts, do not privilege visual experiences: I do not want to imply that Africans have no aesthetic response to landscape, simply that 'seeing' *per se* generally goes unremarked in oral accounts. Meanings attached to places in these tales are often specific rather than generic. It is not the remarkableness of pools in general that is noteworthy, but of a specific pool with a name, such as Fufu, where ancestors could be heard and seen, unlike other named pools where they could not; a baobab tree appears in oral histories not as beautiful in itself (though it may well have been seen as such), but as a marker of a particular shrine or grave. Features were picked out for their historical value, not their scenic value, because they invoked memories of ancestors named and unnamed and

---

[46] Colson recalls a Gwembe woman saying to her in 1956 'You think it is good [the river]. It is bad. It takes people.' She notes that, in Mwemba area, there were places in the Zambezi where outcasts were thrown, such as witches, or children who cut wrong sets of incisors first. This place was a place of fear, to be avoided. E. Colson, pers. comm. See also, Tremmel, *The People of the Great River*, p. 22.

[47] Called *Simusinsi* by the Dombe/Nambya in Hwange and *Simwaba* by the Tonga in Binga.

past ways of life, not their geological or artistic value. Sometimes 'seeing' was explicitly forbidden; after rain ceremonies at the river, for example, communities leaving the place were not permitted to look back at the river.[48]

Interventions in the colonial period and the end of a river-focused life

The colonial era brought an end to this river-focused way of life. Narratives of change in this period have a common theme in the marginalisation of the river people – and of the broader ethnic and linguistic groups, Tonga, Dombe, Leya and Nambya. Here I will focus on changing relationships with the river, and how aspects of these changes can be encapsulated in the idea of the desacralisation of the landscape of the valley and of life with the river. This is, of course, a selective view of history, and only one of many possible narratives. The themes of marginalisation and of desacralisation are, however, common both to those displaced from the Kariba dam, and to those unaffected by the dam, though for different reasons.

The best known aspect of the colonial history of the Zambezi valley is the displacement of those along the river by the waters of the Kariba dam in 1957-8, which brought life with the river to a particularly abrupt and traumatic end for those involved.[49] The displacement affected a part of the valley which had been marginal to colonial economic and political development, and lacked roads, missions and schools: colonial officials on the South bank saw it as a place 'at the edge of beyond', where people were 'untouched and unspoiled by civilization,'[50] still 'leading much the same life as they had when the Livingstones pushed up the river in 1860'.[51] In the wake of the dam, there was a huge increase in the state's presence, as roads, missions and a new district administrative centre in Binga were constructed. District Commissioner Cockroft described how ancient customs died over night and 'the isolation of the Valley has been shattered ... and the Valley baTonka, for better or for worse, have been thrown into the competitive whirlpool of modern development'.[52]

Today, Tonga people displaced by the dam often portray life before the move in glowing and nostalgic terms, and make the move central to an overall narrative of loss and impoverishment. Before the dam is a time when 'there was no hunger' and when 'God was near us ... when we had our *malende* shrines down by the river'.[53] The familiar landscape of the river valley and its islands, holding the memory of the past, was replaced by the new lake shore and the waterless, tsetse- and animal-infested resettlement lands. Elizabeth Colson has described how political and religious leaders were discredited in the aftermath of the move, and how mediums of ancestral spirits

---

[48] This is commonplace in central/southern Africa, after various rain ceremonies, not just those at the river, both among the Tonga and others.

[49] See the classic detailed work of E. Colson, *The Social Consequences of Resettlement: The impact of the Kariba resettlement upon the Gwembe Tonga* (Manchester, Manchester University Press, 1971). Studies on the South bank are M. Tremmel, *The People of the Great River*; A.K.H.Weinrich, *The Tonga People on the Southern Shore of Lake Kariba* (Gweru, Mambo Press, 1977).

[50] H.N. Hemans, *The Log of a Native Commissioner* (London, Witherby, 1935), pp. 7, 13, 64–6.

[51] *The Victoria Falls illustrated: A Handbook to the Victoria Falls, the Batoka Gorge and Part of the Upper Zambezi* (Northern Rhodesia, Commission for the Preservation of Natural and Historical Relics, 1952).

[52] Annual Report, Binga, 1958, S 2827/2/2/6.

[53] Interview, Chief Saba, Sianzyundu, 12 March 2001. See also Tremmel, *The People of the Great River.*

closely connected to the now submerged land of the valley suffered a particularly severe blow.[54] People lost access to fertile fields and to relatives: though they were still allowed to use the lakeshore for fishing and could still cross, both became much more difficult. On the southern bank much of the lakeshore was reserved for tourist or conservationist uses, restricting access to local communities and resulting in further evictions. After Zambia's independence, all crossing of the river and lake was forbidden in the interests of state security, as I shall elaborate further below.

While the hardships and losses of the move were huge and life thereafter very difficult, it is important not to overplay the nostalgia for a past life with the river. Though people often portray life by the river as a time of plenty, when custom was intact and people were close to their ancestors and God, there is often a note of pragmatism to their accounts: life might have been better by the river, but it was dangerous; furthermore, even without the dam, many people would have had to move away from the river as population increased.[55] The combination of demographic pressures and economic changes in the early colonial period had been severe: though the people of the Valley had long engaged in migrant labour, they had been drawn out of the valley in larger numbers as taxes rose, and as older forms of production and exchange collapsed.[56] Fertile riverine gardens may have mitigated hunger, but did not eliminate it completely. Politicians and the younger generation are in many ways now more angry about the subsequent history of state developmental neglect than they are about the state invervening to build the dam and forcing their parents away from the river.

Such anger has come to focus increasingly on the betrayal of promises made in the course of the move by the colonial official responsible – Native Commissioner I.G. Cockroft (known as *Sikanyana*). Cockroft is remembered to have promised the resisting Tonga leaders 'that the water would follow them', meaning the state would provide them with new sources of water after the move.[57] Michael Tremmel describes how, during the meetings he called to compile oral histories of the displacement for his recent book on the topic, 'one of the women, Simpongo Munsaka, kept repeating over and over again, "We left with our property and our bodies, but we left our water behind. We would like our water to follow us. They promised that the water would follow us."'[58] Although the state's presence increased dramatically in the valley after the building of the dam, provision of water, and of schools, clinics and other services proceeded very slowly, and was soon interrupted by the war, leaving Binga one of the most impoverished and poorly served districts in the country, and its people frequently

---

[54] In the wake of the move, new *massabe* possession cults spread, which were not tied to the landscape of the valley. Colson, *The Social Consequences of Resettlement*. See also U. Luig, 'Constructing Local Worlds: Spirit Possession in the Gwembe Valley, Zambia', in H. Behrend and U. Luig, *Spirit Possession: Modernity and power in Africa* (Oxford, James Currey, 1999), pp. 124–42.

[55] This was a recurrent feature of my interviews, see also some of the oral histories in Tremmel, *The People of the Great River*. For a discussion of this pragmatic ethic, see E. Colson, 'Heroism, Martyrdom and Courage: An Essay on Tonga Ethics', in T.O. Biedelman (ed.), *The Translation of Culture: Essays to Edward Evans Pritchard* (London, Tavistock, 1971), pp. 19–35. On movement out of the valley for shifting cultivation, see Scudder, *The Gwembe Tonga*.

[56] On the collapse of local iron and cotton industries, and later commercial tobacco production see Ncube, 'A History'.

[57] As chief Siachilaba recalled 'Sikanyana came with promises, he promised the water would follow behind, but nothing up to now'. Interview, 19 March 2001.

[58] Tremmel, *The People of the Great River*, p. 37.

reduced to dependence on food handouts.[59] Shortage of water was and is one of the most acute problems people faced. Cockroft – and thus the colonial state – is now said by some to have 'blocked' development, to have desired to keep the Tonga away from the modern world and to keep them primitive.[60]

Before returning to the way in which this history is being used today, and how the idea of being a river people has persisted for those displaced in this way, let me first explore the rather different histories of marginalisation of the Dombe, Leya and Nambya communities who lived upstream from the waters of the dam in Hwange district. They still have a riverine landscape into which memories of the past are inscribed and the Dombe/Leya often refer to themselves as river people. However, they too have narratives of loss which relate to the changing role and significance of the river. Rather than being submerged, their sacred places were desecrated or deserted over the course of the colonial period; access to riverine gardens was undermined not by water but by state restrictions and war. The twentieth-century encroachments of modernity were symbolised not by a dam but by the more gradual processes of Christian conversion, commoditisation and state intrusion.

As soon as the Ndebele had been defeated, the Nambya leaders – who did not regard themselves as 'river people' – abandoned their refuge on the North bank of the river and moved southwards with many of their people, back towards the ruins of their former capital.[61] I will focus here on those who remained behind and regarded themselves as more closely related to the river, and who would otherwise have continued to use it. Many people living along the river were forced to move: people in Hwange district were less isolated than the Tonga downstream, being close to the railway to 'the North', and to the urban centres that grew up around Hwange coal mine and the Victoria Falls resort. The Leya/Dombe people of the Falls area were evicted as their land was given over to the tourist resort and 'wildernesses' of the Victoria Falls area between 1900 and 1930: some were told by the colonial state to 'go back' to the North bank, others joined the increasingly crowded populations in the Hwange communal lands.[62] Not only was Hwange District more directly affected by land alienation and the economic changes of the colonial era, but missions also had an earlier impact. As a local educated class emerged through the Catholic and Wesleyan missions in the district from the mid-1930s, and particularly in the 1950s, people gradually ceased swearing on the river and increasingly chose to use the Bible instead.

As life became decreasingly focused on the river, so the river's sacred sites were desacralised. Around the Victoria Falls, the landscape was desecrated because religious sites were taken over by tourists and abandoned by locals. A Leya elder recalled how the vine-covered route down to the sacred place by the boiling point at the foot of the Falls was taken over by 'commercial people' and turned into a tourist path, complete with steps and a handrail.[63] The last religious ceremony he remembered taking place

---

[59] The 1995 Poverty Assesssment Study (Harare: Ministry of Labour, Public Service and Social Welfare, 1996), considers Binga (with one other district) to have the highest levels of poverty in the country: 91% of the population were 'poor' or 'very poor'.

[60] Interview, Andrew Chiumu Mudimba, 11 April 2000.

[61] This paper cannot fully explore Nambya histories and heritage, which are focused on the graves and material remains of former nineteenth-century state capitals, now located in the Hwange National Park and elsewhere. See J. McGregor, 'The Social Life of Ruins: Sites of Memory and the Politics of a Zimbabwean Periphery', *Journal of Historical Geography* (forthcoming).

[62] Elaborated in McGregor, 'The Great River'.

[63] Interview, Maxon Musaka Ndlovu, Chidobe, 27 March 2000.

there was in the 1950s, since when the light at the foot of the Falls and sounds of ancestors at the waterside have neither been seen nor heard. Another place for propitiating ancestral spirits was the famous big baobab tree at the Victoria Falls municipal camp site, access to which was difficult for local people. Ceremonies ceased to be held there and the tree itself was increasingly inscribed with travellers' initials and surrounded by crowds of visitors. Sacred pots by the river were destroyed. Other sites were disturbed as developments stretched downstream: the Wankie Colliery pumping station and the angling club, built on the river banks by the Deka confluence in the 1950s, for example, meant that some of Mapeta's sacred places were on private property.[64]

But it was not only tourists who ignored the religious associations of riverine sites. Fishing sites close to the Falls, where it was necessary to respect ancestral spirits, were regularly abused by labourers at the resort, who were drawn initially from a wide area of Central Africa: as jobs went to 'outsiders' and foreign languages (first Lozi, and then Ndebele) dominated the town and its schools, locals felt increasingly marginalised. Ndebele immigrant communities were dumped in the area by the colonial authorities in the late 1950s: they were ignorant of sites sacred to the evicted former river people, most of whom were by then in Northern Rhodesia.[65] Leya and Nambya people still living in the area complain that these Ndebele newcomers were not inclined to respect their religious sites and practices.

The growing Christian influence in the District was also important in desacralising the landscape, while the pressures of time and work further undercut traditional practice.[66] As church attendance grew, large community events in particular were increasingly difficult to organise, though family-level ceremonies often continued. The last time the Nambya chiefs organised a crossing of the river as part of the pilgrimage to former rulers' graves was in the 1950s.[67]

The decreasing importance of community rituals along the river is also explained in terms of the corruption of ritual leaders who have commodified their practices. This can be illustrated most vividly by the fate of the medium Kasoso, whose immersion in the Zambezi after her birth I have already described. She is widely criticised for joining a Luvale fortune teller in the Victoria Falls craft village, where 'she started working for cash not the ancestors'. After her death in 1974 a baobab tree sprouted on her grave, which should have become an important ritual site. However, it was cut down by Victoria Falls council workers clearing a strip of land for telephone poles.[68]

As the liberation war intensified, so ZAPU established itself in the two districts of Hwange and Binga. Local people with knowledge of how to cross the river were crucially important to ZAPU and to the guerrillas. As a result state controls over crossing were harsh. They were particularly harsh in Hwange, where the narrowness of the river upstream of the lake made crossing easier: in 1972 the security forces moved along the river banks destroying canoes, not only making it more difficult for local people to cross, but also preventing access to some sorts of fish and undercutting other trades. Some people burnt their boats, some sank their craft, others untied the canoes and let

---

[64] Interview, Mankonga Mapeta, Simangani, 24 March 2000
[65] For a history of these evictions, see J. Alexander, J.McGregor and T. Ranger, *Violence and Memory. One hundred years in 'the dark forests' of Matabeleland* (Oxford, James Currey, 2000).
[66] One Leya pool used for immersion south of the Falls, was renamed 'Jordan' by Christians.
[67] Interviews, chief Shana, Jambezi, 15 March 2000; Chief Nekatambe, Dinde, 3 March 2000.
[68] Interviews, Maxon Musaka Ndlovu, Chidobe, 27 March 2000; Esinath Mambaita Kasoso, Milonga, 11/4/2000.

them be carried downstream by the current. As one elder recalled: 'All canoes were captured by the government: before that we crossed a lot, but it became political and everything was destroyed. On the Zambian side, they still have canoes and are allowed to fish from them, only here everything was banned.'[69] Another remembered 'It was during the time when tensions were running high, we were forbidden to cross. We didn't want to see our boats destroyed by the government, so we launched them into the river, casting the canoes downstream. It was a sad thing to see them go. We have not built canoes since that time, we are still waiting for the country to cool down.'[70] In the final years of the war, the entire riverbank population of the Hwange communal area was moved into a protected village, and the banks were mined along their length.

As controlling the river became more important to the state's military effort, so local use of it was ruled out completely for two years in the Hwange District, while use of the lake was also greatly curtailed in Binga by the presence of security forces and guerrillas. This marked a culmination of the appropriations of the colonial period, the legacies of which have been far-reaching. De-mining teams are still working close to the Victoria Falls and have scarcely begun to extend the 100km or so downstream where people have been living with landmines which continue to reap their harvest of cattle and children. The effects of landmines have been compounded by continuing state restrictions on crossing in the interests of controlling Zambian poachers.

The development of tourism and wildlife conservation in the two districts after independence, has often competed with local uses of the river and lake. It is only since the 1990s that development plans have begun to advocate the protection and support of local livelihoods as a fundamental principle in the development of the Zambezi Valley for conservation and tourism. Likewise, plans for the Victoria Falls have only belatedly begun to emphasise local concerns and cultural values.[71] While the desacralisation of life with the river over the course of the colonial period was the concern of the older generation, younger people were often more concerned about their marginalisation; about restrictions on their access to resources, on immigration from other parts of the country, about jobs in tourism and in the public sector, as well as commercial opportunities going to outsiders.

Memories of the river in contemporary politics

Given that a river-focused way of life came to an end over the course of the colonial era, for the reasons I have briefly described, it is perhaps surprising that people who no longer live with the river should still persist in regarding themselves as river people.[72] Moving around the two districts of Binga and Hwange, one often hears people talk about themselves as such. This is the case both for the Tonga displaced from the Kariba dam, and the Dombe/Leya above the dam's throwback. Here, I explore some of the reasons for this persistence, and the ways in which remembered interactions with the river are used today. Aside from the expressions of nostalgia and loss, which have

---

[69] Interview, Sungani George Munkuli and Nelson Nengwa Munzabwa, Simangani, 14 March 2000.

[70] Interview, Petrus Dixon Shoko, Makwa, 24 March 2000.

[71] See the new *Kariba Lakeshore Combination Master Plan* (Kariba, Kariba Lakeshore Master Plan Preparation Authority, 1998) and *Strategic Environmental Assessment of Developments Around Victoria Falls* (Geneva, IUCN, 1996).

[72] Elizabeth Colson has also noted this among those displaced on the Zambian side, pers. comm.

already been explored, this is particularly apparent in constructions of Tonga and Dombe identity and in conflicts over access to resources, especially those of the river and lake. These have shaped aspects of the historical narratives I have described above, in ways that will become apparent.

From the late 1970s, and particularly in the 1980s, there has been a defensive assertion of cultural difference on the part of Tonga communities in Zimbabwe, who constitute one of the country's official 'minority' groups. This has been in part a reaction to a profound sense of political and economic marginalisation, and to a related sense of being looked down upon by others.[73] Not only are the districts of the Zambezi Valley lagging far behind in terms of development (a fact of which local people are very aware), but the name 'Tonga' itself remains a by-word for the primitive and backward in Zimbabwe.[74] Since independence in 1980, local leaders and politicians have pushed for development with an acute sense of urgency, and have also pushed for cultural recognition – particularly for Tonga to be a medium of instruction in local schools and a subject in itself, as well as for Tonga history to be a recognised part of Zimbabwean history.[75] Politicians have demanded the creation of 'Tongaland' or a new 'northern province' along the Zambezi, so that Tongas are not subsumed in Matabeleland. Tonga and Dombe intellectuals have emphasised how Tonga people were the first Bantu people in Zimbabwe, not only in the river valley, but also in a broader stretch of the plateau.

Current Tonga oral and written histories, and the notions of heritage they deploy, tend to look to the river.[76] By making the river a unifying centre, Tonga history appears in a different light from Ndebele, Shona or Nambya-focused histories, in which the Tonga appear on the margins as raided, enslaved and running away, as uncouth and as labelled with various derogatory names.[77] A Tonga-centred history, revolving around the river, as I have illustrated, shows river people commanding the crossing points, islands and river banks. It puts Tonga leaders in a position of power, even in relation to 'warriors' from larger, more centralised polities. While Tonga intellectuals and politicians have found a mouthpiece to promote Tonga culture, history and development through the institutions of Binga District, where Tonga people are a majority, and support from sympathetic NGOs has been significant, the situation in Hwange District is rather different. In Hwange, Dombe contributions to this Tonga assertion have come into conflict with Nambya cultural nationalism, and Nambya speakers are more prominent in the district. The Dombe case is complex partly because they had historically been incorporated into the Nambya state, had little tradition of centralised authority of their own and the colonial state therefore did not appoint any Dombe chiefs. Now, as Dombe intellectuals are emphasising their Tonga identity rather than their past incorpo-

---

[73] The timing reflects the expectations of independence, but also the belated emergence of a local educated elite. The Nambya also asserted themselves in a similar way, in a cultural nationalist movement that began earlier, and which I shall not elaborate here.

[74] See discussion in Tremmel, *The People of the Great River*, p. 9.

[75] Detailed, for example, in CCJP, 'A Report on the Education-Related Problems in Binga District', July 2000. Minutes of the Tonga Language Committee (TLC), and of the Binga Rural District Council's (BRDC) efforts to promote Tonga culture, through full council resolutions, are available in BRDC.

[76] In addition to the oral sources cited above, see the (handwritten) volumes produced by Mathias C. Mnzabwa (court interpreter, Hwange and member of the Tonga Writers Committee), which include two novels in the Tonga language and a book of letters, intended for school use.

[77] Nambya-centred histories, including a number of written texts, have been produced by the Nambya Cultural Association, based in Hwange. On Ndebele experiences of their encounter with Tonga and Nambya, see Alexander and McGregor, 'Understanding Difference'.

ration under the Nambya, they are pushing for Dombe chiefs and the Tonga language. In this, the history of Mapeta the ferryman (recounted above) is central and much contested: Nambya histories do not recognise Mapeta as a significant character before his assistance to them, and emphasise how he achieved his status, his honorary name and leadership through their gratitude. Dombe histories, however, now talk of 'Mapeta-land', ruled by a nine-deep lineage of Mapetas. Their histories have a strongly territorial emphasis, with Mapeta commanding approaches to the river, hills and islands.[78]

This example is revealing of the divisive potential of such cultural assertions, which often imply an exclusivity. The marginalisation of those who live in this part of the Valley undoubtedly requires state developmental attention, as a combination of past interventions and past neglect have resulted in unacceptable levels of impoverishment and disadvandage. As the ruling party ZANU(PF) has failed to live up to the expectations of independence, so Binga and Hwange Districts have turned to the new political opposition, registering the highest opposition majorities for any rural constituencies in the country.[79] However, the cultural dimensions of local efforts to redress this history have often involved setting Tonga against others, particularly members of majority groups, such as Ndebele immigrants, but it has also set them against another minority group – the Nambya.

The displacement from the Kariba dam has come to occupy a central place in these new assertions of Tonga history, identity and heritage, even though many Tonga (as well as Dombe and Leya) were not affected by it. Thus leaders of Binga District instituted an annual commemoration of the displacement in 1997: this was conceived as a cultural event and celebration of Tonga culture, involving speeches, performances by local drumming teams, school drama groups and the like. As noted above, commemorating displacement from the dam is more than a backward-looking exercise remembering what is lost, it is also a reminder of broken promises by Native Commissioner Cockroft and the colonial state, of the failures of the post-independence state, and of Tonga rights to compensation and development.[80] Memories of the broken promises have been invoked in more than rhetorical gestures and performances such as these. For example, the Catholic Commission for Justice and Peace recently investigated the problems leading to the closure of a small irrigation scheme, in chief Siansali's area of Binga District. They reported that when the Lungwalala dam was built in 1992 by the government, the people regarded it as compensation for their removal in 1957. For the first two years they had not been charged for water, but then payments were demanded, and 'people could not understand why, as the DC had promised them that water would follow them to the new areas where they were made to settle'. This attitude had contributed to the refusal to pay rates, and the failure of the scheme.[81]

These arguments about the relationship between Tonga identity and past interactions with the river have a particular relevance in relation to conflicts over access to the resources of the river and lake. As noted above, developments in the wake of the dam were governed by the assumption that tourism and conservation were to be the future

---

[78] Reactions to my earlier seminar paper 'The Great River', from members of the Dombe and Nambya Cultural Societies were instructive on the controversy surrounding this story.

[79] See J. Alexander and J. McGregor, 'Land, Elections and the Politics of Opposition in Matabeleland, Zimbabwe', *Journal of Agrarian Change* 1, 4 (2001), pp. 510–34.

[80] Ppeople are very aware that compensation, although minimal, was received in Zambia.

[81] CCJP, 'Report on the problems that led to the closure of Lungwalala Irrigation Scheme', October 2000. Held in File AGR 16. Binga Rural District Council.

income earners in this region, and, together with the development of commercial fishing, these uses were prioritised over local access to and use of the river and lake. People feel (with considerable justification) that wild animals, tourists and large-scale commercial fishing are being favoured over their own needs; that whites and recent immigrants from other parts of the country are getting preferential and undue access. The idea of the Tonga being the true and exclusive owners of the river/lake, as they are river people and suffered the disadvantages of the creation of Kariba, has a particular relevance in demands for enhanced access to the resources of the river and lake for locals. As one young fisherman, born after the displacement, told me:

> It pains us to see others using the lake freely when we are the owners. We Tongas, we lived along the river. I can't say this is not my land. There was no compensation for our parents when they were forced to move out because of the dam. Now others are getting the land freely but we have to pay.... I can't say where I learnt to fish, I grew up fishing. We are Tongas, people of the river.... I could fish as soon as I could herd cattle, and we started in canoes as early as that.... I was born on the river bank – I was born in this industry like my fathers before me. What I know is that I found myself fishing ... when I started school I was already a fisherman. You don't have to teach a Tonga to fish.[82]

Similarly, in Hwange, Dombe/Nambya along the river have only just secured rights to have a fishing camp, to own boats and practise gillnet fishing after more than two decades of prohibition.[83] They still struggle to use riverbank gardens, cultivation of which is deemed illegal in places by the Department of Agriculture and local council by-laws. People justify evading state restrictions (and have been encouraged to do so by some development workers) with the argument, 'God gave us this river, it is for us to use by right'.[84]

Conclusion

This discussion of how marginalised minorities have invoked a relation to landscape in their claims to resources and other rights has shown how memories of past ways of life and past interactions with the environment can have a persistent relevance even when day-to-day life has changed profoundly. In this case, ideas about relationships with the landscape are more than statements of idealised cultural norms about the past: they are ways of creating meaning at a personal and family level, often in contexts of dispossession and hardship. At another level, they are a means by which marginalised minorities have tried to redefine who they are and create a place for themselves – both physical and cultural – within a nation from which they feel politically and economically excluded. The narratives I have described are being deployed in the creation of a heritage in which oral traditions are combined with biblical idiom and memories of recent events such as the displacement from the dam and promises betrayed. It is a heritage that has a powerful sense of geography and focuses in particular on the landscape of the river, past and present. The history invoked by this geography and remembered interactions with the environment is one that implies both ownership and injustice, and which demands a new dispensation from the central state.

---

[82] Interview, Sanders Mwinde, Mlibizi, 25 March 2001.
[83] Even now, there is only one legal fishing camp in the District, and not one around the Falls.
[84] Interviews, Simangani; Msuna, March 2000.

Part II

Colonial Science, the State
& African Responses

6

African Environments & Environmental Sciences

The African Research Survey, Ecological Paradigms
& British Colonial Development
1920–1940[1]

HELEN TILLEY

This chapter is concerned with a project of the 1930s – the African Research Survey – which on the face of it had all the trappings of imperial hegemony.[2] Its initial aim was to co-ordinate and, if possible, standardise colonial policies in Africa across not only the British but also the French, Belgian, and Portuguese territories. In its pursuit of more effective colonial control, it embraced both the application of scientific knowledge and its complement, scientific colonialism. It championed new forms of 'aerial reconnaissance' to conduct inventories of Africa's vast natural resources. It also sought to develop those resources through widespread experimentation, drawing on methods and practices learned in other parts of the Empire. In private negotiations, its promoters manoeuvred to exclude and de-emphasise more radical voices concerned with Africa's future. The use of new cultural technologies – such as film and radio – was recommended in order to infiltrate more efficiently the heterogeneous inhabitants of the continent. The Survey accepted, almost without question, the need to modernise African ways of life – especially agricultural and medical practices – and to incorporate the various territories into the international economy. It recognised the need for colonial administrators to learn Africa's many vernacular languages because, without such knowledge, controlling the different local populations was next to impossible. In sum, it was a project designed, at least on one level, to master Africa's environments and its human populations through scientific management and planning.

An interpretation of the African Research Survey from this perspective alone, however, fails to appreciate the complexity of the historical record. Throughout the course of the project – from its shaky inception in 1929 to the outbreak of the Second World War – there existed among its many advisers a subtext of criticism, dissent, and debate, which at times challenged the very foundations of British colonial rule in

---

[1] I would like to thank the editors and Nancy Leys Stepan for helpful comments on previous drafts.

[2] In their volume on the pertinence of Antonio Gramsci's concept of hegemony to colonial settings in India and Africa, Engels and Marks define it thus: hegemony 'suggests the ways in which colonial ideology served the ruling class by helping it to make their rule appear natural and legitimate; ... hegemonic colonial ideologies reflected the material and cultural conditions of both the dominant and dominated classes. To be successful, imperial hegemony had to come to terms with, incorporate and transform Indian and African values.' Dagmar Engels and Shula Marks (eds), *Contesting Colonial Hegemony: State and society in Africa and India* (London, British Academic Press, 1994), p. 3.

Africa. It was a project with multiple origins and a multiplicity of authors. An analysis that emphasised only those elements perceived to reify or increase colonial domination would be forced to ignore key shifts in colonial ideology which the Survey embraced and helped to codify. It would also overlook the fact that at this historical moment, following on the heels of the Great Depression, a series of alternative visions and models for colonial development were emerging in Africa that paid a great deal of attention to local conditions, needs, environments, and even knowledge.

The African Survey was initiated in Britain in 1929 to remedy the dearth of information relating to Africa as a whole.[3] By 1938, it had resulted in three official publications, amounting to over three thousand pages: *An African Survey* credited to Lord Hailey, *Science in Africa* by E.B. Worthington, and *Capital Investment in Africa* by S.H. Frankel.[4] At the time of its launch, the Survey's promoters argued that a comprehensive analysis of 'modern knowledge' regarding Africa would help to reconcile contradictory policies across the continent.[5] Throughout the 1930s, the project involved nearly three hundred scientists as advisers, many of whom had first-hand research experience in Africa. These individuals spanned nearly all the disciplines: meteorology, botany, soil science, geology, zoology, medicine (human and veterinary), nutrition, psychology, and anthropology. While several historians have discussed the African Survey in the context of development, native administration, and African affairs, they have often overlooked the scientific dimensions of the Survey's history, despite the fact that one of the official volumes, *Science in Africa*, was an encyclopedic survey of environmental, medical, and anthropological research.[6]

As John Hargreaves has noted, when the results of the Survey were published, they 'not only inspired signposts and stimuli to enquiry and problem-oriented research in all sorts of directions, but exercised a substantial liberalizing effect on official policy'.[7] The two greatest 'scientific' legacies of the African Survey were the creation of the Colonial Research Fund in 1940, which dramatically increased British support for applied science both in and on its colonies, and the consolidation of a network of research institutes in British East Africa following the Second World War.[8] By examining the scientific dimensions of the Survey's history, in conjunction with its relationship to trends in Africa itself, this chapter highlights both the transnational

[3] My analysis of the Survey's origins counters some of the arguments made by John Cell in his article, 'Lord Hailey and the Making of the African Survey', *African Affairs* 88 353 (1989): 481–505. Since these details are not immediately relevant to this paper I will not reiterate them here; they can be found in chapter 2 of my doctoral thesis, 'Africa as a "Living Laboratory" – The African Research Survey and the British Colonial Empire: Consolidating Environmental, Medical, and Anthropological Debates, 1920–1940', University of Oxford, 2001.

[4] Lord Hailey, *An African Survey* (London, OUP, 1938); E.B. Worthington, *Science in Africa: A review of scientific research relating to tropical and Southern Africa* (London, OUP, 1938); and S.H. Frankel, *Capital Investment in Africa: Its causes and effects* (London, OUP, 1938).

[5] Philip Kerr [Lord Lothian] to Frank Aydelotte, 14 November 1929, File 2792, Rhodes Trust Archives, Rhodes House Library, Oxford.

[6] See John Cell, 'Lord Hailey and the Making of the African Survey', and chapter 15 in *Hailey: A Study in British Imperialism, 1872–1969*, (Chapel Hill, NC, University of North Carolina Press, 1994); and also John Hargreaves, 'History: African and Contemporary', *African Research and Documentation*, 1 (1973), pp. 3–8; and Kenneth Robinson, 'Experts, Colonialists, and Africanists, 1895–1960', in J.C. Stone (ed.), *Experts in Africa* (Aberdeen, Aberdeen University African Studies Group, 1980), pp. 55–74.

[7] Hargreaves, 'History: African and Contemporary', p. 7.

[8] E.B. Worthington, *A Survey of Research and Scientific Services in East Africa, 1947–1956* (Nairobi, East Africa High Commission, no date [1952]).

nature of imperial knowledge production and the existence of intellectual traditions often dismissed or ignored in literature concerned to document the ways in which 'colonial scientists' 'misread' the African landscape.[9] Not only have historians fallen short in evaluating the Survey on its own terms, but they have also allowed research trends critical to the period – involving African agriculture, soils, health and disease, social anthropology, land planning, and scientific surveys – to go unnoticed.

This examination of the African Survey, then, is a case study of the research undertaken by environmental scientists and their effect on the overall orientation of the project.[10] It argues that this group – many of whom served in the agricultural service as ecologists, botanists, entomologists, zoologists, soil scientists, and even veterinarians – drew attention to the extreme regional heterogeneity and complexity of Africa's environments. Their emphasis on careful study of local knowledge simultaneously undermined more popular, pejorative opinions of Africans' practices and bridged the gap between 'indigenous' and imported cognitive frameworks. The 'scientific' studies they produced were thus often a blend of insights gained through unusual disciplinary training, on the one hand, and extended African experiences, on the other, creating an intellectual milieu surprisingly critical of past interventions. This new research laid the groundwork for socio-ecological critiques that in many respects culminated in the classic works by William Allan (*The African Husbandman*) and John Ford (*The Role of the Trypanosomiases in African Ecology*), both of whom began their research in British colonial Africa in the 1930s.[11] Central to their work was a recognition of Africans as active agents in the management of their environments; also pivotal was a set of insights concerning non-human nature garnered from ecological science. Both intellectual developments, this chapter argues, were a product of the inter-war engagement with Africa and gave credence to 'bottom-up' development strategies that were to exist in dynamic tension with such large-scale post-war endeavours as the Tanganyikan Groundnut scheme, the Green Revolution, and massive disease eradication campaigns. Scientists' active involvement in the African Survey not only prevented more exploitative colonial agendas from gaining sway, but simultaneously codified a transdisciplinary, humanistic approach to colonial development that continues to be overlooked and little understood in the secondary literature today.[12]

Epistemologies of science and empire: the 'machinery of knowledge', economic development, and inter-war research trends

Studies of Africa's colonial past must contend with rapid and, at times, extreme social, ecological, and epidemiological changes. The 'scramble for Africa' occurred during a period in human history when the technologies of Empire – steamships, railroads,

---

[9] See James Fairhead and Melissa Leach, *Misreading the African Landscape* (Cambridge, CUP, 1996); and Melissa Leach and Robin Mearns (eds), *The Lie of the Land: Challenging received wisdom on the African environment* (London, James Currey for the International African Institute, 1996).

[10] On medical and anthropological debates see chapters 5 and 6 of my thesis where I address nutrition, epidemiology, tropical medicine, eugenics, and social anthropology.

[11] Technically, Allan began work as an 'agricultural research officer' in Northern Rhodesia in 1928. Ford's first trip to Africa was in 1934 with a British Museum Expedition to East Africa; in 1938 he was appointed to a permanent post with the Tsetse Research Department in Tanganyika.

[12] An exception is Paul Richards, 'Reviving the Green Revolution: A Technographic Approach', in P. Hebinck

firearms, the telegraph, and quinine – were firmly established and part of a daily expansion of networks of power.[13] Coinciding with this, the ideology of *scientific colonialism* – or the view that African societies could be, in essence, socially engineered – was becoming widespread.[14] In fact, the formal colonisation of tropical Africa occurred at a time when the sciences themselves were professionalising at a rapid pace and generating new insights into the human and natural worlds.[15]

Recent histories of the relationship between science and empire have drawn attention to three central issues: the power colonialism conferred on science, the way in which the sciences were used as 'tools of empire', and finally, the agency of non-European peoples and places to shape the sciences. Many of these studies have under-scored the point that several disciplines were inextricably linked to imperial processes; practitioners in these fields in turn often benefited from asymmetrical relations of power. These patterns are especially pertinent for sciences of the field, such as anthropology, natural history, tropical medicine, and geography, to name only a few.[16] Travel, exploration, voyages of discovery and formal colonialism have all played a key role in creating what could be called *diasporas of science* across the globe.[17] A fourth theme, which has remained marginal in the secondary literature and which receives greater attention in this chapter, concerns the possibility that scientific epistemologies in colonial contexts at times served to alleviate, rather than reinforce, social and environmental 'hegemonies'.

The inter-war period marked the point in British colonial history when scientific experts first began to grapple extensively, and collectively, with African realities.[18] Through imperial research institutes, co-ordinating conferences, and expanding technical services across the territories, the British and colonial governments slowly

[12] (cont.) and G. Verschoor (eds), *Through the Thicket of Development: Theory, practice and the actor-oriented approach* (Assen: van Gorcum, 2001).

[13] Daniel Headrick, *The Tentacles of Progress: Technology Transfer in the Age of Imperialism, 1850–1940* (Oxford, OUP, 1988).

[14] Lucy Mair, 'Colonial Administration as a Science', *African Affairs*. 32 (1933), pp. 366–71.

[15] How this professionalisation occurred in the context of imperial processes is explored in Roy MacLeod (ed.), *Nature and Empire: Science and the colonial enterprise* (Chicago, University of Chicago Press, 2000) *OSIRIS*, v. 15; many more useful references on this theme can be found in the bibliography.

[16] See, for instance, Henrika Kuklick and Robert Kohler (eds), *Science in the Field* (Chicago, University of Chicago Press, 1996) *Osiris* v 11; Janet Browne, 'Biogeography and Empire', in N. Jardine, J.A. Secord and E.C. Spary (eds), *Cultures of Natural History* (Cambridge, CUP, 1996), pp. 305–21; Matthew H. Edney, *Mapping an Empire: The geographical construction of British India, 1765-1843* (Chicago, University of Chicago Press, 1997); Roy MacLeod and Philip Rhebock (eds), *Nature in Its Greatest Extent: Western science in the Pacific* (Honolulu, University of Hawaii Press, 1988); John MacKenzie (ed.), *Imperialism and the Natural World* (Manchester: Manchester University Press, 1990); Maryinez Lyons, *The Colonial Disease: A social history of sleeping sickness in Northern Zaire, 1900–1940* (Cambridge, CUP, 1992); and Megan Vaughan, *Curing Their Ills: Colonial power and African illness* (Cambridge, Polity Press, 1991).

[17] Two theoretical pieces which have influenced my thinking considerably on this point are Roy MacLeod's, 'On Visiting the "Moving Metropolis": Reflections on the Architecture of Imperial Science', *Historical Records of Australian Science* 5 (1982): 1–15; and Bruno Latour, 'Centres of Calculation', chapter 6 in *Science in Action* (Cambridge, MA, Harvard University Press, 1992), pp. 215–57.

[18] Joseph M. Hodge, 'Development and Science: British Colonialism and the Rise of the "Expert", 1895–1945', Ph.D. Thesis, Queen's University, Belfast (1999); and Michael Worboys, 'Science and British Colonial Imperialism, 1895–1940', Ph.D. Thesis, University of Sussex (1979).

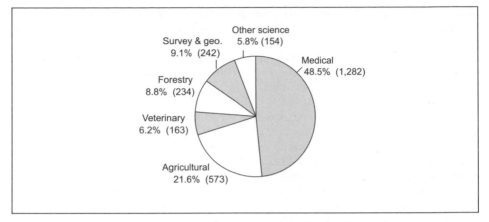

Figure 6.1 Colonial service recruitment 1920–1939 totals (n = 2,648)
(Source: Anthony Kirk-Greene, *On Crown Service* (London, I.B. Tauris 1999), pp. 22, 24, 26, & 37)

established an infrastructure for 'applied' research. One of the more important features of this infrastructure was the technical departments themselves, which dealt with the areas of medicine, agriculture, forestry, geology and land surveys, and game and veterinary concerns. Numerically, individuals in the technical services, and in the scattered array of research stations and institutes, represented an even thinner 'white line' in Africa than their administrative counterparts, being both unevenly and some-what randomly distributed.[19] Nonetheless, their ideas and actions could, and often did, have far-reaching effects.

For the promoters of the African Survey it was precisely this 'machinery of know-ledge' that they wanted to see augmented and co-ordinated more effectively. In their eyes, 'science' provided the key to solving 'general human and administrative problems'. An empirically grounded approach, they believed, would not only serve as a foundation for better-informed government policies, but would also lead to more rapid human 'progress'.[20] Among the inner circle of the African Survey were included some of the best known names of the period in relation to Africa (Lord Lugard and Joseph Oldham), imperial affairs (Lord Hailey, Reginald Coupland, William Ormsby-Gore, and Malcolm MacDonald), international politics (Lord Lothian, Lionel Curtis, and Sir Arthur Salter), and science (Sir Richard Gregory, Julian Huxley, John Boyd Orr, and Bronislaw Malinowski). To achieve a comprehensive picture of sub-Saharan Africa, these individuals called upon literally hundreds of professionals to consult on various pieces of the project. Although it was in principle an independent undertaking, in practice the Survey had close links with the British Colonial Office throughout; while these relations were at times uneasy and strained, they helped to ensure that the Survey's final recommendations had a direct link to decision-makers.

One of the distinguishing features of the African Survey was not only that its instigators were concerned from the start to incorporate the natural and social sciences

[19] See A.H.M. Kirk-Greene, 'The Thin White Line: the Size of the Colonial Service in Africa', *African Affairs*. 79 (1980), pp. 25–44.
[20] All quotations, [Joseph Oldham], 'African Research', no date [May 1931], GD40/17/121, Lothian Papers (LP), National Archives of Scotland.

into their analytical framework, but that they wished to use ecology, the science of 'super-coordination', as the primary bridge between these fields.[21] Julian Huxley, the evolutionary theorist, was insistent upon this point and played a key role in recruiting E.B. Worthington, a zoologist with 'a broad ecological outlook', who ultimately became the longest serving specialist on the project.[22] The preparatory work on science, in fact, far out-stripped all other areas of interest to the African Survey, including economics and 'native administration'. Unlike these other realms, Worthington's work warranted its own sub-committee, was allocated the largest share of the budget, and had at least three times the number of advisers. Even when there existed sharp disagreements among the protagonists regarding key issues, usually involving African versus settler rights,[23] all parties could still agree on the need to augment research facilities both in Britain and Africa. The African colonies, in their view, offered a 'unique laboratory' for scientific study and experiment.[24] Just what these 'experiments' would yield was in many respects the question they wished to answer.

There exists, however, an essential paradox of the inter-war period. Despite lofty rhetoric and ambitious plans, many proposals that would have coupled science and colonial development more concretely were unable to find their way into official policy, and several were in fact rejected outright. Even those that were approved often remained only partially implemented for want of funds.[25] This was true not only of the suggestion to create an integrated scientific and research service within the Colonial Office,[26] but also of a series of recommendations, endorsed by the participants at the 1927 Imperial Agricultural Research Conference, to establish a chain of research institutes within the colonial territories themselves.[27] On the one hand, colonial and African administrators increasingly endorsed the idea that scientific research was a necessary component of colonial statecraft; on the other, projects that would have ensured more systematic integration of such efforts usually faced enduring obstacles in practice. Britain, and its African territories, inadvertently continued to be 'reluctant patrons' of the sciences, even of those fields with explicit economic and sociological aims.[28]

Part of the problem lay in the sheer difficulty of co-ordinating research and applying

---

[21] Charles Elton to Julian Huxley, 9 March 1932, Box 2, File 4, Joseph Oldham Papers, Rhodes House Library, Oxford.

[22] Comments by Julian Huxley in 'Minutes of Meeting of African Research Survey, July 15 & 16 1933', Box 149, File 4, Lord Lugard Papers, Rhodes House Library. In my thesis I discuss the links between ecology and social anthropology as framing, panoptic sciences for the continent; my discussion here is limited to ecology.

[23] See, for instance, Joseph Oldham, *White and Black in Africa – A critical examination of the Rhodes lectures of General Smuts* (London, Longman, Green & Co, 1930) and Jan Smuts, *Africa and Some World Problems* (Oxford, Clarendon Press, 1930); also relevant is the debate between Margery Perham and Lionel Curtis, *The Protectorates of South Africa: the question of their transfer to the Union* (London, OUP, 1935).

[24] Philip Kerr *et al.*, 'Suggestions for an Institute of Government at Oxford', 1 July 1929, File 2792, 'Oxford University Institute of Government', Rhodes Trust Archives.

[25] Hodge, 'Development and Science', p. 358.

[26] *Summary of the First Colonial Office Conference.* Cmd. 2883 (1927).

[27] *Imperial Agricultural Research Conference, 1927 – Report and Summary of Proceedings* (London, HMSO, 1928), pp. 8–13, 223–6.

[28] Peter Alter, *The Reluctant Patron: Science and the State in Britain, 1850-1920* (Oxford, OUP, 1987) and Charles Jeffries (ed.), *A Review of Colonial Research, 1940-1960* (London, HMSO, 1964), p. 13.

its results across very different territories with equally different needs, a constraint often recognised by those involved.[29] Related to this was the fact that territorial governance, and by extension research, was overseen by separate administrative structures. This meant that regions like the Anglo-Egyptian Sudan, Southern Rhodesia, and the Union of South Africa achieved semi-autonomous status compared with the dependent territories that remained under the jurisdiction of the Colonial Office. The creation of the League of Nations further complicated colonial governance by adding the Mandate territories of Tanganyika, Togoland, and the Cameroons to Britain's imperial mix.[30] Such geopolitical dynamics made inter-territorial collaboration and co-ordination all the more difficult. It was largely a growing recognition of this fact that inspired the African Survey to be launched in the first place.

Research efforts were also stymied by the onset of the world economic depression during which recruitment for the technical services alone experienced a 92 per cent decline between 1929 and 1933.[31] Even with attempts to recover pre-Depression numbers, overall appointments in the 1930s were still 46 per cent lower than those of the 1920s. Such declines in appointments had a recognised effect on the capacities of colonial governments to conduct long-term applied research. As the nutritional scientist John Boyd Orr, one of the members of the Survey's general committee, observed, 'Primary producing countries [in Africa] have been practically bankrupt since 1931.'[32] The problem of widespread 'retrenchment and curtailed research,' according to Boyd Orr, had to be seen as just one by-product of a more serious and long-lasting financial crisis for the African territories.[33]

'Native agriculture,' soil science and tropical infertility

In the years preceding the First World War, the organisation of the technical services in British colonial Africa was a small-scale and *ad hoc* affair. Only in the early 1920s did colonial states and the British Government begin to expand and standardise the functions and operations of the various departments, with medicine and agriculture receiving the lion's share of attention. There were several driving ideologies behind these changes: the notion of the 'development of wealth', the idea of social 'improve-ment', the concept of trusteeship, and the parallel, though sometimes conflicting, aim of African paramountcy. Although it is tempting to view economic imperatives as the primary force behind 'colonial development', an examination of trends in the technical departments, which were ostensibly responsible for this work, reveals an equally strong

[29] See, for instance, the discussions on co-ordination of research for East Africa in the *Proceedings of Agricultural Research Conference Held at Amani Research Station, February 1931* (Nairobi, Government Printer, 1931); and *Conference on Tsetse and Trypanosomiasis (Animal and Human) Research*, Held at Entebbe, November 1933, (Nairobi, Government Printer, 1933).

[30] Michael D. Callahan, *Mandates and Empire: the League of Nations and Africa, 1914–1931* (Brighton, Sussex Academic Press, 1999).

[31] Anthony Kirk-Greene, *On Crown Service: A History of HM Colonial and Oversease Civil Services, 1837-1997* (London, I.B. Tauris, 1999), pp. 22, 24, 26, 37.

[32] John Boyd Orr to Hilda Matheson [for Scientific Sub-Committee meeting], no date [November or December 1935], LP, GD40/17/127.

[33] For an analysis of some of these trends, see the contributions in Ian Brown (ed.), *The Economies of Africa and Asia in the Inter-War Depression* (London, Routledge, 1989).

impulse to 'protect the precious lives of the native races' and 'to see that their native industries … [were] not destroyed by any extraordinary untried measures to open the country to British or foreign exploiters'.[34] This suspicion of 'selfish exploiter's capital' was itself a defining feature of the period, resulting from pre-war critiques of the Belgian Congo and post-war condemnations of 'economic imperialism'.[35]

By the time of the economic depression, which drew explicit attention to colonial treasuries and their declining profits, most of the dependent territories had already made Africans, at least in principle, their primary concern. To explore how this took place, and with what consequences, it will help to examine the activities of a single 'environmental' service in greater detail: the agriculture departments. Such an examination helps to reveal three intersecting developments of the inter-war period that became apparent to the African Survey itself as it undertook its own review of the continent: departmental emphasis on research into African cultivation techniques and crop types; burgeoning investigations of soils and fertility; and the adoption of concepts from ecological science in dealing both with African agriculture and with soils. While these trends do not appear to have predominated in all territories equally – Kenya, for instance, with its powerful settler population, proved an exception – their cumulative effects in non-settler territories were certainly visible by the mid-1930s.[36]

Agriculture departments began to pay greater attention to African 'husbandry' for a variety of reasons. In some cases, their intent was simply to increase primary production for export; in others, it was to expand upon the base of local production to prevent famines and raise domestic trade; in others still, it concerned more far-reaching issues of land tenure and settlement policies; many were also concerned with the issues of soil erosion and nutrition. The motives aside, this new approach produced an unintended, yet significant, consequence: it tempered more widely held opinions concerning Africans' 'wasteful' and 'unsound' practices. The pejorative view was perhaps most succinctly put by a businessman and settler in Kenya, Major E.S. Grogan. 'The African people,' he testified to the 1933 Kenya Land Commission 'have never established a symbiotic relationship with land. They are, in the strict scientific sense, parasites on the land, all of them.'[37]

Yet, when research scientists in the agriculture departments began to undertake their own investigations, they typically refuted such beliefs and strove to demonstrate that existing practices were not only sound, but even innovative and worth replicating. V.A. Beckley, Kenya's soil chemist, for instance, wrote in 1930 that while the 'methods of agriculture in the native reserves often are adversely criticized … [m]ore often than not, the methods employed are more suited to the conditions than those suggested; any change in methods would involve the use of manures and fertilizers, which at present are out of the reach of the native cultivator.'[38] H.R. Hosking, one of the botanists in Uganda's Department of Agriculture, offered a similar perspective: 'The question of improving native food crops is beset with difficulties. With long established crops it is probably true

[34] R.E. Dennett, 'Agricultural Progress in Nigeria', *African Affairs* 18 (1918–19), pp. 266–89.

[35] Dennett, 'Agricultural Progress', p. 289; see also Leonard Woolf, *Empire and Commerce in Africa: a study of economic imperialism* (London, Allen and Unwin, 1920).

[36] See Fiona Mackenzie, *Land, Ecology and Resistance in Kenya, 1880–1952* (London, Edinburgh University Press, 1998), especially chapter 4.

[37] Major E.S. Grogan, cited in Sir A. Daniel Hall, *The Improvement of Native Agriculture in Relation to Population and Public Health* (London, OUP, 1936), p. 29.

[38] V.A. Beckley, quoted in Mackenzie, *Land, Ecology and Resistance*, p. 104.

to say that the native can teach us more than we can teach him.'[39] On the subject of soil erosion, B.J. Hartley, a research officer in the Tanganyika territory, remarked that the 'Erok method of sowing a listed crop between the ridges carrying rotting crop residues is a development which would well repay investigation elsewhere under varying conditions of rainfall. Soil movement within the plot under this system is reduced to a minimum while at the same time loss from the terrace is adequately controlled.'[40] Perhaps the most unqualified endorsement of African practices came from the director of Northern Rhodesia's Agriculture Department, John Lewin, in an editorial written in 1932:

> Were a history of attempts to improve native agriculture written, it is certain that many passages would substantiate the truth of the proverb concerning the impetuosity of fools and the timidity of angels. Recognition of the inherent soundness, under natural conditions, of native agricultural practice has only become general in recent years. Practices apparently contrary to the accepted principles of good farming, usually prove on investigation to be the best possible in the circumstances under which the native cultivator works. Shifting cultivation is frequently condemned, yet what more easy method of raising food could be devised where cultivation is done by hand and abundance of land is available? ... [I]t behooves an agricultural department to investigate local practices with the utmost care before presuming to attempt to improve them.[41]

Lewin's orientation to African agriculture had been developed first in Nigeria where, as Paul Richards has documented, the Agriculture Department had undergone a marked transition in the 1920s away from 'concentration on export cash crops with little or no thought for indigenous food supply', and towards 'a greater emphasis on peasant farmer food crops and farming systems'.[42] Richards credits these changes to the outlook of the department's director, Odin Faulkner, who had been appointed in 1921 direct from work in India where 'peasant agriculture' had been under systematic investigation since the turn of the century.[43] In 1933, Faulkner and the assistant director, James Mackie, published a volume on *West African Agriculture* in which they summarised much of the research done to date and echoed the comments made by Lewin on the importance of building upon existing (African) practices rather than substituting entirely new ones.[44]

Faulkner and Mackie were particularly critical of Agriculture Departments that had attempted to secure 'quick returns' by the adoption of 'new crops' without first studying 'local farming and local conditions': 'Europeans have gone much further than

---

[39] H.R. Hosking, 'The Improvement of Native Food Crop Production by Selection and Breeding in Uganda', *East African Agricultural Journal* 4 (1938), p. 84.

[40] B.J. Hartley, 'An Indigenous System of Soil Protection', *East African Agricultural Journal* 4 (1938), p. 66.

[41] Editorial, *Second Annual Bulletin*, Agricultural Department of Northern Rhodesia (Livingstone, Government Printer, 1932), pp. 3–4; also see U.J. Moffat, 'Native Agriculture in the Abercorn District', *Second Annual Bulletin*, pp. 55–62; Moffat's study, discussed below, formed the basis of Lewin's editorial.

[42] Paul Richards, *Indigenous Agricultural Revolution – Ecology and food production in West Africa* (London, Hutchinson, 1985), p. 19.

[43] On India's influence on the Nigerian Agricultural Department, see *The West Africa Commission, 1938-39, Technical Reports* (London, Leverhulme Trust, 1943), pp. 31–3.

[44] O.T. Faulkner and J.R. Mackie, *West African Agriculture* (Cambridge, CUP, 1933); the book was written 'especially for candidates for Government service in West Africa in the Administrative and Agricultural Departments', p. vii.

merely to suggest, and have recommended, advised, persuaded, almost forced, the
farmer to adopt their proposals, often without having first attempted to ascertain
whether they were acceptable to him.' Many such efforts were 'a complete failure' and
caused the 'native farmer' to have a 'justifiable suspicion of all new ideas'. They
warned, further, of the 'great dangers' in creating dependence upon single permanent
crops that would be vulnerable both to fluctuating international markets and to local
'pests and disease'.[45] So significant was Faulkner and Mackie's book to African affairs,
that it was immediately included in a list of books of 'first importance' for Malcolm
Hailey to read when he assumed the role of director of the African Research Survey in
1933.[46]

Emphasis on African agricultural methods in the inter-war period coincided with a
second development for the British African territories: the introduction of soil scientists
to the ranks of agriculture departments. Much has been written on the question of soil
erosion, and in particular, on the colonial state's use of the threat of erosion to intervene
in the lives of its African subjects.[47] Very little, however, has been written on the subject
of research into African soil conditions by soil scientists themselves. The 'soil' had
been a unit of analysis within agricultural science since the early nineteenth century. It
was not until the 1920s, however, that the discipline of soil science, or pedology, came
into its own on the international stage.[48] This professionalisation coincided not only
with a similar trend in tropical agriculture, but also in tropical or 'imperial' forestry. A
lynchpin question for all three applied sciences was what created the conditions of
optimum fertility. The tropics had long been depicted as a region of abundant
vegetation.[49] Yet attempts to produce high yield cash crops in the tropics often met with
biological and economic failure. William Nowell, the Director of the Amani East
African Agricultural Research Institute in Tanganyika, made just this point during an
address to the Royal Society of the Arts in 1934.[50] For more than thirty years, he told
his audience, both the Germans and the British had been attempting to develop coffee
plantations in East Africa. While some efforts met with success, attempts in the
Usambaras and Rungwe districts in Tanganyika, among other places, proved to be
'puzzling' and 'expensive failures ... under what seemed highly favourable conditions'.
Amani was charged with the task of unravelling this puzzle. What they discovered was

[45] Faulkner and Mackie, *West African Agriculture*, pp. 3–4, 7, 41–2.
[46] Joseph Oldham [in consultation with Julian Huxley and William Macmillan] to Sir Malcolm Hailey, 19 July 1933, Oldham Papers, Box 1, File 3.
[47] See, for instance, David Anderson, 'Depression, Dust Bowl, Demography, and Drought: the Colonial State and Soil Conservation in East Africa in the 1930s', *African Affairs* 83 (1984), pp. 321–43; William Beinart, 'Soil Erosion, Conservation, and Ideas about Development: A Southern African Exploration, 1900–1960', *JSAS* 11 (1984), pp. 52–83; Kate Showers, 'Soil Erosion in the Kingdom of Lesotho: Origins and Colonial Response, 1830s–1950s', *JSAS* 15 (1989), pp. 263–85; and Michael Stocking, 'Soil Conservation Policy in Colonial Africa', *Agricultural History* 59 (1985), pp. 148–61.
[48] See I.A. Krupenikov, *History of Soil Science: From its inception to the present* (Rotterdam, Brookfield, 1993); Dan Yaalon and Simon Berkowicz (eds), *History of Soil Science: International perspectives* (Reiskirchen, Catena Verlag, 1997); and *Fifty Years Progress in Soil Science*, Special Volume, *Geoderma* 12, 4 (1974).
[49] On the French context see Christophe Bonneuil, 'Crafting and Disciplining the Tropics – Plant Science in the French Colonies', in John Krige and Dominique Pestre (eds), *Science in the Twentieth Century* (Amsterdam, Harwood Academic Publishers, 1997), pp. 77–96.
[50] William Nowell, 'The Agricultural Research Station at Amani', *Journal of the African Society* 33 (1934), pp. 1–20.

that the East African territories exhibited such 'extreme variations in soil and climate' that it 'localised both the problems and the value of experience in dealing with them'. Only when Geoffrey Milne, Amani's soil scientist, undertook a chemical study of soil acidities was it ascertained that the Tanganyikan failures had to do with 'the high acidity of the soil' which in turn caused unfavourable adaptations in coffee plants' root systems.[51]

During the inter-war period, these failures were beginning to be openly acknowledged, and their causes more systematically investigated. Ultimately, it was the fallacy of tropical fertility to which many researchers wished to draw attention:

> [L]and, even if the soil *per se* is very poor, in most cases brings good harvest at first due to the nutrient reserves accumulated over centuries and millennia. Catastrophe sets in usually during the third or fourth harvest. Numerous abandoned plantations in almost all colonial countries serve as vivid proof of what has been said…. More than 75% of all disasters suffered in tropical and sub-tropical agricultural enterprises must be related to improper selection of the soil. In the tropics and subtropics where the external appearance is quite misleading and confusing, only a thorough acquaintance with soil science can protect the farmer from grievous errors entailing great material losses.[52]

Yet, it was precisely knowledge of the soil that African populations seemed to possess already. In a letter to the editor of *Nature* in September of 1936, Milne, commenting on the great variety of African soils, observed that 'some six or seven of the main types are of sufficiently general occurrence [in Tanganyika] … to have given rise to a well-developed soil nomenclature in the Sukuma language'.[53] In a more comprehensive analysis undertaken as part of the Ecological Survey of Northern Rhodesia, Colin Trapnell and J.N. Clothier observed that there was a close correlation between 'vegetation types and agricultural practice'. 'In particular it was found,' they wrote, 'that native agriculture is built up upon a very definite method of choice of land, which is expressed in the use of certain trees and grasses as indicators of soil potentialities.'[54] Calling this knowledge 'intuitive ecology', Trapnell and Clothier were quick to stress that it depended on a high degree of self-determination which, once disrupted by European intervention, was difficult to recover. They also noted that such agricultural knowledge co-existed with elaborate social practices such as 'a surprisingly developed trade system' and a complex gender division of labour.[55] For beneficial economic development to occur, they argued, such agricultural and trading practices would need to be well-understood.

That same year, Northern Rhodesia's soil chemist, H.B. Stent, published an article

[51] *Ibid.*, pp. 6, 8.

[52] Paul Vageler, from his 1935 volume (in German) *Basic Concepts of Soils of the Subtropical and Tropical Countries* quoted in Krupenikov, *History of Soil Science*, p. 250; also see Vageler, *An Introduction to Tropical Soils* (London, Macmillan, 1933). Vageler worked as a soil scientist in German East Africa before the First World War.

[53] G. Milne, 'Normal Erosion as a Factor in Soil Profile Development', *Nature* 138 (Sept 1936), pp. 548–9, quotation, p. 549.

[54] C. Trapnell and J.N. Clothier, 'Report of the Ecological Survey for 1933', *Annual Report for the Year 1933*, Department of Agriculture, Northern Rhodesia, pp. 23–7, quotation on p. 23.

[55] Trapnell and Clothier, 'Report of the Ecological Survey', p. 25. Also see Henrietta Moore and Megan Vaughan, *Cutting Down Trees: Gender, nutrition, and agricultural change in the Northern Province of Zambia, 1890–1990* (London: James Currey, 1994), especially chapter 2.

on the 'chitemene' system of agriculture.[56] Chitemene was the name Bemba-speaking people gave to a method of shifting cultivation that relied heavily on cutting and burning trees in circular sites prior to cultivation; considered a technique of 'slash and burn' by many colonial administrators, it had been under attack as inefficient and wasteful. To test these views, Unwin Moffat, the agricultural officer for the Abercorn District, initiated, in 1928, a series of 'experimental plots' in which 'native methods' and 'local cultural details could be imitated'.[57] Although he was concerned that the practice of chitemene could exacerbate deforestation and soil erosion, especially in the context of the limited space of 'native reserves,' he also recorded that the initial results seemed to indicate that there were many benefits from the burning process itself.

Moffat's approach was to compare three different agricultural methods: one following the European, or 'normal,' practice of straight-line cropping, a second mimicking the mound-cropping and fallow-rotation techniques of the Mambwe peoples, and a third reproducing chitemene practices. The results were startling. The crop yields for the straight-line test plots, compared to chitemene, were 'markedly inferior'; the latter produced a yield of 1,200 pounds per acre while the former produced only 400.[58] The mound method proved more productive, but even these plots were outstripped by the chitemene plots by an average of 500 pounds per acre. After preliminary tests on the effects of particular fertilisers, artificial and organic, Moffat conjectured that burning produced certain changes in the soil composition and rid the plots of the seeds that caused weeds. His study was inconclusive, however, with respect to the actual fertilising effect of burning and for that reason, Stent was called upon to formulate a new experiment. Once again, the results were fascinating. '[T]he phosphate and potash status of these soils,' Stent reported, 'is appreciably enhanced by the process of wood burning.... [T]he ash from the burning does add large quantities of mineral plant food' and causes a 'beneficial effect which shows itself in an increased mineral content in the grain and consequently in the improved dietetic properties in the meal, which forms the staple food of the people.'[59] These findings only reinforced the Agricultural Department's belief that 'the best and most natural way for introducing any improved methods should be by using [Africans'] own established methods as a basis on which to build'.[60]

Recognition of tropical Africa's soil deficiencies, defined in terms of low fertility, was an important product of British pedologists' and agriculturalists' research in the 1920s and 1930s. At least among this population, optimistic rhetoric concerning Africa's agricultural potential was noticeably dampened and was often replaced with subtle critiques of existing European thought and practice. A former mycologist from the Nigerian Agriculture Department, G. Howard Jones, wrote a book on 'native farming on the West African Coast', in which he noted that early

> explorers spoke of the intensely fertile virgin soils of West Africa which they implied were the cause of the prolific vegetable growth that they saw everywhere towering in masses

[56] H.B. Stent, 'Observations on the Fertilizer Effect of Wood Burning in the "Chitemene" System', *Third Annual Bulletin – Agricultural Department of Northern Rhodesia* (Livingstone, Government Printer, 1933), pp. 48–9; the spelling 'chitemene', rather than citemene, is used to be consistent.

[57] Moffat, 'Native Agriculture in the Abercorn District', p. 55.

[58] The particular crop was *eleusine coracana* or finger millet.

[59] Stent, 'Observations on the Fertilizer Effect of Wood Burning', p. 49.

[60] Moffat, 'Native Agriculture in the Abercorn District', p. 55.

around them. One would not suggest that it is yet possible to measure the fertility of a soil with absolute accuracy, but researches have certainly shown that tropical soils, as assessed by modern methods, are not in themselves remarkable for their richness.... [O]ne must realise that in comparing the yields of temperate and tropical crop plants one is dealing with things which are not properly comparable.[61]

Taking these themes into a discussion of the causes of soil erosion at the second conference of Colonial Directors of Agriculture in 1938, John Lewin noted that the papers presented seemed to show, contrary to popular opinion, that 'erosion was almost invariably due primarily not to the native but to the European who had introduced tillage in certain areas and had encouraged the production of economic crops'.[62]

Critiques of agricultural policies and practices were thus made along two fronts. The first was directed at European and settler misconceptions of tropical agricultural fertility. While researchers in the technical services maintained the importance of agriculture for African economies, they challenged the ease with which such financial rewards could be reaped. In fact, they argued, African soils varied greatly in different environments.[63] To assume that methods that worked in one locale could be replicated across all territories was erroneous. The second critique was both sociological and ontological: if current African agricultural practices had been adapted to different natural conditions and if the philosophy of indirect rule prescribed a certain degree of respect for such practices, then improvements of 'native agriculture' should be built upon the best of what already existed. Both critiques were reflected in the pages of *Science in Africa* and *An African Survey* and helped to legitimate, in the imperial metropole, developments that were already under way in Africa. 'The African tradition of cultivation,' concluded the *Survey*, 'teaches methods of rotation of crops, of usage of soils, and means of fertilization and even sometimes anti-erosion measures, which, though they may not be suited to modern demands on the soil, are often well adapted to the prevailing conditions of labour and climate.'[64] E.B. Worthington's summary offered a more resounding endorsement of African practices and in many respects reflected the insights of agriculture departments' recent research.

The soil-vegetation unit as a controlling factor in environment is only now being recognized by scientists, but it is significant that the Africans themselves still know more about it than we, for every cultivator bases his selection of plots for different crops on recognized associations between certain plants and certain types of soil. The deterioration and erosion of soil is perhaps the best example of any to show the rapidity of environmental change. This likewise has been recognized by African farmers for centuries, and on it have been built up the complicated systems of shifting cultivation which so admirably suit the soils and climate, provided the area of land is sufficiently large. There are many examples of individual tribes which have apparently evolved methods of avoiding soil erosion which could hardly be bettered by science.[65]

[61] G. Howard Jones, *The Earth Goddess – A study of native farming on the West African coast* (London, Longmans, Green & Co, 1936), pp. 43–4.

[62] *Report of the Proceedings of the Conference of Colonial Directors of Agriculture, Colonial Office, July 1938* (London, HMSO, 1938), p. 42.

[63] See, for example, G. Milne et al., *A Provisional Soil Map of East Africa, Amani Memoirs* (London, Crown Agents, 1936).

[64] Hailey, *An African Survey*, p. 881.

[65] Worthington, *Science in Africa*, pp. 7–8.

Just how these insights were folded into a wider 'scientific' framework for colonial development is explored below.

Ecological science, natural resources, and the complexity of African environments

Scholars concerned with Africa are, by now, accustomed to hearing that 'expert knowledge', during the colonial era, served to undermine 'ecological specificity' and African 'survival strategies'.[66] A familiar criticism of this specialist knowledge was that it ignored divergences between European and African environments and gave undue authority to scientific epistemologies which rested on faulty or flawed premises. While these patterns certainly did occur, and were perhaps most significant with respect to gendered divisions of knowledge production,[67] this paper argues that they were accompanied by complementary trends in which researchers worked to 'discover', scientifically, what was 'rational' or 'sound' about indigenous practices. This process depended heavily on 'localising knowledge' and challenging the universal applicability of agricultural and environmental interventions. It also necessitated that the 'colonisers' pay much more attention to Africans' 'traditional knowledge'. One of the sciences that grew in tandem with these trends was ecology.

In his professional memoirs, E.B. Worthington wrote that 'one way or another, [the African Survey] initiated a good deal of ecological thinking and the application of ecological principles. This was related not only to the biological sciences, but also to the development of natural resources and to the affairs of mankind.'[68] Ironically, few historians have ever noted this dimension of the African Survey's work.[69] The interest in ecological science was an enduring feature of the Survey's history and came from both scientific and administrative quarters. More to the point, a critical mass of Worthington's advisers, including individuals in the technical services as well as Fellows of the Royal Society, were early adherents to this newly crystallising field.[70]

The way in which Britain's colonial apparatus embraced ecological science in the twentieth century has only just begun to be explored.[71] Like the institutionalisation of

---

[66] Expert knowledge here includes the activities of all technical officers, not solely researchers; for these critiques see J. Ford, *The Role of the Trypanosomiases in African Ecology: A Study of the Tsetse Fly Problem* (Oxford, Clarendon Press, 1971); Helge Kjekshus, *Ecology Control and Economic Development in East African History: the case of Tanganyika, 1850–1950* (Berkeley, University of California Press, 1977); Douglas Johnson and David Anderson (eds), *The Ecology of Survival: Case studies from Northeast African history* (London, Lester Cook Academic Publishing, 1988); Fairhead and Leach, *Misreading the African Landscape*; Richards, *Indigenous Agricultural Revolution*; and Mackenzie, *Land, Ecology and Resistance in Kenya*.

[67] Moore and Vaughan, *Cutting Down Trees*, and Mackenzie, *Land, Ecology, and Resistance in Kenya*.

[68] E.B. Worthington, *The Ecological Century: A personal appraisal* (Oxford, Clarendon Press, 1983), p. 36.

[69] An important exception is Peder Anker, *Imperial Ecology: Environmental Order in The British Empire, 1895–1945* (Cambridge, CUP, 2002), pp. 214–18.

[70] Of Worthington's 275 advisers, 21 were members of the British Ecological Society; their influence, however, was disproportionate to their actual numbers, in large part because Worthington himself adopted ecological methods and was assisted actively by the field's promoters including Arthur Tansley, Charles Elton, Julian Huxley, Robert Troup, Charles Swynnerton, John Phillips, and Colin Trapnell.

[71] Anker, *Imperial Ecology*; Libby Robin, 'Ecology: a science of Empire?' [on Australia] in Tom Griffiths and Libby Robin (eds), *Ecology and Empire: Environmental history of settler societies* (Edinburgh, Keele

science itself, the process increased in pace in the 1920s and saw the initial fruits of its labours throughout much of the 1930s. The importance of South Africa to this process is undeniable if only for the scale of research undertaken there. Other African territories, however, such as Tanganyika, Uganda, Northern Rhodesia, the Gold Coast, and Nigeria were also important and have either been overlooked or have been examined without an historical appreciation of the novelty of the research. In these locations, work was done not just on agriculture, forests, and pastures, subjects which have been most thoroughly explored in the history of ecology, but also on insects, parasites, and disease. The inter-war period in these territories saw a transition from 'amateur' to 'professional' ecologist, but, perhaps more significant, it also marked the advent of medical ecology and ecological entomology.

Ecology was still a young and fragmented scientific discipline at the start of the 1930s. It was arguably most established in Great Britain and the United States – where the British Ecological Society and the Ecological Society of America had been founded (in 1913 and 1915, respectively) – but it had active adherents, often working in very different intellectual and research traditions, in Soviet Russia, France, Sweden, Germany, the Netherlands, Australia, New Zealand, South Africa, and India.[72] The new discipline's nineteenth-century antecedents were heterogeneous, ranging from botany, natural history, and biogeography, on the one hand, to marine biology, zoology, entomology, and even epidemiology and medical geography on the other.[73] In the early decades of the field's history (1890-1910), however, its proponents began to highlight those properties of ecological science that they argued distinguished it from other disciplines. The broad consensus seemed to be that ecology was the study of the adaptation and interdependence of organisms in relation to their surrounding environ-ments. Unlike practitioners in many other disciplines, such as morphology, anatomy, zoology, and physiology, who at the turn of the century conducted most of their work in laboratories and museums, adherents to ecology often justified their activities on the basis of work in the 'field': in the realm of nature itself.

Arguably one of the most meaningful properties of the burgeoning field was its emphasis, again working against the dominant trends in science, of trans-disciplinary and synthetic research. At just the time when scientific specialization was increasing at a rapid pace, ecological science was being positioned to 'unite originally separate branches of science in a new and natural doctrine.'[74] 'More perhaps than any other

[71] (cont.) University Press, 1997); and Thomas Dunlap, *Nature and the English Diaspora: Environment and History in the United States, Canada, Australia, and New Zealand* (Cambridge, CUP, 1999).

[72] To provide a full list of sources would be impractical; see Douglas Weiner, *Models of Nature: Ecology, conservation, and cultural revolution in Soviet Russia* (Bloomington, Indiana University Press, 1988); Kaat Schulte Fischedick, 'Practices and Pluralism: A Socio-Historical Analysis of Early Vegetation Science, 1900–1950', PhD Thesis, University of Amsterdam (1995); Gregg Mitman, *The State of Nature: Ecology, community, and American social thought, 1900–1950* (Chicago, University of Chicago Press, 1992); Thomas Söderqvist, *The Ecologists: From merry naturalists to saviours of the nation* (Stockholm, Almqvist and Wiksell, 1986); and Malcolm Nicolson, 'The Development of Plant Ecology, 1790–1960', Ph.D. Thesis, University of Edinburgh (1984).

[73] Robert McIntosh, *The Background of Ecology: Concept and theory* (New York, Cambridge University Press, 1985); few historians of ecology have yet explored the epidemiological connections.

[74] Oscar Drude, 'The Position of Ecology in Modern Science', in Howard J. Rogers (ed.), *Congress of Arts and Science – Universal Exposition, St Louis, 1904, v. 5,* (Cambridge, MA, Riverside Press, 1906), pp. 177–90, quotation on p.190.

branch of biological investigation,' asserted one of its early promoters, ecology 'calls for the most varied and thorough preparation.'[75] Given the broad canvas ecology was asked to cover, it was small wonder that some contemporaries, in reviewing its scope, could comment that 'the boundaries of this science are a little hard to delimit'.[76]

Questions over what constituted appropriate units of analysis in ecological studies were at the core of several debates in the 1920s and 1930s. In this context, terms like equilibrium, balance, succession, and system took on multiple meanings and were themselves quite flexible. Attempts to fix nomenclature were no less important to ecological efforts than they were to other emerging disciplines and occupied a central place at national and international meetings.[77] Such debates notwithstanding, a general consensus among the participants did exist with respect to the overwhelming complexity of their studies. As Charles Elton expressed it in his book *Animal Ecology*, 'Any ecological problem which is really worth working upon at all, is constantly leading the worker on to neighboring subjects, and is constantly enlarging his view of the extent and variety of … life, and of the numerous ways in which one problem in the field interacts with another.'[78]

Calls by British and South African scientists for greater attention to Africa's 'ecology' and for 'ecological surveys' developed considerable momentum in the 1920s and were part of a wider appeal for naturalists to serve the British Empire.[79] By the early 1930s, these calls were consolidated into a single article by the South African, John Phillips, who was then Assistant Director and Ecologist for the Tsetse Research Department in Tanganyika. One of the 'principal scientific objects' of Phillips' proposal was to 'evolve the methods of ecological investigation best suited to the conditions holding in Africa'. His suggested 'research programme' aimed to be inter-disciplinary and comprehensive, yet still pragmatic, '[k]eeping in touch with the broader needs of agriculture, officers concerned with pasture management, veterinary work and forestry'.[80] At precisely the same time, two of Phillips' British colleagues, Huxley and Elton, were proposing to establish a 'Bureau of African Ecology' as part of an Institute of African Studies at the University of Oxford. Like Phillips, they envisaged a broad cross-section of investigations that would address 'the scientific problems of Tropical Africa' and 'give advice in connection with regional and territorial surveys if undertaken by colonial governments in Africa'.[81] Such a bureau would operate both as a clearing-house for information on 'African ecology' and would also 'correlate' new research in order to present a more comprehensive picture of the entire continent. While both proposals sparked considerable interest among a handful

[75] V.M. Spalding, 'The Rise and Progress of Ecology', *Science* 17 (1903), pp. 201–10, quotation on p. 205.
[76] Walter Taylor, 'What is Ecology and What Good is It?', *Ecology* 17 (1936), pp. 333–46, quotation on p. 334.
[77] See, for instance, discussions at the International Botanical Congress (1930) at which a committee was established to attain 'general agreement on some of the more important concepts and terms'. F.T. Brooks and T.F. Chipp (eds), *Report of Proceedings of Int'l Botanical Congress*; also Anker, *Imperial Ecology*, pp. 131–5.
[78] Charles Elton, *Animal Ecology* (London, Sidgwick and Jackson, 1927), p. 188.
[79] See, for instance, several of the contributions in A.G. Tansley and T.F. Chipp (eds), *Aims and Methods in the Study of Vegetation* (London, British Empire Vegetation Committee, 1927).
[80] John Phillips, 'Ecological Investigation in South, Central and East Africa: Outline of a Progressive Scheme', *Journal of Ecology* 19 (1931), pp. 474–82, quotations on pp. 474 and 480.
[81] Julian Huxley, 'A Proposal for a Bureau of Ecology for Africa', April 1930, Folder 3 16/26d, 'African Research Survey', Royal Institute of International Affairs, London.

of scientists and administrators, neither was able to overcome the financial and institutional obstacles necessary for success.[82] What they did prompt, however, was the less permanent, but equally far-reaching survey of scientific research undertaken, from an 'ecological' point of view, by E.B. Worthington for the African Survey.

By the time Worthington's work was fully under way in 1934, a trickle of ecological research had begun to appear in annual reports, scientific periodicals, and conference proceedings: the very texts Worthington himself was examining. Besides several independent studies on forestry, agriculture, and tsetse flies in West Africa,[83] three large-scale research projects in East and Central Africa were already making significant contributions to the subject: the Amani Agricultural Research Institute and the Tsetse Research Department (both in Tanganyika), and the Ecological Survey of Northern Rhodesia. All three were state-supported endeavours designed to shed light on appropriate measures for improved economic development; all were also committed to the principle of scientific 'team-work'.[84] What makes these endeavours so relevant to the African Survey is that several of their leading staff – Charles Swynnerton, Geoffrey Milne, and Colin Trapnell – all served as advisers to Worthington during his tenure with the project and shared with him an interest 'to realize Africa as a single entity ... [of] closely inter-related parts'.[85] Their respective reports, most of which were published in 1936 and 1937, formed an important cornerstone for a burgeoning, if relatively unco-ordinated, tradition of 'scientific surveys' in colonial Africa, which concentrated not just on agriculture, natural resources or land management, but also on human health and social organisation.[86]

The 'ecological' units of analysis for each organisation differed in several respects. Amani's researchers developed their expertise primarily in vegetation and soil studies, although the ornithologist and librarian, R.E. Moreau, was particularly keen to examine relationships between climate, vegetation, and fauna, while the botanist, Peter Greenway, developed the first Swahili/English botanical dictionary, which made important links between African botanical knowledge and medical practices.[87] The Tsetse Research Department, on the other hand, concerned itself with the 'dynamic ecology' and 'inter-relations of the fly, plant, and animal communities, and the physical environment,' and thus paid a great deal of attention to population fluctuations and

[82] For reactions in the Colonial Office, which were largely negative on financial and institutional grounds, see CO/847/2/1 and CO847/4/2, Public Records Office (PRO), London.

[83] See, for instance, T. F. Chipp, *The Gold Coast Forest; a study in synecology* (Oxford, Oxford Forestry Memoirs, 1927); A.S. Thomas, 'The Dry Season in the Gold Coast and its Relation to the Cultivation of Cacao', *Journal of Ecology* 20 (1932): 263–9; and J.R. Ainslie, 'Forestry and tsetse control in Northern Nigeria', *Empire Forestry Journal* 13 (1934): 39–44.

[84] The early history of each can be found in CO691/91/8, CO533/601, and CO795/34/2, PRO.

[85] Comments by G.A.S. Northcote after hearing Worthington's presentation of his research on 'The Lakes of Kenya and Uganda', *Geographical Journal* 79 (1932), pp. 275–97, quotation on p. 294.

[86] In addition to 'ecological' surveys, there were also agricultural, geological, forestry, nutrition, health and hygiene, and sociological surveys.

[87] The list of Amani publications is too extensive to detail here; for Peter Greenway see *A Swahili Botanical English Dictionary of Plant Names* (Amani, East African Agricultural Station, 1937); also Greenway, 'Report of a Botanical Survey of the Indigenous and Exotic Plants in Cultivation at the East African Agricultural Station, Amani, Tanganyika Territory, from fieldwork, September 1928 – January 1933', unpublished manuscript, June 1934, Kenya Agricultural Research Institute Library, Muguga, Kenya; and Greenway, 'The vegetation of Mpwapwa, Tanganyika Territory', *Journal of Ecology* 21 (1933), pp. 28–43.

migrations.[88] Finally, the Ecological Survey of Northern Rhodesia 'extended the application of ecology to native crops and agricultural customs and ... to native agricultural development,' and was intended to be as much about human as 'natural' conditions in the territory.[89]

The studies produced by each of these organisations, however, defy simple categorisation since all were conscious attempts to bridge disciplinary boundaries.[90] It was this feature of their research that often drew commentators' attention. 'The Tsetse Research Team,' observed Nigeria's director of the Medical Services in 1929, had undertaken a programme that was 'objective, dynamic, comprehensive, balanced, the outcome of the vision sufficiently broad, sufficiently penetrating'.

> *[A]ny attempt to lessen the conceptional scope of the investigation, would result in a general weakening of the possibility of the team's ultimate success....* A concept embracing [a] purely pathological, histological, veterinary, medical, or entomological basis of research it is believed, would fail to achieve more than a fraction of that knowledge which the biological-ecological concept outlined in this communication should lay before us.[91]

Likewise, the technical advisers to the West African Commission of 1938–9 referred with praise to the 'pioneering work undertaken by C.G. Trapnell and J.N. Clothier' and proposed a similar scheme of ecological surveys for West Africa. 'We have in mind,' they wrote,

> something much more far-reaching than the mere co-ordinating and filing of an indigestible mass of facts. We regard the central purpose of the proposed organisation as the ecological interpretation of the country and its mode of life.... This type of work has the great merit that it utilises the same kind of observations as the native uses instinctively in assessing the value of land. It is able to use local tradition and to employ African assistants to do work for which they are already well qualified.[92]

The need for such surveys was not lost on Worthington as he wrote his early drafts of *Science in Africa*. In his chapter on botany, he asserted that 'the only way to produce ... a good knowledge of the natural resources of Africa,' on which appropriate economic development depended, was through 'ecological surveys'. These would consist not only of careful elucidation of relationships between 'soil-vegetation units' but also of 'native agriculture ... and animal husbandry [which were] among the most

---

[88] 'Research on Tsetse Fly Control in Africa', *Journal of Ecology* 10 (1929), pp. 359–60, quotation on p. 359.

[89] C. Trapnell and J.N. Clothier, *The Soils, Vegetation and Agricultural Systems* (Lusaka, Government Printer, 1957), p. ix.

[90] See G. Milne, 'A Provisional Soil Map of East Africa', *Amani Memoirs* (London, 1936); C.F.M. Swynnerton, *The Tsetse Flies of East Africa: A first study of their ecology with a view to their control* (London, Royal Entomological Society, 1936); and Trapnell and Clothier, *The Soils, Vegetation and Agricultural Systems*.

[91] W.B. Johnson, *Notes Upon a Journey Through Certain Belgian, French and British African Dependencies to Observe General Medical Organisation and Methods of Trypanosomiasis Control* (Lagos, Gov't Printer, 1929), p. 38; emphasis in original.

[92] H.C. Sampson and E.M. Crowther, 'Crop Production and Soil Fertility Problems', *West Africa Commission, 1938-39 – Technical Reports*, p. 53 and more generally, 'Ecological Survey', pp. 52–4.

[93] Worthington, second draft of chapter 5, 'Botany', *Science in Africa* (London: African Research Survey, no date), pp. 95 and 99; in Royal Institute of International Affairs archives.

important natural factors in African ecology'.[93] By the time he published his final book in 1938, he had come to realise that the only way to reflect the natural and social complexity of the continent was through an 'ecological' framework. 'The picture really presented by Africa,' he wrote, 'is one of movement, all branches of physical, biological and human activity reacting on each other, to produce what biologists would refer to as an ecological complex.'[94]

Ecologically appropriate development and
Worthington's contribution to the African Research Survey

Given what is now known about the way in which both volumes *Science in Africa* as well as *An African Survey* were produced, with hundreds of advisers who had several opportunities to comment on and criticise the content, it should come as little surprise that a tone of moderation pervades these texts. The process itself was one which discouraged easy generalisations, sweeping solutions, and unfounded claims. It forced the authors to stress particularity, local specificity, and heterogeneity in African conditions. The *Survey*'s contributors and advisers negotiated among various strands of scientific research, public opinion, and official conviction to arrive at their conclusions. They skirted between dominant and dissenting views on almost every issue, crafting unexpectedly moderate positions given their proximity to the centres of colonial power. This pattern reflected a broader characteristic of the inter-war period in Britain during which the drive to control and improve colonial Africa's natural and human environments was tempered by a sensitivity to the immediate and long-term consequences, and particularly to a recognition of past failures. 'The exaggerated beliefs' in 'natural riches of the territories,' the *Survey* pronounced, echoing the very words of Faulkner and Mackie from Nigeria, had led to 'the loss of vast sums in misguided attempts to reap quickly without sowing.'[95]

A sense of anxiety concerning African environments cannot be avoided when reading *Science in Africa*. The book opens with a long discussion of Africa's 'changing environment'; what is interesting is how widely defined this concept is – encompassing, quite explicitly, environments 'both inside and outside' humans.[96] The book's recommendations for active intervention usually stemmed equally from a desire to increase economic development and to prevent potentially irreversible damage. The problems brought to the reader's attention are ones familiar to today's readers as well: soil erosion, over-stocking, deforestation, new methods of cultivation, and the general spread of disease and changing epidemiological patterns. Such changes Worthington introduced in the context of 'constructive and destructive factors' involved in the 'balance of nature'. 'In a mechanical sense the balance of nature is not a simple balance, but a complex system of levers and links all balanced with each other, so that extra weight placed on any part of the system may cause the whole to change its equilibrium.'[97]

The ecological system Worthington described was neither static nor linear. Constituting that picture were eighteen different subjects – organised in many respects

[94] Worthington, *Science in Africa*, p. 15.
[95] Hailey, *An African Survey*, p. 1313.
[96] Worthington, *Science in Africa*, 'The Changing Environment', pp. 4–15, quotation on p. 15.
[97] Worthington, *Science in Africa*, p. 4.

as ecologists of the period represented food chains – and encompassing the inorganic world of geology, meteorology, and soil science; the plant world of forestry, botany, and agriculture; the animal world of fisheries, zoology, entomology, and animal industry; and the human world of health, human diseases, population and anthropology. To best study and understand the full picture, he argued, a good deal of research could 'only be carried out in Africa itself'.[98] A recurring theme of the book, in fact, was the need for further 'local study' as well as sensitivity to African knowledge. The hubris of past epochs seemed to be giving way to a modicum of humility in scientific circles at least.

The guiding principles which emerged from Worthington's synthesis of science were: (i) that knowledge of existing conditions was a necessary precursor to any intervention; (ii) that economic development strategies should build upon African methods already in place; (iii) that balance should be sought between attempts to maximise economic yields and sustain environmental fertility; (iv) that policies did not necessarily need to be uniform across very different 'localities'; (v) that 'quick results' in research were 'impossible' which meant that 'team-work,' 'interterritorial co-operation,' and long-term efforts should be the model; (vi) that, due to their interconnections, management of particular problems was inherently complex; and finally, (vii) that such complexity inevitably led to competing claims on Africa's land and natural resources which would have to be adjudicated with caution.[99]

An important feature of these principles was that in many respects they attempted to strike a balance between an 'ecological' and a 'sociological' reading of Africa's environments.[100] In other words, development was prescribed and constrained by both human and non-human conditions. With respect to the non-human, in his memoir Worthington wrote that 'The ecology of land use could only be learned on the spot and the environment had a way of kicking back at mistakes.'[101] This was an important insight of the Survey and had much to do with the kinds of development strategies it promoted. On the question of animal industry, for instance, Worthington described successive failures with European cattle because of their susceptibility to disease: in most territories, 'imported cattle [were] not successful'. 'In the tropical parts of Africa,' he concluded, 'it appears desirable to breed local stocks selected for qualities appropriate for varying economic conditions, and for resistance to different diseases … It is also thought that breeding will have to be carried out for each different locality, on account of the prevalence of particular diseases in different areas.' The 'naturally acquired immunity' of indigenous stocks and their adaptations to different environments were therefore an important research agenda the Survey endorsed.[102]

Science in Africa adopted similar positions with respect to fishing and native agriculture. 'The chief consumer of African fish, … at any rate in the tropical regions, is the African native, and he is likely to obtain the best, most continuous, and cheapest

[98] Worthington, *Science in Africa*, p. 144.

[99] Worthington, *Science in Africa*, quotations on pp. 423, 337, and 22; on the tensions he wrote (p. 15), 'Every branch of human activity, including cultivation, grazing, forestry, game preservation, mining and administration, involves the utilization of land, and the claims of various activities often come into conflict.'

[100] The examples which follow deal predominantly with 'environmental' issues; other issues including epidemiology, nutrition, and social anthropology I discuss more fully in my thesis.

[101] Worthington, *The Ecological Century*, p. 42.

[102] Worthington, *Science in Africa*, pp. 420, 423, 425, 446.

supplies by the gradual improvement of the existing indigenous trade, rather than by the introduction of large-scale industries organized on modern lines.' As this passage and others convey, Worthington and many of his advisers expressed a general mistrust of vast commercial enterprises because such efforts were rarely driven by concern for people or their habitats.

There is a strong body of opinion, that [corporate agricultural] schemes of this nature are not entirely beneficial, and may even prove disastrous to native life in the regions concerned. The development of export crops at the expense of native food crops, which characterizes the company system, can easily lead to an unbalanced system of agriculture.[103]

Regarding the changing assumptions concerning fertility, Worthington wrote critically, that in 'tropical conditions' it was once assumed that one needed only to 'remove indigenous vegetation and introduce crop plants. How far this idea is from the truth is shown from the mass of intricate research which has become necessary with almost every crop. As knowledge concerning tropical soils progresses, it becomes more and more evident that to judge them from a European standpoint is entirely misleading.' But it was not just comparisons with European environments that were dangerous, European methods – characterised as capital-intensive, large-scale production – also had adverse effects. This was particularly true in the context of soil deterioration.

[The European cultivator] may be even more destructive than the native since he works on a larger scale and aims at keeping a cleared area permanently under crops … European cultivation also is usually cleaner from weeds than that of the natives and, therefore, is more liable to wash, as there are only the roots of the crop to hold the soil. It is certainly regrettable that some European-owned land in Africa is worked on a principle which is not worthy to be designated farming, but can only be termed soil exploitation.

Africans were themselves already active in plantation agriculture, in particular in West Africa where there were few European settlers. To draw a line between European and African methods of production, was therefore, in some sense arbitrary. '[T]he real division,' Worthington wrote, 'probably lies between those methods which do and do not involve the investment of capital.'[104]

What becomes clear from a close reading of *Science in Africa* is that scientists and technical officers were themselves often quite critical of the way in which colonial territories in Africa had been managed. In many instances, in fact, they seemed willing to draw attention to the fact that most regions had been *poorly* planned and *inappropriately* developed. Their comments, summarised in Worthington's introduction, served to highlight the contradictions and tensions that existed between the colonial aims of conservation, development, and scientific research: 'A development based on a real understanding of Africa's potentialities,' Worthington concluded, 'has hardly yet begun, and will be impossible until the necessity of scientific knowledge is recognized.'[105]

It would be difficult to read these words and not also be reminded that in many

[103] Worthington, *Science in Africa*, pp. 237, 399.
[104] Worthington, *Science in Africa*, pp. 124, 404–5, 302.
[105] Worthington, *Science in Africa*, pp. 23–4.

respects the continent of Africa, during the colonial period, served as a 'fruitful field ... for experiment'.[106] This was, in fact, an enduring motif throughout the *African Survey* and was stated explicitly in both final volumes. 'Africa,' wrote Lord Hailey, 'presents itself as a living laboratory, in which the reward of study may prove to be not merely the satisfaction of an intellectual impulse, but an effective addition to the welfare of a people.'[107] To deny or overlook the abundant evidence that many such experiments had adverse effects, however unintended, would be arrogant in the extreme. This is not the purpose. What this chapter has tried to draw attention to, however, were the multiple ways in which the production and use of scientific knowledge in the inter-war period had progressive and liberalising effects, relieving rather than concentrating inappropriate colonial interventions.

The project had its start at the close of the 1920s when the question of further European settlement in colonial Africa was still open for debate; by its conclusion, in 1938, such a question was irrelevant in official circles. The African Survey tracked the shift in research away from European and toward native agriculture. It witnessed the optimism concerning Africa's abundant natural resources fade, in the face of agricultural and soil research, into a pragmatic approach regarding the kinds of schemes particular regions could support. It observed first the rise, and then the fall, of technical departments in the territories in the wake of the world economic depression and lamented the effects retrenchment had on the pursuit of original research. It saw the growth of ecological science in both Britain and the colonies and endorsed future research and development based on its methods. It took part in the transition from an ideology of colonial self-sufficiency and extractive exploitation toward one of human welfare and bottom-up development strategies. Finally, it recognised the need to analyse past failures, accept the complexity of problems, and proceed with development cautiously. The problems encountered in Africa, the *Survey* concluded, 'require[d] a special knowledge, which [could] only be gained by an intensive study of the unusual conditions'.[108] That special knowledge included new epistemological insights into both the human and non-human worlds and was organised largely under the rubric of ecology.

Such a reading of the Survey's history does not negate the fact that external imperial control in British colonial Africa was still often autocratic, coercive, and bound to an ideology of European superiority. Nor does it deny that efforts to mobilise scientific advisers had the simultaneous effect of drawing such individuals, and their institutions, more squarely into the colonial apparatus. What it does do is complicate that picture by exploring the heterogeneous ideas and proposals that emerged from this process, many of them bearing a striking resemblance to alternative agendas and critiques of the present day.

[106] Worthington, *Science in Africa*, p. 17.
[107] Hailey, *An African Survey*, pp. xxiv–v.
[108] Hailey, *An African Survey*, p. 1662.

7

Soil Conservation Policies in Colonial Kigezi, Uganda

Successful Implementation &
an Absence of Resistance *

GRACE CARSWELL

Kigezi, in the southwestern corner of Uganda, is an area of intensive agricultural production with a dense population that has, for decades, been perceived to be at risk from serious environmental degradation. Colonial officials put forward a number of policies to try to deal with problems as they saw them – namely, land degradation, land shortage and fragmentation. This paper considers one such set of policies: those of soil conservation from the 1930s.[1] It aims to shed light on how policies were successfully implemented in Kigezi, where there was little large-scale resistance. It argues that the scheme's success can be explained by precolonial methods of preventing soil erosion, the gradual introduction of the policies, the emphasis on propaganda and incentives, and the efficient working of the structure of chiefs. The chapter also compares the case of Kigezi with three other schemes in East Africa, which had very different experiences. The article raises a number of questions around the technical success of conservation policies, the continued sustainability of agricultural systems in the face of increasing population, and the social costs of such transformations.

From the 1930s the colonial state in East Africa became increasingly concerned with the environment.[2] Such concerns can be seen all over colonial Africa and there are a number of studies of areas where these concerns played a major influence in the formulation of agricultural policy.[3] Many of these studies examine soil conservation policies in the context of the growth of nationalism and their role in this political process, and thus examine the success or failure of these policies in essentially political

---

* This paper has benefited from comments from Bill Adams, David Anderson, William Beinart and JoAnn Mcgregor.

[1] On other policies see G. Carswell, 'African Farmers in colonial Kigezi, Uganda, 1930–1962: Opportunity, Constraint and Sustainability', PhD. thesis, SOAS (1997).

[2] D.M. Anderson, 'Depression, dust bowl, demography and drought: The colonial state and soil conservation in East Africa during the 1930s', *African Affairs*, 83 (1984): 321–43.

[3] See, for example, F. Mackenzie, *Land, Ecology and Resistance in Kenya, 1880–1952* (London, Edinburgh Unversity Press, 1998); J.L. Giblin, *The Politics of Environmental Control in North-Eastern Tanzania 1840–1940* (Philadelphia, University of Pennsylvania Press, 1993); G. Maddox, J.L. Giblin and I. Kimambo (eds), *Custodians of the Land: Ecology and culture in the history of Tanzania* (London, James Currey, 1996). W. Beinart and C. Bundy, *Hidden Struggles in Rural South Africa: Politics and popular movements in Transkei and Eastern Cape* (London, James Currey, 1987).

or social terms.[4] Few examine the methods used by the colonial state to ensure their implementation, and even fewer look at success or failure of these policies in environmental, agricultural or technical terms.[5] This is perhaps unsurprising, as there are few examples where these policies were implemented successfully for long enough to enable technical measures of success to be made. But Kigezi is an area where a number of soil conservation policies were implemented successfully and this is the first study of the process of implementation and the reception given to the policies by the local population in Kigezi.[6]

Background to the area

Kigezi lies at an altitude of between 1500m and 2759m above sea level. The mean annual rainfall of 1000mm is bimodal and precipitation is usually gentle and evenly distributed. Temperatures range between 9°C and 23°C. The district has undulating hills with steep slopes and many of the valley bottoms were once papyrus swamps, although most have been drained during the last 50 years, and are now cultivated or grazed.[7] Kigezi has an extremely long history of human settlement and in migration, and agriculture concomitant with more permanent settlements was probably established around 2,000 years ago.[8] Southern Kigezi is densely settled, and the population more than doubled between 1921 and 1959.[9] Early statistics suggest substantial increases in population and high rates of in-migration from Rwanda until the early 1940s.[10] These high population densities, combined with the system of land inheritance, have led to

[4] See L. Cliffe, 'Nationalism and the reaction to enforced agricultural change in Tanganyika during the colonial period', in L. Cliffe and J. Saul (eds), *Socialism in Tanganyika* (Vol. 1) (Dar-es-Salaam, East Africa Publishing House, written 1964, publ 1972); G.A. Maguire, *Towards 'Uhuru' in Tanzania: the politics of participation* (London, CUP, 1969); I.N. Kimambo, *Penetration and Protest in Tanzania: The impact of the world economy on the Pare, 1860–1960* (London, James Currey, 1991).

[5] Exceptions include S. Feierman, *Peasant Intellectuals: Anthropology and history in Tanzania* (Madison, WI, University of Wisconsin Press, 1990) and K. Showers, 'Soil erosion in the Kingdom of Lesotho: Origins and colonial response, 1830s–1950s', *Journal of Southern African Studies (JSAS)* 15, 2 (1989): 263–86. Technical assessments are developed in J.C. de Wilde, *Experiences with Agricultural Development in Tropical Africa*, 2 Vols, (Baltimore, MD, Johns Hopkins University Press, 1967). Also see M. Tiffen, M. Mortimore and F. Gichuki, *More People, Less Erosion: Environmental recovery in Kenya*, (Chichester, Wiley and Sons, 1994).

[6] See J.W. Purseglove, 'Land use in the overpopulated areas of Kigezi District, Uganda', *East African Agricultural Journal* 12 (1946), pp. 139–52; J.W. Purseglove, 'Resettlement in Kigezi, Uganda', *Journal of African Administration* 3 (1951), pp. 13–21; and E.R. Kagambirwe, 'Causes and consequences of land shortage in Kigezi' (Makerere, Department of Geography, Occasional Paper 23, 1973). These do not consider historical context, solutions put forward by the colonial state, or farmers' responses.

[7] J.D. Jameson (ed.), *Agriculture in Uganda* (Oxford, OUP, 1970) 2nd edn, p. 47.

[8] A. Hamilton *et al.*, 'Early forest clearance and environmental degradation in South West Uganda,' *Nature* 320 (1986), pp. 164–7; D. Taylor, 'Late quaternary pollen records from two Uganda Mires: Evidence for environmental change in the Rukiga highlands of southwest Uganda', *Palaeogeography, Palaeobotany and Palynology* 80 (1990), pp. 283–300. D.L. Schoenbrun, 'The contours of vegetation change and human agency in Eastern Africa's Great Lakes region: ca 2000 BC to ca. AD 1000', *History in Africa* 21 (1994), p. 302.

[9] From 206,090 in 1921 to 493,444 in 1959, Kigezi District. Kabale Uganda Govt Statistical Abstracts, 1966.

[10] B. Langlands, 'Population geography of Kigezi', Occasional Paper 22 (Dept. of Geography, Makerere, 1971); J.W. Purseglove, 'Report on the Overpopulated Areas of Kigezi' (ms 1945).

relatively small and fragmented land holdings.[11] By the mid-1940s the average area under cultivation was under 3 acres per taxpayer.[12]

The people of Kigezi are Bakiga, Banyaruanda and Bahororo. But the focus here is on the present-day Kabale area, where Bakiga predominate. The Bakiga have been categorised as a segmentary lineage society,[13] which differs from the stratified societies of the Banyaruanda and Bahororo. Both long-term permanent migration and short-term labour migration have been historically significant in the area.[14] There is a long history of movement by families on their own initiative.[15] Labour migration from Kigezi to southern and central Uganda was also very important to the economy of Kigezi (in 1959 an estimated 40-50% of the total adult male population was absent from Kigezi at any one time), although migration from Ruanda-Urundi into Uganda has to some extent overshadowed other movements.[16]

While there was no formal system of chieftainship amongst the Bakiga, authority was exercised at a lower level, although sources disagree as to whether this authority was through the household (as argued by Edel), the clan, or the lineage.[17] Of these, Edel's findings have been the most widely accepted.[18] Colonial administrators thus found no systems of government that they could recognise. This, however, did not alter the way they established their administration; they did what they did elsewhere in Uganda, initially appointing Baganda agents as administrators. Civil administration of Kigezi District began relatively late compared with the rest of the Uganda Protectorate, only after the Anglo-German-Belgian Boundary Commission of 1911.[19] The district's peripheral status persisted throughout the colonial period, and its relative isolation (both geographical and political) had implications for the success of colonial policies, which were never harnessed by nationalist movements as they were elsewhere in East Africa.

Kigezi was divided for administrative purposes into counties (*sazas*), sub-counties (*gombolola*), parishes (*miluka*: pl; *muluka*: sing) and sub-parishes (*mukungu* or

---

[11] J.M. Byagagaire and J.C.D. Lawrance, *Effect of Customs of Inheritance on Sub-Division and Fragmentation of Land in South Kigezi, Uganda* (Entebbe, Uganda Government, 1957).

[12] J.W. Purseglove, 'Kigezi resettlement', *Uganda Journal* 14 (1950), pp. 139–52.

[13] P.T.W. Baxter, 'The Kiga', in A.I. Richards, *East African Chiefs: A study of political development in some Uganda and Tanganyika tribes* (London, Faber and Faber, 1960), p. 283.

[14] B. Turyahikayo-Rugyema, 'A history of the Bakiga in south western Uganda and northern Rwanda c1500–1930', PhD thesis, University of Michigan, 1974); P.G. Powesland, 'History of migration' in A.I. Richards (ed.) *Economic Development and Tribal Change: A study of immigrant labour in Buganda* (London, 1954).

[15] M.M. Edel, *The Chiga of Western Uganda* (Oxford, OUP, 1957), p. 18.

[16] Western Provincial Annual Reports [hereafter WPAR]; Richards, *Economic Development and Tribal Change* and C.C. Wrigley, *Crops and Wealth in Uganda: a short agrarian history* (Kampala, Institute of Research, Makerere, 1959).

[17] Edel, *The Chiga*, p. 3; J. Roscoe, *The Bagesu and Other Tribes of the Uganda Protectorate. The Third Part of the Report of the Mackie Ethnological Expedition of Central Africa* (Cambridge, CUP, 1924); B. Turyahikayo-Rugyema, 'Bakiga institutions of Government', *Uganda Journal* 40 (1982), pp. 14–27.

[18] For example B.K. Taylor, *The Western Lacustrine Bantu: Nyoro, Toro, Nyankore, Kiga, Haya and Zinza* (London, International Africa Institute, 1962). Also Baxter, 'The Kiga', 278–310. On contemporary Kabale see J. Bosworth, 'Land, Gender and Ideology: the case of Kabale', PhD. thesis, Oxford University, 1996).

[19] See W.R. Louis, *Ruanda-Urundi 1884–1919* (Oxford, Clarendon Press, 1963), pp. 79–91, 194–9. Also J.M. Coote (with postscript by H.B. Thomas), 'The Kivu Mission 1909–10', *Uganda Journal* 20 (1956), pp. 105–12; H.B. Thomas, 'Kigezi Operations 1914–17', *Uganda Journal* 30 (1966), pp. 165–73.

mutongole). With chiefs appointed at each level, a hierarchy of authority was established, each chief being directly accountable to his superior. All the chiefs (except the lowest rank) were salaried employees of the Administration, and for some years *bukungu* also received a small salary.[20] Initially Baganda agents were used at *saza* and *gombolola* levels, but from 1922 this was phased out, and by 1930 three *saza* chiefs and all the lower chiefs were indigenous to Kigezi.[21]

The Native Authority Ordinance of 1919 set out the role of chiefs and gave them both executive and judicial powers.[22] The chiefs supervised tax collection and public works, and worked in the courts. From the beginning of British rule, the Administration, through the chiefs, extended its control into a wide range of matters including private concerns such as bridewealth, famine reserves and methods of cultivation.[23] The chiefs were placed in an extraordinarily powerful position:[24] for the first time men from the area could be appointed with power over non-family members, and over people from different clans and lineages. Younger men could have authority over older men and this new local elite could intervene in what had previously been entirely family matters. For many years chiefs were able to execute their powers with little reference to anyone else. From the mid-1940s changes were introduced so that some of the powers of the chiefs were handed over to councils of both chiefs and elected members, the latter eventually forming the majority. In some cases chiefs succeeded in continuing to dominate their councils, and it could still be said in the mid-1950s that 'chiefs, in their various capacities, are judges, legislators and executives'.[25] It was not until the mid-1950s that the power of the chiefs was to change to any significant extent, when the process of separating the judiciary from the executive began to take place.[26]

African chiefs thus had significant powers. In addition, Kigezi had high levels of European administrative personnel throughout much of the colonial period. From 1934, in addition to the District Commissioner and Assistant District Commissioner, a District Agricultural Officer was dedicated to the district.[27] From then onwards staff levels increased continuously and the District Team consisted of the DC, ADC, DAO, DVO (District Veterinary Officer) and DMO (District Medical Officer). In the Department of Agriculture there were Assistant Agricultural Officers (AAOs), who until 1954 were all Africans. There was one AAO for each of the five *sazas* of Kigezi: they provided the link between the DAO and farmers, and their reports kept the DAO informed of all the agricultural news in the counties, alerting him to any problems.[28] In

[20] Baxter, 'The Kiga'.

[21] B. Turyahikayo-Rugyema, 'The British imposition of colonial rule on Uganda: The Buganda agents in Kigezi, 1908–30', *Transafrican Journal of History* 5 (1976), pp. 111–33; A. Roberts, 'The Sub-imperialism of the Baganda', *Journal of African History* 3 (1962), pp. 435–50; D.J.W. Denoon, 'The allocation of official posts in Kigezi 1908–1930', in D.J.W. Denoon (ed.), *A History of Kigezi in South West Uganda* (Kampala, National Trust, Adult Education Centre, 1972); Baxter, 'The Kiga'.

[22] K.T. Connor, 'Kigezi', in J.D. Barkan et al., *Uganda District Government and Politics, 1947–1967* (Madison African Studies Program, University of Wisconsin, Madison, 1977).

[23] Edel, *The Chiga*, pp. 125–7.

[24] Baxter, 'The Kiga', pp. 289–90.

[25] Baxter, 'The Kiga', p. 289.

[26] Kigezi District Annual Report 1915–16 and WPARs 1925, 1931, 1945, 1949 and 1956.

[27] Except for a two-year period, 1939–41, when Kigezi shared a DAO with neighbouring Ankole District.

[28] For example, Monthly reports 1949–51 to DAO from Ag Asst, Kabale District Archives, Papers of the District Agricultural Office [KDA DoA] 19/B/2.

1954 the Agricultural Productivity Committee recommended increased staffing levels for Kigezi, and some of the *sazas* were allocated European officers, who were known as Field Officers. This relatively high level of administrative support, and the policy of working through chiefs as much as possible, can be seen as fundamental to the successful administration of the district.

Kigezi was quickly incorporated into the Uganda administration through, for example, tax collection. From 1935 payment of both compulsory labour obligations (*luwalo*)[29] and poll tax was commonly in cash.[30] Cash was earned through wage labour[31] and the sale of hides and of livestock (mainly small stock).[32] Kigezi was intricately tied into wider flows of salt and livestock in the region and was central to a food production system and market that straddled international boundaries and encompassed Ruanda and the neighbouring Ankole District. The main crops grown were sorghum, peas, beans and sweet potato, and peas and beans in particular were traded. Throughout the colonial period the British attempted to introduce a variety of non-food 'cash crops' but none was a success as the British consistently failed to appreciate the vitality of the food crop sector in Kigezi.[33]

Indigenous methods of soil conservation and early colonial encounters

This section will focus on Kigezi's situation during the very early stages of colonial rule, outlining indigenous methods of erosion prevention and examining the earliest policies. Given that Kigezi is an area with a long history of agriculture and in-migration, it is probable that the precolonial Bakiga agricultural system was highly adaptive to demographic pressure through agricultural change, relatively innovative and included significant soil conservation practices.[34] Roscoe visited Kigezi in 1919-20 before any colonial measures had been introduced and remarked how 'ridges' formed by gathering together weeds and stones resulted in the fields forming 'regular plateaux' that looked like terraces.[35] An administrative officer, Elliot, wrote of the period 1920–25 that 'there was not much pressure on the land at that time but some people were already starting terrace cultivation' and 'had some idea of soil conservation'.[36] Snowden, an Agricultural Officer visiting the district in 1929, described how on the hillsides 'cultivation starts at the bottom of the plot, so that the soil is gradually brought down and banks are formed on the foot of each plot. These banks tend to stop soil erosion to some extent.'[37]

Discussing soil fertility in 1935, the Director of Agriculture wrote: 'In many densely

[29] This initially involved each adult male working for 10 days, later 30 days. WPAR 1933.
[30] Introduced from 1912 and 1915 respectively. Initially payments were made in labour, cash was widespread after 1935.
[31] WPAR, 1922.
[32] See Kabale District Archives, Papers of the District Commissioner's Office [KDA DC] MP23 1923 and KDA DC GENPOL.
[33] See Carswell, 'African Farmers'.
[34] On precolonial agricultural technologies, see special issue on 'History of African Agricultural Technology and Field Systems', *Azania* XXIV (1989).
[35] J. Roscoe, *The Soul of Central Africa: A general account of the Mackie ethnological expedition*, (London, Cassell and Co., 1922), p. 101. Visit to Kigezi (1919–20).
[36] Papers of J.R. McD. Elliot, Rhodes House [RH], Oxford, MSS Afr s 1384, #33 and 2A.
[37] Snowden, Report to Director of Agriculture on Tour of Kigezi District, 16 Nov. 1929. RH MSS Afr s 921, ff258.

populated counties the inhabitants have been driven by dire necessity to terrace their lands, and this practice already obtains in parts of Kigezi',[38] suggesting that the indigenous system included aspects aimed at longer-term sustainability. The benefits of these methods were recognised, and officials observed that in the Kigezi highlands 'the native has developed his own anti-erosion measures: he grows his crops in strips across the slopes, with intervening strips of uncleared land, and this system leads to the formation of natural terraces. In addition some individuals have built small terraces.'[39]

Although evidence from the precolonial period is scanty, there seems little doubt that at this time the Bakiga agricultural system was highly adapted to local conditions. Bakiga sited their narrow plots along the contour and left strips between plots, so that over time 'ridges' or steps formed, the steepness of the plot gradient was reduced and terraces of sorts (or at least plots of a lower gradient) built up. Crops were planted along the contour, while the system of mixed cropping and use of legumes (with peas and beans being amongst the principal crops) helped to preserve soil fertility. In addition, the use of trash lines and 'rough tillage' had the same effect.[40] Photographs from 1911,[41] 1935[42] and 1938[43] all illustrate indigenous agricultural practices, two examples of which are reproduced below.

The perception amongst colonial officials of 'a problem' with Kigezi agriculture grew during the 1930s, and policies were put into place at a local level to address this. In 1929 concerns were recorded about the insufficiency of land for the population around Kabale,[44] and in 1935 District Agricultural Officer (DAO) Wickham observed that crop yields were falling because of soil exhaustion in a 10-mile radius of Kabale. He observed that it was probable that

> all crops in this area are ... deteriorating in yield, or quality.... The reason for this state of affairs is clearly overpopulation and soil exhaustion. There is not enough land available for the essential item in the rotation – fallow – to be included at the proper intervals ... nearly all the land where crops are grown is on a steep slope, causing heavy erosion.[45]

He estimated that the area cultivated by the average household had halved from 12 to 6 acres in the previous decade, and predicted that as yields fell there would be an increased tendency to encroach on land that should be left to fallow. Wickham saw the problem as having two related aspects: soil erosion due to the use of steep hillsides, and soil exhaustion due to continuous cultivation.[46] He warned that 'the position will

---

[38] 'Notes on Preservation of Soil Fertility' prepared by Dir of Ag, Entebbe National Archives, Uganda [ENA] H175/1/II ff5 or H218/I ff16(1), quote re Kigezi para 24.

[39] J.D. Tothill, *Agriculture in Uganda* (London, 1940), p. 87.

[40] Tothill, *Agriculture in Uganda*, p. 127.

[41] Photographs of Major R.E. Jacks (Surveyor on Anglo-German-Belgian Boundary Commission, 1911). Public Records Office, Kew [PRO] CO 533/57.

[42] Photographs of D.W. Malcolm, (Secretary to Lord Hailey, Visited Uganda Dec. 1935 to Jan. 1936). RH MSS Afr s 1445. Box 3, Album II – photo of Lake Bunyonyi with terraces in the background. Also Box 4, Album III – photo of hillsides showing contour cultivation, with strips or trash lines along contour.

[43] Photograph in collection of Miss Edith Baring Gould, Church Missionary Society [CMS] Acc 28z5. Lake Bunyonyi, 1938. 'Steps' can be seen in background on hills around Lake Bunyonyi.

[44] Note on 'Land insufficiency around Kabale', 1929, by J.E. Phillips, KDA DC MP69 ff34.

[45] Report for Year 1935 by Wickham, KDA DC AGR-MNTH ff53.

[46] Letter to DC from Wickham, DAO, Kabale, 5 Sept. 1935, KDA DoA 009exp-c ff10. Soil 'erosion' (sheet or gulley erosion) and falling soil fertility are sometimes used interchangeably.

7.1 (Right) Bunds, steps and trashlines on hillsides.

(Source: photographs of D.W. Malcolm (Secretary to Lord Hailey, Visited Uganda Dec. 1935 to Jan. 1936). RH MSS Afr s 1445 (Albums II and III). Reproduced with permission of the Rhodes House Library, Oxford)

7.2 (Below) Contour cultivation on hillsides in Kigezi before colonial policies were implemented.

(Source: Photograph in collection of Miss Edith Baring Gould, CMS Acc 28z5. Lake Bunyonyi, 1938. Reproduced with kind permission of the CMS collection, Birmingham University Library)

inevitably and steadily become worse', and feared the area might cease to be self-supporting in food.[47]

G.B. Masefield,[48] who replaced Wickham as DAO in 1937, made similar observations and expressed concern about the effect falling yields were having on the ability to collect sufficient famine reserves.[49] In some areas he found little cultivable land resting and 'scarcely any' available for expansion, while grazing land was contracting and the number of stock increasing.[50] Masefield quickly established a programme of propaganda and anti-erosion measures and began advising missionaries as to ways of protecting land they leased.[51]

By late 1937, Masefield was concentrating propaganda work on anti-erosion measures.[52] He asked the DC to help in 'spreading knowledge of these measures, whether by speaking in lukikos or otherwise'.[53] The notes he circulated to his staff and chiefs included advice that plots should be in strips across the slope and should be no more than 30 yards down a slope (or 20 yards on steep slopes) and that there should be a 5-yard strip of grass between plots. He recommended building 'ridge terraces' at the bottom of the plot, running along the contour, and using a 'sod bank', hedges or grasses, contour rows of mulch, weeds and crop debris to help terraces form. The introduction of improved crop rotations was also advised.[54] It is clear that these measures, in particular having plots along the contour with strips of grass between plots and 'ridge terraces' at the bottom of the plots, were actually adaptations of methods already in use. This may explain why the policies were relatively readily accepted by farmers.

Masefield's policies were carried out not merely through Agricultural Department staff but largely through the network of chiefs.[55] Thus by 1938, before soil conservation policy had been formalised in Uganda as a whole,[56] the concerns of local officials and the presence of Masefield, a recently trained, dynamic DAO with a particular interest in soils, meant that soil conservation measures had begun in Kigezi and were one of the routine subjects discussed by officials while on tour.[57]

[47] Report for Year 1935 by Wickham, KDA DC AGR-MNTH ff53.
[48] Masefield was DAO in Kigezi from Feb. 1937 to June 1938. He had been educated at Oxford and received a Colonial Agricultural scholarship (first year at Cambridge and second at the Imperial College of Tropical Agriculture in Trinidad), was posted to Uganda, and after periods as DAO in Ankole, Kigezi and Mbale, became Soil Conservation Officer in Buganda. His interest in soils began as an undergraduate: 'I was thrilled with soils … I don't know why, but I just took to soils and that is why I took to soil conservation.' Interview, 18 April 1996. He later went on to an Oxford lectureship and wrote several books on tropical agriculture.
[49] G.R. Masefield, 'Notes on Food Crops and Famine Reserves in Kigezi', May 1937. KDA DC AGR-MNTH ff81.
[50] Monthly report, July 1937, by G.B. Masefield, KDA DC AGR-MNTH ff87.
[51] Letter to Dr N.M. James, CMS, Syira, PO Kabale from Haig, Sen. Ag. Off., Kampala, 13 July 1937; letter of 30 Aug. 1937 to Sen. Ag. Off. from Masefield, KDA DoA 009crops.
[52] Monthly Report for Oct. 1937 by Masefield, KDA DC AGR-MNTH ff95.
[53] *Lukikos* were meetings held by officials with the local population during safaris around the district. Letter to DC from Masefield, DAO, 23 Oct. 1937, KDA DC AGR6I ff2.
[54] Letter to DC and DMO from DAO, 18 March 1937. KDA DoA 010 crops.
[55] Interviews with elderly men and women, Kabale District, July–September 1995. For details see Carswell, 'African Farmers'; interview with Masefield, 18 April 1996.
[56] In other parts of the colonial world, soil conservation policy had already been formalised. See W. Beinart, 'Soil erosion, conservationism and ideas about development: A Southern Africa exploration, 1900-1960', *JSAS* 11, 1 (1984), pp. 52–3.
[57] Subjects covered at *lukikos* on safari included: coffee mulching, timber and black wattle planting and the

In addition to such propaganda, demonstration plots were also used. Masefield believed that talking about anti-erosion measures was of limited use, and that the use of demonstration plots that were 'properly terraced' was much more effective.[58] By mid-1938 about seven demonstration plots had been established.[59] He suggested that the training of agricultural instructors be made more relevant to districts outside Buganda, and that more attention be paid to the agricultural instruction of women. In later years efforts to reach women were increased and, as will be seen, they were, for example, included as participants in courses. Archival sources did not reveal anything specifically about the reactions of women to conservation policies, which is unfortunate as they probably did the greater proportion of physical work in the fields, including maintaining soil conservation measures.

Masefield's successor in 1940 – Stuckey – expressed concern about soil erosion on land leased to Europeans for pyrethrum cultivation[60] and to missionaries.[61] He recommended that more land be fallowed, that strip cultivation be introduced to enable land to be fallowed, and that very steep and badly eroded areas be taken out of cultivation altogether.[62] Commenting on these recommendations, the PAO said that

> bunding has not been suggested as to attempt this would be a work of considerable magnitude. I think that this strip cropping will serve the purpose, and if a success it will be a useful demonstration of something which other people in Kigezi are much more likely to follow than bunding.[63]

However, as we shall see, both strip cropping and bunding[64] were ultimately used in Kigezi, and it was bunding that was more acceptable to Bakiga farmers, being closer to indigenous methods and taking less land out of production.

At a national level concerns over the threat of soil erosion also emerged, although Kigezi received little attention and it was not until after a tour in July 1941 by the Deputy Director of Agriculture that the extent to which anti-erosion measures were already being carried out in Kigezi was fully appreciated by senior officials. He reported that Kigezi was 'intensively cultivated with plots on very steep slopes.... There has, however, been an almost spectacular development of lines of elephant grass at the tops and bottoms of plots.'[65] In 1951 the Deputy Director of Agriculture, Watson compared the district then with 1938 when 'the farming pattern was ... a "patchwork"

---

[57] (cont.) planting of contour erythrina hedges to avoid soil erosion. See ADC, Wright's Safari in Rukiga, 15 Feb. 1937 to 3 March 1937, KDA DC MP139 ff34.

[58] Letter to Sen. Ag. Off. from Masefield (on leave), 26 May 1938, KDA DoA 11/A/1 ff4.

[59] Interview with Masefield, 18 April 1996.

[60] Letter to Sen. Ag. Off. from Stuckey, DAO, 25 Jan. 1940, KDA DoA 008. Also enclosure to Letter to Stafford from H.B. Thomas, Land Officer, 23 Jan. 1940, KDA DoA 008.

[61] For example, Bwama Island in Lake Bunyonyi, which was established by the CMS as a hospital and treatment centre for lepers in 1930/31. Letter to Sen. Ag. Off. from G.F. Clay, Dir. of Ag., 7 Feb. 1940, KDA DoA 008. Referring to letter to Director of Agriculture from Director of Medical Services.

[62] Letter to Sen. Ag. Off., WP from Stuckey, 18 April 1940, KDA DoA 008.

[63] Letter to Dir. of Ag. from E.F. Martin, Senior AO, WP, 1 May 1940, KDA DoA 008.

[64] Strip cropping is the method of resting and cultivating alternate strips of land. Bunds are vertical steps between plots of land. In situations where steps or banks already exist between plots bunds are relatively easy to adopt. Introducing bunds from 'scratch' is labour-intensive.

[65] Report on Tour of Western Province, 7–19 July 1941, by Deputy Director of Agriculture, KDA DoA 11/A/1 ff6.

type, with no attempt being made to preserve or improve the land'. He noted 'it is obvious that spectacular advances have been made in the matter of reorientation of holdings coupled with a more rational type of general agriculture'.[66] His comment reveals something very important about the attitudes of the colonial authorities, namely the failure to recognise that, while the indigenous system might have resulted in 'patchwork' cultivation, it was not necessarily ignorant of soil conservation. Although, as shown above, some officials such as Elliot (in 1920–25) and Snowden (in 1929) did recognise the benefits of the indigenous system. McCombe, DAO in 1941–2, saw the benefits of the system in place and observed that 'Kigezi had an established system of planting elephant grass on the contour and what I have introduced is an addition to and not a disturbance of the older system'.[67]

As we have seen, the indigenous system of Bakiga agriculture included a number of important elements to ensure the sustainability of the resource base. The first anti-erosion measures put in place by Masefield (elephant grass strips and a recommended plot width of 30 yards) and McCombe (similar to the earlier measures but with narrower plots) were modifications to the indigenous system, and so could be adopted by the local population with relative ease. As the colonial period progressed there was a gradual move towards a more orderly system of agriculture. Up to the early 1940s, Kigezi, not being a major cotton or coffee producing area, was not a part of wider national discussions about the threat of soil erosion.[68] The lack of attention given to Kigezi was to change quite suddenly and before long Kigezi's soil conservation measures were held up as an example to the rest of Uganda, indeed to the colonial world.

Implementation of soil conservation measures
The Purseglove era – 1944–53

This section will look at the implementation of soil conservation measures during Purseglove's era. The state employed the stick and the carrot in introducing these policies: the 'stick' of enforcement in which chiefs and regulations played a prominent role, and the 'carrot' of propaganda, competitions and educational courses. Adverse weather conditions resulted in food shortages across much of Uganda in 1943. Marketing regulations were tightened up and the purchase of African foodstuffs for resale or export was prohibited. The 'famine' as it was called[69] brought Kigezi's agricultural system under closer colonial scrutiny, and the district quickly became a model for the successful implementation of conservation measures. This coincided with Purseglove's arrival as DAO. He was a catalyst for many new development initiatives, in particular the resettlement scheme and soil conservation policies that collectively became known as *plani ensya,* 'The New Plan'. This phrase entered the

---

[66] Letter to DAO from T.Y. Watson, Deputy Director of Agriculture, 2 Oct. 1951, KDA DC AGR6I ff67.
[67] Letter to Sen. Ag. Off. from McCombe, DAO, 18 Jan. 1943. KDA DC AGR6I ff11 and other letters from McCombe, KDA DoA 11/A/1 ff7.
[68] See Carswell, 'African Farmers'.
[69] The assertion that shortages were 'imminent' justified marketing regulations, which acted as a constraint on production and ultimately did more harm than good. Attempts to introduce marketing controls over foodstuffs need to be seen in the light of colonial efforts to introduce a range of cash crops. See Carswell, 'African Farmers'.

Rukiga language, and is still remembered today. Purseglove, who has been described as a 'Pioneer of Rural Development',[70] had graduated in 1936 from the Imperial College of Tropical Agriculture in Trinidad. Having developed an acute awareness of soil erosion, he was only too keen to put this knowledge into practice. He was appointed Agricultural Officer in Uganda in 1936 and DAO in Ankole and Kigezi in 1938–9, before being appointed DAO in Kigezi in 1944, where he remained until 1952. The longevity of his stay may in part explain Purseglove's influence and impact.[71] His enthusiasm was also important: he learnt Rukiga and was interested in Bakiga customs. The impact that he made on Bakiga farmers is striking and many informants remembered him: Byagagaire told of songs written about Purseglove,[72] while Ngologoza praised him, recalling his nickname 'Kyarokyezire' meaning there is plenty of ripe ready food in their area.[73]

In November 1944 a committee was established to investigate and report upon Kigezi's overpopulated areas.[74] The committee – which comprised officers from the Administration, Forestry, Veterinary and Agriculture Departments – held only one meeting; thereafter all the work was left to Purseglove. He carried out a series of traverses in a 12-mile radius of Kabale town to assess whether the areas were 'over-populated', and if so to what extent. It is, however, clear that before the study had even begun it had been decided that these areas *were* overpopulated, and the survey confirmed this. The population density of Kigezi District as a whole was found to be 155 people per square mile, while Ndorwa, one of the southern *sazas*, had a density of 210 people per square mile.[75]

Purseglove found that 'The main problem at the moment is soil exhaustion … it would appear that overcultivation has resulted in soil exhaustion and a deterioration in soil structure, with a consequent reduction in the amount of water absorbed by the soil.'[76] Quoting from Jacks and Whyte, *The Rape of the Earth*, he stated that 'although serious erosion is not yet a problem we cannot afford to be complacent and wait for it to become so'. He concluded that the area around Kabale could not continue to support an increasing population and that it would be 'most unwise to continue under the present conditions in the hope that further soil deterioration and erosion will not take place'.[77] Purseglove believed that grass fallows were essential to soil fertility maintenance. He suggested moving people out of the 'overpopulated' areas into less populated areas to the north in order to increase the proportion of land resting, and introducing a policy of strip cropping with every third strip resting. In the areas left behind there would be

---

[70] E. Clayton, *Purseglove: A pioneer of rural development* (Wye, 1993). Purseglove was the subject of the first monograph to be produced by Wye College on important individuals in tropical agriculture.

[71] CV and Aide Memoir – RH MSS Brit Emp s 476.

[72] Interview, J.M. Byagagaire, Kampala, 21 Sept. 1995. Byagagaire worked alongside Purseglove during vacations while doing a diploma in agriculture at Makerere. He was AAO in Kigezi 1953–7 and the first African DAO in Kigezi, from May 1962.

[73] Ngologoza, *Kigezi and its People* (Dar-es-Salaam, East Africa Literature Bureau, 1969), p. 94. Ngologoza was a Mukunga Chief from 1923, Chief Judge in Kigezi in 1956 and Chairman of Appointments Board in 1959. Interviews with elderly informants, who were ordinary farmers and remember Purseglove in a similar light. Interviews July–September 1995.

[74] Purseglove, 'Report on the Overpopulated Areas of Kigezi' (1945).

[75] *Ibid.*, para 17.

[76] *Ibid.*, para 13.

[77] *Ibid.*, paras 13 and 93.

some 'reorganisation'[78] of agriculture, the distance between bunds would be further reduced (thus narrowing the strips) and a more orderly system of alternate strip cropping would be introduced. These policies, which collectively became known as *plani ensya*, differed from those of the earlier period in that they increased the proportion of land taken out of cultivation and demanded greater labour inputs.

It should be stressed that, although Purseglove played a crucial role in bringing Kigezi to centre stage, his findings were not particularly groundbreaking or innovative. On the contrary, many officials had previously discussed the problems of over-population, soil erosion and falling yields and by the time Purseglove arrived Kigezi's reputation as an 'overpopulated' district was firmly entrenched. Purseglove, however, greatly increased the attention that was focused on the district. The reputation of being seriously overpopulated and threatened with serious environmental degradation that Kigezi gained in this period is one that it has never been able to shake off. Researchers have consistently repeated many of these ideas, often without substantiation,[79] and it is only recently that some of these myths, such as continuous cultivation, have been put to the test.[80]

Following Purseglove's report a great deal of energy went into the resettlement scheme[81] and the policies of *plani ensya,* central to which was strip cropping. Purseglove proposed taking all land on slopes of over 20^0 out of cultivation and introducing a system of strip cropping in which land would be rested in rotation, with two years cultivation and one of rest under grass (or four and two respectively). The resting strip could be grazed. Plots would be a width of 16 yards on slopes of up to 15^0 and narrower on steeper slopes, with bunds between the plots of at least 3 feet. Purseglove noted that 'Once the system of strip cropping ... has been established, automatic control of the number of people on the land will be accomplished. One strip in three must always be resting and this can be maintained by the minimum of supervision by the Administration, agricultural staff and chiefs.' Purseglove acknow-ledged that the main difficulty would be reorganizing strip lines, which would cut across existing plots and necessitate some reorganisation of tenure.[82] As the 1940s progressed the soil conservation measures undertaken included strip cropping, bunding, introducing more organised fallow systems, encouraging manure use, com-post pits and the fencing of paths.[83] Below I explore how the Administration ensured that these measures were carried out.

[78] *Ibid.*, para 94.
[79] For example *State of the Environment Report for Uganda* (Ministry of National Resources, 1994), p. 26; E.M. Tukahirwa (ed.), *Environmental and Natural Resource Management Policy and Law: Issues and options, summary* (Washington, DC, MISR and Natural Resources and World Resources Institute, 1992); and F.D.K. Bagoora, 'Soil erosion and mass wasting risk in the highland areas of Uganda', *Mountain Research and Development* 8 (1988): 173–82.
[80] K. Lindblade, G. Carswell and J.K. Tumahairwe, 'Mitigating the relationship between population growth and land degradation: Land-use change and farm management in southwestern Uganda', *Ambio* 27, 7 (1998): 565–71. See also G. Carswell, 'Farmers and fallowing: agricultural change in Kigezi district, Uganda', *Geographical Journal* 168, 2 (2002), pp. 130–140.
[81] On the Resettlement Scheme see Carswell, 'African Farmers'. On its effects on the family see R.E. Yeld, 'The Family and Social Change: A study among the Kiga of Kigezi, south west Uganda', PhD thesis, Makerere (1969).
[82] Purseglove, 'Report on the Overpopulated Areas of Kigezi', paras 98–9 and 102.
[83] Details of soil conservation measures in KDA DoA 11/A/1.

The role of chiefs

By the late 1940s most soil conservation work was a matter of routine, and colonial appointed chiefs played a crucial role in its implementation. This emerges clearly from archival sources such as monthly reports sent to the DAO. For example, it was reported that following a visit to an area where soil conservation measures had been neglected

> steps were taken by the chiefs to see that new grass strips were well laid out.... The chiefs and the Agricultural instructors were reminded about [the use of elephant grass] ... it is hoped that good results will be achieved if the gombolola chief and muruka chief ... remain industrious and devoted. ...progressive work about soil conservation measures ... is mainly due to the organising ability of the muruka chief.[84]

Purseglove wrote in 1948 that the success of soil conservation measures 'has been achieved through the direct approach of departmental officers and the district team generally to the peasant farmers concerned working through the medium of the native authority'.[85] Colonial authorities thus placed much responsibility on chiefs for ensuring that their 'patch' followed the required measures; if they failed to do so, they were punished. In addition, chiefs at each level (*saza, gombolola*, etc.) were responsible for ensuring that all the chiefs at the level below them carried out the work expected of them.

By working through this hierarchy the administration ensured that conservation measures were carried out, and it is clear that chiefs were punished without hesitation. In 1949 the *saza* chief of Ruzhumbura reported that he had 'dealt with' the *gombolola* chief of Kagungu, his minor chiefs and the Agricultural Instructor of the area concerning the 'negligency of the Soil Conservation work'. He tried the chiefs in the *saza* court and found that the *gombolola* chief was not helping his sub-chiefs and the Agricultural Instructor, and so he was warned that if he did not improve he would be fined.[86] Just a few days later the *saza* chief took the case further, reporting that as no improvements in soil conservation measures were seen he had sacked one *muluka* chief and two *bakungu* chiefs, and fined four other chiefs.[87] Oral sources have confirmed that work was supervised by *muluka* or *gombolola* chiefs along with agriculture department staff.[88]

Force of law

It is widely believed today[89] that a soil conservation byelaw was in force throughout the colonial period, but in fact there was no such byelaw until 1961. Instead 'Agricultural Rules' made under the Native Authority Ordinance were enforced in the lower courts,

[84] Report on Agriculture in Bukinda by AAO, Rukiga sent to DAO, 25 Nov. 1949, KDA DoA 19/B/2, ff56.

[85] Letter to Provincial Agricultural Officer (PAO) from Purseglove, DAO, 9 June 1948, KDA DoA 11/A/1 ff51.

[86] Letter to DAO from Kitaburaza, Saza Chf Ruzhumbura, 12 Nov. 1949, KDA DoA 16/A/1 ff87.

[87] Letter to DAO from Kitaburaza, Saza Chf Ruzhumbura, 28 Nov. 1949, KDA DoA 16/A/1 ff90. Also KDA DC AGR6I ff38. On actions against other chiefs e.g. Bubale, Ndorwa in 1950 – See Report by AAO, Ndorwa, 1 May 1950, KDA DoA 19/B/2, ff92.

[88] Interviews, Kabale District, July–September 1995.

[89] For example amongst District Officials, interview with Mutabazi, DAO, July 1995.

and these Rules alone proved to be quite sufficient to ensure implementation. [90] They were only clarified in 1954 when it was decided that all rules should be 'codified', consolidated into a pamphlet and issued to chiefs. [91] The fifteen Agricultural Rules of 1954 stated that: contour strips should be 16 yards wide or 10 yards on steep slopes, bunds must be 2 yards wide and permanent, alternate strip cropping should be practised where possible, grazing areas should be set aside where possible, and grass burning should be carried out only with the permission of a chief. [92] The Agricultural Rules were enforced by the lower courts and it is perhaps for this reason that no court returns, or details of punishments imposed, have been located.

The authority that chiefs had in Kigezi is striking. If an individual failed to follow the soil conservation rules – for example, if bunds were dug over and not replaced – that person was logged in the 'warning register' by the local chief and given 14 days to comply. Those who still failed to follow the rules would be taken to court and if found guilty would be fined, and ordered to comply within 7 days. [93] No archival evidence has been found as to precisely how work on *plani ensya* measures was enforced and informants were inconsistent in their replies as to who actually did the work. [94] Some said that it was just male taxpayers, while others said that women and children also had to work. No court records survive of the punishments imposed for failing to carry out the measures, but oral evidence suggests that fines and short terms of imprisonment were the most common punishments, while working for the *gombolola* chief was also mentioned. It seems that the threat of a fine alone was usually enough to make a farmer carry out the measures required. [95]

On occasions some chiefs were over-enthusiastic in their efforts to ensure that measures were implemented. In 1951 the Secretary General wrote to all *saza* chiefs stating that it was 'not desirable that married women should be compelled to work on the "plani ensya" ... [nor should] ... work on "plani ensya" be done daily. This work should be done by men, girls, and boys only, and should only be done once every week.' [96] That such a warning was needed supports the view that chiefs had the authority to ensure that people turned up for *plani* and that some used this authority with over-enthusiasm. [97] It is also of interest that, while adult women were being excused from working on soil conservation measures, it was felt that they should attend agricultural education courses. This suggests some ambivalence in the colonial policies towards women's involvement in soil conservation.

The successful implementation of measures in the Kigezi scheme was noted with surprise by a Kenyan official following his visit to Kigezi. He was clearly particularly impressed with the degree of co-operation noting:

[90] Telegram, DAO to PAO, 5 Sept. 1950, KDA DoA 16/A/1 ff113.

[91] Letter, DC to DMO, DVO, DFO and DAO, 6 Jan. 1954, KDA DoA 11/A/2, ff1.

[92] Memo on 'Agricultural Rules' in letter, DAO to DC, 5 Feb. 1954. KDA DoA 11/A/2 ff5.

[93] Letter, DC to Saza and Gomb Chfs, 3 Aug. 1951, KDA DC AGR6I ff62.

[94] Interviews in Kabale, July–September 1995.

[95] Interview with Kazlon Ntondogoro. Interviews in Kabale, July–September 1995.

[96] Letter to Saza Chfs from Ngologoza, SecGen, 23 Oct. 1951, KDA DC AGR6I ff70.

[97] Here the Secretary General checked the actions of over-zealous chiefs, unlike Chief Tengani in the Shire Valley of Nyasaland, whose 'dictatorship' is described by Mandala and who demanded strict compliance. His zealousness succeeded in 'breaking resistance' to the scheme, generating support for nationalism and illustrating 'the potential of Indirect Rule for creating tyrants out of traditional rulers'. E.C. Mandala, *Work and Control in a Peasant Economy* (Madison, WI, University of Wisconsin Press, 1990), pp. 232–4.

The central administration seem able to persuade the tribal leaders of the desirability of soil conservation practices and good husbandry generally, and once persuaded, the chiefs and councillors seem to have little difficulty in enforcing good agricultural behaviour on their people. In the case of a particularly recalcitrant person, a fine of a shilling is apparently enough to make him change his ways.[98]

The official, who was himself in charge of the Makueni Settlement scheme, put forward a number of explanations for the high level of co-operation between the District Team and chiefs: firstly, the degree of continuity in administration; secondly, the power and prestige of chiefs; and thirdly, the fact that chiefs were also members of the native courts, so that they were often prosecutor, judge and jury. His comment on this was that, while it might 'seem an odd legal conception … in the case of soil conservation measures, it appears to produce results. The senior native courts have powers of corporal punishment which they regularly exercise.'[99]

Education and propaganda

In addition to regulations, much effort was also expended on encouraging conservation through education, competitions and propaganda. Purseglove established courses at Kachweckano, an experimental farm near to the Kabale belonging to the Department of Agriculture that had been established in 1938. Attended by chiefs, employees of the Agricultural Department, schoolteachers and others, these courses taught the rudiments of conservation methods.[100] Chiefs had to attend at least one course, at which lectures and practical demonstrations were given by the DAO. In the examination held at the end of the course the emphasis was on erosion and soil fertility. Lower-level chiefs also attended lectures, given by Agricultural Assistants, on a monthly basis.[101]

Purseglove himself regarded the Kachweckano courses as 'an important factor in the scheme…. This approach [is] of greatest significance as no lasting result can be achieved unless the mass of the people understand the fundamental reasons behind the charge [sic change].'[102] Byagagaire, an AAO in the 1950s, recalled that the most important thing was to 'first of all teach chiefs and public opinion leaders … [about] why [the policies] were necessary. These are elders in the village – old men – they are not chiefs or councillors, but they are highly regarded in the village, their word is highly respected … you had to convince them.'[103]

Oral evidence confirms the widespread impact of these courses upon chiefs and ordinary farmers alike. It is noteworthy that by the 1950s many women were attending such courses. At the same time, however, women were excused from participating in

---

[98] Balfour (Officer in Charge, Makueni, PO EMALI) to the Commissioner, ALUS, Nairobi, 15 Sept. 1950 reporting on Visit to the Kigezi Resettlement Scheme. PRO CO 892 15/8 ff1. Kenyan officials were interested in the light of similar efforts in the Makueni and Machakos Settlement Areas, in Kenya.

[99] Report by Balfour on Visit to the Kigezi Resettlement Scheme, 15 Sept. 1950, PRO CO 892 15/8 ff1.

[100] The first course, (1–6 July 1946), was attended by 11 Gombolola chiefs; 16 Muluka chiefs and 3 instructors, KDA DoA 16/A/1 ff21; the second was attended by 17 Gombolola, 20 Muluka chiefs and 6 members of Ag. Dept., letter from Purseglove, 4 Nov. 1946, KDA DoA 16/A/1 ff31.

[101] Letter, SAA i/c Ruzhumbura to DAO, 25 Feb. 1953, KDA DoA 16/A/1 ff133.

[102] Letter, Purseglove to PAO , 9 June 1948, KDA DoA 11/A/1 ff51.

[103] Interview, J.M. Byagagaire, Kampala, 21 Sept. 1995. He also recalled that they never toured the area by car, but always walked and camped.

weekly soil conservation work, and it seems that colonial officials were unsure of what stand to take with regard to women's involvement in these activities. The courses were an efficient way of 'spreading the word'. As one elderly informant Bishisha recalled: 'when they came back they organised public gatherings to tell people about what they had learnt [at Kachweckano].' The fact that people were well informed about the reasons behind the soil conservation measures suggests that the propaganda campaign to explain the measures was generally effective. [104] Many informants confirmed that explanations of the reasons for the measures, combined with the threat of punishment, together ensured that the majority of people complied. [105]

Competitions were another popular feature of the campaign. In 1946 Purseglove introduced an annual soil conservation competition, which became an important event in the local calendar.[106] A cash prize was awarded to the *gombolola* judged to have made the biggest advance in soil conservation work during the year, which was spent on a feast attended by people living in that *gombolola*, as well as by District Officials. In addition, small cash prizes were awarded to the *gombolola* chief, *muluka* chiefs and the Agricultural Assistant,[107] which acted as an additional incentive to ensure that the measures were carried out.

Whenever other agencies of propaganda could be employed they were harnessed to Purseglove's scheme. The missions were involved in implementing soil conservation measures in so far as it was their responsibility to follow the guidance of the Agricultural Department on land they leased, or on which they had schools. The AAO in particular worked through mission employees and teachers,[108] school farms were targeted and in 1949 a school garden competition was introduced.[109] The Western Province Demonstration Team also had a role to play. During the Second World War Army Mobile Propaganda Units had toured Uganda giving displays and film shows and it was decided that these should be adapted for use in peacetime.[110] There was one entirely self-contained and fully mobile team in each Province composed of a leader and 12 members, all Africans, mainly ex-service men. They aimed, through films, plays and demonstrations, to 'arouse interest in and stimulate action towards improved standards both in the home and on the farm'.[111] From 1947 this team worked in Kigezi giving performances on agricultural matters, amongst other things.[112] Following these performances, leaflets in the vernacular were distributed, which explained the causes of soil erosion and suggested ways to check it.[113]

The Western Province Demonstration Team played an important part in promoting the one aspect of soil conservation policies that ran into particular problems: planting

---

[104] See also articles in 'Kigezi Newsletter' (also known as 'AGANDI'), produced in Rukiga by the district administration from Oct. 1950. KDA DC SCW7-1-I ff38a.

[105] Interviews with elderly men and women, Kabale, July–September 1995.

[106] Letter, Purseglove to PAO 19 July 1946, KDA DC AGR6I ff14. Also interviews.

[107] Results of 1958 Soil Competition, KDA DoA 218A ff30.

[108] Report on Agriculture in Bukinda by AAO, Rukiga, 25 Nov. 1949, KDA DoA 19/B/2, ff56.

[109] KDA DC AGR6I ff39.

[110] On the background to the Colonial Film Unit created in 1939 see R. Smyth, 'British Colonial Film Policy 1927–1939', *Journal of African History* 20 3 (1979), pp. 437–50.

[111] Memo on role of Demonstration Teams, by CMA Gayer, Dir of PR and SW, 2 Jan 1947. KDA DoA 11/A/1 ff38.

[112] Memo re organisation of WP Demo Team from Snowden, ADC, 21 May 1947, KDA DoA 11/A/1 ff43Enc.

[113] Letter to Purseglove from Dennis Carr, PR and SW Dept, Mbarara, 26 April 1947, KDA DoA 11/A/1 ff40. Leaflet on 'Soil Erosion', KDA DoA 11/A/1 ff40Enc.

temporary grass leys for grazing on resting strips. The policy was introduced in 1949 and presented the administration with some of its greatest difficulties. From the beginning there were reports of the Demonstration Teams having problems getting land on which to plant the leys and collecting people to work with them. In 1951, the Secretary General wrote to the *gombolola* chief in the area concerned encouraging him to gather his people on *plani* day to plant grass leys.[114] But problems continued and it was reported that in some areas 'much if not most' of the work was being nullified by inadequate weeding, and the demonstration plots were poorly located, being too scattered over the *gombolola* for people to appreciate their existence and usefulness. The plots often belonged to people with 'very little interest in grazing them [who] therefore are not bothering to weed and maintain them properly. They seem to have very little idea of the underlying reason for the planting of these leys.'[115] As might have been expected, the chiefs were criticised for not making enough effort to encourage people to maintain and graze the plots, but it seems that the problems went deeper and that this aspect of the soil conservation work was very badly thought out. From the lack of references to the policy of planting leys in the years that followed, it seems that this aspect of soil conservation was quietly dropped from the agenda. Another aspect that largely failed was the 'reorganisation' of land left behind by resettlers, as suggested by Purseglove. This policy was also abandoned, largely because it involved changing plot boundaries and thus had implications for land tenure. In contrast to other areas (see below), agricultural officers in Kigezi both planned and implemented the measures to be introduced in the district. They were in a position to adapt or change the measures if problems arose and had the sense to drop interventions that were ill-conceived.

In most respects, however, soil conservation policies were implemented success- fully. By the early 1950s it was reported from Kigezi that 'cultivation has been developed on true strip cropping lines, which is now generally practised throughout the district'.[116] In 1950 the DC wrote of the 'universal adherence' to rules requiring both strip-cropping and bunding and stated that they were 'well understood and diligently followed by the great mass of the people'.[117] In this respect, the experience of Kigezi stood in stark contrast to other parts of East Africa. Aside from the two minor policies discussed above, no references to any widespread feelings of opposition to the policies in Kigezi have been found.[118]

Reassessment in the 1950s

From the early 1950s there was a shift in conservation policies as colonial concerns about agricultural productivity became increasingly linked to issues of land tenure.[119]

[114] Letter, Sec. Gen. to Gomb Chf Kitumba, 6 Oct. 1951, KDA DC AGR6I ff68.

[115] Letter, G. Symons DVO to DAO, 27 March 1952, KDA DC AGR6I ff75.

[116] Notes on Shifting Cultivation in Western Province, by Purseglove. Prepared for EARC. PRO CO 892 15/7. Also letter to DAO from T.Y. Watson, (Deputy Director of Agriculture) 2 Oct. 1951. Following visit to Kigezi. KDA DC AGR6I ff67.

[117] Notes on the System of Land Tenure in Kigezi written by DC, for EARC, 1950. PRO CO 892 15/9 p. 47.

[118] In the early 1950s there was some criticism in the vernacular press about soil erosion measures in Buganda. Monthly Political Surveys: Uganda (EAF 96/15/01/A) SECRET file, PRO CO 822/381 – 1951–3. Even without a vernacular press in Kigezi one might expect to find references to discontent in the district archives, in for examples files on 'Petitions and Complaints' which were examined closely.

[119] See Carswell, 'African Farmers'.

This coincided with Purseglove leaving Kigezi, and with a change in the DAO, the policies of the 1940s were reassessed. King, the DAO who replaced Purseglove, observed that the value of the resettlement scheme was often overstated, as it had never managed to keep up with the natural increase in population.[120] From the time resettlement began in 1953, 22,000 people had been resettled, while the population was estimated to have increased by 64,000 in the same period; it was therefore 'obvious that the problem had only been scratched'.[121] The scheme had also failed to reorganise the agricultural system in the way suggested by Purseglove. Like officials before him, King spoke of the problems of growing land pressure and decreasing areas for grazing. With a clear hardening of attitude he proposed further resettlement. Estimating that at least 50,000 people needed to be removed from Kigezi, he recommended that married seasonal emigrants (to Buganda and elsewhere) should be made to take their families with them. As a marked decline in the birth rate was unlikely, he felt that resettlement was the only answer but noted that it would 'not succeed unless very strong pressure is brought to bear and severe penalties inflicted on those who subsequently return'.[122]

Other officials agreed that, while the resettlement scheme had led to a 'lessening of pressure', the figures were totally inadequate. To get a 'real breathing space', about 100,000 people (i.e. 7 years increase) would have to be moved, which would 'require a colossal organisation and an expenditure of about £250,000'.[123] DC Fraser felt, however, that 'resettlement by itself is a somewhat sterile solution to the district's problems', as it would have to continue indefinitely on a very large scale. Instead, he suggested more effort should be put into finding ways for Kigezi to support a greatly increased population,[124] and the emphasis on soil conservation remained.[125]

At around this time concerns over loss of grazing were increasingly expressed. The DVO Symons calculated that 'within 8 years at the present rate, there will be no uncultivated land remaining'.[126] Symons was strongly critical of the strip cropping policy, observing that grass on resting strips was often of inferior quality compared with natural grazing, with much weed and bush growth. Moreover, it was very difficult to graze cattle, especially larger herds, on resting strips. He observed that often, particularly in grazing areas of northeastern Kigezi, a hill was opened up for cultivation and after three years, rather than cultivating the intermediate strips, further land was opened up higher up the hill. He wrote that 'the obvious reason for this is that the Chiefs like to produce an orderly pattern of alternate strips and the more strips then the more points they consider they will score for the Agricultural Competition. This is an obvious waste of grazing lands.'[127] The Agriculture Department itself admitted in the early 1950s that alternate strip cropping was a 'wasteful method of land utilisation' and it was virtually impossible to graze the resting strips. Instead a 'block layout' was suggested with parallel strips along the contour separated by grass washstops or bunds

---

[120] Letter, King DAO to PAO, 7 May 1953, KDA DoA 012-3 ff8. Further assessment re Resettlement Scheme in KDA DoA 012-3 ff11, ff14 and ff17.
[121] Memo on Resettlement by Sub-Committee of Kigezi District Team (1953) KDA DoA 11/A/1 ff115.
[122] Letter, King DAO to PAO, 7 May 1953, KDA DoA 012-3 ff8.
[123] Letter, Todd DAO to Dir of Ag., 8 March 1954 'Kigezi Ag.al Policy'. KDA DoA 11/A/2 ff9.
[124] Letter, Fraser DC, to PCWP , 3 Feb. 1954. KDA DoA 11/A/2, ff3.
[125] Letter, DAO to 'All in charge, Sazas', 2 Sept. 1954 re tour of Kigezi during August. KDA DoA 11/A/2 ff27.
[126] Letter, G.B. Symons, DVO to DC, 12 March 1953, KDA DoA 13/A/1 ff318.
[127] *Ibid.*; letter, King DAO to Saza Chf Ruzh, 8 May 1953, KDA DC AGR6I ff201.

of about 3 yards.[128] This marked a return to something much closer to the precolonial indigenous system, and a system of horizontal plots separated by strips or bunds exists today, although the bunds or washstops are significantly narrower than 3 yards.

The evidence thus suggests that the system of alternate strip cropping introduced during Purseglove's time in office had been applied too broadly and over too wide an area. In applying a single formula, grazing lands had in fact been excessively reduced in some areas. The shift in policy towards the promotion of block cultivation had been suggested by the Deputy Director of Agriculture as early as 1951 following a visit to Kigezi,[129] but it was not until 1954 that experiments began in Ruzhumbura to test the effectiveness of block cultivation.[130] In 1956 it was agreed that in certain areas 'better use can be made of the land if the system of alternate resting and cultivating strips is abolished and block cultivation introduced'.[131] During the mid-1950s there was an increased emphasis on a 'more rounded' approach to soil conservation, and this meant a return to something closer to the precolonial indigenous systems.

East African comparisons

To appreciate the exceptionality of Kigezi's experience of colonial soil conservation policies we need to consider the broader picture of colonial rural development programmes throughout eastern Africa.[132] The striking contrast with other places where soil conservation measures were implemented on so large a scale is the lack of opposition to the proposals in Kigezi. This section will explore Kigezi's apparently anomalous position. There are a number of reasons that might contribute to the success or failure of a soil conservation scheme, and they fall broadly into three categories: firstly, the nature of the measures being introduced (for example their closeness to the indigenous system of agriculture and the amount of labour required to carry them out); secondly the methods of implementation (the use of propaganda and education and the length of time taken); and thirdly, the effects of such measures on existing social and political structures (including the effect of existing systems of land tenure and the presence of local political tensions and of nationalist politics). With these broad categories in mind, three other schemes[133] will be outlined and contrasted with Kigezi.

Uluguru Land Usage Scheme, Tanganyika[134]

The Uluguru Land Usage Scheme (ULUS), introduced during the early 1950s, was designed to 'improve' the land in the Uluguru Mountains through the construction of bench terraces and the introduction of other conservation measures. Discontent over terracing became a 'vehicle of protest against Native Authority,'[135] led to rioting in

[128] Annual Report, Department of Agriculture, 1953, pp. 42–3. Also Annual Reports for 1954 and 1955.

[129] Letter ,T.Y. Watson to DAO, 2 Oct 1951. KDA DC AGR6I ff67.

[130] Extracts from Minutes of Kigezi District Team Meetings in KDA DC AGR6I and KDA DoA Teammins.

[131] Letter E.W.King, DAO to Sec.Gen., Saza Chfs and Field Officers ,23 May 1956, KDA AGR6II ff30.

[132] M. Stocking, 'Soil conservation policy in colonial Africa', *Agricultural History* 50, 2 (1985).

[133] See Carswell, 'African Farmers' for further comparisons with the Usambara Scheme, the Sukumaland Scheme and the Pare Development Plan.

[134] See also A. Coulson, 'Agricultural Policies in Mainland Tanzania', in J. Heyer (ed.), *Rural Development in Tropical Africa* (London, Macmillan, 1981), pp. 52–89; L. Cliffe 'Nationalism and the reaction to enforced agricultural change'; and Giblin, *The Politics of Environmental Control*.

[135] See R.A. Young and H.A. Fosbrooke, *Smoke in the Hills: Political tension in the Morogoro District of*

1955, and the scheme had to be abandoned. Various reasons have been put forward for the failure of the scheme, and the first major study, by Young and Fosbrooke, looks at reactions to the scheme in terms of local political dynamics and conflicts fed by discontent over terracing. While it is impossible to say if the discontent would have become apparent had it not been for the existence of these local political tensions and divisions, it is clear that the conservation scheme played a significant part. Over most of the area the difference between the bench terracing being introduced and the methods already in place was much greater than was the case in Kigezi. The exception to this was in Mgeta on the western side of the mountains where, as Maack has observed, residents had practised terracing since the early 1900s, and its benefits were clear in this environment.[136] In this area the people were in general 'sympathetic with the broader ULUS',[137] and the measures were more successfully implemented, supporting the view that closeness to the existing system of agriculture was important.

The labour inputs required for the construction of bench terraces were large and colonial officials initially introduced targets of 'yards of terraces' to be built. When this failed, all taxpayers had to work on the terraces for three days a week.[138] This was an extraordinarily high demand to make and it is entirely unsurprising that the policy was hugely unpopular. In addition to being very costly to introduce in labour terms, it was found that bench terraces were actually totally inappropriate for the area; indeed, with the exception of the western side, they were detrimental to the soil. Tests showed that bench terraces were unsuitable, given the fragility and thinness of the soil,[139] and officers in the field themselves questioned their suitability. These officers, however, were not in a position to adapt, change or abandon policies when problems arose, as were those in Kigezi. In Uluguru bench terraces had a largely negative effect on the productivity of the area, with yields on treated plots actually declining. Again the exception was the western area of Mgeta, where farmers could produce high-value foodstuffs on these terraces and thus 'for them terracing was a worthwhile effort'.[140] Iliffe has suggested that the failure to offer incentives in the form of cash crops to farmers, meant that it was never while farmers investing time and labour in the measures proposed, and this contributed to the scheme's failure.[141] In Maack's words, 'the Waluguru resisted efforts to combat soil erosion because they derived few benefits from their labour.'[142] Overall, therefore, the measures being introduced were ill thought out and unsuited to the area, and lacked the incentives of high-value crops to make them worth carrying out.

The methods used to implement these measures have not been examined in great detail, and how much 'persuasion' was used is unclear. Young and Fosbrooke have observed that 'the attempt to enlist the support of the clan leaders had limited

---

[135] (cont.) *Tanganyika* (Evanston, IL, Northwestern University Press, 1960).

[136] P.A. Maack, '"We Don't Want Terraces!" Protest and Identity under the Uluguru Land Usage Scheme' in G. Maddox (ed.), *Custodians of the Land*, p. 159.

[137] See Young and Fosbrooke, *Smoke in the Hills*, p. 147.

[138] Maack, '"We Don't Want Terraces!"', p. 158.

[139] *Ibid.*, p. 156.

[140] *Ibid.*, p. 160. Similarly in parts of Nyasaland there were cases of successful promotion of ridges in Northeastern Chikwawa,the Lulwe plateau, and the Tchiri highlands. In areas of steep hillsides farmers found it 'reasonable' to adopt contour ridging, unlike the rest of the Shire Valley where opposition was strong. Mandala, *Work and Control*, pp. 227–9.

[141] John Iliffe, *A Modern History of Tanganyika*, (Cambridge, CUP, 1979), p. 474.

[142] Maack, '"We Don't Want Terraces!"', p. 153.

success'[143] and the short timetable used to introduce the scheme may have been its greatest downfall. The scheme was first proposed in 1947 and the ambitious terracing programme introduced in 1950. This was very different from the gradual implementation of measures seen in Kigezi and was perhaps a case of 'too much, too soon'. The existence of local political tensions and rising nationalist politics must have assisted the articulation of discontent, and Iliffe has observed that 'drudgery and political conflict also killed the Uluguru scheme'.[144] Maack has noted that the Wuluguru felt betrayed by the Native Administration at a time when new forms of political expression were becoming available. In addition, the measures became associated with loss of land (as forced migration had been discussed earlier in connection with soil conservation measures), which added to suspicions about the scheme.[145]

The officials failed to understand fully the Wuluguru land system, which included individual rights of ownership, individual use rights and complex patron-client relationships. Unsurprisingly, farmers were unwilling to invest large quantities of time and labour on land that was not theirs. Young and Fosbrooke have observed that the ULUS 'struck at two sensitive topics: the land ... and the social system which governed the use of the land.'[146] Crucially, in the case of Kigezi, this was avoided. Individual security of tenure was strong in Kigezi, and although measures were attempted that would have threatened the system of land tenure in place (such as the 'reorganisation' of agriculture suggested by Purseglove following resettlement), these were quickly dropped by the administration.

Central Province, Kenya

In Central Province a scheme of terracing was carried out by means of communal labour.[147] The system of implementation was one of coercion, not persuasion; people were required to work two mornings a week, and those who failed to do so were fined.[148] As Throup has observed

> the alternative strategy of attempting to educate the population to follow approved techniques of 'sound' land use was dismissed as too slow, since it was considered that immediate action was necessary. Consequently the palliative anti-erosion measures were introduced without the understanding and support of the peasantry. This was a fatal error.[149]

In Murang'a narrow-based terraces, which initially took less labour to build, but in the long term incurred greater labour demands because of high maintenance needs, were considered by the administration to be most appropriate, but in fact were particularly unpopular. In addition, there was little incentive to carry out terracing, as production of high-value cash crops was not an option for these farmers. Elsewhere – at Meru and Embu – broad-based terraces and the opportunity to grow coffee meant that the measures were worthwhile and therefore more acceptable.

[143] Young and Fosbrooke, *Smoke in the Hills*, p. 147.
[144] Iliffe, *A Modern History of Tanganyika*, p. 474.
[145] For further details of the disturbances in Uluguru see PRO CO 822/807.
[146] Young and Fosbrooke, *Smoke in the Hills*, p. 146.
[147] D.W. Throup, *The Economic and Social Origins of Mau Mau, 1945–53* (London, James Currey, 1988); D.W. Throup, 'The origins of the Mau Mau', *African Affairs* 84 (1985), pp. 399–433.
[148] T. Sorrenson, *Land Reform in the Kikuyu Country – A study in government policy* (Nairobi, 1967).
[149] Throup, *The Economic and Social Origins of Mau Mau*, p. 70.

The high level of male migration meant that most work fell on women and they mobilised against the colonial regime. In April 1948 2,500 women marched to the District headquarters to inform officials that they refused to do the twice-weekly communal work.[150] Kenya African Union activists, under Kenyatta, played a crucial role in mobilising opposition to communal terracing which fed into wider discontent.[151] Thus 'resistance to soil conservation schemes became a rallying point in the struggle against the administration, and its adherents'.[152] By the 1950s the Agricultural Department's belief that progressive cultivators should be rewarded with the right to grow high-value crops began to be accepted by the administration, and there was a move towards encouragement of individual enterprise, and in 1954, with the Swynnerton Plan, a commitment to the positive role to be played by small-scale African producers. The Swynnerton Plan was in part a political device implemented as a counter-insurgency measure to the Mau Mau uprising. However, 'compulsory terracing had destroyed any chance there might have been of gaining new collaborators as [the Kikuyu] had been irredeemably alienated from the colonial regime'.[153]

Machakos, Kenya

Efforts were also made to control soil erosion in the semi-arid Machakos District.[154] The rehabilitation programme included closing areas for rehabilitation, compulsory soil conservation works and destocking. Some years earlier in 1938 a policy of compulsory destocking had met with total non-co-operation and 1,500 Akamba marched to Nairobi, camping there for six weeks until the order was rescinded and the policy abandoned.[155] This, combined with concerns about loss of land to Europeans, meant that the Akamba were deeply suspicious of government policies.

The first attempts to introduce a mechanical soil conservation unit in 1946 met with popular resistance, with people throwing themselves in front of the tractors.[156] Initially all able-bodied adults were obliged to work communally for two days a week under the direction of chiefs and headmen but, as cultivation gave ownership rights under traditional law, people did not want soil conservation work done on their land by others even if it was for free. As in Murang'a, the type of terrace being introduced in this area was the narrow-based terrace which was easier to build initially but, because of maintenance needs, required a larger long-term labour input, and was liable to collapse in storms. Bench terraces were thought to be inappropriate for African farmers due to the lack of tools and the time needed to build them, but once constructed they were more permanent and stable. From about 1949 some farmers began building bench terraces for the growing of vegetables and by the mid to late 1950s, when market access had improved, the adoption of bench terraces increased. Similarly there was a 'much greater and continued interest in bench terracing in higher hill areas, when this work could be directly associated with the introduction of new and profitable crops

[150] Mackenzie, *Land, Ecology*.
[151] *Ibid.*, pp. 152–3.
[152] *Ibid.*, p. 2.
[153] *Ibid.*, pp. 209–10.
[154] Tiffen *et al.*, *More People, Less Erosion*.
[155] See J.F. Munro, *Colonial Rule and the Kamba: Social change in Kenya Highlands 1889–1939* (Oxford, Clarendon Press, 1979).
[156] de Wilde, *Experiences with Agricultural Development*, Vol 2.

such as coffee'.[157] Machakos in the 1940s, however, did not offer the attractive farming opportunities seen for example in Nyeri, where from the 1950s bench terraces became acceptable as they were associated with the introduction of coffee, a highly profitable crop. This evidence therefore supports the argument that incentives in the form of market opportunities are crucial, combined with tenurial security, a persuasive approach and choice of technologies.[158]

Conclusion

That soil conservation policies were implemented in Kigezi without opposition is in stark contrast to other areas where similar attempts were made. Comparisons with such cases highlight some of the reasons for the apparently successful implementation and lack of opposition to the measures. The degree to which the measures being introduced differed from indigenous methods of erosion control; the amount of additional labour input that was necessary to implement the measures; the extent to which local conditions were taken into account in the formulation of these schemes;[159] and the extent to which officials on the ground were able to adapt the measures to local conditions were all critically important. In Kigezi the earliest colonial policies were essentially modifications of the Bakiga agricultural system. As the colonial period progressed, the authorities' obsession with the threat of soil erosion and their desire for 'orderliness' in agricultural systems grew, and further far-reaching measures were brought in, which coincided with the appointment of Purseglove as DAO. But the measures had begun some years before Purseglove arrived, and this gradual introduction was crucial to their successful implementation. In comparison with similar schemes elsewhere, in Kigezi greater effort was put into education, propaganda, and the provision of incentives, and thus the reasons behind the conservation measures were generally understood. Purseglove's role is also significant: not only was he a particularly dynamic individual, but his period of service in Kigezi was prolonged. By working directly through chiefs, placing responsibility on them, and giving them authority to both judge and punish, the administration was broadly successful in getting conservation measures carried out. In addition, suspicions of the government's motives, fears of losing land to Europeans and the rise of nationalism were critical ingredients missing in Kigezi, which in other areas facilitated the articulation of discontent. Finally and crucially, the Agriculture Department was flexible enough to abandon those parts of the scheme that proved inappropriate (such as the planting of grass leys on resting strips and the 'reorganisation' of land left behind by resettlers), suggesting that greater attention was paid to local responses to policies than elsewhere. The success was such that Kigezi became a 'show piece' for the administration and a visit to Kigezi became part of many official visitors' itineraries. The 'carrot and stick'

---

[157] Ibid., p. 97.

[158] Tiffen *et al.*, *More People, Less Erosion*, p. 256.

[159] Mackenzie notes that with few exceptions (all in Tanganyika) 'local conservation systems, their ecological specificity and their integration of biological with technical measures, were completely ignored in attempts to resolve the growing environmental crisis in colonial Africa.' Mackenzie, *Land, Ecology*, p. 15. The evidence presented here suggests that Kigezi is another such exception.

method of implementation appeared to be successful and the success story of Kigezi has been repeated many times, including by outside observers.[160]

In this paper, therefore, I have argued that Kigezi's soil conservation policies were successfully implemented. There are examples of the successful implementation of schemes being reported where very little changed on the ground,[161] but in Kigezi there is enough strong evidence to rule this out. There are, however, a number of different measures of 'success', and in the colonial situation manifestations of success or failure were being judged on political or social terms (as distinct from assessments on agricultural or environmental terms). It may be that Kigezi was seen as successful because the policies were introduced without strong resistance from local populations, and so it was seen as politically and socially successful in the short term. Whether the policies were a success in the long run in the technical or agricultural sense, is, however, a different question: was it the implementation of policies that was successful, or the policies themselves that were a success? This question is difficult to answer, although research has shown that, contrary to popular belief, farmers have continued to maintain fallow periods in the face of growing population pressure, and have successfully maintained the sustainability of their agricultural system despite a steadily increasing population.[162] The social costs of the transformation that Kigezi has undergone are likely to include an increased differentiation in the ownership of land and livestock, an increased occurrence of landlessness or effective landlessness, the loss of land types such as swamps that reduce vulnerability in times of drought, an increased reliance on remittances and possibly increased outmigration. There is need for an examination of these factors in order to understand more fully the consequences of the changes that have occurred in Kigezi. There is no doubt that in the past farmers in Kigezi have been remarkably responsive to challenges to the sustainability of their production system. Whether they can continue to be so remains to be seen.

[160] Wrigley, *Crops and Wealth*, p. 77.

[161] For example, Thackwray Driver, 'Soil conservation in Mokhotlong, Lesotho, 1945–56: A success in non-implementation'. Paper presented at African History Seminar, SOAS, 1996.

[162] Lindblade *et al.*, 'Mitigating the relationship'; Carswell 'Farmers and fallowing'.

8

Conservation & Resistance
in Colonial Malawi

The 'Dead North' Revisited*

JOHN McCRACKEN

At midnight on Sunday 22 February 1959, K.J. Waterfield, the agricultural supervisor in the remote Misuku Hills in the extreme north-west of Nyasaland, abandoned his post. Leaving his African staff to cope as best they could in the face of an increasingly hostile local population, Waterfield fled by Landrover with his wife and children to the comparative sanctuary of the provincial capital, Mzuzu, driving with no lights for the first 25 miles in order to avoid attention. Five days later he attempted to retrieve his possessions with the aid of a police patrol, only to be driven off by an irate crowd. That was his final opportunity. On 5 March, in an act of ritual cleansing through fire, local people burnt his house and belongings along with the houses of all six African members of the agricultural staff.[1] So ended the Misuku Land Usage Scheme, a pioneering project introduced in 1938 and the subject of a great deal of favourable colonial attention.

It is more than thirty years now since historians first emphasised the importance of colonial conservation policies in explaining the eruption of anti-colonial peasant protest in Malawi in the late 1950s.[2] In all that time, however, attention has been firmly focused on state intervention in the Southern Province and, in particular, the Lower Shire Valley, leaving developments elsewhere virtually undiscussed.[3] This paper attempts to rectify the balance by extending the focus of attention away from an area of extensive land alienation and cash-cropping, where large-scale schemes for social

---

* This chapter would not have been written without the pioneer work of Leroy Vail who so often asked the right questions.
[1] Rhodes House Library, Oxford [hereafter RHL], Devlin Commissions Papers, Box 8, K.J. Waterfield, 'Nyasaland Disturbances NW Karonga', 6 May 1958; Zimbabwe National Archives [hereafter ZNA] F236 CX 27/3/1 Governor, Zomba to Colonial Secretary, 8 March 1959.
[2] John McCracken, 'African Politics in Twentieth-Century Malawi' in T.O. Ranger (ed.) *Aspects of Central African History* (London, Heinemann, 1968), pp. 204–5; Roger Tangri, 'From the Politics of Union to Mass Nationalism: the Nyasaland African Congress, 1944–1959', in Roderick J. Macdonald (ed.), *From Nyasaland to Malawi* (Nairobi, East African Publishing House, 1975), pp. 262–81.
[3] Elias C. Mandala, *Work and Control in a Peasant Economy* (Madison, WI, University of Wisconsin Press, 1990), pp. 191–268; William Beinart, 'Agricultural Planning and the Late Colonial Technical Imagination: the Lower Shire Valley in Malawi, 1940–1960' in Centre of African Studies, *Malawi: An alternative pattern of development* (Edinburgh, Centre of African Studies, 1984), pp. 93–148.

engineering abounded, to the altogether different social and economic environment to be found in Nyasaland's 'dead North'. This was a region, as Waterfield discovered to his cost, where the near complete absence of settlers did not prevent the emergence of a peasant-based nationalist movement more violent in its acts and tenacious in its resistance than anywhere else in Malawi – or indeed in British Central Africa as a whole – in the late 1950s and early '60s. As late as October 1958, no less than 48 of the Nyasaland African Congress's 63 branches were sited in the Northern Province.[4] They provided the organisational base for a campaign of sabotage and arson, focused in particular on the conservation strategies pursued by the colonial government, which left 26 bridges damaged, 10 completely destroyed and 79 houses burnt to the ground (out of a total of 100 houses destroyed in the whole of Nyasaland) during the first few weeks of the emergency up to 23 March 1959.[5] Elsewhere, the arrest of nationalist leaders on 3 March was quickly followed by the suppression of overt resistance. But in the Northern Province, and particularly in the Karonga district and the Misuku hills, armed gangs of young men led by 'General' Flax Musopole roamed the hills, building roadblocks and evading arrest with the active support of what the Governor, Armitage, described as a 'generally very truculent' population.[6] Not until August 1959 was Musopole finally captured.[7]

In a larger study I am writing, I hope to explore the inter-relationships between peasant protest on the ground and Flax Musopole's militant strategies, developed in part through his contacts with radicals in Johannesburg and Cape Town from the late 1940s. Here, however, my central focus is on the conservation ideas and policies developed by a succession of observers, among them administrators, missionaries and agriculturalists, struggling to make sense of the process of environmental and economic change taking place before their eyes in the rolling hills and abrupt ridges of northern Malawi. As my investigation has proceeded I have become increasingly sceptical of the conventional view of the 'making of the dead North', initially shaped by Scottish missionaries in the 1890s but given its most authoritative form in a typically powerful and imaginative essay by Leroy Vail, published in 1981.[8] Nevertheless, I have also become aware of the formidable difficulties involved in reaching firm conclusions on the extent and causes of environmental degradation over a substantial period of time, given the striking absence in Northern Malawi of the type of detailed information on agricultural systems that Moore and Vaughan have used to such effect in their study, *Cutting Down Trees*.[9] If even these two find it necessary to present their findings not as a single narrative but, rather, as an exploration of a variety of locally and externally produced discourses, how much more should a student of

[4] Public Record Office, Kew [hereafter PRO] CO 1015/1749, Political Intelligence Report for October 1958.

[5] ZNA F 236/CX27/3/3, Federal Intelligence and Security Bureau, report on sabotage in Nyasaland, 8 July 1959.

[6] PRO CO 1015/1494, Armitage to Colonial Secretary, 30 March 1959. See also PRO CO 1015/1494, MILLIA, Salisbury to Troopers Force, Nairobi, 17 March 1959.

[7] Philip Short, *Banda* (London, Routledge and Kegan Paul, 1974), p. 117.

[8] Leroy Vail, 'The Making of the 'Dead North': A Study of Ngoni Rule in Northern Malawi, c. 1855–1907' in J.B. Peires (ed.), *Before and After Shaka: Papers in Nguni history* (Grahamstown, Institute of Social and Economic Research, 1981), pp. 230–65.

[9] Henrietta L. Moore and Megan Vaughan, *Cutting Down Trees. Gender, nutrition, and agricultural change in the Northern Province of Zambia 1890–1990* (London, James Currey, 1994).

environmental change in northern Malawi resist the temptation to provide easy answers to what, in the present state of our knowledge, are dauntingly difficult questions.

Conservationist ideas and the apocalyptic vision: the 'Dead North' revisited

Conservationist anxiety has a long history in colonial Malawi. The first Commissioner and Consul General, Harry Johnston, was a passionate naturalist, as much at home in the world of plants and insects as he was in that of imperial politics. It was, therefore, not surprising that he arrived in the British Central African Protectorate in 1891 with a keen sense of conservationist concern.[10] His central belief, no doubt influenced by the ideas of Scottish surgeons and missionaries in India and South Africa about whom Richard Grove has written, was that desiccation was already proceeding rapidly as a consequence 'of the ravages of the bush-fires and the destruction of the forests'.

> I think it may be taken … as a fact that the rainfall of South-central Africa is slowly decreasing, and that in past ages all this country was far more heavily forested than at present, and probably received a supply of rain scarcely inferior to that of West Africa. I still maintain that the chief cause of this deterioration lies in the bush-fires which year by year widen their area of destruction and are by degrees practically reducing the whole country to prairie condition.[11]

Johnston's concern at the degrading effect of the use of fire by agriculturalists was more than shared by the Scottish Presbyterian missionaries of the Livingstonia Mission who set up stations at Njuyu and Ekwendeni in the Ngoni highlands[12] of northern Malawi from the 1880s. This was an area inhabited predominantly by Tumbuka agriculturalists, who had been subjected to an invasion by Mbelwa's branch of the Ngoni people in the mid-1850s. Livingstonia agents such as Robert Laws and the civil engineer James Stewart, who visited the main Ngoni villages in 1878 and 1879, less than twenty-five years later, contented themselves with largely descriptive accounts of 'a gently undulating country, flanked by hills on all sides, and cut up by several watercourses dry except in the rains'. Stewart noted that 'The Kasitu itself is the only running stream. The land is cultivated to a considerable extent. Maize is chiefly grown. Trees are few and those of a stunted growth.'[13] Laws added that 'Each village along the road seems to have its herds of cattle, some twenty or thirty, others about one hundred.'[14] Stewart provides a detailed account of a *citimene*-type form of shifting cultivation in which 'The natives cut down branches of trees and collect them in a large

---

[10] For Johnston's wider conservationist concerns see John M. Mackenzie, *Empire of Nature and The Nature of Empire* (East Linton, Tuckwell Press, 1997), pp. 42–4.

[11] *Report by Commissioner Johnston of the First Three Years' Administration of the Eastern Portion of British Central Africa*, 1983, Cmd. 7504; Richard Grove, *Green Imperialism* (Cambridge, CUP, 1995) pp. 380–473; Grove, *Ecology, Climate and Empire* (Cambridge, White Horse Press, 1997), pp. 5–36, 86–123.

[12] This is probably the least unsatisfactory term to describe the highlands west of Lake Malawi and south of the Nyika plateau. Colonial authorities from 1904 wrote of the 'Mombera district' and later of 'Mzimba district'. Historians have veered between 'Northern Ngoniland' and uNgoni'.

[13] Jack Thompson (ed.), *From Nyassa to Tanganyika. The Journal of James Stewart CE in Central Africa 1876–1879* (Blantyre, Central Africana Malawi, 1989), entry for 17 September 1879, p. 74.

[14] Robert Laws to Convenor, Livingstonia Committee, February 1897, *Free Church of Scotland Monthly Record*, 2 June 1879, p. 136.

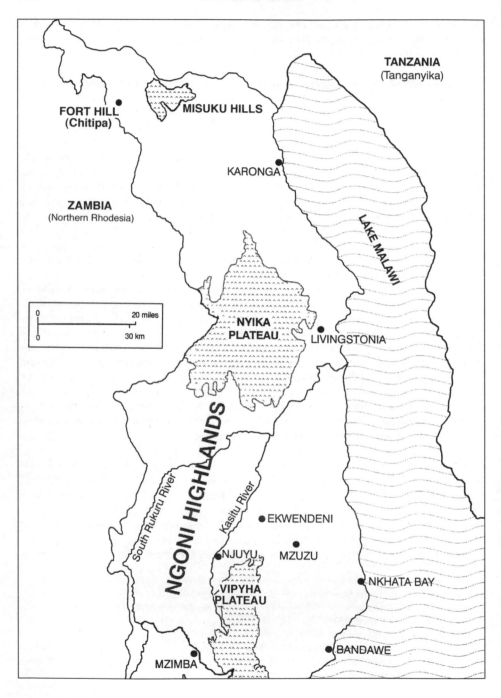

Map 8.1 Malawi: the North

heap perhaps two feet high.... This they burn and then hoe the ashes into the soil of their gardens.' It is important to note, however, that this account is drawn from observations made north of Karonga in the vicinity of the Misuku hills and not among the Ngoni.[15]

The shift from this descriptive mode to a new powerful representation of environmental decline was associated with the establishment of permanent mission stations in the area. In the late nineteenth century, as Markku Hokkanen has recently noted, Scottish churchmen were deeply influenced by ideas of evolutionary degeneration and regeneration.[16] These were given popular form in the work of Professor Henry Drummond, a Free Church preacher and scientist who visited the Malawi region in 1883,[17] and, as they applied to Africa, of Dr James Stewart, the founder of Livingstonia, whose Duff Lectures were published in 1903.[18] Central to this thesis was the belief in a perpetual struggle between evolutionary progress and decline, in which African societies were depicted as being constantly dragged down by the degrading customs which they practised, yet with a potential for regeneration which Christianity alone could tap.

For W.A. Elmslie, who established himself permanently at Njuyu in 1885, and even for the more moderate Donald Fraser, defective agricultural practices could thus be placed alongside social evils such as polygamy, slavery and beer-drinking in building up a portrait of a society in a state of moral and economic collapse.[19] Writing in his influential study, *Among the Wild Ngoni*, Elmslie described the Ngoni highlands as a land 'once covered by dense forests of large trees, which have been ruthlessly cut down for firewood or, as is more frequently the case, to be burned to the ground as manure for new gardens'.[20] This in turn, so Fraser argued, resulted in the carrying away of topsoil and the subsequent decline of rainfall.

> The heavy tropical rains carried the loosened soil down the slopes and filled the river beds, until the once loamy ground became hard, sun-baked and sterile, and the clear streams disappeared, leaving only waterless sandy channels. [21]

In the first of what was to become a regular series of critical comments, Fraser signalled out the *visoso* system of cultivating millet, used by the Ngoni in the production of beer, as particularly destructive of woodland:

[15] National Library of Scotland, Edinburgh (hereafter NLS) 7904, James Stewart C.E., 'Report on a Journey of Exploration, September to December 1879'.

[16] Markku Hokkanen, 'Moral Education as Medicine – An African Case Study: the Livingstonia Medical missionaries in Nyasaland, 1875–1914', (unpublished paper, 1999).

[17] Henry Drummond, *Natural Law and the Spiritual World* (London, Hodder and Stoughton, 1884); Drummond. *Tropical Africa* (London, Hodder and Stoughton, 1889). For an excellent introduction to Drummond's ideas see D. W. Bebbington, 'Henry Drummond, evangelicalism and science', *Records of the Scottish Church History Society* 28 (1998), pp. 129–48.

[18] James Stewart, *Dawn in the Dark Continent* (Edinburgh, Oliphant Anderson and Ferrier, 1903),

[19] It should be stressed that Fraser in particular significantly modified his views in later years. See John McCracken, *Politics and Christianity* (Cambridge, CUP, 1977), pp. 194–97; T. Jack Thompson, *Christianity in Northern Malawi. Donald Fraser's missionary methods and Ngoni culture* (Leiden, 1995), pp. 151–3, 271–73.

[20] W. A. Elmslie, *Among the Wild Ngoni* (Edinburgh and London, Oliphant Anderson and Ferrier, 1899), p.32.

[21] Donald Fraser, *The Autobiography of an African* (London, Seeley, Service and Co., 1925), p. 20.

The ground has to be carefully prepared, trees are hewn down in the hot season, and left to dry in the blazing sun. The whole patch of garden is covered with these trees and the branches, then when the first clouds appear the wood is fired. For a day it blazes, and then during the gathering of the clouds the atmosphere is thick with the smoke of burning trees. The rain comes and washes the carbon into the soil, and it makes an excellent fertiliser. But the crop exhausts the ground in two or three years, so another patch of forest is cut down and burnt, and another garden cultivated and so the country is rapidly being deforested.[22]

The recognition that the crop was largely used in the making of beer brought the twin issues of moral and environmental degradation together.[23] 'We have had to denounce the beer drinking as a menace to the social order of the country, and ... we have preached against the deforesting of the land as a wicked improvidence', Fraser informed his Scottish audience in 1900. He added that, 'The native church has, of its own initiative, taken up the question and enjoined on the members total abstinence and the preservation of forests.' One Christian sub-chief, so he claimed, had formed his own police force with the express intention of preventing people cutting down trees.[24]

Elmslie's emphasis was rather on the disintegration of the Ngoni kingdom as a political entity – an event that he believed would result from the destruction of the land as much as from external pressures. Writing in 1886 he relished the prospect that:

The end of the Angoni kingdom as a marauding tribe is not far distant. Hemmed in on every side, they must give in soon and the fact that they are looking for an uncultivated country as a new settlement means a great deal in the history of a tribe which has never broken ground for itself but swallowed the gardens of other tribes.[25]

The subsequent drift of an increasing stream of Ngoni settlers south from the Kasitu valley, the original home of the kingdom, to the undulating plains of the Mzimba district was regarded by Elmslie as confirmation of his warning, though whether in fact this moving of villages was evidence of economic collapse or adaptability, as some historians have argued, is difficult to prove.[26] What is the case is that by the mid-1890s, many new villages had been opened south in the area known as Mzimba and that, in Elmslie's words, 'already hundreds of square miles of good bush – not forest as the bush is all growth from former trees cut down by Tumbuka or Tshewa [Chewa] – is being cleared for lupoka [millet] gardens'.[27] 'For many years back the Northern Ngoni have been gradually moving away from the Kasitu basin seeking new gardens in the wooded valleys to the south especially along the basin of the Rukuru and its tributaries', another missionary noted in 1902. 'The failure of the crops this year has

---

[22] Donald Fraser, 'The Zulu of Nyasaland: their Manners and Customs', *Proceedings of the Philosophical Society of Glasgow* 32 (1900–01), pp. 69–70.

[23] For the formulation of similar views by Scottish missionaries in South Africa see Richard Grove, 'Scottish Missionaries, Evangelical Discourses and the Origins of Conservation Thinking in Southern Africa, 1820–1900', *Journal of Southern African Studies* (*JSAS*) 15 (1989), pp. 163–87.

[24] Fraser, 'Zulu of Nyasaland', pp. 70; 74.

[25] Edinburgh University Library (hereafter EUL), Shepperson Collection, Elmslie to Laws, 22 November 1886.

[26] For an alternative view which emphasises the efficiency of Ngoni agricultural practices, but unfortunately without engaging with Vail's thesis, see Thompson, *Christianity in Northern Malawi*, pp. 22–4.

[27] NLS 7648, Elmslie to Laws, 9 December 1895.

intensified the desire to move. And when the chief intimated his intention of going, a large number of the *indunas* who lived in his neighbourhood said they would follow.'[28]

It is an indication of the marginality of northern Malawi to the colonial government that official concern for environmental issues began to emerge there only in the 1920s, more than thirty years after the intervention of the missionaries. The initial spur appears to have been the evidence given by Dr Laws to the 1920 Land Commission which vividly contrasted the disastrous ecological conditions of the Ngoni highlands at that time with an imagined golden era half a century earlier. In 1879 Laws and Stewart had written that there were few trees in the district and that the Kasitu was the only perennial stream.[29] Looking back in 1920, however, Laws remembered 'that the northern areas now peopled by the invading Angoni were well wooded only fifty years ago and that streams flowing all the year round were plentiful'. 'At that time', according to the Assistant Director of Agriculture, A. J. Hornby, 'he [Laws] knew of at least twenty large streams in the country of Mombera which formerly flowed all the year round but which, in consequence of the vast destruction of forests, have now ceased to flow at all, rendering vast tracts of land uninhabitable.'[30]

Laws's concerns were taken up by Hornby, who quoted him in full, and also by the district administrator in the Mzimba District, Ion Ramsay, from 1932.[31] In his pioneering survey of soil erosion in Nyasaland, Hornby gave special attention to the *visoso* method of cultivating finger millet, which he described as involving the destruction each year of large areas of woodland in the north. This in turn provided the ecological justification for intervention for which the Mzimba DC was waiting. An amateur historian, Ramsay had already written a potted history of the area, emphasising the culpability of the Ngoni for denuding the land of trees and making it waterless and infertile.[32] Now, in an action that mirrored that of Fraser back in the 1890s, he called a special meeting with chiefs and headmen at Mzimba in August 1932, aimed at bringing 'the system of uncontrolled *visoso (Ntewele)*' to an end. Chiefs were informed that the cultivation of finger millet would still be allowed but only on condition that a modified form of *visoso* was employed in which the best coppice shoots would be left to grow undamaged. [33]

This must be regarded as an essentially rhetorical statement at a time when the coercive forces available to the DC were limited to little more than a dozen policemen, most of them heavily involved in following up tax defaulters. Nevertheless, it does constitute the beginning of a more interventionist approach that was to be given further ideological backing through the findings of the *Report of the Agricultural Survey of the Five Most Northerly Districts of Nyasaland* that was published in 1938. Commissioned

---

[28] *Aurora* [Journal of the Livingstonia Mission], June 1902, p. 2.

[29] Thompson (ed.), *Journal of James Stewart*, entry for 17 September 1879, p. 4.

[30] A.J. Hornby, *Denudation and Soil Erosion in Nyasaland* (Zomba, Government Printer, 1934), pp. 7–8. I have not been able to locate a verbatim record of this evidence. However, a summary of broadly similar views, not identified with any individual, is contained in *Report of a Commission to Enquire Into and Report Upon Certain Matters Connected with the Occupation of Land in the Nyasaland Protectorate* (Zomba, Government Printer, 1921) pp. 20–1.

[31] Hornby, *Denudation and Soil Erosion*.

[32] Malawi National Archives (hereafter MNA), NNM 1/14/6, D.C. Mzimba, 'Suggested Application of a System of Indirect Rule in the Mombera District', 27 January 1930.

[33] MNA Mzimba District Book, Vol. 4, August to December 1932, Report on a Council Meeting, Mzimba, 26 August 1932.

as a follow-up to the 1935 Report on Emigrant Labour, the Agricultural Survey was conducted under the general charge of Hornby and largely represented his views. Once more attention is drawn to 'the results of uncontrolled and unwise clearing of land' and once more the *visoso* system involving the burning of large quantities of timber and brushwood on finger millet gardens is seen as the major source of trouble. What is new is the tone of urgency that Hornby brings to his conclusions: 'It may again be asked if in twenty years time the bulk of the people will not in the normal year suffer from actual starvation and be incapable of real efforts in the improvement of their living conditions.'[34]

In his pioneering study, 'The Making of the "Dead North"', Leroy Vail follows the Scottish missionaries in depicting the impact of the Ngoni as being ecologically disastrous. Prior to the 1850s, in his view, 'the Tumbuka had achieved an ecological balance' through the employment of 'a longfallow system of agriculture' combined with a dispersed pattern of settlement. But with the coming of the Ngoni, land was ruined through the over-grazing of cattle, the creation of centralised villages in 'an island of fairly dense human and animal settlement' and, above all, through 'the denudation of the countryside of its bush and tree cover'. Immense numbers of trees were consumed, the water table in consequence declined and the result was that 'the ecological balance between man and his environment was upset'. In the years after 1906, hut tax and labour migration were to acerbate the crisis but it was one that the Ngoni had created.[35]

Vail's views are always worthy of respect, but in this case there is evidence to suggest that he has too easily accepted the complex set of assumptions, some false, some questionable and some in part true, created by missionaries and officials to explain ecological decline in a key area of northern Malawi. Whether it is likely that in the space of less than 30 years a relatively small group of invaders, equipped with hoes and only some thousands strong, would have inflicted the damage envisaged must remain a matter of doubt.[36] What is more certain is that there is no justification for the assumption, made by Fraser and subsequently elaborated, that *visoso* was an agricultural technique introduced by the Ngoni and utilised only by them. In fact, as a careful reading of contemporary sources indicates and as the work of agricultural scientists like William Allan confirms, the practice of cutting trees and burning the branches into ashes was employed in a variety of forms by a substantial number of peoples in northern Malawi and north-eastern Zambia both prior to and following the Ngoni invasion.[37] Even Elmslie, as we have seen, notes that it was Tumbuka and Chewa cultivators rather than Ngoni who were responsible for destroying forests in southern Mzimba; further north *visoso*-like techniques were being used by cultivators in the Misuku Hills by at least the late 1870s.

Just as important, descriptions of forest loss often took a ritualised and exaggerated

---

[34] *Report of the Agricultural Survey of the Five Most Northerly Districts of Nyasaland* (Zomba, Government Printer, 1938), p. 79.

[35] Vail, 'Making of the "Dead North"', pp. 237–43.

[36] Vail's emphasis on the destructive impact of the Ngoni economy is strikingly at odds with most recent research on 'Nguni' societies including J. Guy, *The Destruction of the Zulu Kingdom* (London, Longman, 1979) and most other articles in Peires, *Before and after Shaka*.

[37] William Allan, *The African Husbandman* (Edinburgh, Oliver and Boyd, 1965), pp. 66–76, 99–137. See also G. G. Trapnell, *The Soils, Vegetation and Agricultural Systems of North Eastern Rhodesia* (Lusaka, Government Printer, 1943).

form.[38] As we have seen, Elmslie and Fraser in their published accounts emphasise the treeless state of northern Ngoniland by the 1880s in contrast to the forests that had existed prior to the coming of the Ngoni only three decades earlier. But these accounts are implicitly contradicted by Laws's testimony from the 1920s, which contrasts the 'well wooded' valleys and plains of fifty years earlier with the vast tracts of uninhabitable land that existed when he spoke. This again can be contrasted with the views of the Provincial Commissioner for the Northern Province, writing in 1948 of the Kasitu Valley which Stewart had visited in 1879. The Provincial Commissioner declared his intention of bringing the unofficial members of the Legislative Council to the Valley 'to see on the ground the appalling erosion, and to hear at first hand from living Africans that sixty or seventy years ago this great valley, nearly 70 miles long, was a graceful parkland of great trees, deep soil and wavering grasses'.[39] Yet Stewart in 1879 had noted of the Valley: 'Trees are few and those are of a stunted growth'.[40] This, of course, is not to deny that the quality of the soil may well have deteriorated over the decades as a result of intensive cultivation. It is to suggest, however, that the 'graceful parkland of great trees' was the product of the Provincial Commissioner's imagination, an idealised landscape drawing for its inspiration on England as much as Africa. Not until the changing vegetation forms of the highlands have been studied in detail will it be possible to state with any degree of conviction when forest loss took place and how extensive it has been. Here, it is only necessary to say that, by the 1930s, much of the Northern Province was being depicted in colonial circles as a region facing imminent environmental collapse as a result of the ravages imposed upon it by African cultivators.

Colonial intervention: the first stage

The transition from conservationist concern to colonial intervention took place in a number of stages. Schemes aimed at stream bank protection and the establishment of forest reserves were developed by the Forestry Department from the early 1920s, but these were soon to be dwarfed by the more interventionist approaches that resulted from the development of the tobacco industry in the Southern and Central Provinces. In the initial stages, A. J. Hornby was particularly concerned with encouraging planters to grow their tobacco on terraced ridges.[41] But from 1934 the Native Tobacco Board turned its attention to African tobacco growers, who were instructed to cease from growing their crops on mounds or *matutu,* which were believed to be susceptible to erosion, and to cultivate instead on terraced ridges. Efforts were also made to get tobacco growers to construct contour bunds, 'large ridges with a base of a few feet which contour the fields at a grade of one in four hundred and are spaced on an average forty yards apart', designed to prevent the rains sweeping away topsoil. In 1935 it was claimed that 'Under the direction of Capt. Antill of the Native Tobacco Board 2,500

---

[38] For a similar discussion from West Africa see J. Fairhead and M. Leach, *Misreading the African Landscape. Society and ecology in a forest-savanna mosaic* (Cambridge, CUP, 1996), pp. 24–54.

[39] Acting Provincial Commissioner Northern Province to Chief Secretary, 18 July 1949, MNA 2/17/7F/879.

[40] Thompson, *From Nyassa to Tanganyika,* p. 74. On a previous visit to the Ngoni highlands in 1878 Stewart noted: 'Chipitula's country is not so desolate and weird as Chikuse's [near modern Ncheu] but the soil is poor and wood very scarce.', p. 62.

[41] *Annual Reports of the Nyasaland Agricultural Department,* 1930 and 1931.

acres of gardens have been protected against erosion'.[42] A year later, 6,454 acres of land in the Lilongwe District were said to have been bunded and in addition several village demonstration plots had been opened, designed to demonstrate the advantages that manuring and crop rotation would bring.[43]

From the mid-1930s concern over erosion was heightened as a consequence of official reactions to the 'dust bowl' disaster of the American plains caused by a combination of drought and the ruthless application of capital-intensive farming methods.[44] Up to then, ideas on conservation had largely been drawn by Nyasaland officials from their contacts with agriculturalists in South Africa and Southern Rhodesia.[45] Now, however, the American example was brought to the fore and administrators and agriculturalists reacted with alarm. In October 1935 the Colonial Advisory Council on Agriculture and Animal Health, meeting at the Colonial Office in London, called for the appointment of wholetime soil erosion officers in each of the East African colonies to take preventive measures against erosion 'with the minimum of delay'.[46] The Governor in Nyasaland was glad to concur. And the result was that, in May 1936, approval was granted for the secondment of Paul Topham from the Forestry Department to act as Soil Conservation Officer.[47] On 1 January 1937 Topham took up his post at the start of a three-year campaign involving increasingly coercive methods of intervention. No attempt was made by Topham to penetrate into northern Malawi; instead a series of campaigns was launched in hilly areas in the Ncheu, Zomba, Cholo [Thyolo], and Lower Shire districts designed to impose the construction of ridges and bunds on an increasingly hostile local population.[48] In what was to become a familiar pattern, Native Authorities were induced to pass orders enforcing the construction of ridges, which they then failed to enforce in the face of the opposition of their people. Topham then demanded that District Commissioners should over-rule these Authorities and issue supplementary orders themselves.[49] 'It is my considered opinion', he stated, 'that, to enforce the orders already given, either every offender must now be prosecuted and heavily punished, or else supplementary orders setting a near time limit must be issued.'[50]

For the northern province, Topham's intervention was less important than a shift in the direction of government policy that took place in the 1930s. In the previous decade, colonial officials, aided and abetted by the Native Tobacco Board and the British Cotton Growing Association, had been responsible for thwarting two of the most promising initiatives in peasant agriculture in the province: the attempt to develop tobacco growing north of Kasungu, which ended with the closure of the market at Ngara in 1930, and the attempt to grow cotton on the Karonga flood plain, which was halted following the discovery of the pink bollworm in 1925.[51] In 1928, however, the

[42] *Annual Report of the Nyasaland Agricultural Department*, 1935, p.17.

[43] *Annual Report of the Nyasaland Agricultural Department*, 1936, pp.46–7.

[44] John McCracken, 'Experts and Expertise in Colonial Malawi', *African Affairs* 81, 322 (1982), pp. 110–14.

[45] See William Beinart, 'Soil Erosion, Conservation and Ideas about Development', *JSAS* 11, 1 (1984).

[46] See file on Soil Erosion, MNA FE 1/4/1.

[47] MNA FE 1/4/1, H. B. Kittermaster to J.H. Thomas, Secretary of State for Colonies, 26 March 1936.

[48] MNA NS 1/2/4, P. Topham to PC, Southern Province, 15 September 1937.

[49] MNA NS 1/24, Topham to DC, Cholo District, 29 November 1938.

[50] *Ibid.*

[51] MNA S1/61/32 and S1/112/340, Kasungu District Annual Reports for 1931 and 1935; MNA S1/1751/25, 'Cotton, North Nyasa, 1925–1940'.

British South Africa Company, which for more than thirty years had claimed ownership to over 2 million acres of undeveloped land in the North Nyasa district, indicated that it was finally ready to withdraw. The government, in consequence, established the North Nyasa Reserves Commission under the chairmanship of Judge Heythorn Reed to investigate conditions;[52] at the same time, the BSAC began belatedly to sell off land to European settlers, two of whom took the lead in planting coffee in the Misuku Hills overlooking the Tanganyikan border.[53] Faced by the evidence of a striking absence of local opportunities in the north, Reed's Commission came to the conclusion that these remote hills, inhabited lightly by the Sukwa people whose origins lie across the Songwe in Tanzania, were specially suited to the production of robusta coffee, to be grown by peasants who had already indicated their eagerness to become involved.[54] The disadvantage was that these abrupt ridges were perceived to be particularly vulnerable to soil erosion as a result of heavy rain washing away topsoil. The Commission therefore recommended that, while coffee growing should be fostered, it should be a condition that peasants should terrace the ground on which it was planted.[55] By 1930 the Department of Agriculture had begun to distribute seed and establish coffee nurseries. Six years later, Dennis Smalley was appointed to the district to develop the Misuku Land Usage Scheme, one of the earliest examples of a comprehensive, state-directed, agricultural scheme designed to radically restructure peasant society.

All texts require interpretation; Smalley's accounts of the Misuku Land Usage Scheme require more interpretation than most. A former First World War major, who still used his title, Smalley appears to have drawn on East African discourses of Environmentalism and Betterment in developing his military-style campaign.[56] An inspired self-publicist, he succeeded for over a decade in convincing a range of agriculturalists of the remarkable success of the scheme he masterminded. But it is by no means easy to determine how far what he describes relates to objective reality and how far to a fantasy world of his own imagining.[57]

Smalley's accounts of the Misuku scheme divide into three main parts: a description of the havoc wreaked by 'primitive' Sukwa farmers (mixed agriculturalists and pastoralists) on the natural environment; an account of the strategies he, Smalley, introduced to rectify the problem; and a discussion of the beneficial results as perceived by Sukwa peasants and British agriculturalists alike. The problem, as he saw it, was that by the mid-1930s overpopulation, deforestation and the mismanagement of cattle had resulted in chronic soil erosion in the Misuku hills. This had come about in particular from the Sukwa strategy of producing finger millet on land fertilised through the

---

[52] See PRO CO 525/123, file entitled 'British South Africa Company Land in North Nyasa District'.

[53] PRO CO 525/123, Governor Nyasaland to Secretary of State for Colonies, 15 May 1928; W. O. Mulwafu, 'The development of the coffee industry in the Misuku hills of Chitipa District, 1934–1964' (Chancellor College, History Seminar Paper No. 12, 1986–7).

[54] MNA COM 4/1, Interim Report of the North Nyasa Reserves Commission, 1929.

[55] *Ibid.*.

[56] See Fiona D. Mackenzie, 'Contested Ground: Colonial Narratives and the Kenyan Environment, 1920–1945', *JSAS* 26 4 (2000), pp. 679–718.

[57] Smalley's accounts appear in three forms: in an article entitled 'The Misuku Land Usage Scheme' published in the *Nyasaland Agricultural Quarterly Journal* 4, 3 (1944) and in two unpublished papers with similar titles though rather different forms entitled 'The Misuku Land Usage Scheme North Nyasa District, Nyasaland 1938–1943' and 'The Misuku Land Usage Scheme, 1938–1947', Rhodes House Library Oxford, Mss. Afr. S. 918.

felling of trees and burning of branches (a form of *visoso* or *citimene* already described). In addition, however, Smalley accused Sukwa farmers of constructing vertical ridges on steep slopes and of grazing cattle and goats on drying riverbeds – both activities that resulted in heavy gully erosion. The remaining rainforest was being rapidly depleted. Timber for firewood was hard to find.

Smalley's solution, which he introduced in successive stages over a five-year period, involved a comprehensive restructuring of peasant society based in part on the revival of an indigenous agricultural technique once employed widely but now largely abandoned. This was the Vingonyeka system of hill cultivation, described by Smalley as a form of box ridging in which ridges running from the top to bottom of a hill were interrupted by the construction of bunds placed at right angles to them. Stream banks were protected through the introduction of protective vegetation such as bananas and sugar cane. Millet growing was prohibited except under strict supervision. Cattle were banned from homesteads and were restricted to designated grazing zones. Evergreen forests were protected by being designated as reserves.[58]

At first, so Smalley records, many Sukwa people strongly resented this massive interference with their methods of farming and fled across the Nyasaland border into Tanganyika and Rhodesia rather than submit to the new demands. By 1942, however, these doubts had been largely overcome; contour bunding and contour ridging had been widely introduced and gullies were being protected. All cattle, with the exception of a few milch cows, had been moved to communal kraals; grass burning no longer took place; forest reserves had been established. So remarkable was the progress that by the mid-1940s groups of chiefs from other areas were regularly brought to the Misuku hills to admire the progress made.[59] Thriving forest areas had now been established; abundant supplies of bamboo existed in villages and along stream banks; cattle had assumed a more balanced place in the economy of the locality; soil erosion had been almost halted. Virtually no growing of millet took place. In what is almost an aside, Smalley admits that, in 1947, several offenders against agricultural rules had been punished in Native Authority Courts. But he adds that, 'Today the Asukwa people marvel at their past stupidity and praise what has been done for them.'[60] A population which once had to emigrate in search of food, so he claims, was now the fortunate possessor of a well-balanced food supply, with the surplus being sold in neighbouring markets.

In 1948, less than a year after Smalley had written his account, the intelligence report for the Karonga District undermined his easy optimism by noting that 'there is still great opposition to agricultural policy in the area.... The opposition is not against contour ridging so much as against the rules which make millet cultivation from their point of view so difficult.'[61] For colonial strategists in the 1940s, however, such reservations were less important than the example of successful conservationist planning that the Misuku Scheme appeared to provide. It was, in part, with Smalley's achievement in mind that the planners entered on a new and infinitely more dynamic phase of colonial intervention in the aftermath of the Second World War.

[58] Smalley, 'Misuku Land Usage Scheme, 1938–1947'.
[59] Mulwafu, 'The development of the coffee industry in the Misuku hills'. See also *Annual Reports of the Nyasaland Department of Agriculture,* 1940–42.
[60] Smalley, Misuku Land Usage Scheme, 1938–1947'.
[61] MNA NN 4/2/11, Intelligence Report, Karonga District for 1948.

Conservation strategies and peasant resistance in the post-war era

In Malawi, as in other colonies in East and Southern Africa, the determination to increase agricultural productivity while coping with a perceived crisis of accelerating soil erosion was a key factor in explaining the intensification of state intervention that took place following the Second World War.[62] R. W. Kettlewell, the architect of the new policy of intervention, had been deeply influenced by the alarming account of environmental degradation world-wide contained in Jacks' and Whyte's 'semi-racist and inaccurate' book, *The Rape of the Earth,* published in 1939.[63] On his appointment as Senior Agricultural Officer for the two northern provinces in 1943, he therefore took the lead in calling for the implementation of comprehensive land usage legislation.[64] Shortage of staff and money, combined with the reluctance of Ellis, the Provincial Commissioner, to risk provoking the opposition of African cultivators, prevented any major initiatives being taken at the time.[65] But when Kettlewell returned to the attack in the aftermath of the war, his policy was rapidly approved. In a last ditch stand, the liberal-minded Director of Agriculture, P. B. Garnett, made clear to Kettlewell 'that I was not prepared at this stage to be responsible for, or associated with, the enactment of any mass legislation in respect of soil conservation on Native Trust Land'.[66] But with the arrival in 1948 of a new interventionist governor, Geoffrey Colby, the opposition was finally stilled. A strong admirer of Kettlewell's energy and commitment, Colby engineered Garnett's humiliating transfer to the Gambia and Kettlewell's appointment in his place.[67] New Natural Resources legislation was introduced with the specific aim of bypassing the Native Authorities. Funds were made available on a much larger scale than previously for the enactment of soil conservation measures. The resources of the District Administration were committed to the task of agricultural extension. And with new staff in place, large-scale schemes were introduced, designed 'to substitute contour and box ridging for the indigenous system of flat and mound cultivation over as wide an area as possible'.[68]

In a narrative no less moralistic than those once presented by Scottish missionaries, Kettlewell justified increasingly draconian state intervention on Malthusian grounds by depicting peasant farmers as wreaking terrible havoc on the environment through their inability to adjust their farming methods to the rapid growth of population:

> It is a regrettable fact that the radical change in environment which the rapid increase in population has brought about has not resulted in the natural evolution of better agricultural

---

[62] Useful comparative accounts include John Iliffe, *A Modern History of Tanganyika* (Cambridge, CUP, 1979), pp. 436–84; Steven Feirman, *Peasant Intellectuals* (Madison, WI, University of Wisconsin Press, 1990), pp. 163–67.

[63] G. V. Jacks and R. O. Whyte, *The Rape of the Earth: A world survey of soil erosion* (London, Faber and Faber, 1939); Grove, *Ecology, Climate and Empire*, pp. 34–5. I owe this observation to William Beinart who interviewed Kettlewell in 1982.

[64] MNA NC1/30/1, Kettlewell to Provincial Commissioner Northern Province, 31 January 1944.

[65] MNA NC1/30/1, Ellis to Kettlewell, 15 June 1944.

[66] MNA NCL 1/30/1, Garnett to Kettlewell, 16 October 1947.

[67] In fact there was a year's delay, filled by short-term appointments, before Colby succeeded in getting Kettlewell promoted. See Colin Baker, *Development Governor. A Biography of Sir Geoffrey Colby* (London, British Academic Press, 1994), pp. 116–18; RHL Mss Afr.S. 1811, R.W. Kettlewell, 'Memories of a Colonial Career' (unpublished typescript).

[68] *Annual Report of the Nyasaland Department of Agriculture for 1944.*

practice to cope with it. The change has been too rapid and the traditional methods contain scarcely even the foundation on which improvement might naturally develop.There was no consciousness of erosion; crop rotation did not exist since maize with a few interplanted legumes provided a fairly adequate diet; livestock were regarded simply as wealth; land tenure was on a communal basis; and in the majority of tribes the matrilineal system of marriage prevailed.[69]

Matrilocality, ensuring, as it did, the access of land to women, was a particularly pernicious obstacle in the southern and central provinces: 'There is no doubt that this system, by removing the man's personal interest and responsibility in the land he cultivates, is one of the greatest stumbling blocks to agricultural progress.'[70] By the mid-1950s Kettlewell had come to the conclusion that it was only through a social revolution imposed from above resulting in the emergence of 'a class of [male] yeoman farmer with security in the land he farms' that the problem would be solved. This he accepted, would have to be combined with the creation of 'a landless class of workers' and the mass 'emigration by family units' to Southern Rhodesia, made all the more possible through the recent creation of the Federation.[71]

In much of the Southern Province, schemes for soil conservation were closely associated with the introduction of ambitious land settlement programmes involving the forced movement of thousands of Malawians onto new areas of land.[72] In the Northern Province, however, land settlement schemes were few in number and instead the initial impetus focused on the prohibition of mound cultivation and of the *visoso* method of growing finger millet, condemned by missionaries and administrators alike for its destructive effect on indigenous woodlands. The first concerted steps appear to have been taken in 1947 but, a year later, it was claimed: 'in Ngoni country opposition to contour ridging was general. Rules had been made to prohibit *visoso* and mound cultivation but they had not been properly enforced.'[73] Similar reactions were expressed in the Karonga District where the new DC noted in his diary: 'God, how these people loathe the agricultural department.'[74] And a comparable response was recorded in the Chikulamayembe area with the Chief Conservation officer noting: 'Regarding the ridge cropping programme, it is doubtful if this would be maintained without constant supervision by Agricultural Instructors backed by Native Administration Chiefs.'[75]

Even Kettlewell, in drafting comprehensive Soil Conservation orders in 1948, accepted that 'Order No. 3 requiring general ridging might not be applied on Trust Land and in Mzimba district at the outset, as lack of supervision and general opposition make it impracticable at present.'[76] But Kettlewell was insistent that the practice of *visoso* should be prohibited, though he introduced a provision that the planting of

---

[69] R.W. Kettlewell, *An Outline of Agrarian Problems and Policy in Nyasaland* (Zomba, Government Printer, 1955), p. 2.

[70] *Ibid.*

[71] *Ibid.*, pp. 3, 7.

[72] For this process in the Lower Shire Valley see Mandala, *Work and Control in a Peasant Economy*, pp. 191–268.

[73] *Annual Report of the Nyasaland Departments of Agriculture*, 1947 and 1948.

[74] Henry Phillips, *From Obscurity to Bright Dawn* (London, Radcliffe Press, 1998), p. 22.

[75] W. J. Badcock, Chief Conservation Officer to Director of Agriculture, 31 December 1946, MNA 1.17.7F/879.

[76] R. W. Kettlewell, memo on 'Soil Conservation Orders', 6 May [1948?], MNA 2.17.7F/879.

finger millet on the flat would be allowed. Not until the end of 1949 were the first gardens in the Mzimba district ridged and this resulted only from a herculean effort by newly appointed rangers who toured the area seeing that work on ridging had been carried out and punishing offenders.[77] Some success in this draconian policy was noted in 1950 when 32,000 gardens in the Mzimba district were ridged, according to the agricultural authorities. But this was only a prelude to the great push of 1951 when 6,400 miles of bunds were said to have been constructed in the Northern Province alone.[78]

Something of the flavour of the debate over soil conservation policy in the 1950s can be obtained from the remarkably frank *ulendo* diary kept by Griff Jones, District Commissioner in the Nkhata Bay area, on his tour of the district with the Agricultural Officer, Ted Wilmot, in 1952.[79] This was a district that had been deliberately excluded from the provisions of the 1951 Natural Resources Rules. But that did not prevent the lakeside people, at meeting after meeting, vociferously criticising the government's conservation campaign and its local representatives.

Jones's notes are particularly interesting because they reflect what has been described elsewhere as a 'counter-narrative' – an account responsive to the knowledge and concerns of local Tonga villagers and yet one reluctant to abandon support for the official 'scientific' discourse which Jones's colleague, Wilmot, was attempting to propagate.[80] 'The Kasitu Valley bunding [in the Mzimba district] is held up as an awful example and they are quite definite that they want none of that nonsense here', he noted following his visit to Chisadizi village in January 1952.[81] These views were elaborated on at Vimaso village where, according to Jones, men and women objected to:

(1) Contour ridging because in these steep hills the ridges are washed flat. Fair enough.
(2) Strip gardens, because the gardens cease to look like gardens & I understand the boundaries of the gardens would no longer be clear. Balls.
(3) Bunds because they brought starvation in Mzimba. Blood pressure!
(4) Not planting on stream banks, because only there do vegetables grow in the dry season, & vegetables essential because they have no *ndio* [relish] hereabouts (?)
(5) The wretched Agricultural Officer, because he brought bunds and hunger to the Angoni. More blood pressure.[82]

As the tour progressed, Jones's unease at the policies he was required to advocate became increasingly clear. 'I DO THINK that T.W. should not stuff bunds down their throats until he can show them successful gardens of his own, contrasted, side by side, with gardens cultivated by African methods', he noted after yet another rancorous meeting dominated by the common complaint that the construction of bunds resulted in a reduction in available fertile land and hence a fall in production. 'T.W. should settle

---

[77] *Report of the Nyasaland Agricultural Department for 1950*, pp. 11–12.

[78] *Report of the Nyasaland Agricultural Department for 1951*.

[79] RHL Mss Afr. V 123, Griff Jones, 'Ulendo Diary', 19521–53. For a more composed view by Jones, written after his retirement from the Colonial service see Griff Jones, *Britain and Nyasaland* (London, 1964).

[80] The concept of 'counter narratives' as they apply to Kenya in the 1940s is usefully discussed in Mackenzie, 'Contested Ground'.

[81] Jones, 'Ulendo Diary', entry for 14 January 1952.

[82] *Ibid.*, 5 April 1952.

down to being a better farmer than the Africans; if he can, he will have a hope of teaching them, & if he can't he's got nothing to teach. And if he won't I'm afraid my sympathy is with the Tonga.'[83]

Everywhere Jones went, people complained that they 'were afraid of fines and imprisonment, which I could do nothing to counter – & did not try.'[84] Villagers were insistent that if cassava was grown on ridges it would rot – as had happened in 1942 during an earlier experiment.[85] Time and again, they warned that the recently completed bunding campaign in the Ngoni highlands to the west of them had resulted in nothing but 'trouble & hunger.'[86] As Jones wryly noted, attempts by the agricultural officer to invoke the Bible on his side in a faint echo of earlier Scottish missionary discourse were refuted by Tonga military veterans with direct experience of the Biblical lands:

> Ted said that Garden of Eden was now a desert, because they hadn't put in any bunds, & nobody lived there any more. An old soldier got up & said T. was talking balls; he'd been to Aden & they still had lots of people living there, with gardens too. Ted had to take refuge in the Gobi desert, where nobody had been.[87]

Elsewhere, there were complaints concerning the excessive labour involved in digging bunds, the loss of fertile land, and above all the fear that bunding would serve as a prelude for European settlement in the area.[88]

Griff Jones's experiences are of value in demonstrating the depth of resentment against government intervention that could be felt even in an area where coercive measures were reduced to a minimum. In the northern highlands, where the attempt to ban *visoso* was construed as an assault on cultural identity, the effects were even more damaging. In 1951, the Northern Provincial Commissioner reported that Native Authority orders imposing conservation measures were 'not being strictly enforced due to the erratic and half-hearted support of most of the Native Authorities concerned'.[89] The attempt to switch to government Natural Resources legislation proved highly unpopular, however, as was noted in an intelligence report of July 1951:

> It is reported from the Northern Province that many Africans consider the Natural Resources Board rules a greater danger than Federation because of the cumulative effect on their way of life. It is said that Federation plays on their fears but Natural Resources rules are an ever present source of trouble.[90]

With the outbreak of the Cholo disturbances in the Southern Province in 1953, tension increased, leading to a crisis of legitimacy in which young men and sometimes women repeatedly challenged the authority of the local representatives of the colonial

[83] *Ibid.*, 7 June 1952.
[84] *Ibid.*, 9 June 1952.
[85] *Ibid.*, 11 June 1952.
[86] Jones, Ulendo diary, 8 June 1952.
[87] Jones, Ulendo diary, 2 August 1952.
[88] For the expression of similar fears by Tumbuka farmers in the Henga valley see R.E. Gregson, 'Agricultural Change in the Henga Valley', *Society of Malawi Journal*, 23, 2 (1970), pp. 46–8.
[89] MNA 4.13.8F/3091, PC Northern Province to Chief Secretary, 13 October 1951.
[90] PRO CO 1015/464, Political Intelligence Report, October 1951.

state. No evidence is currently available that traditional religious institutions comparable to those operating in the Lower Shire Valley at this period were mobilised against the ridging campaign.[91] But in an ironic and increasingly prevalent move, young members of the Presbyterian Church were active in a public protest against the bunding campaign held at Livingstonia in August, which resulted in seventeen arrests.[92] With only a handful of policemen stationed in the northern province, however, the coercive power of the state was limited. More and more Native Authorities gave their support, direct or tacit, to the protesters with the result that the government lacked the means to respond.[93] In the Misuku hills, hundreds of cultivators went unpunished when they flouted bunding rules; elsewhere Natural Resources legislation was routinely ignored.[94] By 1955, hundreds of small-scale and hence largely ignored contests were being fought throughout the northern highlands. Near the mission station at Ekwendeni, for example, L.N. Gondwe was leader of a soil conservation team charged with marking bunds that local villagers were then required to build. Gondwe's report to his supervisor captures the strained atmosphere in which he worked:

> No garden owner assisted in the work of cutting pegs each one entirely refused, so the team had to provide pegs and marked all the gardens, no work has been done from that time. Only few people have made traces. Often and often we are visiting this village but we cannot find people at the village or in their gardens; they always desert when they have seen or heard us coming.... The village has given us troubles for a very long time, since 1950 they have been accused for many times and fined many times in Mtwalo's court but no change.[95]

The agricultural supervisor complained at the low level of fines that Mtwalo's court imposed (five to ten shillings for an offence against bunding regulations; fifteen to twenty shillings for those found guilty of cultivating *visoso* gardens). But with his authority in the balance there was no question of the chief imposing more.[96]

From 1955 the focus shifted to the Karonga district and particularly to the Misuku hills, the foremost arena of confrontation in the late 1950s. As we have seen, this district was the locus for one of the earliest and ostensibly one of the most successful of Nyasaland's land usage schemes. Even by 1948, however, state intervention in the Misuku hills was provoking considerable opposition. And, with the return of Flax Musopole to his homeland in 1955, this opposition was given a central direction. Earlier Congress leaders had frequently supported soil conservation measures as part of

---

[91] For the impact of the Mbona cult in the Lower Shire valley see J. Matthew Schoffeleers, *River of Blood* (Madison, WI, University of Wisconsin Press, 1992), pp. 107–8; Mandala, *Work and Control in a Peasant Economy,* p. 229.

[92] PRO CO 1015/464, Political Intelligence Report, October 1953.

[93] John McCracken, 'Coercion and Control in Nyasaland: aspects of the history of a colonial police force', *Journal of African History*, 27 (1986), pp. 138–9; McCracken, 'Authority and Legitimacy in Malawi: policing and politics in a colonial state', in David M. Anderson and David Killingray (eds), *Policing and Decolonisation. Nationalism, politics and the police 1917–65* (Manchester, Manchester University Press, 1992), pp. 172–8.

[94] RHL Devlin Commission Papers Box 8, Waterfield, 'Nyasaland Disturbances N.W. Karonga', 6 May 1959; PRO CO 1015/465, Political Intelligence Report October 1953.

[95] MNA 9.4.11F/16100, L.N. Gondwe to Agricultural Supervisor, Zombwe, no date [1955].

[96] MNA 9.4.11F/16100, Agricultural Supervisor, Zombwe to Agricultural Officer, Mzuzu, 29 October 1959.

a modernising project.[97] Musopole, however, a radical Marxist who had been politically active in Cape Town and Johannesburg, had no hesitation in using grievances over conservation as a means of building a peasant base.[98] Faced by a resentful Sukwa peasantry, an almost invisible police force and an ineffective administration weakened by constant changes in personnel, Musopole was ideally positioned to act. As a member of one of the leading coffee-growing families in the district he was well placed to seek to utilise the recently created coffee co-operative society as a base for his operations.[99]

By 1956 he had begun to organise opposition to coffee rules. The next year he carried this further, holding frequent branch meetings of the Nyasaland African Congress throughout the Karonga district and calling on the people to boycott dipping tanks and to flout agricultural rules.[100] By August 1958, membership of Congress in the Karonga district had risen from less than two hundred a few months earlier to 2,200. In a studied rejection of government policy, bush fires were lit all over the Misuku hills, so that when Dr Banda visited the area in September, the Misuku was indeed 'ringed with fire'.[101] 'At the same time, palm trees were cut without permit and widespread *visoso* cultivation was practised in the Karonga hill area.'[102]

This was the background to the outbreak of violence that virtually paralysed the Northern Province from late February 1959, bringing colonial rule in the area to a standstill. Only a few days before the state of emergency was declared, the Provincial Operations Committee reported that, from 15 February, all branches of Congress in the district 'were engaged in activities to arouse people to illegal disturbances'.

> The degree of support is 100% in the Misuku area and widespread in all other areas. This has resulted in attacks on Karonga and occupation of the Fort Hill airstrip. The standard of Congress leadership is comparatively very high and the organisation of women and children is growing rapidly. The power of the Chiefs is insufficient to overcome Congress leadership.[103]

With the security forces 'thin on the ground', little or no attempt was made to detain Musopole and his companions during the military-style campaign, 'Operation Sunrise', in which more than 570 Congress leaders were arrested.[104] And with his freedom

---

[97] See Presidential address by C. J. Matinga delivered at Nyasaland African Congress conference, 23 September 1946, MNA PCC 1/4/1. This point is also made by Megan Vaughan in D. Birmingham and P. M. Martin, *History of Central Africa. The contemporary years since 1960* (London, Longman, 1998), p.174.

[98] Musopole was awarded a scholarship to study Russian language and literature at Moscow State University in 1957 but was prevented by the Nyasaland authorities from taking it up. PRO CO 1015/1748, Political Intelligence Digest, August 1957.

[99] Mulwafu, 'The development of the coffee industry'; Waterfield, 'Nyasaland Disturbances N.W. Karonga'.

[100] PRO CO 1015/1749, Nyasaland Intelligence Report for quarter ending 31 March 1958.

[101] RHL Devlin Commission Papers, Box 8, Waterfield, Nyasaland Disturbances N.W. Karonga'; C. Haskard, Provincial Commissioner's 'Report on the Disturbances in the Northern Province of Nyasaland, February/ April 1959 and the events leading up to them'. Banda frequently claimed that he had 'set the whole of Nyasaland on fire' but this is usually read metaphorically. *Report of the Nyasaland Commission of Inquiry* (London, HMSO, 1959) Cmd 814, p. 35.

[102] Haskard, Provincial Commissioner's Report ... February/April 1959.

[103] RHL, Devlin Commission Papers, Box 8, Appreciation of the Situation as at 0900 hour, Monday 25 February 1959 by the Provincial Operations Committee, Mzuzu.

[104] PRO CO 1015/1494, Nyasaland Operations Committee, Operation Instructions nos. 2 /59 and 3/59.

secured, Musopole travelled widely over the area, appearing 'one day at Ngerenge, another at Misuku, another at Bulambya', leaving behind him a trail of torched buildings and sabotaged bridges.[105] As late as June the security situation in the Karonga district continued to alarm the Governor, Armitage, though by this stage military reinforcements from Southern Rhodesia were fanning out from Karonga putting Musopole and his supporters on the defensive.[106]

In the weeks following the declaration of a state of emergency, agricultural officers made an attempt to calculate what remained in the Northern Province of the ambitious schemes introduced a decade earlier. Ridge cultivation, by this time, was widely employed on hill slopes for the cultivation of maize, not cassava, but the marking and construction of bunds was restricted to the occasional master farmer holding. In several areas the illegal practice of *visoso* was spreading unchecked in the absence of field staff. In the Misuku hills agricultural work was limited to the support of coffee growing; other types of extension work had been entirely abandoned. Shifting cultivation continued, notably in the Mzimba and Karonga districts. This, coupled with the problem of widespread burning of timber for *visoso* cultivation was seen as contributing to accelerated erosion.[107] Eighty years on from the first missionary analyses of ecological decay, 'experts' continued to promulgate the same prescriptions of environmental doom.

Conclusion

This paper has had two main aims: the first to review the variety of cultural interpretations that were made of environmental change in the northern region of Malawi in the colonial era and the second to relate these interpretations to peasant resistance in the north in the 1950s. From the 1880s onwards, external perceptions of the northern Malawian environment were powerfully influenced by the belief of Scottish missionaries that the Ngoni impact on Malawi was culturally and environmentally destructive and that this impact appeared most dramatically in agricultural techniques involving the cutting down and burning of trees. These views were reinforced from at least the 1930s by the spread of conservationist ideas developed in Southern Africa and America. But they were given extra authority in the north through the ability of experts to utilise the views of earlier witnesses in the area, thus building a powerful perception of environmental degradation that officials were unwilling to challenge. This, in turn, gave rise to the emergence of a new interventionist model of regeneration developed most imaginatively in Smalley's reports on the Misuku Land Usage Scheme and subsequently employed in the conservation campaign of the 1950s. By this time, some administrative officers, typified by Griff Jones, were beginning to question whether the techniques employed were in fact counter-productive. But these criticisms remained isolated and failed to dent the prevailing orthodoxy.

It is against this background that an analysis of peasant-based anti-colonial protest

---

[105] EUL, Helen Taylor Papers, Report on a visit to Karonga for Easter Services, 27 March to 2 April 1959, unsigned.

[106] ZNA FX 236 CX 27/2, Governor Nyasaland to Secretary of State for the Colonies, 6 July 1959.

[107] MNA 5.14.10R/11906, Provincial Agricultural Officer, Mzuzu to Director of Agriculture, 14 April 1959; MNA 9.4.11F/16100, Provincial Agricultural Officer, Northern Province to Director of Agriculture, 27 June 1960.

must be placed. The Northern Province was the most peripheral area of Malawi in the 1950s – the region least affected by land alienation or the development of cash cropping. But, after 1956, it was also an exceptionally volatile area politically – the only one in which colonial authority was successfully challenged for any length of time. A variety of factors explain this state of affairs, among them the fragility of colonial authority in the north and the political influence of the Livingstonia Mission, both direct and indirect.[108] These, however, were intimately related to peasant attempts to resist government conservationist interventions in an area where the interests of men and women were equally involved. In that sense, the symbol of the burning bush, emblem of the Church of Scotland of which Livingstonia was a part from 1929, has a particular resonance for my story. The symbol of the church, the burning bush, can also be seen as representing the ultimate in environmental degeneration in the imagination of a succession of external observers. How appropriate, then, that when peasant leaders looked for a means of dramatising their resistance, they did so by setting the bush on fire and ringing the Misuku hills with flames.[109] After all, in one tradition, the very term *Malawi* is said to derive from the Chichewa word for *flames* and in particular from the burning grasslands observed by Phiri newcomers when they entered the Malawi region several hundred years ago.[110]

[108] I have discussed both these themes elsewhere. See McCracken, 'Authority and Legitimacy'; McCracken, *Politics and Christianity in Malawi*; John McCracken, 'Church and State in Malawi: the Role of the Scottish Presbyterian Missions, 1875–1964' in H. B. Hansen and M. Twaddle (eds), *Christian Missionaries and the State in the Third World* (Oxford, James Currey, 2002), pp. 176–93.

[109] Waterfield, 'Nyasaland Disturbances N.W. Karonga'.

[110] For an interesting discussion of the symbolism of fire among the Maravi peoples see J.M. Schoffeleers, 'The Meaning and Use of the Name *Malawi* in Oral Traditions and Precolonial Documents' in B. Pachai (ed.), *The Early History of Malawi* (London, Longman, 1972) pp. 91–103.

9

Representations of Custom, Social Identity & Environmental Relations in Central Tanzania
1926–1950[1]

INGRID YNGSTROM

Introduction

This chapter examines the origins and content of colonial ideas about 'traditional' land practices, and related ideas about development in central Tanzania. The specific context is the formulation and implementation of agriculture and livestock policies in Dodoma District among people known as the Gogo. In juggling the demands of territorial agricultural policy while tackling locally-specific problems, the District administration constructed a framework – a script of Gogo identity – for explaining and trying to solve the problems the district was experiencing. In particular, officials identified soil erosion and the small size of Gogo fields as hampering colonial efforts to increase production. The 'tradition' of livestock-keeping prevented the Gogo from farming sufficient acreages. 'Traditional' land use management methods, in particular pasture management, were deemed the main causes of soil erosion, which also affected productivity. The framework posited these relationships in a downward spiral of decline. To reverse this decline, modern forms of production would be required. These policies were targeted at men, for women were not viewed as participants in the development process. Thus not only was environmental improvement associated with modernity, modernity was constructed as a specifically masculine process.

This paper situates these policy processes in the context of historical transformations in the district as local economies were integrated into wider economic systems. The ahistorical model of development – which posited social change as a transition from 'traditional' to modern forms of production – was inadequate as an explanatory tool and officials became increasingly frustrated as their efforts to transform production failed, increasingly relying on the script of Gogo identity to justify and explain the recurring problem of food shortages. The chapter evaluates the content of colonial ideas about customary land use in Dodoma District and asks how and why the script of Gogo identity continued to be reproduced after the 1940s in the face of failing policies and evidence that contradicted it.

[1] I would like to thank my supervisors Megan Vaughan and Gavin Williams for their intellectual guidance in the writing of my doctoral thesis from which this paper derives. I am grateful to the Economic and Social Research Council, Nuffield College and St Antony's College, Oxford for doctoral and post-doctoral research funding and support.

The incorporation of Gogo debates over custom and social identity into colonial thinking were limited until the mid-1940s. This argument, and indeed the approach, may seem at odds with recent work that emphasises the incorporation of African ecological knowledges and debates over custom into colonial structures and debates.[2] Colonial efforts to acquire knowledge of Gogo land practices were limited in Dodoma District in the early years of colonial rule when efforts were geared towards understanding political authority in order to exercise the implementation of indirect rule.[3] At the same time, contact with Gogo through colonial intermediaries, such as chiefs, was limited because staff numbers were low for many years and because government-appointed 'chiefs' lacked local legitimacy.[4] Interactions between colonial officials and the Gogo were also limited to the extent to which colonial officials were willing, and had the resources, to tour in the district. More significantly perhaps, economic interest in the area was limited and therefore few resources were put at the disposal of officials to investigate these issues systematically. However, evidence presented in this paper, albeit limited, shows that debates over rights and interests in livestock were incorporated into the structures of colonialism after the 1940s. Detailed documentation with which to demonstrate this more conclusively, particularly from court proceedings, is either missing or absent.[5]

The foundation of the script of Gogo identity

The 'tribe' was a key concept in the construction of African social identities. The importance of 'tribe' emerged in the context of indirect rule which was founded on the use of 'traditional' tribal authorities and 'customary law' to provide social stability. In the meantime, colonial 'development' would bring Africans into the colonial market economy. Colonial development discourse constructed 'tradition' and 'custom' in direct opposition to modernity. The eradication of 'tradition' was necessary for modernisation to occur. But in the pursuit of locally legitimate 'traditional' forms of control, tradition and custom had to be maintained even as modernisation was pursued

[2] Sara Berry. *No Condition is Permanent* (Madison, WI, University of Wisconsin Press, 1993); Martin Chanock. *Law, Custom and Social Order* (Cambridge, CUP, 1985); Kristin Mann and Richard Roberts. (eds), *Law in Colonial Africa* (London, James Currey, 1991); Fiona Mackenzie. *Land, Ecology and Resistance in Kenya, 1880–1952* (Edinburgh, Edinburgh University Press for the International Africa Institute, 1998); Terence Ranger, 'The Invention of Tradition Revisited: the Case of Colonial Africa', in Terence Ranger and Olufemi Vaughan (eds), *Legitimacy and the State in Twentieth Century Africa* (London, Macmillan, 1993); Terence Ranger, 'The Invention of Tradition in Colonial Africa', in Eric Hobsbawm and Terence Ranger (eds), *The Invention of Tradition* (Cambridge, CUP, 1983).

[3] *Ibid*. For a study of Gogo systems of political authority by a colonial intermediary see Mathias E. Mnyampala. *The Gogo: History, Customs and Traditions*. Translated by Gregory H. Maddox (New York, 1995).

[4] Ingrid Yngstrom, 'Gender, Land and Development: Rural Dodoma, 1921–1996', unpublished DPhil. thesis, University of Oxford, 1999, chaps 2 and 5.

[5] Although a number of the records of colonial court proceedings in Dodoma District are recorded in the catalogue at the National Archives of Tanzania, they were reported as either missing or unavailable at the time of fieldwork in 1997. Documentation of court proceedings would be particularly valuable, given that currently the most common cases brought to the lower court in Mvumi Division of Dodoma District are those concerning divorce and conflicts over the return of brideprice. The historical antecedents of these conflicts may have been played out in the colonial customary courts.

as a development strategy. At times, 'custom' – frequently invented – was applied by the administration in the customary courts in an attempt to enforce unpopular policies. This was the contradictory and unsustainable nature of the colonial project to which the 'tribe' was an essential tool.[6]

Tribal identities were frequently tied to specific agricultural practices and production systems. As Moore and Vaughan's study of *citemene* – a form of shifting cultivation practised among the Bemba of Northern Zambia – shows, *citemene* was intimately tied to Bemba 'tribal' identity. But, as Moore and Vaughan argue, this was not a gender-neutral formulation: Bemba identity was constructed as explicitly masculine.[7] In other contexts, such as the one described in this paper, it was not the practice of shifting *cultivation* as such that was constructed as masculine, although land-clearing was seen to be, and predominantly was, a male activity. Rather, the colonial association of masculinity with 'shifting cultivation' came from the idea that Gogo men were pastoralists who cultivated, rather than agriculturalists who also practised livestock-keeping. The practice of 'shifting' around was not compatible with good farming practices and soil conservation. This idea was combined with a further belief that Gogo men were unwilling to cultivate: to 'develop', they should be made to cultivate. In this context, whether they were seen as idle or hard-working, it was men who were seen as the principal agents of development and change.

In constructing social identities, colonial officials drew on a range of debates concerning African agricultural practices. Colonial discourse characterised African traditional production methods as backward. This underpinned the civilising mission of colonial intervention. These ideas, although evident in the early twentieth century,[8] became common currency only in the 1920s. Colonial officials were particularly disparaging about shifting cultivation. According to one of Lugard's sources, a 'high authority' on the subject: 'the acreage taken up for [shifting] cultivation is five to nine times in excess of the requirements of a cultivator under a less "wasteful system", one which was only tolerated in "uncivilised parts of the world"'.[9] African agricultural practices were not only constructed as 'wasteful'. In the late 1920s and early 1930s, fuelled by conservationist ideology in North America, and dovetailing with existing beliefs about the poor agricultural methods of Africans, these practices became characterised as destructive.[10] In the 1930s, soil erosion had emerged as a central preoccupation of governments in East Africa.[11] Within this discourse, Africans were constructed as 'unscientific exploiters' with a poor understanding of the local ecology and production techniques, in contrast to colonial agricultural knowledge generated

---

[6] Kate Crehan, *The Fractured Community: Landscapes of power and gender in rural Zambia* (Berkeley, University of California Press, 1997).

[7] Henrietta Moore and Megan Vaughan. *Cutting Down Trees: Gender, nutrition and agricultural change in the Northern Province of Zambia, 1890–1990* (London, James Currey, 1994).

[8] Moore and Vaughan, *Cutting Down Trees*.

[9] Sir Frederick D. Lugard. *The Dual Mandate in Tropical Africa*. 3rd edn (Edinburgh and London, William Blackwood and Sons, 1926), p. 299.

[10] William Beinart, 'Soil erosion, conservationism and ideas about development: a Southern African exploration, 1900–1960', *Journal of Southern African Studies (JSAS)*, 11, 1 (1984). See also account by Moore and Vaughan, *Cutting Down Trees*, pp. 94–122; Mackenzie, *Land, Ecology*.

[11] David Anderson. 'Depression, Dustbowl, Demography and Drought: The Colonial State and Soil Conservation in East Africa during the 1930s', *African Affairs* 83, 332 (1984).

from its own modern 'scientific' research base.[12] As Fiona Mackenzie has shown, this involved the silencing of local – especially women's – ecological knowledge.[13]

Despite these ideologies, individual colonial agricultural officials and ecologists were, at times, sensitised to the localised nature of local production systems. Grace Carswell (this volume) argues that colonial and indigenous ideas about soil conservation frequently coincided, and that is a major factor in explaining the success of anti-erosion measures in Kigezi, Uganda. Other studies have also drawn attention to the complexities of colonial ideas about conservation, and the depth of knowledge acquired by agricultural officers about local ecologies and farming systems.[14] Such accumulated knowledge was more likely to occur in areas of economic interest to the colonial administration. Dodoma District was not of economic or political interest to the administration and, as a result, suffered from a shortage of personnel until the mid-1950s. The district covered an area of 6,600 square miles, and had a scattered population of roughly 128,000 in 1928, rising to 220,000 in 1950.[15] As part of the 'tribally' defined area Ugogo within the larger administrative zone of Central Province, it had only one Administrative Officer.[16] Between 1934 and 1937, there were no agricultural staff working in Central Province.[17] The African population of Central Province was estimated to be 820,551 by the late 1940s,[18] by which time the entire Province still had only six agricultural staff: two agricultural officers, two agricultural assistants, and two crop supervisors.[19]

According to Lumley, a District Administrative Officer (DAO) in Tanganyika between 1923 and 1944, the DAO's two most crucial tasks were to supervise chiefs in the 'dispensing of justice' and customary law in the Native Courts, and to ensure that sufficient crops were planted across the district.[20] In order to carry out his duties effectively, the DAO was supposed to tour the district three times in each year. Lumley admitted that during the depression in the 1930s, the 'touring allowance' was withdrawn and 'only the more dedicated men carried out the duty of touring'.[21] Despite this, Lumley maintained that, in carrying out his touring duties, the DAO would become 'conversant with almost every inch of their district, and was in contact with most of its people'.[22] Given the large size and scattered nature of populations in most districts, this was almost certainly an exaggerated claim.

[12] William Beinart, 'Introduction: The Politics of Colonial Conservation', *Journal of Southern African Studies* 15, 2 (1989), p. 159.

[13] Mackenzie, *Land, Ecology*; Fiona Mackenzie, 'Selective Silence: A Feminist Encounter with Environmental Discourse in Colonial Africa' in Jonathan Crush (ed.), *The Power of Development* (London, Routledge, 1995).

[14] Beinart, 'Soil Erosion'; Anderson, 'Depression'; Mackenzie, *Land, Ecology*; Moore and Vaughan, *Cutting Down Trees*.

[15] Population figures from Gregory Maddox, 'Environment and Population Growth in Ugogo, Central Tanzania' in G. Maddox *et al. Custodians of the Land: Ecology and culture in the history of Tanzania* (London, James Currey, 1996); Land mass figures from Carl Christiansson. *Soil Erosion and Sedimentation in Semi-Arid Tanzania* (Uppsala, 1981).

[16] Ugogo comprised two further districts: Manyoni to the west and Mpwapwa to the east. Combined with Singida to the north-west and Kondoa to the north, they came under the administration of Central Province.

[17] *Tanganyika Agricultural Reports*, 1938 (University of Dar es Salaam (DSM), 1939).

[18] Lord Hailey, *Native Administration in the British Territories*, Part 1 (London, 1950).

[19] Annual reports of the Provincial Commissioners (hereafter ARPC), Central Province, 1950, Tanzania National Archives (TNA) A2/1.

[20] E.K. Lumley, *Forgotten Mandate: A British District Officer in Tanganyika* (London: Hurst & Co., 1976), p. 11.

[21] *Ibid.*

[22] *Ibid.*, p. 12.

Although the establishment of chiefs, courts and customary law theoretically paved the way for institutional forms of control, there was little possibility of this being exercised in practice. In areas such as Ugogo, colonial chiefs could rarely exert any significant control over scattered populations and most were unable to establish sufficient legitimacy to implement often unpopular government policies.[23] The courts exercised only limited customary jurisdiction over local populations, and did not provide the appropriate institutional context from which to extract the principles of customary law. But knowledge was the means to control and officials had to develop methods of knowing. Relying on sporadic contact with the Gogo, administrative and agricultural officers drew on existing colonial ideologies in order to try to understand and explain particular patterns of behaviour, and to exercise control over scattered populations. It was for these practical, rather than ideological, reasons that the script of Gogo identity was able to thrive.

The idea of 'Gogoness' was not a colonial invention. The precursor to the script of Gogo identity appears to have originated among the Swahili-speaking caravans in the nineteenth century.[24] The idea of the 'Gogo' was taken up by European travellers passing along the caravan routes from the late 1850s to the late 1870s. Even though it was difficult to draw boundaries around the peoples of pre-colonial Tanzania because ethnic relations were constantly in flux, it was European travellers who bound tribes into single identifiable entities.[25] On the fringes of western Ugogo – or as Hore described it, 'the debatable border beyond Western Ugogo' – where the Gogo mixed 'in friendly intercourse' with neighbouring groups, 'they all seem to retain markedly their tribal characteristics'.[26] Maddox has suggested that Ugogo was a permanent physical frontier 'surrounded on the west, south and east by better watered lands where cattle-keeping was problematic, and bordered on the north where agriculture was not possible'.[27] Linguistic evidence suggests that this may have been the case.

Agricultural policy and 'traditional' land practices

Dodoma District has one short 3-4 month rainy season and 'a long and severe dry season'.[28] Rainfall averages at about 500mm per annum, with a potential annual evapo-transpiration rate of between 2,000mm and 2,500mm.[29] Commonly referred to as a 'semi-arid' environment, Dodoma District has supported both agriculture and livestock since at least the middle of the nineteenth century, if not before. The main grain crops under cultivation in Ugogo at the end of the nineteenth century were *uwele* (millet) and *mtama* (sorghum). Other crops, including a variety of legumes – such as groundnuts –

[23] Yngstrom, 'Gender, Land'.

[24] Peter Rigby, *Cattle and Kinship among the Gogo* (Ithaca, NY, Cornell University Press, 1969); Robert Jackson and Gregory Maddox, 'The Creation of Identity: Colonial Society in Bolivia and Tanzania', *Journal of the Comparative Study of Society and History* 35, 2 (1993).

[25] Juhani Koponen. *People and Production in Late Pre-colonial Tanzania: History and Structures.* (Helsinki, Monographs of the Finnish Anthropological Society, no. 23, 1988), pp. 188–91.

[26] Edward Coode Hore, *Missionary to Tanganyika 1877–1888*, edited by J.B. Wolf. (London, 1971), p. 137. The 'tribal characteristics' to which Hore referred were particular facial markings and adornments, rather than specific agricultural practices and production systems.

[27] Maddox, 'Environment and Population'.

[28] William Allan, *The African Husbandman* (Edinburgh, Oliver and Boyd, 1965), p. 208.

[29] Christiansson, *Soil Erosion.*

were grown in smaller quantities in different parts of the region. The central more densely populated areas where the early caravan routes passed, had become particularly dependent on agriculture by the early 1900s.[30] Livestock were kept for particular kinds of transactions such as bridewealth exchange, for ceremonial purposes and as a security against hardship.

Cash crop production was the mainstay of economic policy under the British administration. With its large cattle herds, its central position in the existing transportation network, and its potential for grain and pulse surpluses, Dodoma District was generally considered by the administration to be suitable as a food-producing region.[31] Food crop production was generally high throughout the 1920s in Dodoma District and the Gogo took increasing amounts of food crops – grains and groundnuts – as well as livestock to the markets.[32] Groundnuts were the principal cash crop competing with millet in these early years. Production for household consumption was also considered paramount to ensure household food security, and prohibitions on the sale of crops were common during famine years.[33]

Food traders, most of them either Indian or Arab, exchanged grains with African producers through barter exchange, although the colonial government attempted to check this by legislation. In 1942, owing to a variety of problems with the staple food supply, the government reversed its liberalised trade policy and producer price regulation was introduced across the country. This involved the setting of guaranteed minimum prices for both maize and groundnuts and, in 1943, the control of produce exchange at designated trading posts. Even stricter controls were placed on the transfer of crops from one district to another.[34] Although this policy remained in place until 1957, the restrictions were difficult if not impossible to enforce, especially in more remote areas, and 'informal' networks and market relationships almost certainly remained a central part of the exchange nexus.[35]

In 1929, world prices for commodities had slumped dramatically and sales of all crops declined.[36] Increasingly reliant on export crops to support the depressed economy at home, the government began a drive for increased crop production with the 'plant-more-crops' campaign. By the early 1930s, the campaign against soil erosion was also well under way across the territory, including Central Province.[37] Although the campaign lost some of its momentum during the mid-1930s, it remained on the agenda in Central Province. By 1937, by-laws for the enforcement of soil conservation measures were introduced in the Province.[38]

---

[30] Carol Sissons, 'Economic Prosperity in Ugogo, East Africa, 1860–1890.' Unpublished PhD dissertation, University of Toronto (1984).

[31] Dodoma was at the intersection point of the newly constructed railway running from the coast to Lake Tanganyika and the north to south trunk road.

[32] Gregory Maddox, 'Leave Wagogo! You have no food! Famine and survival in Ugogo, Tanzania, 1916–1961'. Unpublished PhD dissertation, North-Western University (1998), p. 172.

[33] Tanganyika, Annual Reports of Provincial Commissioners on Native Affairs (hereafter *ARPCNA*), 1936/1944 (DSM, 1937/1945); Deborah Fahy Bryceson. *Food Insecurity and the Social Division of Labour* (London, Macmillan, 1990), p. 66.

[34] Bryceson, *Food Insecurity.*

[35] *Ibid.*; Maddox, 'Leave Wagogo!'.

[36] Maddox, 'Leave Wagogo', p. 173.

[37] John Iliffe, *A Modern History of Tanganyika* (Cambridge, CUP, 1979), p. 348; 'Soil Erosion', Public Records Office (PRO) CO 691/141/13.

[38] *Central Provincial Books*, Rhodes House Library (RH).

Erosion control in Dodoma District

In 1938, a government agriculturist, A. H. Savile, was appointed to carry out a soil survey in Central Province. He found the worst soil erosion in the north of the Province in Kondoa and in some of the central more densely populated areas of Dodoma District. Savile was quick to blame African cultivation and livestock-keeping practices for the erosion and the lack of government efforts at regulating these activities:

> A disinclination to interfere with the improvident habits of the native is resulting in the needless destruction of thousands of acres of fertile forest and agricultural lands.... Over cultivation, over-grazing, and the removal of all tree growth have led to the most appalling gulleying.

He further claimed – in the absence of any evidence – that: 'nearly all this destruction has taken place within the last decade'.[39]

Nevertheless, this analysis of the situation provided colonial officials with both an explanation of the problem and a way of dealing with it. As the out-going Provincial Commissioner, Partridge, explained it:

> Speaking generally, the natives of this Province are pastoralists rather than agriculturalists. The normal method of agriculture ... is most wasteful and inevitably results in soil erosion. They take three crops only off a piece of land and then abandon it, clearing a further piece each year for the following year's crop. Unfortunately, they do not abandon their waste land entirely, but allow their cattle, sheep and goats to continue to use it until there is nothing left growing on it except weeds and thorn scrub. Cultivation is on the flat so that no protection whatsoever to the land is afforded and all that will grow on it after it is abandoned is thorn scrub, and what is generally described as secondary thicket.[40]

In 1938, the anti-soil erosion regulation enforced the construction of contour ridges on personal plots of sorghum and millet. Village leaders were expected to present an example to their people: every chief, sub-chief and village headman in those chiefdoms where erosion was considered at its worst were to cultivate groups of five contour ridges across their millet or sorghum fields at intervals of 15 yards.[41] In the same chiefdoms, the administration put their soil reclamation schemes into action: 'three areas of a total acreage of some six hundred acres, were cleared of bush, contour banked and the gullies stopped by means of check dams'.[42] After 1943, these public works – the so-called 'communal labour' turnouts – were frequently used by the administration during famines to acquire labour in exchange for food. Officials maintained that 'communal labour' was a customary practice, and it was enforced under the Native Authority Ordinance, but the work was highly unpopular.

Savile left for the war in 1939. His work was continued by R.R. Staples who estimated that 2,000 miles of contour-banking was needed in Dodoma District alone. Staples was a government ecologist who had already worked in Tanganyika for some time, and who also had experience of working in Basutoland (now Lesotho), an area of

[39] A. H. Savile, 'Agricultural Problems of the Central Province, 1938', TNA 46/20/22.

[40] Partridge, 'Handing Over and Taking Over Statements and Report', 1943, TNA 46/A4/6/ Vol. IV.

[41] Savile, 'Agricultural Problems of the Central Province, 1938', Annexure 2, 'Résumé of anti-erosion rules and orders made in the Central Province by the Native Authorities during 1938', TNA 46/20/22.

[42] Annual Report for the Agricultural Officer, Central Province, 1939, TNA 46/20/22.

extensive livestock-keeping and soil erosion. Staples' recommendations for livestock control did not differ substantially in either Dodoma or Basutoland. Recommendations included the introduction of block and rotational grazing, cast as customary in both areas.[43] In Dodoma District, the plans were enforced through the Native Authority Ordinance under the section dealing with 'Native Law and Custom'.[44] By 1945, in Dodoma District, it was clear that the grazing controls were not being 'strictly observed'.[45]

Contour-banking on individual plots and tie-ridging on hillsides continued to be enforced up to 1950.[46] But the measures often proved valueless, either because the ridges collapsed in the heavy downpours, or simply because they did not improve yields as had been intended.[47] Sword, an agricultural officer working in the District in 1949 and 1950, admitted as much.

> Tie-ridging in Dodoma which was introduced on a large scale this year suffered a setback as crops grown on the flat gave higher yields ... it seems that the poor results of the ridged land were due to the more rapid drying out of the soil during the various long dry spells. [48]

In many areas visited by Sword, soil erosion measures had barely begun or had been neglected. On tour in Makangwa, having noted that 'they don't like making contour banks', Sword went on: 'Told them what they could do about the latter'.[49] Following a meeting with leaders where the new cultivation orders had been explained, Sword remarked:

> The argument was then produced that if this method of cultivation [contour-banking] was to be adopted, the size of *shambas* [plots] would have to be decreased as cultivators would lack sufficient strength to complete the work. When little work is done in the field from May to December, this is not convincing.[50]

Soil erosion and the 'plant-more-crops' campaign

Throughout the 1930s and 1940s, economic policy remained production-oriented under the 'plant-more-crops' campaign, in spite of the observation in 1939 by the agricultural officer, W.F. Baldock, that increased production and anti-soil erosion policies were not readily compatible. The soils, he argued, would not be able to replenish because of lack of fallow. 'No doubt the area under cultivation each year may be decreased by improved agricultural methods but the plant more crops campaign will

[43] R.R. Staples and W.K. Hudson, 'An Ecological Survey of the Mountain Area of Basutoland', TNA 26281, 1938/9. In Dodoma District, this was operated within a 3-mile radius of the administrative capital where there was no surplus grazing available (Michael Patton, 'Dodoma Region, 1929–1959: A history of famine', Bureau of Research Assessment and Land Use Planning, Research Report No. 44 (University of Dar es Salaam, 1971).

[44] Central Provincial Books, RH; See also 'Native Land Tenure', Ugogo (no author, no date), TNA 49/39/3.

[45] Tanganyika Annual Reports of Provincial Commisioners on Native Affairs (TARPCNA), Central Province, 1945 (UDSM, 1946).

[46] J. M. Sword, 'Handing Over Notes', 1949/50, RH Mss. Afr. s. 972.

[47] J. M. Sword, 'Safari Notes', 1949/50, RH Mss. Afr. s. 972. Various references.

[48] Sword, 'Handing Over Notes'.

[49] *Ibid.*, 'Safari Notes', Safari no. 6.

[50] *Ibid.*, Safari no. 8.

more than counteract this'.[51] Despite the apparent contradictions, the PC for Central Province, Partridge, drawing on statistical evidence of local carrying capacity, seemed at pains to demonstrate their compatibility:

> It is estimated that a rough average acreage for a family's food requirements with their present methods of agriculture is as great as eight acres and that the amount of grazing required per beast is somewhere between eight and twelve acres, and even with this enormous acreage there is a starvation period of some weeks at the end of the dry season. What I have been trying to aim at is to reduce the acreage under crops so as to free land for grazing. Our attempts at increased production are directed towards better methods of cultivation rather than increased acreage, and it is confidently expected that if total cultivation is followed by manuring, it will be possible to obtain the same yield from a very reduced acreage.[52]

The encouragement of intensive agricultural practices was only half-heartedly pursued in Dodoma District. High-yielding crop varieties which were not drought-resistant were not suitable for the hostile environment of Dodoma, even though some seeds were distributed in the late 1920s.[53] Manuring fields was also supposed to be encouraged.[54] But in 1943, the senior agricultural officer complained that the Gogo did not apply manure, and argued for extending acreages on this basis.[55] Most officers seemed unaware that in areas of livestock plenty, farmers applied manure anyway.[56] In any event, amongst agricultural officers there was no question of reducing acreages in order to open up more land for grazing, as Partridge had claimed was the case. All the agricultural reports indicate that extending acreages was the principal policy goal.

In the 1930s, the average planted by a 'family' in Ugogo was believed to be around three acres.[57] In 1941, Staples had commented on the large size of fields in Central Province and Ugogo, noting an average of 6 acres, but also commenting that family fields could be as large as 15 acres.[58] Two years later in 1943, Rounce, the senior agricultural officer for the Province, cited the figure of 1.14 acres cultivated by each adult in Dodoma chiefdom, a figure lower than any he had computed in the entire territory.[59] This produced a figure of 6.5 acres cultivated per homestead of approxi-

---

[51] W.F. Baldock to Director of Agriculture, Morogoro, 27 March 1939, TNA 46/20/22. The 'plant-more-crops' campaign was contested both at a territorial and regional level. As Iliffe, *A Modern History*, p. 349, points out, in certain regions, especially those impoverished such as Dodoma and Lindi, Provincial Commissioners thought the plant-more-crops policy to be 'a blatant exploitation of Africans'.

[52] Partridge, 'Handing Over and Taking Over Statements and Report, 1943'.

[53] L.E.Y. Mbogoni, 'Ecological Crises and Food Production in Dodoma District: 1920–1960', unpublished MS dissertation, University of Dar es Salaam (1981).

[54] Monthly Reports of District Agricultural Officers (MRDAO), Dodoma District, TNA 46/20/22; ARPC 1943, TNA, A.2/1; Oral testimonies, Mvumi, Dodoma District, November 1996 to February 1997.

[55] Senior Agricultural Officer to PC, Central Province, 2 December 1943, TNA 46/A20/1.

[56] Oral testimonies, Mvumi, Dodoma District, November 1996 to February 1997; Maddox, 'Leave Wagogo', Annex: oral testimony, Ernest Musa Kongola; Rigby, *Cattle and Kinship*.

[57] DAO, Dodoma District, to PC, Central Province, 19 May 1937, TNA 46/20/1/Vol. II, cited by Mbogoni, 'Ecological Crises', p. 73.

[58] R.R. Staples, Monthly Agricultural Report, 14 January 1941, TNA 46/20/31, cited by Maddox, 'Environment and Population', pp. 54–5.

[59] Published later in N.V. Rounce, *The Agriculture of the Cultivation Steppe* (Dar es Salaam, Longman's Green, 1949).

mately nine individuals.[60] Maddox notes that colonial officials began to remark on small fields cultivated in Ugogo after 1944, up to which time they had commented on the large fields under cultivation, indicating a drop in agricultural production in the district around this time.[61] Maddox argues that a drop in acreages under cultivation in the early 1940s can be explained by an increase in labour migration out of Ugogo. This may be part of the explanation for this apparent drop in acreages under cultivation in certain parts of the district. However, the differences in the colonial figures can also be explained in other ways.

The differences could be indicative of a variation in actual acreages under cultivation within the district at any one time, as well as in people's ability to extend cultivation over time. The script of Gogo identity was primarily an explanatory framework, and could not accommodate differentiation and variation in production and agriculture within the district. Probing beneath this script, using the limited evidence available on variation in production and on patterns of migration and settlement within the district, shows that a series of important transformations in migration, settlement and production were occurring at precisely the time when officials were commenting on the small size of Gogo fields.[62] Since the mid-nineteenth century, producers had been attracted to the central belt area, a strip running from east to west, incorporating the late nineteenth-century caravan routes, the railway and Dodoma Town. These areas had become increasingly congested. By the 1930s and 1940s large livestock owners from these areas had begun to migrate to more remote parts of the district where grazing was more plentiful. The decline in livestock availability in the central areas also coincided with the integration of the local economy into the cash economy. Men began to seek out cash with which to purchase livestock but were unable to acquire sufficient to accumulate livestock to the same extent as their fathers. In Mvumi, in the central part of Dodoma District, the permanent migration of livestock owners did not keep pace with the natural rate of population increase, and access to arable land also went into decline. Thus, in this area, a gradual decline in the size of fields under cultivation may have been evident from around the 1940s and 1950s,[63] rather than the dramatic decline indicated by the colonial figures.

In 1944, agricultural officers produced an annex to their monthly report which showed that at least 23 per cent of the land in Dodoma District was under 'fairly dense cultivation', the majority lying within the central belt area.[64] The 1944 annex provided statistics on areas under 'fairly dense cultivation' from within each of the 14 chiefdoms of the district. The evidence from this annex and from a touring report from 1949/50 suggests that agricultural officers were aware that different production systems were operating throughout the district.[65] But the evidence could not be accommodated into officials' attempts to explain the recurrent food shortages which had become a feature of the district by the 1940s. Armed with Rounce's figures and those from a number of

[60] MRDAO, Dodoma District, July 1944, TNA 46/20/22. If Staples' 'family' is the methodological equivalent of Rounce's 'homestead', the figures would show virtually no difference in acreages under cultivation.
[61] Maddox, 'Environment and Population'.
[62] Yngstrom, 'Gender, Land', chapter 4.
[63] *Ibid.*, chapter 7.
[64] MRDAO, May 1944, Annex, TNA 46/20/22.
[65] Sword, 'Safari and Handing Over Notes', 1949/50.

localities in the central belt area,[66] officials complained that the Gogo hampered efforts towards greater production. In 1944, after almost three years of recurring food shortages, the PC incorrectly cited Rounce's figures maintaining that the Gogo cultivated 1.14 acres *per family* rather than per adult individual, and stating categorically that 'these people have never had enough food because they have never been able to cultivate an adequate acreage'.[67] One senior agricultural officer complained that the Gogo only produced enough to last for eight months,[68] and another attributed under-production to the fact that the Gogo were 'cattle, not crop conscious'.[69]

In 1942, the cultivation of one to two extra acres was ordered under the Native Authority Ordinance.[70] In 1944, out of a total of 2,949 convictions across the three districts of Ugogo, 545 people were convicted in the Native Courts of failing to cultivate a large enough acreage and a further 1,185 of failing to produce an 'adequate supply of food for maintenance of dependants'.[71] By 1944, the chief agriculture officer for Dodoma District had noted that cultivators had not extended their acreages by the required extra two acres. Rather, 'they probably cultivated an average of one and a quarter acres extra'. He further advised that 'great pressure should be put on them not only to maintain the extra acres put under crop, but to make it up to the original two acres'.[72] Even in 1950, officers were still insisting on extended acreages. On tour in Mwitikira, Sword asked to see the 'big shambas' which were situated at some distance from the homestead. The local farmers, however, declined, assuring him that they were 'very very large and a very long way away.'[73]

Anti-famine production policy

Throughout the late nineteenth and first half of the twentieth century, people used a variety of strategies to insure against years of poor crops. Grains were stored in granaries and livestock were also used as a security against famine. Through livestock exchanges such as bridewealth, individuals and groups invested in social relationships which they could draw on in times of food shortage. During more generalised food shortages, individual men and women worked for food, or went themselves to other areas in search of food. Sometimes the entire homestead would leave - a risk especially for households without livestock which had to forge social and economic ties with new groups in neighbouring localities.[74] In the last resort, livestock could be given up in exchange for food. During the 1930s and early 1940s, many of these strategies were going into decline. By the 1950s, farmers in central Dodoma District had turned over fields set aside for grain crops to groundnuts for cash and begun to use this cash to acquire livestock, leaving them more vulnerable to grain shortage. When severe

---

[66] Studies conducted in Dodoma, Mvumi, Buigiri and Bahi chiefdoms in the 1940s lay within the central belt area. Mvumi figures: Senior Agricultural Officer to Provincial Commissioner, 5 August 1944, TNA 46/20/22; Buigiri and Bahi figures: Patton, 'Dodoma Region,' Appendix 3. Dodoma chiefdom figures are those cited as 1.14 acre per adult (MRDAO, Dodoma District, July 1944, TNA 46/20/22).

[67] ARPC, Central Province, 1944, TNA A2/1.

[68] Senior Agricultural Officer to PC, Central Province, 2 December 1943, TNA 46/A20/1/vol. X.

[69] MRDAO, Dodoma District, July 1944, TNA 46/20/22.

[70] *Central Provincial Books*, RH; ARPC, Central Province, TNA A2/1.

[71] *Dodoma District Book*, RH.

[72] MRDAO, Dodoma District, July 1944, TNA 46/20/22.

[73] Sword, 'Safari Notes', Safari no. 28.

[74] Interviews, Mvumi 1996/7. See also Rigby, *Cattle and Kinship*, on the history of settlement in Dodoma District.

hardship struck, livestock were more likely to be sold for cash rather than exchanged for food.[75]

Government policy in the early 1930s regarding famine relief was to provide relief issued as a loan to the Native Authorities.[76] These loans were difficult to recover and concerns over the cost of famine relief grew. In 1941, Maguire, PC for Central Province, designed a scheme which would force each farmer to contribute grain to a 'tribal' grain reserve controlled by the Native Authorities.[77] This scheme was claimed to be 'broadly-speaking in accordance with native custom as it operated in Tanganyika'.[78] Although in some parts of the territory, chiefs had controlled grain reserves prior to colonial rule,[79] there is no evidence that this was ever customary in Ugogo. Enforcement of the new controls once again entailed the invention of custom. The small amounts of food in the tribal reserves suggest that this policy was not systematically enforced. It required that people give up grain, often left to rot if the following years produced good harvests.[80] As food shortages became more common, it also became increasingly difficult for Native Authorities to claim back food issued on loan.[81] Not all officials believed in food relief during famine periods. Wyatt, acting PC for Central Province in 1947, believed that relief measures made the Gogo more 'famine-minded'; they discouraged farmers from cultivating sufficient acreages and, according to another agricultural officer, encouraged beer-brewing.[82]

During the severe famine of 1943, which affected most of the territory, concerns over food supply intensified. A worldwide grain shortage pushed up grain prices, and Tanganyika was forced to rely on domestic production rather than expensive foreign imports. Food insecurity became a widespread feature of the Tanganyikan economy, and its alleviation pivotal to the administration's economic policies.[83] At this juncture, the government intensified efforts to increase the food supply through various methods including enforced cultivation.

In 1943, the administration introduced plans to enforce the cultivation of drought-resistant 'anti-famine' root crops, such as cassava and sweet potatoes.[84] But the policy did not meet with much success. One agricultural officer noted that it was only successful in certain areas of the district, and that 'stock, vermin, white ants and the people themselves are against it'.[85] In 1938, the chief agriculture officer had identified livestock as constraining root crop production:

> There appears to be a close correlation between scarcity of root crops and density of livestock. One reason for this is that the extreme shortage of pasture in the over-stocked areas encourages stock owners to allow their herds to browse in their own (and other

[75] Yngstrom, 'Gender, Land.'

[76] Mbogoni, 'Ecological Crises,' p. 86.

[77] Maddox, 'Leave Wagogo!', p. 280.

[78] Mbogoni, 'Ecological Crises', p. 98.

[79] See Bryceson, *Food Insecurity*, pp. 82–3.

[80] Maddox, 'Leave Wagogo!'.

[81] *Ibid.*

[82] TARPCNA, Central Province, 1943 (UDSM, 1944); MRDAO, July 1948 TNA 46/20/22.

[83] Bryceson, *Food Insecurity*, p. 119.

[84] Maddox, 'Leave Wagogo', p. 300; Mbogoni notes that other drought-resistant seed varieties were distributed in Central Province. It is unclear how many of these reached Dodoma District, but the total amounts were small. 'Ecological Crises', pp. 94–6.

[85] ARPC, Central Province, 1943, TNA, A.2/1; See also Mbogoni, 'Ecological Crises', p. 92.

people's) root crops. The result of this is that there is a perpetual shortage of planting material at the commencement of each planting season.[86]

But it was the Gogo themselves, rather than the cattle, who were widely seen to impede their own food security. The Gogo were used to 'scatter[ing] far and wide in search of food in times of scarcity, probably jeopardising the new season's production'.[87] Those with livestock were forced to sell some of their stock and purchase food. Those in famine-stricken areas who owned no livestock were to enter famine camps in order to cut down on the demand for food relief.[88] One agricultural officer claimed that the camps would ensure hungry people would 'not *hemera* [shift] and so denude those areas which do have some food'.[89] The practice of 'shifting' around in search of food was thus not viewed as a food security mechanism. Rather, the practice was seen to disrupt food security mechanisms.

Beer-brewing was also seen to impede food security. Restrictions on beer-brewing had been introduced in the early 1930s under the Native Authority Ordinance. In the 1940s, these regulations were more aggressively enforced.[90] The administration viewed beer-brewing as a waste of grain, and to some extent a cause of food shortages. Beer-drinking was a leisure activity but it was also an important form of sustenance, and the means to acquire labour parties for intensive work, such as field preparation and harvesting. Some of the chiefs tried to reason with officers. Sword reports in 1950:

> Received a request that they should be allowed to brew pombe at cultivation time. It is said to be necessary and that it will be done anyway (!) and that to imprison offenders simply means that food production will suffer.[91]

Attempts to control beer-brewing met with little success because, as African leaders pointed out, it was necessary in order to maintain production during times of intensive agricultural activity.

Colonial explanation and policy formulation

Land policy in Dodoma District was formulated on the basis of territorial requirements which were contradictory. Policies which aimed, on the one hand, to combat soil erosion and, on the other, to increase production were not compatible, as one or two more enlightened officers pointed out. At the same time, policies had to be adapted to suit the particular problems the district or wider locality was experiencing. The process of formulating policy was therefore a question of balancing these problematic and contradictory objectives, at the centre of which was a preoccupation with the effects of soil erosion on production. In 1943, the out-going PC for Central Province, Partridge, declared that 'practically every problem which faces us [in the Province] is concerned in some way with that of soil erosion', identifying the causes as 'the wasteful methods of agriculture' and the 'absence of any kind of pasture management'.[92] Officials were unaware of the historical processes which had created the conditions for 'over-

---

[86] Annual Report of the Agricultural Officer, Central Province, 1938, TNA 46/20/22.
[87] MRDAO, Dodoma District, July 1944, TNA 46/20/22.
[88] Maddox, 'Leave Wagogo', p. 288.
[89] 'Provincer' to Dar es Salaam, 15 September 1943, TNA 46/A20/1/vol. X.
[90] TARPCNA, Central Province, 1934, (UDSM, 1935); TARPCNA, Central Province, 1944, (UDSM, 1945).
[91] Sword, 'Safari Notes', Safari no. 8.
[92] Partridge, 'Handing Over and Taking Over Statements and Reports', 1943.

grazing', and that soil erosion had been under way in the central areas of the district from at least the mid-nineteenth century.[93] In these areas, grazing was in short supply and farmers were forced to graze their livestock on their own fields or the fields of their neighbours. According to farmers in Mvumi, this was used as a method of manuring the fields that were not abandoned but left to fallow.[94]

In explaining the problems of the district the ahistorical tribal model emerged as an especially powerful framework. Low levels of production were seen to be caused by the declining productive potential of the soils and the low productive potential of Gogo agricultural practices. The Gogo themselves caused soil erosion through poor land-use management practices, especially over-grazing of livestock and unsustainable agricultural practices. As food shortages became more frequent from the early 1940s, officials were anxious to apportion blame. It is at this juncture that debates over the impoverished nature of traditional Gogo land practices, and how to eradicate or transform them, became especially intense (although invented 'custom' continued to be applied in order to implement unpopular policies). The rationale for these interventions lay in the colonial goal of modernising production. The intention was to draw the Gogo deeper into the colonial economy through forcing exchanges of cattle and grain. This would provide new and more modern forms of self-sufficiency for the Gogo, and tackle the problem of over-grazing once and for all.

Gender, livestock and development in Dodoma District

Gogo livestock-keeping practices were an important factor in the colonial explanation of soil erosion and low yields in Dodoma. By the 1940s, these practices were also identified with a reluctance on the part of the Gogo to participate in the colonial market economy. The 'cattle complex' which, as Beinart notes, was given formal definition by anthropological work in the 1920s provided colonial officials with a model to explain the seemingly irrational value attached to cattle.[95] According to this model, livestock were 'overvalued' for cultural reasons; any economic significance attached to cattle was down-played. A 1934 memorandum on 'The economics of the cattle industry' declared:

> Cattle are necessary to the fulfilment of many tribal customs, and it is because of the indispensable part they play in the life of the tribe, and for the distinction which is conferred by ownership, rather than for what they represent in the way of meat, milk and manure, that these animals are prized so highly.[96]

The colonial bipolar model of livestock-keeping practices posited 'two autonomous sectors': one of livestock within the 'traditional' sector, and the other of cash within the 'modern' sector – i.e., the colonial market economy. In reality, cultural and economic processes interacted as individuals, differentiated by gender and seniority, attempted to maintain control over dwindling resources in a transforming economy. In this process, it was the interests of senior male livestock keepers that were reproduced. In the

[93] Christiansson, *Soil Erosion.*
[94] Oral testimonies, Mvumi, Dodoma District, November 1996 to February 1997.
[95] Beinart, 'Soil Erosion', p. 67.
[96] Memorandum on 'The Economics of the Cattle Industry', 1934, PRO CO 169/138/22.

'prestige complex' – as Ferguson refers to it – livestock remain concentrated in the hands of senior men mainly through brideprice transactions and life-long livestock accumulation.[97] In the early twentieth century, Gogo men acquired livestock in exchange for grain and through bridewealth which compensated households for their loss of female labour. Senior men wealthy in cattle loaned cattle to more impoverished, often junior, households in exchange for access to labour. The more livestock a man could acquire, the more labour he could procure to produce grain to exchange for more livestock. In this way, livestock came to be concentrated in the hands of senior men.

In his Lesotho study, Ferguson found that a 'socially-created "one-way barrier" between cash and livestock' existed in order to enable men to protect livestock assets from those who were able to make claims on cash.[98] For men who controlled livestock, their herds represented a retirement fund – a form of savings – and the barriers which prevented their sale were there to protect what were essentially male assets. Once cattle were converted into cash, a whole range of new claims could be made on the cash that could not have been made on the livestock. Women in particular had interests in converting their husband's livestock into claimable assets such as cash. However, in emergencies, livestock could be sold to provide a safety net for the entire household.[99] In a context where cattle were always of benefit to the community at large, rather than only to individual men, the 'prestige complex' endured. This did not imply static 'traditional values'. The 'prestige complex' was an arena where 'traditional' values were 'constantly at issue', where livestock practices were daily 'challenged, defended and re-established'.[100] Nevertheless, it was specifically men's interests that were reproduced in struggles over livestock control and over the customs regulating livestock activities, rather than women's. Accounts of normative arrangements over livestock transactions suggest that this barrier almost certainly operated, in principle, in the first half of the twentieth century in Dodoma District.[101] Only in times of extreme food shortage did the one-way barrier break down. By the 1950s, as local economies became more deeply integrated into the cash economy, some men started to sell livestock to make new investments, mainly in the education of family members.[102] However, bridewealth remained the principal means to forge social and economic relationships across households, and the 'prestige complex' endured.[103]

Livestock and the cash economy

When food production levels dropped off in Dodoma District between 1932 and 1934 due to locust invasions, cattle were sold in order to make up for the shortfall in cash.[104] This was actively encouraged by the administration, fearful that the Gogo would have no money to pay taxes, and anxious to reduce stock numbers in the region as a preventative measure against erosion.[105] In the 1920s, sales of cattle in Dodoma did not

---

[97] James Ferguson. *The Anti-Politics Machine: Development, depoliticization and bureaucratic power in Lesotho* (Minneapolis, University of Minnesota Press, 1994). In his Lesotho study, senior men acquired livestock through resources from migrant labour contracts.

[98] Ferguson, *Anti-Politics*, chapter 5, 'The Bovine Mystique'.

[99] *Ibid.*

[100] *Ibid.*, p. 162.

[101] Oral testimonies, Mvumi, Dodoma District, November 1996 to February 1997.

[102] Yngstrom 'Gender, Land'.

[103] *Ibid.*

[104] Maddox, 'Leave Wagogo!'.

reach beyond 4,000.[106] There are no district figures with which to compare these in later years, but in 1939, *Provincial* cattle sales reached 37,472.[107] Given the importance of cattle to food security, and on the basis of oral testimonies from one part of the district, it seems likely that a small proportion of these sales took place among cattle-keeping *cultivators* among whom a one-way barrier operated to prevent these kinds of trans-actions. It is more likely that there was an increase in sales among livestock *producers* operating in areas where grazing was plentiful, some of whom may have been 'Gogo', and others from communities who had traded livestock with the Gogo in the late nineteenth and early twentieth century.[108] Between 1939 and 1943, the number of cattle sold in Central Province rose from 37,472 to 96,893 and the PC noted in 1944 that the heavy sales of cattle over the famine period had reduced considerably the number in Kondoa and Dodoma.[109] Much of the livestock sold through official markets was exported out of the region, and made up for war-time meat shortages in Britain. Sales were stimulated by Leibigs, livestock traders from Kenya, who purchased over 15,000 head of stock in 1940.[110] Money, the PC noted in 1940, had been 'plentiful in Ugogo, owing to the greater war-time demand for native produce, particularly slaughter-stock'.[111]

Although 1944/45 saw a drop in livestock sales, officials were not unduly concerned since the shortfall had been 'more than made up for by wages brought home by labourers conscripted for rubber and essential civil labour in 1945 and remittances from natives in the forces'.[112] In 1944, the PC commented that, although his annual report had suggested a situation of generalised poverty, this was 'in fact, not the case, … the natives have more money in hand than they have had for many years'.[113] He failed to place the comment in the context of the inflationary pressures of depression and war.[114] During the war, imported goods were in very short supply; the price of imported cloth, by then widely worn among the Gogo, almost doubled between 1939 and 1942.[115] Tax remained at Shs. 10. Meanwhile, the price of one head of cattle in 1941 was £1.12. In 1947, it was £2.41, jumping to £7.26 in 1951.[116] In the west Usambara rubber estates, where many of the Gogo went to work, a labourer earned less in 1948 than in 1929 – Shs. 18 as against Shs. 15-30 a month. By the mid-1940s, the Gogo labourer may have been poorer than he had ever been.

The mid-1940s were a time of crisis for the more central areas of the district. Livestock now had to be bought with cash at prices beyond the means of most labouring Gogo. In this context, the value of livestock rose relative to other resources, and conflicts over rights and interests in livestock became intense, as senior men

---

[105] TARPCNA, Central Province, 1931–4, (UDSM, 1932–5).

[106] *Dodoma District Books*, RH.

[107] ARPC, Central Province, 1943, TNA A.2/1.

[108] Yngstrom, 'Gender, Land.'

[109] ARPC, Central Province, 1944, TNA A.2/1.

[110] TARPCNA, Central Province, 1940 (UDSM, 1941).

[111] *Ibid.*

[112] ARPC, Central Province, 1944, TNA A.2/1.

[113] TARPCNA, Central Province, 1944 (UDSM: 1945).

[114] Avis Richardson, a missionary in Mvumi, comments on dramatic price rises over the same period (Avis I. Richardson, 1986, 'Hold high the torch: a history of the life and works of women in African education at Mvumi Girls' School, Tanganyika, 1926–79', unpublished manuscript).

[115] Iliffe, *A Modern History*, p. 354. These are the prices for Dar es Salaam. The prices in the interior are likely to have been higher.

[116] Patton, 'Dodoma Region'. Central Province Cattle sales, Appendix III, p. 60.

attempted to maintain the prestige complex. Rigby's early 1960s' evidence documents detailed struggles between fathers and sons over the distribution of livestock for brideprice.[117] In the late 1940s, Hans Cory, the government anthropologist, undertook a study of 'Gogo Law and Custom' which undoubtedly reflected similar concerns by senior men to maintain the 'prestige complex'.[118]

By the mid-1940s, the administration's concern to 'modernise' customary livestock practices had begun to take shape and it is in this context that struggles over rights and interests in livestock were being incorporated into colonial policy debates over how exactly this could occur. In 1943, the administration attempted to reduce bridewealth from the 'excessive' figure of '27 cows'.[119] In 1946, the administration managed to get the chiefs to agree that only seven could be returned in a divorce suit; the report also notes that this had 'the support of all the tribe except the wealthy cattle owners'.[120] They were unable to persuade chiefs – who had generally acquired large herds – to lower brideprice, attesting to the enduring nature of the 'prestige complex'. An attempt to tax wealthy cattle-owners from 1944 probably met with little success for similar reasons.[121] In 1948, the acting PC for Central Province remarked that 'the sale of cattle in order to obtain the wherewithal to improve his standard of living does not yet appeal to the tribesman'.[122] Livestock keepers were still reluctant to sell their livestock, and continued to acquire cattle for 'cultural' reasons. These, however, were increasingly acquired with cash.[123]

Incentives to modernise Gogo customary livestock practices were integral to colonial policies during and after the 1930s. Reducing cattle numbers would, in theory, reduce over-grazing and erosion. In particular, officers believed that more cash from sales of cattle would make the Gogo self-sufficient. Stimulating the demand for cash would cause farmers to want to produce a greater surplus. Food shortages would be less frequent and greater cash reserves would enable the Gogo to purchase food in the event of shortage. In 1946, the Director of Agricultural Production, R.W.R. Miller, submitted a Memorandum to the Chief Secretary. In this document, he repeated that soil poverty was the reason for the small surpluses and argued for an improvement in farming methods, and for the need to turn shifting cultivators into permanently cultivating cash-crop producers and consumers.[124]

Gender, modernisation and Gogo identity

In the early 1950s, the administration noted that there had been a dramatic decline in per capita livestock ownership. According to official figures the population of Ugogo increased by roughly 75 per cent between 1931 and 1948. The greatest proportional increase occurred in Mpwapwa. In Dodoma, the increase over the same period was

[117] Rigby, *Cattle and Kinship.*

[118] Hans Cory, 'Gogo Law and Custom', unpublished manuscript, University of Dar es Salaam (1951).

[119] A.V. Hartnoll, ARPC, Central Province, 1943.

[120] *Ibid.*

[121] TARPCNA, Central Province, 1944 (UDSM, 1945). I can find no mention of its actual implementation in later reports.

[122] TARPCNA, Central Province, 1948 (UDSM, 1949).

[123] Yngstrom, 'Gender, Land'.

[124] R.W.R. Miller to Chief Secretary, Memorandum on 'Proposals for Agricultural Investigations, Policy and Development', 19 February 1946, TNA 26054.

about 50 per cent.[125] Before World War II, it was estimated that at least 60 per cent of households owned livestock; whereas by 1953, the figure had dropped to 30 per cent.[126] Although it is unclear from which part of the district these figures were collected, it is highly likely that they come from studies carried out in the central areas of Dodoma District, since the majority of government studies were conducted in these more accessible areas, where an out-migration of large livestock owners outpaced by population growth had caused livestock availability to decline more dramatically than elsewhere.

In this context, colonial ideas about livestock and Gogo identity underwent modification. The government now began to identify certain cattle-owners as industrious and as providers, while non-cattle-owners continued to hamper colonial efforts at increasing production:

> These people [the Gogo] have never had enough food because they have never been able to cultivate an adequate acreage. They have depended for assistance on the *capitalist* cattle owner who could afford to put up 'beef and beer' for starving neighbours.[127]

In 1950, when Bahi chiefdom was short of food, the agricultural officer, Sword, commented on the lack of cultivation: 'Many people have gone from here to do paid labour at Kongwa and left their families – some of them without attempting to provide for them.'[128] In a nearby area he noted that 'the worst problem is caused by people who left the area because of hunger and are now returning to sponge on their more industrious neighbours'.[129]

According to the historian L.E.Y. Mbogoni, during times of food shortage, with no cattle as food security, non-cattle-owners became totally reliant on selling their labour locally or through migration. As a result their own food production suffered, forcing them once again to seek work. The prevention of beer-brewing harmed non-cattle-owners who relied on beer to acquire labour, while cattle-owners could rely on their surplus of food and cash.[130] For Mbogoni, a virtuous cycle of accumulation for large (male) cattle-owners was coupled with a vicious cycle of decline for (male) non-cattle-owners. Mbogoni's argument is drawn from colonial accounts of social differentiation, hidden behind which were a set of assumptions about the masculine orientation of capitalist transformation. In reality, there were quite different patterns of cattle acquisition and decline throughout Ugogo. There were probably a minority of cattle-owning Gogo men in the central, more populous belt, of Dodoma District, who were consistently able to maintain control over large herds and production. In this part of the district, livestock control was a fluctuating situation, rising and falling with the acquisition and payment of brideprice and with the loss of cattle through famine.[131] Senior men wealthy in livestock continued to maintain control over production. However, they

[125] Maddox, 'Environment and Population', p. 44. Maddox computes figures from the official census, and estimates the 1948 figure at a time when Dodoma and Manyoni Districts were amalgamated into one administrative unit.
[126] H. S. Senior, 'Gogo Development Plan.'
[127] ARPC, Central Province, 1943, TNA A.2/1. Emphasis added.
[128] Sword, 'Safari Notes', Safari no. 12.
[129] *Ibid.*, Safari no. 18.
[130] Mbogoni, 'Ecological Crises', p. 74.
[131] Yngstrom, 'Gender, Land'.

needed to participate actively in existing social relations and institutions in order to do so, preventing the kind of accumulation that would create a separate class of wealthy producers, benefiting from an underclass of impoverished labourers.

In the context of greater interaction with the cash economy, the out-migration of young men to colonial plantations, and the simultaneous decline in livestock holdings, all Gogo farmers found it more difficult to acquire labour. Shortages of labour increased the need for women to brew beer,[132] and resistance to enforced cultivation and prevention of beer-brewing became more overt as the agricultural officer, Sword, had found (see above). This only served to reinforce government beliefs about the 'backward', 'lazy' and 'improvident' male farmers who had no desire to improve their lot. Women, on the other hand, were viewed rather differently. Much of what colonial officials observed was coloured by their own beliefs about women's roles. Women were responsible for household reproduction; officials only rarely referred to women's valuable involvement in production. However, the administration were not unaware of the increased burden of work on women as men migrated out to work in other districts, or went in search of food in times of famine.[133] Sword reports that women only were cultivating in some areas.[134]

The most frequent references to women in the colonial records occur in relation to famine. The colonial government generally perceived women as victims, abandoned by their husbands during famine, and unable to participate in plantation labour or any of the heavy famine works. During the 1940s and 1950s, the colonial government did not provide famine relief to women whose husbands were away working, although some ended up in the famine camps, where they were provided with food for work.[135] In 1943, one agricultural officer noted that some of the camps had a large percentage of women.[136] In the 1950s when free issues of famine relief were more common, women, if they could claim destitution, were supported by the state. In 1954-55, in Dodoma, one officer noted that 'women, nearly all with young children, with husbands on sisal estates elsewhere, with husbands in jail, and many with no husbands at all, formed a hard core for whom assistance is essential'.[137]

It is quite clear that women and men were affected by famine in different ways, and that women often suffered disproportionately as men grabbed opportunities for work outside the district to escape poverty.[138] But if women felt the sting of colonial policies, they may have developed new strategies for survival, using their 'victim' status for their own ends. In 1954, a colonial official reported that 'the number of women presenting themselves to the District office claiming destitution and absent husbands showed a significant increase towards the end of the month'.[139]

[132] Oral testimonies, Mvumi, Dodoma District: Rachel Meda; Elina Msanjila, November 1996.
[133] Sword, 'Safari Notes'.
[134] *Ibid.*; Jellicoe, 'Notes on the Position and Role of Women', RH Mss. Afr. s. 2038.
[135] Gregory Maddox, 'Gender and Famine in Central Tanzania, 1916–1961', *African Studies Review* 39, 1 (1996).
[136] Maddox, 'Leave Wagogo', p. 288.
[137] TNA 184/A3/42, 1944–55, cited by Maddox, 'Gender and Famine', p. 97.
[138] Maddox, 'Gender and Famine'; Megan Vaughan, *The Story of an African Famine* (Cambridge, CUP, 1987).
[139] MRDAO, Dodoma District, November 1954, TNA 46/20/22.

Conclusion

Colonial ideas about Gogo land-use practices, drawn from colonial ideas about generic forms of African land use, gave primary shape to the script of Gogo identity. In the context of colonial descriptions of *citemene* shifting cultivation among the Bemba in northern Zambia, Moore and Vaughan note there was a tension between 'a wish to describe complexity, adaptability, and variability and the wish to typologize, systematize and make comprehensible'.[140] In Moore and Vaughan's study, there was a specific scientific and anthropological interest in *citemene* and thus an extensive literature describing agricultural practices and social organisation in the area. In Dodoma, this was not the case. The need to systematise emerged more in the context of the limited and sporadic nature of 'knowledge' about local production systems in the early days of colonial rule. In these early years, the script of tribal identity provided a means to 'know' where 'knowledge' was partial, fragmented and frequently absent. Later reports from the mid-1940s show that at least some agricultural officers were aware of heterogeneity in production systems within the district. But the script proved difficult to dislodge. The power of the tribal model lay in its ability to transcend variation and complexity. Faced with the difficult task of juggling the contradictory demands of territorial policy with locally specific problems, the script was a powerful policy tool.

But it was the colonial model of development which shaped explanations of the causes of the problems the district was experiencing. This ahistorical model which pitted the 'traditional' against the 'modern' made a series of assumptions about the forces of change. The most important of these was the 'market'. It was men rather than women who were seen to drive market-oriented change. This model could not capture social and environmental relations and the complexity of gendered rights and interests in productive resources. Throughout this period of change, senior men were almost certainly extending their control over shrinking livestock resources in order to maintain the prestige complex. By the mid-1940s, wealthy livestock owners were using colonial structures in an attempt to shape the content of custom with regard to brideprice to this end. Given colonial interest in matters of livestock, it is highly likely that these debates were incorporated into the structures of colonialism elsewhere, though existing documentation does not provide direct evidence of this.

Colonial ideology pervaded accounts of Gogo land practices and explanations of change, but soil erosion and low production levels were real problems in Dodoma District. Even though the colonial idea of the Gogo 'shifting cultivator' did not exist in Ugogo (if it existed anywhere), Gogo livestock keepers were mobile and migrated to new areas, especially when faced with shortage of grazing or famine conditions. By the 1940s, shortage of grazing was a problem in the central areas of Ugogo but soil erosion was not a new phenomenon, as some officials maintained. Whether or not soils were continuing to deteriorate under the eyes of colonial officials is unclear. In any event, the problems of grazing shortage were being resolved to some extent by the out-migration of large livestock owners from the more central areas of the district to those on the periphery. Those producers that remained were adapting their land-management practices to changing conditions, such as by allowing livestock to graze on fields, thus providing manure to improve soil quality.

[140] Moore and Vaughan, *Cutting Down Trees*, p. 21.

It is at precisely this juncture in the history of the district that colonial debates about 'wasteful' and 'destructive' Gogo land practices, deteriorating soils and associated low levels of production intensified. The low acreages recorded by colonial officials in the early 1940s appear to have come exclusively from the central areas of the district, where a crisis in livestock, labour and land availability was occurring. Elsewhere, outside of this belt where land and livestock were not in short supply, acreages may well have been maintained at higher levels. Nevertheless, the figures provided an explanation for the food shortages which had worsened in those years. These figures, and the ahistorical ideas about 'traditional' male land practices which informed them, mask important questions about gendered processes of migration, settlement and land use as production systems were integrated into the wider economy.

List of Abbreviations

ARPC   Annual Reports of the Provincial Commissioners (unpublished)
ARPCNA   Annual Reports of the Provincial Commissioners on Native Affairs
          (Published)
BRALUP   Bureau of Resource Assessment and Land Use Planning
DSM   Dar es Salaam
MRDAO   Monthly Reports of the District Agricultural Officers
PRO   Public Records Office
RH   Rhodes House Library
TARPCNA   Tanganyika Annual Reports of the Provincial Commissioners on Native
          Affairs (published)
TNA   Tanzania National Archives UDSM University of Dar es Salaam

Part III

*Settlers & Africans;
Culture & Nature*

10

An Unnatural State

Tourism, Water & Wildlife Photography in the Early Kruger National Park

DAVID BUNN

Since its foundation in 1926, the Kruger National Park has played a central role in the fantasy life of South Africans. This wilderness reserve still occasions the most complex welling up of collective opinion about what the South African nation has managed to conserve, protect, and imagine for future generations, suggesting, as it were, an affective link between the state and the state of Nature. At the same time, to function effectively as a place that satisfies the desires of tourists for a particular kind of visual experience and family narrative, the Kruger National Park has always had to hold at bay a variety of contradictions associated with changes in the nature of land tenure, labour, and death in the Lowveld. Nowhere is this clearer than in the attempts of a first generation of English wildlife custodians to write their legacy in water.

A bonfire in the dark

The Kruger Park lies in the north-eastern corner of South Africa's Mpumalanga Province. After its proclamation as a National Park in 1926, the press quickly came to refer to the new wilderness space as 'the world's greatest Game Reserve'.[1] In practice, that meant that African land-ownership claims in the Reserve were finally swept aside, and a newly consolidated form of white national opinion was mobilised around a powerful landscape symbol. This is now familiar history. But the apparent unanimity of white political support for the Reserve becomes less certain when we ask what it was that early visitors actually desired to see.

Shortly before the official opening of the Reserve, the state-run railways inaugurated a series of national tours that came to be known as the 'Round-in-Nine' service.[2] An overnight stop in what was then called the Sabi Reserve soon became the most popular feature of the journey, with the highlight being a bushveld campfire singalong by the tracks. James Stevenson-Hamilton, first Warden of the Park, described the scene: 'the people sat round the huge blaze, alternately singing choruses and shivering

---

[1] Jane Carruthers, *The Kruger National Park: a social and political history* (Pietermaritzburg, University of Natal Press, 1995), p. 55.

[2] U. de V. Pienaar, *Neem Uit Die Verlede* (Pretoria, National Parks Board, 1990).

with delight at the idea of being watched, from the dark bush close at hand, by the hungry eyes of beasts of prey'.[3] Such evenings were also often the occasion for theatrical pranks by stewards, who, throwing a lion skin over their shoulders, would rush into the circle of firelight. Unstructured tourist desire was already being organised around the idea of the bushveld providing a theatrical exaggeration of sensory experience, a *frisson* of delight. The campfire was a primary reference point for the white body imagining itself at risk in majority darkness.

From this point on, 'atmosphere' as much as animals was valued by early visitors to the Kruger Park. For many English tourists, it seems, the bonfire in the dark was also emblematic of a special class of hardy bushveld administrators, an outgrowth of benevolent colonial governance. Consider this 1925 description of the progress of the Prince of Wales's Royal Tour by train through the Lowveld, where what is emphasised is the thrill of finding lone white administrators, suddenly lit by firelight, against a backdrop of oceanic dark:

> [I]n the heart of the wilderness, towards 9 o'clock, we saw a great bonfire blazing by the track, and … the Royal Train paused for the Prince to say a few words to the only four white people living in an area of nearly 40 square miles…. The scene was typically African virgin bush country, and round the fires had assembled 120 shangaans, who sang and chanted as the Prince passed by late in the night.[4]

Night is not simply a primordial backdrop in this description. Rather, the very grammar of the report ('around the fires had assembled 120 shangaans') suggests that the Royal Train has an uncanny attraction for a certain class of loyal native subject, drawn out of the surrounding darkness.

'Waterhole work'

Long before the opening of the consolidated National Park, Stevenson-Hamilton allowed select individuals into the Sabi Reserve. Prominent amongst these first visitors were the early wildlife photographers Paul Selby, Colonel Hoare, Herbert Lang, C. A. Yates, Bertram Jearey, C. P. De L. Beyers, and, most important of all for my argument, the belligerently outspoken P. W. Willis. In the 1930s, 'Pump' Willis, as he was known, was awarded the administrative contract for three of the largest tourist rest camps in the Kruger National Park, and from then on he was able to use his privileged access to the game reserve in service of an obsession with the art of wildlife photography.[5]

Capturing wild animals in photographs and on film was already a popular pastime in the early 1920s. Not all photographers imitated the showmanship of early cinematographers like Martin and Osa Johnson;[6] nonetheless, early wildlife photography in Kruger was still closely associated with the idea of stalking and spectacular

[3] J Stevenson-Hamilton, *South African Eden, The Kruger National Park* 1937, reprint (Cape Town: Struik, 1993), p. 170.

[4] *Cape Times*, 18 June 1925.

[5] A valuable record of his career is contained in the correspondence between Willis and the wildlife artist Charles Astley-Maberley, also a major figure in the education of tourist vision in the early Kruger National Park, in the Kruger National Park Archive (NKW), personnel file for Astley-Maberley.

[6] W. Beinart, 'The Renaturing of African Animals: Film and Literature in the 1950s and 1960s' in P. Slack (ed.), *Environments and Historical Change* (Oxford, OUP, 1999), p. 149.

10.1 Waterhole work   (Photo: P.W. Willis)

capture. Lions were a favourite photographic subject, and semi-professionals like Bertram Jearey stressed danger and proximity above all else. Most of Jearey's studies were extreme close-ups of lion, and his admirers claimed that 'he [held] what [was] believed to be a world's record for a close study of a lion': a camera-to-subject distance of 12 feet. Jearey relied on idiosyncratic methods of stalking his subjects. Positioning himself behind a moveable screen at a waterhole, he would wait for the arrival of lion, then move progressively closer. To attract their attention, and to catch light in the eyes – a trade trick of all wildlife photographers – he would play tunes on a harmonica.

At the top of the food chain, lion epitomised the problem of wildlife management generally, and for many years after the establishment of the Reserve they were still regarded as 'vermin' by old white hunters, rangers, and tourists. However, tourist attitudes to lion, and to photographic approaches to animals generally, changed quite markedly over the first decade. Denys Reitz, Minister of Lands in the Smuts government, recalled some of his first photographic trips to the Lowveld with the American photographer Paul Selby:

In those days game photography was in its infancy. Few people had realized how little attention wild animals pay to motor-cars, and it was a novel experience for us to find that we could drive up to a troop of waterbuck or a herd of wildebeest.... We thought at first that our success was due to the pains we took to cover our ancient Ford from stem to stern with boughs and foliage under which we sat crouched behind an old-fashioned box-camera swivelled on a universal joint like a machine gun.[7]

[7] D. Reitz, *No Outspan* (London, Faber and Faber, 1943). p. 133.

By far the most important and jealously guarded commodity for photographers like these was knowledge of secluded waterholes where animals came to drink. The Willis letters are full of references to what he called 'waterhole work'. Much of his time was spent chasing rumours of these secret places:

> When I go in next week [to the Reserve] I am going to try and locate a buffalo pool where I understand they drink every day along with a lot of other game and this may prove to be the best pool in the Park, if the report is true. I heard of this pool during the Boer War and doubt if Hamilton himself knows of it, or if he does he does not wish to make it known.[8]

For photographers with bulky half-plate cameras and slow film, the waterhole was a predictable locale where, in the dry winter months, a variety of game animals could be relied upon to appear. Moreover, it offered an aesthetically pleasing setting: game seemed to arrange itself for the camera, with mixed, representative herds presenting a fringing display, as in those typical 1930s images by Willis, reproduced in this chapter. Added to this, there was the obvious nervousness of animals approaching to drink. Aware that predators could attack from dense cover at any minute, the herds seemed doubly alive and alert – fully animal.

In the most general sense, therefore, the thousands of waterhole photographs produced by South African photographers in the 1930s and 1940s, and marketed internationally in magazines like *The Field*, all refer to the same broad themes: a sense of ontological fullness, of sensory acuity, and of natural hierarchies. The essentially concentric nature of the waterhole arrangement lent itself to powerful visual analogies: privileged viewers, intruders upon Eden, sharing the predator's view but choosing not to act; and a representative cross-section of game, driven to this place by the primary needs of environmental influence and biology.

Waterhole photography extended the project of museum habitat-group dioramas, developed by Akeley in New York's American Museum of Natural History. South African museums began to make the transition from glass display cases to dioramas in the 1930s. A visit to the United States by E. C. Chubb, curator of the Durban Natural History Museum, stimulated interest in modern habitat-group displays, though the museum's first, hugely successful diorama of a lion family group was only installed in 1939.[9] The similarities between diorama and waterhole photography go beyond their compositional frame, and their shared reliance on implied connections between animal behaviour and landscape contexts. Both emphasise the intimacy of a secret perspective not normally available to the average viewer. This, in turn, is frequently associated with the idea of donorship. Akeley's theatrical displays were closely associated with his own hunting prowess; similarly, in Durban, displays of African mammals were identified with the largesse of sugar baron William Alfred Campbell, who owned a private lowveld reserve, and who generously allowed specimens to be collected and preserved on his estate.

Like many English-speaking South Africans in the years before and during the Second World War, photographer P. W. Willis had a deep distrust of Afrikaners. Trying to preserve a monopoly over access to prime photographic sites, Willis fulminated

---

[8] NKW, personnel files: Charles Astley-Maberley, P.W. Willis to Charles Astley-Maberly, 30 June 1932.

[9] C. Quickelbridge, *Collections and Recollections: the Durban Natural History Museum, 1887–1987* (Durban, Durban Natural History Museum, 1987), p. 56.

[10] NKW, Willis to Astley-Maberly, 5 January 1941.

against his chief Afrikaner rival C. P. de L. Beyers, and relied instead for information on English-speaking Kruger section rangers and photographers like Selby and Knight. As war approached, however, national politics impinged more and more on the English administrative structures in Kruger. When the conflict broke, and volunteers streamed up North, the old photographer-naturalists found themselves in isolated occupation of the Park, and a considerable portion of their war anxiety was directed against Afrikaners like ranger L. B. Steyn: 'I should bet,' wrote Willis, 'that Steyn is a "General" in the Ossewaga [*sic*] Brandwag as he is a bad and bitter swine and always has been.' [10] Fear of the Ossewabrandwag, an extreme right-wing, Nazi-supporting, anti-British mass movement was widespread during the war.

After 1948, the Kruger National Park came into complex association with different fractions of the new Afrikaner Nationalist state, its spaces penetrated and managed at different levels by the military, government, police, army, and state labour recruiters. For the English amateur naturalists of the 1940s, it was a death knell. Having imagined themselves in an individually privileged relationship to the spirit of pristine Nature – an empathy epitomised in their wildlife photography – they had now come to be regarded as bumbling, sentimental amateurs. Their last champion, also a military man, the luckless post-war Warden Sandenbergh, was drummed out of the Reserve on trumped-up charges of mismanagement. Tellingly, it was the anti-English ranger L. B. Steyn who took over the vacant management position. The Afrikanerisation of the Kruger National Park spelled the end of waterhole work, and broke the patronage system that sustained the first photographers. As I shall show, it also marked the end of the metaphoric link between wildlife photography and the idea of *donation*: gone were the enlightened few who had access to 'secret' pools, and who thought of themselves as giving the public a magnanimous gift of a view.

Brooding and looming

The idea that wildlife photography is a kind of gift springs directly from the conception of benevolent authority that was thought to hold sway in the Game Reserve before 1948. This was a period symbolically bracketed by the two Royal Tours of 1925 and 1947. By the time of the Royal Family's visit in 1947, the box Brownie camera had become ubiquitous, and the sight of the young Princess Elizabeth photographing hippo at the pool near Crocodile Bridge caused a flurry of imitative photographic touring.

Warden Stevenson-Hamilton imagined himself guarding over the primal essence of the bushveld, what he often refers to as the 'Spirit of the Wild,' which, without his custodianship, 'would have spread wings, and with averted face would have fled forever from the Lowveld'. [11] Prompted no doubt by his frequent use of such tropes, his wife Hilda painted an allegorical representation in which the female guardian looms out of the soft density of a cumulo-nimbus cloud, and her nurturing presence is associated with the provision, or withholding, of water, represented in the waterhole scene beneath her. This was in some senses Hilda's own fantasy about the role of the Warden's wife. Whereas she appears as an apotheosised feminine form, the Warden or his ranger companions, in her other paintings, were active landscape presences, moving with ease on horseback, like unobtrusive centaurs, amongst the game animals.

The custodial spirit that was thought to reign benevolently in Kruger before 1948 is

---

[11] Stevenson-Hamilton, *South African Eden*, p. 250.

an interesting form of what Foucault called 'pastoral power,' and which comes into association with other types of state administration.[12] Thus the Kruger National Park, I would argue, was a manifestation both of the individualising and totalising aspects of the South African state: it exhibits forms of governmentality, not only in its administration of game laws and combating of poachers, but also through the control of animal populations. Success in the field of wildlife population management then becomes metonymically associated with the ability to govern other populations elsewhere. Secondly, this administrative capacity was built on an ideology of custodial care, for the health of species, of 'natives', and of individual visitors. Pastoral power, force presenting itself as care, was figured in the looming feminine presence in the clouds.

The idea of benevolent, invisible control was refined over centuries in the Whig landscape traditions of Britain, and modulated through the imperial nostalgia of generations of white settlers in the Lowveld. A considerable lobby in Kruger's early years was from an older class of colonial civil servant eager to preserve the picturesque elements of the Reserve, including old pontoons rather than bridges, and peopling by a certain class of African resident. This conception was then spliced on to a view of therapeutic national wilderness spaces inherited from the American national parks movement, which was closely studied by Stevenson-Hamilton and Minister of Lands Piet Grobler in the lead-up to the 1926 proclamation.[13] Revisionist accounts of Kruger's history have emphasised, quite correctly, that its founding represented a consolidation of white nationalist opinion in the 1920s, although this consensus was not accompanied by the same rhetoric around scenic grandeur as in the United States.[14] Nonetheless, South African conservationists learned a great deal from the American experience. Railways enabled the popularisation of the Sabi Reserve, and, just as in the case of photographer William Henry Jackson some two decades earlier, Paul Selby's photographic portfolios 'helped the public to realise what was in danger of being lost … [and] attracted considerable attention in Parliamentary circles'.[15]

Stevenson-Hamilton was not the only intellectual to describe the Lowveld as a source of authentic, unalienated wilderness experience. Another common source for many descriptions of Lowveld harmony, are the philosophical ramblings of Prime Minister Jan Smuts. Smuts was a keen amateur botanist and photographer; he wrote an influential introduction to Stevenson-Hamilton's widely read *The Low-Veld: Its Wild Life and Its* People, in which he spoke at length about the existence of a Lowveld 'Earth Spirit':

> [Greater] even than its wonderful fauna, its sub-tropical flora, its unrivalled scenery, is the mysterious eerie Spirit which broods over this vast solitude, where no human pressure is felt, where the human element indeed shrinks into utter insignificance, and where a subtle Spirit, much older than the human spirit, grips you and subdues you and makes you one with itself.[16]

---

[12] Hubert L. Dreyfus and Paul Rabinow, *Michel Foucault: Beyond structuralism and hermeneutics* (Brighton, Harvester, 1982), 'The Subject and Power', pp. 208–26.

[13] W. Beinart and P. Coates, *Environment and History: the taming of nature in the USA and South Africa* (London, Routledge, 1994), p. 78.

[14] Carruthers, *The Kruger National Park*.

[15] *Star*, 1926.

[16] J. Stevenson-Hamilton, *The Low-Veld: Its wild life and its people* (London, Cassell, 1934), pp. i–ii.

Common to all these descriptions, and far more elaborately in Smuts's own philosophical writing, there is the underlying belief that certain classes of people are rewarded for their sensitivity to landscape aesthetics by the appearance of benevolent phantoms. For the Spirit of the Lowveld to manifest itself, in other words, a specific form of evolved consciousness, associated with the art of refined looking, had to be present.

Smuts was also famous as the inventor of 'holism'. His political writings frequently harnessed evolutionary theory to an anti-Spenserian new liberalism: 'Smuts ... denied the equality of individuals', argues Kate Fletcher in her gloss of his reasoning, 'ascribing to each ... animal instincts, as well as higher powers of reason and conscience, all correlated and harmonised ... according to the progress of the personal evolution of the individual'. For the Prime Minister, this also meant that there were strict hierarchies in the order of governance:

> The unity of character which the holistic movement aims at does not invoke the destruction of the lower by the higher ethical factors, but the clear undisputed hegemony of the latter over the former, and the reduction of the former to a subordinate and servile position in the whole.[17]

This association between social division and natural selection is quite complicatedly present in a variety of early segregationist discourses in South Africa, especially in references to overpopulation in protected 'native reserves'. Even in the period before major apartheid legislation, the state supported Lowveld farmers' claims that Africans on unsupervised Crown Land were an unruly surplus, proliferating beyond control and with catastrophic results for environmental degradation.[18]

There are homologies between the philosophical principles of holism, the fantasy of the Warden guaranteeing peace between lower species at the waterhole, and, indeed, as we shall see later, the rhetoric of benevolent custodianship that underpinned efforts by other state agencies like the Native Affairs Department.[19] In all three cases, good administration is likened to the harmonious agency of a higher consciousness, directing the distribution of resources within a landscape system and admiring the naturalness of the result. In stark contrast, white farmers in the region were completely intolerant of this idea, in as far as it encouraged a class of Africans resident on Crown Lands who were not available as agricultural labourers.

Neurasthenia, synaesthesia, and looking

For most of its history, Kruger was like many national parks elsewhere in that visitor experiences were mediated first and foremost through travel in private motor vehicles. Still today, for the average tourist, the motor car is essentially a mobile viewing platform. At the same time, the early landscape design of the Kruger National Park was

---

[17] K. Fletcher, ':The Culture of the Personality": Jan Smuts, Philosophy and Education', *South African Historical Journal* 34 (May 1996), pp. 106–26.

[18] C. Mather, 'Environment as Weapon: Land, Labour and African "Squatters" in Rural South Africa' in Tony Binns (ed.), *People and Environment in Africa* (New York, John Wiley, 1995), pp. 231–8.

[19] S. Dubow, *Racial Segregation and the Origins of Apartheid in South Africa, 1919–1936* (London, Macmillan, 1989), p. 36.

10.2 The role of the car   (Photo: J.J.E. Gill)

determined to a lesser degree than in the United States by the needs of motor tourism. American national parks evolved in lockstep with a system of national roads and freeways; some roads, particularly 'the nature parkways begun in the 1930s, [barred] commercial traffic and in the design of their curves and rest areas [instructed] drivers about how best to appreciate the scenery out the window'.[20] The Lowveld was not entirely immune to the American idea of a scenic approach to the national parks. Even in 1928, newspapers were advocating the creation of 'a defined route through the Northern Transvaal to pass the native location, game reserves, scenery and other interests that appeal to overseas visitors'.[21] For the Reserve itself, however, the public actively resisted the 'Coney Island' experience of American national parks, which were presumed to be 'over-civilised for the comfort of the tourists'.[22] Until after the Second World War, roads in the Kruger Park were rough and unpaved. Moreover, South African tourists – compared with those in many major East African game parks, where organised safaris were the order of the day – had a high degree of relative autonomy, in that they planned their daily motor routes and game-viewing strategies independently.

For many years pleasure consisted in the amateur ability to maximise game sightings from the vehicle, while the sensory delights of the unenclosed bushveld experience were limited to rest camps and a handful of official picnic sites. It might be said, then, that car tours and rest camps were part of one visual system, a combination of mobility and framed, stationary views that fell within the classical definition of landscape experience not only in the apprehension of picturesque views, but also in the implied metaphor of a wandering subject who pauses, from time to time, for contemplation.[23]

[20] A. Wilson, *The Culture of Nature* (London, Blackwell, 1992), p. 29.
[21] *Star,* 25 September 1928.
[22] *Pretoria News,* 16 October 1934.
[23] Alan Liu, *Wordsworth: the sense of history* (Stanford, CA, Stanford University Press, 1989), pp. 61–137.

The landscape system I am describing, consisting of the intense concentration of the touring car view and the bottled-up, atmospheric pleasure of time spent back at the tourist camp, was not in place in the first years of the Park. In fact, it is intriguing to see that early tourists were completely unsophisticated and unstructured in their desires. For the first few years, many of them came armed with rifles and camped freely in the bush.[24] Nevertheless, most visitors to the Park also thought of themselves as travelling back in time, away from the city and its modernity. Novelist Ethelreda Lewis, for instance, describes Kruger as 'a place of ancient stillness streaked by many rivers flowing in primeval beauty'.[25] Especially at dawn and dusk this primitive quality was communicated directly to the viewer. The bushveld mise-en-scène allowed the visitor to be part of a different spatio-temporal experience: instead of the day determined by the rhythms of work, its contours were defined by more primitive, affective associations. The dying of the light triggers a far wider range of responses, from mature depression to slight fear, and the dawn is full of joy, as though one were able to inhabit, for a brief time, an older, pre-modern subjectivity attuned to the nuances of the environment.

In these accounts, Kruger is a therapeutic environment that 'reserves' an older form of time and value. This is consistent with many of the compensatory, primitivist land-scapes of European and American modernism. With the generalisation of the com-modity form, the abstraction of labour as a commodity, and the proliferation of Fordist work regimes, global modernity expresses an intense, compensatory nostalgia for 'reserved' spaces where the remnants of archaic value are to be found: Hemingway's Kilimanjaro, Lawrence's Taos, the Reservation in Huxley's *Brave New World,* van der Post's Kalahari are all examples of symbolically enclaved zones. These writers reworked the contradictions around labour and value intrinsic to metropolitan capitalism by exporting them to fictive colonial environments. The Game Reserve might be said to theatricalise a framing, primal past for modernising Europe, as well as for local metropoles like Johannesburg. In other words, it encapsulated two temporal orders: enlightened modern management and the best remnant traces of the pre-industrial past. Homi Bhabha has explained this double temporality as follows. He speaks of

> The ambivalent historical temporality of modern national cultures – the *aporetic coexistence*, within the cultural history of the *modern* imagined community, of both the dynastic, hierarchical, prefigurative 'medieval' traditions (the past), and the secular, homogenous, synchronous cross time of modernity (the present).[26]

Bhabha was talking about the racialised 'projective past': that European modernity exports the problem of its racism, intrinsic to capitalism, to the colonies, as a way of working it through by imagining it as a problem of the past. Kruger, too, provides a way of working through contradictions inherent to capitalism in South Africa. It is a theatrical space in which the problem of race, and rights, is displaced on to the idea of Nature.

To sum up: what I am suggesting is that Kruger is a typically modernist form of symbolically enclaved space that tries to separate the destructive force of early

---

[24] Stevenson-Hamilton, *South African Eden*, p. 231.
[25] *Star*, 16 November 1929.
[26] H.K. Bhabha, *The Location of Culture* (London, Routledge, 1994), p. 250.

twentieth-century industrialisation, mechanisation, and shocking new experiences of time, from the realm of value. European and American modernists saw the need for special forms of leisure experience that would counter the experience of 'technologically multiplied shock' (to use Benjamin's phrase) characteristic of post-First World War society. There was a broad perception amongst white opinion-formers in South Africa that senses had been maimed by the war, and that the industrial work regimes of mining and manufacture were having widespread negative effects. The effect of this new experience of time, according to philosophers like Benjamin, was to produce a 'defensive numbing of the sensorium' in which the subject created a protective, anaesthetising screen.[27] Wilderness experience would simply restore the deadened, instinctual power of the senses, and the beautiful, mirroring semblance of the waterhole photo was designed to achieve just that sort of sympathetic reawakening. For English-speaking visitors to the National Park, the bushveld could bring 'invigoration and refreshment to nerves … jaded by the humdrum routine of work'.[28]

A trip to the Game Reserve in the 1930s was seen as a 'cure' for the various neurasthenic disorders that follow from industrial work regimes, and the obscure sense of loss attendant on the instrumentalisation of labour relations.[29] Vision, it seems, is the sense that has been especially affected by industrialisation, and Kruger offered a chance for recovery. Seen from a moving car, the bushveld allowed a naive sort of wish-fulfilment, becoming a place of ontologically replete vistas where, for Ethelreda Lewis, 'the whole picture books of childhood come true at last'.[30] This aspect of vision suggests a return to that sense of pre-Oedipal completeness, a childlike pleasure that has its origins in the proximity of animals.

Looked at with new intensity, creatures like giraffe appeared to move in another world of time and space: 'that soft, gigantic, fascinating canter which is like an optical illusion'. 'If your car goes quietly,' Lewis continues, 'you will get near enough to see that in the folds of the skin of the neck perch tick birds.' Ironically, therefore, the recovery of vision depended on the car itself as platform and prosthesis. It is not unlike the contradictory experience of early movie audiences: 'On the one hand,' says Susan Buck-Morss, regarding the movie-going experience, 'there is an extreme heightening of the senses … [while] on the other, there is … a numbing of the nervous system.'[31] Here too, in the exaggeratedly slow passage of the vehicle, with the windows open and occupants straining for a view, technology seems to be in harmony with the goals of conservation. Remarkably, cars also proved to be very effective mobile hides, and wildlife paid very little attention to slowly moving vehicles.

The idea of Kruger as a 'reserve' for reactivating dulled sensory capacities was especially important for the self-conception of white English speakers and for white national identity. In an advertisement for pre-1926 South African railways' game reserve tours, which was published in *The Illustrated London News*, white visitors were being taught to see. A game scout, in that characteristic hunter-gatherer's crouch typical of

[27] M. Hansen, 'Benjamin and Cinema: Not a One-Way Street', *Critical Inquiry* 25, 2 (1999), pp. 306–43.

[28] C.A. Yates, *The Kruger National Park* (London, George Allen & Unwin, 1935).

[29] For a fine account of the belief in 'neurasthenia and of its ubiquity', see Brigid Doherty, '"See: We Are All Neurasthenics!" or, the Trauma and Dada Montage', *Critical Inquiry* 24,1 (1997), pp. 82–32.

[30] *Star*, 16 November 1929.

[31] S. Buck-Morss, 'The Cinema Screen as Prosthesis of Perception: A Historical Account', in C. Nadia Seremetakis (ed.), *The Senses Still: Perception and memory as material culture in modernity* (Chicago, University of Chicago Press, 1996), pp. 45–62.

ethnographic dioramas, points out animals, sighting along his arm. Three white visitors, in various attitudes of timid delight, stand well back from the scene, while a fourth leans into the African's field of vision. Tourism, in this instance, consists in the adventure of the white body rediscovering somatic capacities, through interaction with black bodies. Because this is a British advertisement, the racist association of the Boer, staring into a cooking pot with instinctual dullness, is not surprising, but there is clearly also another transitional form of white subject, epitomised by the man who stands next to the African scout. In the 1920s and 1930s, there was a widespread fantasy that white colonial subjects could be defined by their acute visual capacity. For white modernists like the poet Roy Campbell, this was because South Africans grew up with guns and lived in close proximity to Africans. Hunting, for Campbell, taught South Africans to 'think with [their] eyes', and the descriptive power of his poetry results, he said, from 'the strength of my eyes, used to stroking whole hillsides for the least flicker of a buck's tail'.[32] Sharpened vision, in his understanding, is a precondition for racially adaptive colonial citizenship.

Camera Tyros and Afrikaner pilgrimages

Prominent among the enemies of the landscape harmony described by Smuts and Stevenson-Hamilton, were the unreconstructed, libidinally driven white working-class visitors from neighbouring industrial centres. Often raucous and ungovernable, they arrived in droves, only to be disappointed at the thin entertainment provided by the wilds. What emerged to structure this polymorphous mimetic desire was the spread of amateur photography, and a related, emergent genre of autobiographical tourist writing about Kruger Park encounters.

For the average tourist, being in a game reserve, sometimes within yards of dangerous animals and without supervision, was a bewilderingly intense experience. Within a very short space of time, game spotting became a highly competitive activity, the occasion of male bravado. A surging interest in amateur photography exacerbated the problem. In 1931, a tour leader left his vehicle to take a close-up photo of a sable antelope, and was promptly charged and severely gored. Early rangers' diaries are full of accounts of warnings to young men for taunting lion. Press reports in 1931 and 1932 carry increasing references to the 'extremely mischievous practice of pursuing animals in motor cars in order to obtain a close-up photograph or to see them run'.[33] By 1937, letters to the Johannesburg *Star* went so far as to suggest that 'cameras ... should be banned, because tourists who are too anxious for photographs run a great risk'.[34] An *economy* of wildlife viewing – originally the domain of select amateur naturalists but now more widely available – was seen to be under threat from the increasingly disruptive excesses of white working class tourists.

The National Parks Board responded to the threat of unruly white trippers by imposing spot fines, and by threatening to ban trucks, then taxis from the reserve. One grumpy White River resident took the opportunity to suggest even wider forms of regulatory control: 'If only the ban could be extended to those youths who bring their synthetic blondes down for a weekend, our happiness would be complete.'[35] The battle

[32] R. Campbell, *Broken Record* (London, Boriswood, 1934), p. 85.
[33] *Star,* 18 August 1932.
[34] 'Animal Lover', *Star*, 4 September 1937.
[35] *Star*, 26 August 1938.

lines were laid out clearly: for a middle-class tourist audience, the Park was a compensatory landscape, a system of views organised for therapeutic effect to restore the frayed nerves of city-dwellers. For other classes, it was sometimes a place where pleasure was heightened by a sense of bushveld danger, and sexuality.

Popular photography provided a means for white tourists to structure their unbound desires. From 1927 onwards, newspapers advised readers on what views to capture in Kruger. By 1931 the Johannesburg *Star* was running a photographic competition for the best image taken in the Reserve and offering to record the growing traffic of game reserve anecdotes: 'There is developing a mild game, yet unnamed, when friends who have been [to the Reserve] begin to compare notes on what they have seen.'[36] Apart from disseminating competitive records of animal sightings, these newspaper reports often advanced a peculiar form of family narrative in which mother, father, and children are bound together by the recollection of the intense Game Reserve experience. It was not just the spectacular sightings that passed into memory. More often, typical background and foreground objects were sought after, as in the remark by Marion Archer that 'a beautiful kudu bull standing out against a darker background will remain a memory picture for all time'.[37] These shared and stored memories became an element in the family experience and a renewal of commensality.[38]

Another division in perception of the park was reflected in growing antagonism between English- and Afrikaans-speaking visitors. A cartoon in a 1934 Afrikaans newspaper associated lack of interest in game spotting with English decadence. Emphasis was placed on drunkenness, sexual bravado – a woman in shorts ostentatiously smokes a cigarette – and the camera turned narcissistically inwards upon humans. At the margins of sight, a pride of lion gazed on in astonishment, the chief prize for educated game spotters now sadly neglected. The sarcastic attack on 'uncivilised' English behaviour in the Kruger Park is an indication perhaps of how little we know of Afrikaans attitudes to the Kruger National Park landscape before 1945. Almost all the publicity material for the Reserve was written in English, and debates were frequently monopolised by the anglophone Transvaal press. But Afrikaners were equally intrigued by the image of the Park as a transformative symbolic landscape. In the 1920s and 1930s nascent Afrikaner nationalism was heavily invested in the idea of rescuing 'poor whites' from their ambiguous proximity to working-class black and coloured communities. Christian Nationalist propagandists looked to the past for examples of Afrikaner heroism that could mobilise and consolidate the *volk* in its new task; perhaps surprisingly, the dominant paradigm and reference point in this debate was not the recent past of the Anglo-Boer War, but the past of the farm and the image of honest white pioneers.[39]

Afrikaner intellectuals everywhere returned to the idea of rural harmony as a means of recovering a sense of racial pride. This was the period in which the *plaasroman* [farm novel] flourished, and magazines like *Die Huisgenoot* are full of sentimental accounts of second-generation urban Afrikaner youths eschewing the life of the city and returning home to the family farm.[40] But if the farm was a mobilising symbol in the

[36] *Rand Daily Mail*, 30 August 1932.

[37] *Star*, 15 August 1932.

[38] C.N. Seremetakis, 'The Memory of the Senses, Part II' in Seremetakis, *The Senses Still*, pp. 23–44.

[39] D. O'Meara, *Forty Lost Years* (Athens, OH, Ohio University Press, 1996), p. 41. See Swart in this volume.

[40] J.M. Coetzee, *White Writing* (Johannesburg, Radix, 1988), pp. 91–100; J.A. du Pisani, 'Progression in Perceptions of Masculinity Among the Afrikaans Community, 1935–1995', paper presented at 'Masculinities

1920s and '30s, so too was the bushveld, as a dramatic context for similar exemplary stories of pioneering pluck. As Isabel Hofmeyr has shown, leaders of the Second Language movement like Gustav Preller actively sought to recover authentic trekker narratives, and in their descriptions the Lowveld became a symbolic zone inscribed with the exemplary suffering of nineteenth-century trekker parties.[41]

To some extent, the Afrikaans conception of the Kruger Park as a domain of typicality associated with rural fortitude was present even in the negotiations around the name of the national reserve in 1926.[42] But for the average Afrikaans visitor, this originary wilderness was often also associated with religious presences. The landscape was associated with the dramatic trekker past, and with proximity to God. Most important of all perhaps, it was a means by which a generation of newly urbanised Afrikaner youth could be reminded of the unalienated pastoral family. By the 1950s, many Afrikaans writers routinely described tourist visits to the Kruger Park as pilgrimages and an escape from industrial pollution and materialism.

> Met die werke van sy hande het die mens homself toegebou. In sy stede, dorpe en selfs op sy plase omring sy handewerk hom in so `n mate dat die maan nie meer uit `n polsende oerwout van lewe en dood verrys nie, maar slegs flou skemer deur rookwolk tussen skoorstene; sodat die son nie meer die lumier in `n gloed van rooi en goud aankondig nie, maar slegs `n nuwe werksdag om meer geld to maak.... Dit is om die volk van Suid Afrika jaar na jaar, asof op pelgrimstog, die grootpad na die Krugerwildtuin vat.[43]

English administrators seem to have been largely unaware of this considerable political investment in the idea of the Kruger Park landscape. In the 1930s and 1940s, the Board came in for increasing attack from Afrikaners because the Park was not accessible to white working-class visitors. The *Low Veld Chronicle* of 1937 reported unsympathetically on a Barberton delegation which claimed that 'the Kruger National Park Trustees had locked and barred the Game Reserve on the southern boundary to the poorer man'. Elsewhere, the public complained bitterly about implicit class prejudice in the fact that the Reserve administrators seemed to focus mainly on middle-class white families with private motor vehicles.

By the 1930s, the Kruger National Park had a become a more routine destination for that class of visitor who had access to camera and private motor vehicle. For increasing numbers of middle-class English visitors, good game reserve demeanour entailed obeying regulations, remaining in the vehicle, and not 'robbing the next car to come along of a sight'.[44] A sharp divide emerged between those who believed they had the

---

[41] (cont.) in Southern Africa' conference, University of Natal, Durban, 2–4 July 1997.

[41] I. Hofmeyer, 'Popularising History: the Case of Gustav Preller', *Journal of African History* 29, 3 (1988), pp. 521–35.

[42] Carruthers, *The Kruger National Park*.

[43] R.J. Labuschagne, *60 Jaar Krugerwildtuin* (Pretoria, National Parks Board of Trustees, 1958), pp. 63–4. `By their own work, people have built around them. In their cities, towns and even on the farms, people are so surrounded by their handiwork, that the moon no longer rises from a pulsing, primeval forest of life and death, but merely shines weakly through clouds of smoke between chimneys (smokestacks); so that the sun no longer heralds the dawn in a glow of red and gold, but only a new working day in which to make more money.... That is why, year after year, the people of South Africa, as though on a pilgrimage, take the highroad to the Kruger game reserve.'

[44] *Star,* 12 July 1932.

innate sensibility and civic understanding to appreciate wildlife without intruding upon it, and those who apparently could not see.

With the popularisation of the Kruger Park family holiday, writing about game experiences became one of various means by which middle-class parents advertised their exemplary behaviour. The generalisation of this ethics of appropriate game watching, focused on rules for photography and game reserve behaviour, was so successful, that by 1939 the secretary of the National Parks Board of Trustees described the tourism industry in the Reserve as essentially self-regulating.

> Visitors are beginning to take an almost proprietary interest in the park, and this has resulted in more respect for ... regulations. Indeed, many of those who disregard regula-tions are very firmly dealt with by other visitors who love the park. There is a congenial, friendly spirit among visitors, both in the camps and on the roads.[45]

In the period immediately preceding the war, scores of visitors joined the 'Common-sense League,' an organisation that advocated temperate Kruger Park behaviour and had its members sign a pledge of good behaviour and display a windshield sign reading 'Stay in your car and keep to the road'.[46] Thus for an entire class of visitor, it was by now apparently 'commonsense' to follow the agreed-upon rules of game spotting. As a landscape system, therefore, Kruger was by now beginning to satisfy the desires of a significant minority by regulating the way in which a series of wilderness views unfolded in space and in time.

Ethnicity in the frame

In the first decades of its existence, the Kruger National Park routinised class and race forms of ideological interpellation, and provided a *scene* for significant fantasy investment. The extent to which this framed wilderness space had become a site of intense emotional investment is demonstrated even in minor debates around the aesthetics of rest camps. The considerable exotic appeal of thatched, round, rest-camp huts is captured in the following government information pamphlet:

> The distinctive design of the ... huts is based on the quaint little dwellings of the natives. These hive-shaped huts, called rondavels, fit snugly into the luxurious green background of the undulating plains and hills.... [They never seem] to mar or conceal the harmony of the scene.[47]

Rondavels, as this style of vernacular building came to be called, are an imitation of 'native' dwellings. They are also part of a larger system of homological structures in which the white presence is able to stage itself as though adapted to the African environment. Structurally speaking, they are therefore analogous to the experience of the waterhole photograph, where the viewer sees the plenitude of animals that results from custodial care, but is himself unseen. Throughout the history of the Kruger Park,

[45] *Star,* 14 June 1939.
[46] NKW, Box File 25/1, Briewe van die Publiek, 1936–1979, has an interesting array of sycophantic letters on the subject of good game reserve behaviour.
[47] National Parks Board of Trustees, *Unspoilt Africa* (Pretoria, National Parks Board, 1939).

10.3 African guard at Kruger National Park   (Photo: Miss M. Burton)

an extraordinary amount of public interest was focused on retaining the original form
of these dwellings, and when Stevenson-Hamilton tried to introduce the first
rectangular dwellings, they were generally regarded as ugly.

One way of looking at the history of wildlife photography in the Kruger National
Park is to argue that waterhole photographs, huts, and the Reserve landscape as a
whole, are all homologically related. But the intense national longing evident in these
scenarios finally depends on the management of another framing presence: that of
Africans themselves. Resident Africans were part of the white tourists' experience of
the Kruger National Park up to the 1950s. The approximately 3,000 black workers and
villagers who lived permanently in the Reserve were imagined to be an extension of the
picturesque, tribal fringe that surrounded it. Stevenson-Hamilton quickly came to
appreciate that captured poachers and illegal immigrants 'could be useful to the
conservation effort by providing both labour and funding'.[48]

But Africans were not simply camp help. In many English tourist accounts it is clear
that the experience of proximity to 'raw natives,' as they were called, was a crucial
aspect of enjoyment for whites. The Native Reserves themselves around the Park were
advertised as an appropriately archaic scenic domain that formed a pleasing backdrop
to a motor tour to the Lowveld with the game reserve as its final destination. African
staff in Kruger were representative of another order of time, an older domain of loyalty
and pre-capitalist value that appeared already passed away beyond the borders of the
Game Reserve. They were, as Homi Bhabha puts it, the sign of the ontological

[48] J. Carruthers, 'Game Protection in the Transvaal, 1846-1926', unpublished doctoral dissertation, University
of Cape Town (1988), p. 92. In the 1911 Annual Report for the Sabi and Singwitsi Reserve, Stevenson-
Hamilton estimated a population of 600 tax-paying males, and 3,500 old men, women, and children.

'belatedness' of black identity;[49] existing in a liminal world before rights, it is as though these transitional figures helped to cushion the violent effects of racial modernisation elsewhere. Kruger, in this sense, was a place of primal misrecognition, where whites were investing in the notion of loyal labour that had chosen, so to speak, to give up its rights for the sake of an older fealty. Africans in the employ of the park clearly derived some benefits and were prepared to play such roles; their perceptions will be explored in a separate paper.

There is an entire genre of tourist photography in the 1930s and '40s, that seeks to capture images of gate guards. In these pictures, Africans are theatricalised as static, caryatid figures, wearing uniforms that combine an older colonial house-boy style with that of the imperial military.[50] The apparent fixity of these figures, though, is not just a sign of their loyalty; rather, it is an expression of their status as stereotypes. These liminal figures stand at a symbolic threshold, signalling the transition to an older form of labour relation. In a sense, too, the gate guard's function is primarily photographic, rather than administrative: his is a particularly stylised pose, conscious and responsive to the needs of the camera. In Kruger, moreover, there was a portmanteau term used by tourists and rangers alike to refer to the dutiful native guards who stood at attention: they were called 'Shangaans'.[51]

The term 'Shangaan' has a complex history, and even in its early popular English usages (consider *Jock of the Bushveld*), it was associated with forms of displacement. Whether in reference to migrant Mozambican mine workers, or to 'police boys' in Kruger, the descriptions of Tsonga speakers had in common the perception that Shangaans came from elsewhere, but were fiercely loyal to those they served. When she visited the Kruger National Park in 1935, Karl Akeley's second wife Mary Jobe Akeley gained the impression that 'Tshangane rangers are strong, wild, and brave'.[52] Incidentally, the 'police boy' named Watch at Crocodile Bridge whom she describes as 'courageous and devoted to his white superior and to the cause he serves' is one of a handful who crop up again and again in the personal narratives of English-speaking women visiting the Park. The exploits of hired Shangaan lookouts are a favourite preoccupation of 1930s' tourist anecdotes.

Quarrels over the definition of the African presence in the Kruger National Park were an important indication of the way the Reserve was thought to function as a visual system. Africans were permissible within the landscape frame as long as they were visually pleasing, and as long as they were not engaged in productive agriculture. Anything beyond subsistence crops, or small, unobtrusive herds of cattle destroyed the therapeutic distinction between bushveld wilderness and agricultural modernization that underpinned the entire rationale for the park. Some visitors complained that there were too many Africans in the Park, and that 'their cattle were [monopolising] ... water holes to the detriment of the wild life'.[53] Cattle brought the less palatable (to whites) reality of the 'native reserves' spilling in.

[49] Bhabha, *The Location of Culture*, p. 236.

[50] See John and Jean Comaroff, *Of Revelation and Revolution: the dialectics of modernity on a South African frontier, Vol. II* (Chicago, Chicago University Press, 1997), pp. 218–73, for an excellent account of 'frozen' styles of dress.

[51] See K. Silverman, *The Threshold of the Visible World* (London, Routledge, 1996), pp. 202–19 for a fine analysis of the photographic 'pose'.

[52] M. J. Akeley, *Restless Jungle* (London, George G. Harrap, 1937), p. 97.

[53] *Star,* 9 August 1931.

Mounting aggression towards the presence of settled African families in the Park is especially apparent in the Afrikaans press. The fifth Annual Transvaal Publicity Association Conference in Lydenburg in 1931 was the scene of vigorous protest against resident Africans in Kruger, and in the same year General Kemp, National Party Minister of Agriculture, complained bitterly about the lack of bilingualism in the Reserve, the powers of native police, and the presence of cattle-owning African families. Clearly stung by the criticism, the National Parks Board of Trustees took it upon themselves to publish an 'authoritative statement' on 'Natives in the Kruger National Park'. In it, they make the following critical claim: 'It is quite incorrect to say that the natives are 'farming'. Tribal natives do not farm in our sense of the word. They grow enough grain for the consumption of their families ... and their domestic stock is kept for private consumption, and where cattle are concerned, for barter in connection with their marriage customs.'[54] The implication is clear: natives in Kruger are not surplus to the labour needs of the Reserve, nor do they compete with local white farmers, or the needs of game. Instead, as 'raw natives, living under the tribal system' they are picturesque remnants of an older system.[55]

Ironically, the argument around African residents in the Park was often bracketed with vociferous letters about the growing 'lion problem' in Kruger. Many Lowveld farmers were outspokenly critical of the Warden's decision to halt the culling of lion. Increasing numbers of predators and an imagined proliferation of 'farming natives' were both seen by conservative writers to be evidence of a mismanaged or unscientific system, to which the Board responded with a classic *laissez faire* riposte: 'The Kruger Park is a self-contained organism and its machinery has run smoothly and well for nearly 30 years. To tamper with this machinery ... would be a serious error.'[56]

The problem of resident, cattle-owning Africans in the Kruger National Park relates directly to antagonistic perceptions of those who believed poor whites were being driven off the land, and that Africans on Crown Land were being protected by the Native Affairs Department in the Smuts government, keeping them out of reach of labour markets.[57] Further fuel was added to the fire when the National Party made the spectre of African urban migration ('oorstrooming') a key element of its 1948 election campaign.[58] For Liberal segregationists, however, the image of a settled, picturesque, pre-modern community in harmony with Nature in the Kruger Park also suggested the possibility of beneficial, regulatory white control over neighbouring rural communities. Kruger, with its resident, semi-feudal African population, was a system that worked and appeared to manage animal and human populations with apparent ease. As if in evidence of this gently successful control, the Western boundary of the Kruger Park remained unfenced, with only rudimentary markers. The borders were in large measure legal and symbolic, and there was considerable public opposition in the English press to the idea of a boundary fence. Instead, when pressed by local farmers, Board members like photographer Paul Selby suggested various scenic alternatives, including barrier rows of knobthorn (*Acacia nigrescens*).[59]

---

[54] *Star,* 3 September 1931.

[55] Stevenson-Hamilton, *The Low-Veld*, p. 217.

[56] *Star,* 3 September 1931.

[57] Mather, 'Environment as Weapon'.

[58] O'Meara, *Forty Lost Years*, pp. 24, 34.

[59] S. C. J. Joubert, *Master Plan for the Management of the Kruger National Park* (Skukuza, Kruger National Park, 1986), p. 36.

Until the 1960s, one of the chief defining features of the Park border was precisely its ability to exert a moral influence on those Africans within the irregularly demarcated limits. For Stevenson-Hamilton, the Reserve administration had always effectively protected resident Africans from the corrupting forces of modernisation that afflicted those who lived just beyond its influence. 'I would like to point out,' he said, in his Annual Report of 1929, 'the very noticeable difference in the manners and ways of the Park residents as compared with those living outside.' 'Whereas our natives are always civil and obliging to Europeans,' he continued, 'those living along the Crocodile River especially close outside our borders are just the reverse, and seem permeated with political propaganda.'[60] This is an intriguing claim – probably indirect evidence of the effects of rural Lowveld recruitment campaigns by the Industrial and Commercial Workers Union.[61]

The ambiguities around the visible presence of African employees in Kruger is dramatically demonstrated in the case of the so-called Doispane community. One of Kruger's most famous early rangers was Harry Wolhuter, in Section 1 in the vicinity of Pretoriuskop. He maintained an efficient band of 'police boys' in the Phabene region around the kraal of Doispane and then at Albasini. The Doispane settlement had at its core a group of African rangers, including Sokkies Masinga, Stump Mangani, Ridonga Mongwe, around whom various relatives and followers began to cluster. These were the 'gate guards', 'police boys' and 'lookout men' who were a familiar sight to visitors in the south-west, and despite the fact that they spoke a variety of languages, they were for the most part referred to as Shangaans. Many of them also kept livestock, and their children herded and dipped Wolhuter's own cattle. However, when the group swelled from three to five families, Stevenson-Hamilton ordered some of them to move, and eventually a new settlement grew at Albasini.[62]

The community was further threatened during the foot-and-mouth epidemic of the 1930s when the veterinary authorities finally decided that game and cattle could no longer share the same drinking places. Cloven-hooved game animals, it was believed, transmitted the disease to cattle, which then spread it to other herds sharing watering points. For the Doispane and Albasini families, catastrophe struck in 1939 when, according to Nkayinkayi Samuel Mavundla, all their cattle were slaughtered. The 1939–41 veterinary killing of cattle in the Lowveld, motivated by the fear of spreading foot-and-mouth disease, is vividly remembered. Mavundla recalls how workers dug a huge pit with bulldozers, and Department of Agriculture officials herded the milling beasts to the very brink. Shots rang out repeatedly for an unimaginably long time, and their livelihood was destroyed. The Chief Native Commissioner for the Northern Areas described how in the Kruger National Park 'some 1,200 cattle belonging to its Native population of some 2,000 souls [have] … been slaughtered to establish a cattle free zone between Portuguese territory and the Transvaal'.[63] In the neighbouring Crocodile

[60] Kruger National Park, Warden's Annual Reports, 1927–1950.
[61] H. Bradford, 'The Industrial and Commercial Workers' Union of Africa in the South African Countryside, 1924-1930', unpublished doctoral dissertation, University of the Witwatersrand (1985), p. 229.
[62] Interview with Samuel Nkayinkayi Mavundla, who still lives in the Kruger National Park, in an unprotected kraal near the Albasini ruins. His mother is buried at the ruins, and there are graves of several of the old field rangers in the vicinity. He is one of the oldest surviving members of a generation of 'police boys' who worked for Wolhuter, who had a complicated and ambiguous relationship with the Reserve, and who suffered through generations of rough National Parks Board justice.
[63] National Archives, Pretoria, Native Affairs Department (NTS), Box 6803, file 28/316/8.

River district almost 14,000 animals were shot.[64] Still today, young men explain away their poverty by reference to the fact that once their families had wealth, but this was destroyed when the government shot the cattle.[65]

Whether as part of the dramatisation of archaic time, or as an intrusive force, Africans were a crucial element in the definition of Kruger's borders. Photography worked to maintain this separate sphere for African identity in the Park, distinct from the debased conditions in the Reserves outside. However, in the 1930s, another force intruded upon the system of pastoral power embodied in both the images of statuesque game guards and the waterhole photograph. That force was drought.

The ensuing drought

In the 1930s, periodic waves of drought were not understood, as they now are, in terms of an overall theory of regular recurrence of El Niño cycles. There was some sense of a recurring pattern, but the overall trends were hard to establish and each drought event was experienced as a form of catastrophe.[66] For many conservatives, drought was a sign of a newly destructive order of temporal sequencing intrinsic to capitalism: the industrialisation of agriculture was proceeding out of control, and this seemed to render farmers especially vulnerable to environmental change. For the state, vulnerability to drought was the hallmark of 'backward' white commercial farmers or African peasants not yet integrated into rural betterment schemes. Drought also affected different races and classes very unevenly. In 1913, African residents in the old Sabi-Singwetsi reserve died of starvation caused by drought.[67] In 1930 Stevenson-Hamilton suggested that in two out of three years Africans experienced famine conditions.

There was also intense competition for water resources between white, capitalised farmers, peasant stock farmers, and game reserve authorities. All parties wanted access to the perennial rivers in the area such as the Limpopo, Luvuvhu, Letaba, Olifants, Sabi, and Crocodile which flowed through the Kruger National Park. Responses to limited water resources were shaped by global discourses on desertification, and local South African perceptions that the country was drying up. Kruger came to play a symbolic role in arguments advanced by the state, and by citrus farming concerns in the Lowveld, against the supposedly irresponsible nature of African agricultural practices. 'Significantly,' says Charles Mather, 'the source of many complaints concerning Africans damaging the environment originated from white farmers who could not control rent tenants on Crown land.'[68] The state looked to game reserves for examples of progressive environmental management. In the popular 1954 Department of Information film *Guardians of the Soil,* for instance, an apocalyptic account of the 'bleeding soil', and crude African methods of farming, is juxtaposed against images of Kruger as a scientifically managed but nonetheless natural system, a zone of replenishment where the balance of nature is kept intact.

---

[64] NTS 6803 28/316/8.

[65] Philemon Ngomane, interviewed by David Bunn, Numbi Gate, 14 May 1999.

[66] U. De V. Pienaar, 'Indications of Progressive Desiccation of the Transvaal Lowveld Over the Past 100 Years, and Implications for the Water Stabilization Programme in the Kruger National Park', *Koedoe,* 28 (1985), pp. 93–165.

[67] J. Carruthers, '"Police Boys" and Poachers: Africans, Wildlife Protection and National Parks, The Transvaal 1902–1950', *Koedoe* 36 (1993), pp. 11–22.

[68] Mather, 'Environment as Weapon'.

Stevenson-Hamilton accepted the dominant apocalyptic view of Lowveld desertification. His 1928 annual report focused on problems of water supply in the Park: 'in
view of the prevailing theory that the country is drying up, it is imperative that if the
fauna is to be preserved the first essential is a good and well distributed water supply.' [69]
A major Lowveld drought ran from 1926 to 1933, and in 1932 the Warden noted in his
diary: 'Native crops failed throughout, even in the western border area where this is
unusual.' [70] Early in 1933, the public began to raise its voice against drought conditions
in the Kruger National Park. Intriguingly, it was the photographers who first took up
the cause: Bertram Jearey wrote an open letter to the Warden, complaining about the
appalling sights of dying animals he had witnessed in the Reserve. Across the country,
reports streamed in about massive numbers of weakened game animals trekking in
search of water and grazing. Near Upington, huge herds of wildebeest appeared, so
weak that they could be killed with sticks. The enclosed kingdom of Swaziland was
also invaded by vast numbers of frantic wildebeest, and the government resorted to
mass poisonings of the animals to protect farmlands and grazing.

Around the country, newspapers rallied to the cause of preserving Kruger's camera-
habituated animals, and in 1933 the *Star* launched a vigorous 'Save-the-Game'
campaign to raise money for a string of new boreholes. Stevenson-Hamilton favoured
using the funds to build concrete troughs at windmills, then leading `the overflow water
some distance away in pipes to form ponds which the game love'. 'Some of the new
drinking holes,' he is reported to have said, 'will be made near existing roads, thus
bringing the public in closest touch with the wild life of the Reserve.' [71] This aspect of
the campaign was immensely popular with the public. The new waterholes had the
potential, it seemed, to democratise game viewing in the Park, breaking the monopoly
over views which until then had been the privileged prerogative of specialist
photographers. [72] When some vigilant conservationists complained that tourist desire
for views, rather than the needs of animals, seemed to be determining borehole siting,
the Parks Board responded evasively: 'in no instance … will a borehole be sunk with
the primary object of serving a rest camp'. [73] In the tradition of waterhole work, views
were precious and had to be earned; to recline in a tourist camp and have the game
parade before you was to pervert and commoditise the system of looking.

For the next fifteen years, following the 1933 campaign, debates continued in the
press about the relative aesthetic merits of dams versus boreholes in the Park. This ran
alongside the critique of African peasants and calls for 'the erosion evil [to be] fought
vigorously in the Native areas'. [74] When Colonel Sandenbergh became Warden after the
Second World War, he staked his reputation on being able to manage the relationship
between water supply, erosion, and siltation. Sure enough, another drought cycle
arrived to test him. In 1947, newspaper reports began to complain about the effects of
progressive desiccation on tourist game viewing in Kruger: 'Wild life in the reserve,
which formally grazed at random, has been forced to use the remaining water holes,
thus limiting grazing areas to small zoos which are often great distances from the

---

[69] Pienaar, *Neem Uit Die Verlede*, p. 480. See also Annual Report 1912.

[70] Pienaar, 'Indications of Progressive Desiccation'.

[71] *Star,* 23 August 1933.

[72] *Star,* 26 August 1933.

[73] *Star,* 4 August 1933.

[74] H.R. Roberts and K.G. Coleman, *Betterment for the Bantu* (Pretoria, Department of Native Affairs, 1948),
    p. 11.

sightseeing roads.'[75] The work of drought, in this awkward logic, was now to undo the democracy of that system which had been progressively opening up game-rich territory to the average photographer. Drought broke the new imaginative mirror, and called attention to the frame.

Mindful of the success of the 1933 campaign, Sandenbergh began a new national drive to fund waterholes. In public lectures throughout the country, he spoke of 'the tortures of thirst' and of frantic animals trekking out of the Reserve: 'the banners of dust that rose against the sky from these moving herds, [are] fingers of accusation raised against the Nation for its neglect of this Sanctuary.'[76] Kruger had become like the country itself in time of war or civil strife: drought had produced 'a state of emergency of the Park'. Emergency measures were needed to alleviate the crisis. In this moment, the older rhetoric of pastoral power began to converge explicitly with that of governmentality.

Conscious of the public investment in Kruger as an imaginary landscape, the Warden arranged for each new windmill to have a brass plaque attached to it, and donors had maps sent to them with the location of their borehole marked upon it. Individual letters were then sent to donor families, giving lists of animals drinking at their borehole and inviting them to visit Kruger to view the effects of their generosity. In the early stages of the campaign, though, there were some significant detractors. The irascible P. W. Willis railed against the artificial appearance of boreholes served by windmills: 'I am willing,' he said with characteristic brusqueness, 'to donate £100 for DAMS but not a damn for a borehole.'[77]

In 1951, biologist T. G. Nel wrote to the Board about the need to be clear about why dams were being created. There were, he concluded, five main rationales: for the conservation of water; for the use of animals and to encourage certain forms of vegetative growth; for domestic use; to attract animals for the sake of tourists; and finally, most surprisingly, to act as monuments for donors. This in essence demonstrates one of the main hypotheses of this paper. Water, whether represented in the genre of waterhole photographs or in actual dams and boreholes, had varying symbolic functions, depending on whether it was near the border of the Reserve or distant from it. Far away from the edge, artificial water provision through dams was as much for aesthetic and monumental purposes as for the utilisation of game. Closer to the political borders of the Park, water became part of a different economy. The point is dramatically demonstrated in the plans for new water points in the 1950s. In the absence of a western fence, the Kruger National Park of the 1950s had come to conceive of itself as being in direct competition with African communities to the west. A series of 23 new barrier dams were planned, mainly along the western edge of the Park, effectively taking away the need for game to migrate seasonally to better-watered pastures.[78]

Shortly before his retirement, Sandenbergh conducted a survey amongst his rangers as to the relative merits of dams versus boreholes. Sharp divisions of opinion appeared, with the most outspoken response of all coming from Steyn, the Afrikaner ranger.

[75] *Sunday Times,* 17 August 1947.

[76] NKW 18/1, Water Vir Wild (Algemeen), p. 4.

[77] NKW, Willis to Astley-Maberly, 23 September 1949. S. A. Lombard, the Transvaal Provincial Secretary, was also vociferous in his opposition to the scheme as 'foreign to his conception of a game reserve'. *Star,* 2 June 1949.

[78] Joubert, *Masterplan.*

The whole question of drought and artificial water supplies for W. Life in the Park has been over-emphasized and over-publicized to the detriment of other methods and considerations which are called for in our struggle with our unnatural state and … the resultant measures will fall short of the expectations thus engendered in the 'Public Mind'.[79]

The visible signs of artificial water provision, in the form of windmills, had become the chief means by which successful administration of the wildlife preserve was communicated to a worried public. The older, naturalising landscape aesthetics common among English-speaking administrators were passing. Kruger, it would be admitted, was an 'unnatural' environment. Steyn was aiming his remarks at a tradition of sentimental, amateur authority. He took over Sandenbergh's job and, under his control, the Park perfected a new, ostensibly scientific approach towards the politics of water: water, he argued, was the key 'locality factor' in game distribution, and the overall management of the Reserve should consist in 'first transform[ing] semi-permanent water into permanent water' in a manner 'only restricted by the quantity and quality of the available grazing'.[80] It was a farmer-scientist's response to the older politics of the picturesque. Kruger was now to be managed by Nationalist scientists, with a new muscular bureaucratic authority, akin to the administrative policies of the apartheid state.

[79] NKW, 25/1, L. B. Steyn to J.A.B. Sandenbergh, 14 July 1950.
[80] Joubert, *Masterplan*, p. 140.

11

The Ant
of the White Soul

Popular Natural History, the Politics of Afrikaner Identity
& the Entomological Writings of Eugène Marais[1]

SANDRA SWART

There was an international scandal in 1927, when a South African amateur naturalist, with an unfortunate predilection for morphine, accused the internationally famous, Nobel Prize-winning Belgian author Maurice Maeterlinck of plagiarism.[2] Maeterlinck was accused by Eugène Marais, a South African lawyer and author, sunk in a semi-permanent state of drug addiction, of having used Marais's concept of the 'organic unity' of the termitary in his 1926 book *La Vie des Termites* (*The Life of the White Ant*). Marais had published his ideas on the termitary in the South African Afrikaans-language newspaper, *Die Burger*, in January 1923 and in *Die Huisgenoot,* which featured a series of articles on termites (Isoptera) under the title 'Die Siel van die Mier' (*The Soul of the Ant*), from 1925 to 1926.[3] Supported by his coterie of Afrikaner nationalist friends, Marais sought justice – promoting his side of the story through the South African press and attempting an international lawsuit. This was to prove financially impossible and the case was not pursued.

The incident is highly revealing of Marais's scientific work: a mixture of serious academic findings, scandal and what he saw as his martyrdom, at the hands of a powerful foreign figure. The latter fed into the Nationalist myth that was made of his life, both by himself and Afrikaner culture-brokers. Marais was born to English-speaking parents from the Cape in 1871. His father, however, was disgraced in a white-collar corruption scandal, and the family relocated to Pretoria before Marais's birth, although Marais returned to the Cape to be educated. By the age of nineteen he was editing his own paper, *Land en Volk*. He was an opponent of Paul Kruger's regime and a supporter of the Progressive faction in the Transvaal. Marais studied law sporadically

[1] Many thanks to William Beinart, Stanley Trapido, Albert Grundlingh, Saul Dubow, Andrew Dale, Leon Rousseau, Adrian Ryan, David van Reybrouck, the Plant Protection Research Institute (Agricultural Research Council), Lisa Jenschke and Eugene Marais of the Entomology division of the National Museum of Namibia for their suggestions.
[2] Maeterlinck (1862–1949) was born in Ghent, but lived most of his life in France. He won the 1911 Nobel Prize for literature for his dramatic works, such as *The Blue Bird*.
[3] The collection of articles appeared in book form as *Die Siel van die Mier* in 1934 and by 1948 had undergone four reprints. This paper uses Eugène Marais, *The Soul of the White Ant* (London: Penguin, 1937, 1973) and Maurice Maeterlinck, *The Life of the White Ant* (London, George Allen, 1927, 1928 trans, Alfred Sutro).

in London during the 1890s, returning to the Transvaal after the South African war (1899–1902), to briefly edit a newspaper. He spent the rest of his life writing for the popular press, while he relied on a group of literary friends, particularly the historian and newspaperman, Gustav Preller, for financial support. His addiction to morphine and his increasing depression as he grew older resulted in his suicide in 1936.

At the time of the scandal Marais asked: 'I wonder whether he blushes when he reads such things [critical acclaim], and whether he gives a thought to the injustice he does to the unknown Boer worker?'[4] This paper seeks to explore the context of Marais's work on termites, why the Afrikaans popular press disseminated it, and the manner in which it was used to promote an Afrikaner nationalist agenda.[5]

'Everyone cares about ants'

Entomology was widely used within theoretical discussions of natural history, with disparate socio-cultural implications. From the nineteenth century onwards, the social insects provided scientists and social commentators with analogues for social concerns. Ants and termites were used interchangeably as subjects, because of their similar size and habits. White ants, as termites are commonly but incorrectly called, are not ants at all, but Isopterans, and not white, but earth-coloured – resembling, as Maeterlinck had it, 'a badly drawn ant'.[6]

Once nineteenth-century naturalists had accepted that the distinction between the mental capacities of ants and men was of degree and not of kind, ants were used as an example of sentient organisms. Although Fabre famously said 'the insect has no morality', ants and bees were powerful polemical tools and their social organisations were invested with a variety of socio-cultural meanings.[8] In 1861, Darwin noted: 'every one cares about ants – more notice has been taken of slave-ants in the *Origin* than of any other passage.'[9]

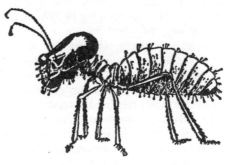

Figure 11.1 Marais's sketch of a termite[7]

---

[4] Quoted in F.G.M. Du Toit, *Eugène Marais – Sy bydrae tot die Afrikaanse letterkunde* (Amsterdam, Swets & Zeitlinger, 1940), p.184.

[5] For recent work on the interaction of South African science and ideology, see Saul Dubow, *Illicit Union – Scientific racism in modern South Africa* (Johannesburg, University of the Witwatersrand Press with Cambridge University Press, 1995) and W.D. Hammond-Tooke, *Imperfect Interpreters, South Africa's Anthropologists* (Johannesburg, University of the Witwatersrand Press, 1997). See also, Special Issue on the Politics of Conservation in Southern Africa, *Journal of Southern African Studies* (*JSAS*) 15, 2 (1998) and Jane Carruthers, 'Towards an Environmental History of Southern Africa: Some Perspectives', *South African Historical Journal* 23 (1990).

[6] Maeterlinck, *The Life of the White Ant* , p.23.

[7] Marais's sketch of a termite. Marais, *Soul of the White Ant*, p.113.

[8] Maeterlinck, *The Life of the White Ant,* p.156.

[9] Charles Darwin to H.W. Bates, 25 September 1861, in Darwin, *More Letters* (London, John Murray, 1903) vol. II, pp.196–7.

The social implications were even more explicit for others like Ludwig Buchner who accorded slavery pre-eminence in his anthropomorphic study of ants.[10] Ant slavery, husbandry and gender were three examples of the nineteenth-century tendency to mix nature and culture. As Clark observes, the ambiguity of the word 'social' in the appellation 'social insect' encapsulated the tension within literature on ants and bees.[11] Natural theologians, social evolutionists and neo-Darwinists all applied varying degrees of anthropocentric and anthropomorphic attributes to these insects.[12]

In the wake of the *Origin of Species*, biology carried intellectual authority and it was from this discipline that social theorists amassed evidence to support their pro-grammes. The general interest in ants seeped into popular fiction. In 1904, H.G. Wells (1866–1946), whom Marais met in London and whose writing Marais admired, wrote a short story called 'The Empire of the Ants', about a remote Amazonian village besieged by ants of human intelligence.[13] In Maeterlinck's work there is a 'grim suggestiveness' of the parallels between man and termite, which makes the latter 'almost our brothers'.[14] In his text no animal is so 'pitiably, so wonderfully, so fraternally human' as the termite.[15] Clearly, the social insects had a special significance for those using biology to make socio-political points. The question remains, however, why did the Afrikaner nationalist press solicit Marais's articles, and why was he besieged with requests for more in the same vein. Why did the people who were working to define themselves as Afrikaners 'care about ants'?

South African entomology

As the nineteenth century passed, the 'science of exploration' came to be replaced by the 'science of settling'. This latter science dealt with the ecological boundaries of development, like tropical medicine, veterinary science, agriculture and entomology.[16] Amateur scientific endeavour came to be replaced by Ministries, and the rhetoric of development was adopted.[17] Government entomology at the time of Marais's writing concentrated predominantly on pest eradication and, to a lesser extent, taxonomic classification.[18] Members of the public were encouraged to post unusual insect samples to the Department of Agriculture and Forestry.[19] Several pest eradication procedures were first devised in South Africa.[20] The anti-termite campaigns were an important part

[10] John Clark, 'Science, Secularization, and Social Change: the Metamorphosis of Entomology in Nineteenth-Century England', unpublished D.Phil. thesis, University of Oxford (1994), p.134.

[11] *Ibid.*, p.142.

[12] John Lubbock, 'On the Habits of Ants', *The Fortnightly Review*, new series, 27 (1 March 1877); John Lubbock, *Ants, Bees, and Wasps: A record of observations on the habits of the social Hymenoptera* (London, Kegan Paul, Trench Trubner, 1915).

[13] du Toit, *Eugène Marais*. For a contextual analysis of Wells's story see David Hughes, 'H.G. Wells: Ronic Romancer', *Extrapolation* 6 (1965), pp.32–8.

[14] *Times Literary Supplement*, 21 July 1927.

[15] Maeterlinck, *The Life of the White Ant*, p.22.

[16] William Beinart, 'Vets, Viruses and Environmentalism: the Cape in the 1870s and 1880s', *Paideuma* 43 (1997).

[17] C.P. Lounsbury, 'The Pioneer Period of Economic Entomology in South Africa', *Journal of the Entomological Society of Southern Africa* 2 (1940).

[18] See Central Archives Bureau, Pretoria, (SAB), Division of Entomology archives (CEN).

[19] SAB CEN, 725, vol. 10.

[20] S.H. Skaife, *A Naturalist Remembers* (Cape Town, Longmans, 1963), p.25.

of this department's work. From 1910 there was government-funded research on termites at an experimental farm in Potchefstroom, and the 1920s saw a great deal of interest in eradicating and resisting termites.[21] Marais was aware of the work of government entomologists, like Claude Fuller, with whom he was well acquainted, and he did make use of the Department's facilities, but appears to have entertained great suspicion of them. In a letter to Preller, he enclosed some termite specimens, asking Preller to have these classified by the Department without mentioning his name.[22]

Preller encouraged Marais to publish in the Nationalist magazines, which were designed to create a distinct Afrikaans cultural identity, to establish and then maintain standards of language purity. As an advertising slogan in *Die Burger* read in 1918: 'Through literature, the nation becomes great.'[23] Magazines were also an attempt to uplift and educate the growing underclass of poor whites, although widespread illiteracy impeded this project. *Die Huisgenoot*, which articulated the aspirations of the Second Language Movement, carried much educational material and was known as 'the poor man's university'.[24] *Die Brandwag* was also devoted to education and upliftment, and designed to reach those in the platteland (countryside) who were beyond urban resources.[25] The writers of the Second Language Movement – Jan F.E. Celliers, Totius, C. Louis Leipoldt, D.F. Malherbe and Sangiro – all contributed to it. One Afrikaner intellectual noted that the national writer must not concentrate on the urban reader and merely leave the rural communities to their own devices: 'ferret out every single Afrikaner, find him a school, a teacher, a book that he can understand and which uplifts and educates him.' Another noted that the population was deteriorating into an ignorant proletariat and it was to 'these people that we wish to speak through books, newspapers and magazines'.[26]

From 1916 to the 1930s, *Die Huisgenoot* expanded in size and readership; after four years it could be found in every province, was bought in the countryside, and was mailed to Afrikaners abroad.[27] By 1921 *Die Huisgenoot* called itself ''*n Tydskrif vir Afrikaners*' (a magazine for Afrikaners), and dealt explicitly with problems of nationalism.[28] By the mid-1920s it was reported to be the most popular magazine in South Africa,[29] and was used as a teaching-aide in Afrikaans schools. Initially, the magazine focused on language concerns, technical notes on spelling and grammar, but it broadened into more general questions of culture, such as the nature of Afrikaner art, and included Afrikaner social questions, like the poor white issue. It is this

[21] TAB (Transvaal Archives Bureau) 639 G2870/43; SAB CEN, 770, Ex 2/120; and Entomology Memoir 2, 'White Ant Experiments: Tests of the Resistancy of Timbers', pp.81–104.

[22] TAB A.787, Preller Collection, p. 95, Marais to Preller, 28 March 1927.

[23] 'Deur die letterkunde word 'n volk groot'. This could also mean 'Through literature, a nation reaches maturity.'

[24] Isabel Hofmeyr, 'Building a Nation from Words: Afrikaans language, literature and 'ethnic identity', 1902–1924', in S. Marks and S. Trapido (eds), *The Politics of Race, Class and Nationalism in Twentieth Century South Africa* (London, Longman, 1987) p.113.

[25] G.S. Preller, 'Ons stig 'n tydskrif', *Die Huisgenoot*, 28 June 1940.

[26] Quoted in Hofmeyr, 'Building a Nation', p.112.

[27] Louise Vincent, 'Mothers of Invention' – Gender, Class and the Ideology of the Volksmoeder in the Making of Afrikaner Nationalism, 1918 to 1938', unpublished D.Phil. thesis, University of Oxford (1997), p.47; see correspondence, *Die Boerevrouw,* August 1919.

[28] *Die Huisgenoot*, July 1921.

[29] 'Huisgenoot' entry in *Standard Encyclopaedia of Southern Africa* (Cape Town, 1972). *Die Brandwag,* however, folded in 1922.

concern with wider cultural issues that produced the series of termite articles. As Dr D.F. Malan noted: 'A healthy national feeling can only be rooted in ethnic [volk] art and science'.[30]

Go to the Ant ... consider her ways, and be wise[31]

Marais's writing on ants, structured around two tenets, was part of this 'ethnic science'. Firstly, he maintained that his work was cutting-edge science and attributed a sophisticated knowledge of arcane scientific academic debates to his rural audience. Secondly, he employed another *leitmotif*, the recurring theme that the Afrikaner was invested with a traditional knowledge of the land. Both tenets reinforced the idea of Afrikaner unity – as 'sons of the soil', inheritors of traditional knowledge, and as a developing nation at the cutting edge of science. Both served to stimulate unity and bolster the national ego. The Afrikaans popular press enthusiastically received his contributions; his entomological formulations served their nationalist agenda.

Marais ascribed to his readership a familiarity with the latest scientific debates to foster the image of the Afrikaner as a progressive citizen and to raise the tone of the articles to that befitting the 'poor man's university'. He had read widely and presented himself as immersed in the late Victorian European entomological milieu. He makes casual and unelucidated mention of De Vries, Henri Fabre, an unnamed Japanese naturalist, Metchnikoff, Dr Durand de Gos, Jean Finot, Grassi, Dr Bugnion, Auguste Forel, Barthellier, Ghesguiere, Wilhelm Bosche, Henri Bergson and Ernst Haeckel.[32] Marais displayed an autodidact's claim to scientific legitimacy and promoted the image of Afrikaners as a nation capable of advanced research, part of the international scientific community. Simultaneously, he persistently undermines European expertise, criticising Fabre, Bugnion, Forel and European scientists in general.[33] And he credits his readers with knowledge. A typical phrase is, for example, 'As a result of that biological knowledge which is almost the heritage of those living in a land so teeming with animal life'.[34]

This antipathy towards European scholars suggests his ambivalence as an amateur naturalist on the periphery, where the evidence was at hand, while European scholars received the credit and maintained their control of mainstream scientific debate. A recent book on S.J. Du Toit has a special section on 'Buitelanders raap Afrikaners se

[30] Cited in T. Dunbar Moodie, *The Rise of Afrikanerdom* (Berkeley, CA, University of California Press, 1975,) p.47.

[31] *Proverbs*, vi, 6. This was quoted in a review of Marais's book by M.S.B. Kritzinger, *Die Volkstem*, 4 April 1936.

[32] Marais had access to the Transvaal Museum library, which contained a wide range of entomological texts. Some of his sources may be traced: Jean-Henri Fabre (1823–1915) wrote many entomological texts, like the eleven-volume *Souvenirs d'un entomologiste* (Paris, Balland, 1986); Elie Metchnikoff (1845–1916) *The Nature of Man; studies in optimistic philosophy* (London, Watts, 1938); Jean Finot, *Modern Saints and Seers* (London, W. Rider, 1920); Édouard Bugnion (1845–1939) *The Origin of Instinct: a study of the war between the ants and the termites* (London, Kegan Paul, Trench, Trubner, 1927) originally written as an appendix to pt. IV of Forel's *The Social World of Ants.*); Auguste Forel (1848–1931), *The Senses of Insects* (London, Methuen, 1908); the many works by the philosopher Henri Bergson (1859–1941) and Ernst Haeckel (1834–1919), *The Evolution of Man: a popular scientific study* (London, Watts, 1910).

[33] See Marais, *Soul of the White Ant*, pp. 59, 112, 120, 131.

[34] Eugène Marais, *My Friends* (New York, Robert M. McBride & Co., 1939), p.108.

eer weg' (Foreigners steal Afrikaners' glory) and mentions the Marais-Maeterlinck case.[35] Marais sets up a direct comparison between the so-called experts whose works 'would fill a library', who failed to ask questions Marais finds pivotal, and his friend, Jan Wessel Wessels, whom he called 'one of the finest of practical naturalists'. Claiming a better familiarity with the material, while at the same time criticising the theoretical constructs of European experts, was arguably integral to the emancipation of South African natural history.

Marais's second tenet had a long legacy. As a journalist in the pre-war South African Republic (ZAR), he had espoused a xenophobic editorial policy. As part of the opposition camp, Marais was heavily critical of Kruger's purported favouritism of Hollanders over those born in the Transvaal. His articles for the Progressive press were saturated with the promotion of the *Landszoonen* (sons of the soil) as autochthonous and genuine. The popularisation of xenophobia was thus wrapped up in issues surrounding land and landlessness. It was at this period, the end of the nineteenth century, that landlessness was becoming a factor in the process of class differentiation in Boer society.[36] As approximately half of the white rural families were non-landowners in the first three-quarters of the nineteenth century, *bywoner* was not a pejorative term. As a result of industrialisation and modernisation, the *bywoner* ceased being an asset and became an albatross around the neck of wealthier landowning farmers.

Following these material changes, an ideology of the land was created in the media. The names adopted by the community, 'Boer' and 'Afrikaner', were themselves loaded with imagery of the land and with farming. Although Cape-educated, Marais referred to himself as a *landszoon* and made much of the right of *landszoonen* to participate in the government of the ZAR, investing them with the rights of authochthony. Marais, like others on the Progressive front, wrapped up this land ideology with the rhetoric of opposition to foreign capitalists. The insistence on the Afrikaners' instinctive knowledge of the veld is an extension of this earlier trajectory. This is made explicit in the *plaasroman* (farm novel) writer C.M. Van den Heever's essay 'The Form of the Afrikaner's Civilization and Culture', when he asserts that 'the slumbering might of the culture of every people' has its basis in 'the bondedness of man to the earth'. The earth is the 'soil of generation' of national culture.[37] The Afrikaans 'colonisation' of the landscape is part of an insistence on the natural right to belong.

Marais's position on these points was not always consistent. When there was talk of a German translation of *Die Siel van die Mier*, he noted revealingly:

> With reference to the proposed publication in Germany I shall without question
> have to revise and recast the articles. They were written primarily for people who
> knew nothing about these things. I was continuously influenced (while writing
> them) by the 'unconscious idea' that I was writing for children.[38]

---

[35] V.E. D'Assonville, *S.J. du Toit van die Paarl, 1847–1911* (Weltevredenpark, Marnix, 1999) p. 254.
[36] Timothy Keegan, *Rural Transformations in Industrialising South Africa: the Southern Highveld to 1914* (Braamfontein, Ravan Press, 1986).
[37] C.M. van den Heever, *Die Afrikaanse gedagte* (Pretoria, Van Schaik, 1935), pp.16, 52–53, quoted in J.M. Coetzee, *White Writing – on the Culture of Letters in South Africa* (New Haven, CT, Yale University Press, 1988) p. 87.
[38] Du Toit, *Eugène Marais*, p.170.

This is at odds with scattered references to the wealth of Afrikaner knowledge about nature that are to be found in his work. Moreover, Marais was not always in sympathy with rural Afrikaners. His family were originally from the Cape and retained disdain for the uneducated Transvaler, the *takhare* (hicks, hayseeds) and particularly for *doppers*, the members of the very conservative Reformed Church.

Nevertheless, deeper reading of Marais's text reveals an insistence on Afrikaners' 'special knowledge'. Marais opened with a discussion of an article published in a South African journal by a Dr Hesse, the result of observations in America and Europe – none of which was, he maintained, relevant to 'our South African termites'.[39] He contended that he wished to present the facts so that South African knowledge could be used by the readers to test European theories.[40] He insisted, with simple national pride, that 'the life-history of most of our South African ants and termites is in every respect just as wonderful and interesting as anything discovered in South America'.[41]

Also worth noting is the fact that in the English translation the text reads: 'The ordinary use of light by the glow-worm and firefly is well known to dwellers in South Africa.'; 'What South African child has never seen the *toktokkie* and heard him make his knock?' and 'our dear little *toktokkie*'.[42] In the original, however, Marais used the word 'Afrikaner' instead of 'South African'. He emphasised the phrases: 'which most Afrikaners know'; 'there are many Afrikaners who know'; 'well-known to all Afrikaners'.[43] He observed how many new admirers of 'our' nature the Afrikaans renaissance had created.[44] This was in line with the trend, which Hofmeyr has dubbed the 'redefinition of everyday life': the pages of Afrikaans magazines featured articles and advertisements that made reference to every available aspect of people's lives and repackaged these as 'Afrikaans'. What had previously been 'furniture' became 'Afrikaans furniture' and what had previously been the natural world became the 'Afrikaners' natural world'.

Marais had originally intended his first ant article as simply a single item, but significantly the editor of *Die Huisgenoot* asked for more.[45] Indeed, the editor endured Marais's broken promises and missed deadlines in order to print more in the same vein.[46] Newspapers and publishers went to unprecedented and even unethical lengths to get hold of Marais's work. It was rumoured that the publisher Van Schaik manipulated Marais's morphine addiction to extort contracts from him.[47] Marais's articles lent themselves to the nationalist project in the way that other social organism theories lent themselves to political agendas. A scientist who inspired both Marais and Maeterlinck was Ernst Haeckel, whose theory of 'monism', for example, was directly absorbed by National Socialism.[48] His pupils were political agitators who used his ideas of holism in

---

[39] Marais, *Soul of the White Ant,* p. 21. This is almost certainly a reference to the article by Dr A.J. Hesse, 'Iets Omtrent Miere' (Something about ants), *Die Huisgenoot*, 18 September 1925.

[40] E. Marais, *Die Siel van die Mier* (Pretoria, J.L. Van Schaik, 1938), p. 24.

[41] Marais, *The Soul of the White Ant,* p. 21.

[42] Marais, *The Soul of the White Ant,* pp. 56, 33.

[43] Translated from Afrikaans. Marais, *Siel van die Mier*, pp. 12, 14, 54, 25.

[44] Translated from Afrikaans. Marais, *Siel van die Mier*, p. 25.

[45] Revealed by S.J. Du Toit in *Ons Eie Boek*, April–June 1938.

[46] J.H. Viljoen, *'n Joernalis vertel* (Cape Town, Nasionale Boekhandel, 1953).

[47] Leon Rousseau, *The Dark Stream – the story of Eugene Marais* (Johannesburg, Jonathan Ball, 1982), p.484.

[48] Daniel Gasman, *The Scientific Origins of National Socialism: Ernst Haeckel and the Monist League* (New York, Elsevier, 1971).

societal contexts.[49] Maeterlinck extended his own hypothesis in the political context, applying it to the corporate state of Portuguese President Salazar.[50] There was no similar uninterrupted link between Marais's writing and social policy. His work had, however, obvious potential for the Afrikaner nationalist programme. It was simultaneously able to claim autochthony and progressiveness for the Afrikaner. The two poles of Marais's ideology served to mirror the twin poles of nationalism itself, the containment of tradition and development within a single ideology. This simultaneous containment of oxymoronic conditions was also reflected in the rhetoric surrounding the Language Movement. On the one hand, Afrikaans was the authentic, unique language of South Africa; on the other, it had a long traceable lineage to the great Graeco-Roman traditions, as D.F. Malan maintained.[51]

Another and more self-evident reason for the termite articles was the everyday experience of the readership. While the role of the middle-class editors as nationalism's motor is undeniable, it can also be argued that the content was partially dictated by the subject. The rural Afrikaner suffered an almost biblical profusion of plagues: ticks, scab, locusts and termites. From August 1924, *Die Huisgenoot* made calls for greater popular participation, maintaining that the magazine was not the possession of Die Nasionale Pers nor of the editors, but could only function if 'every reader feels that he or she is personally a part of it…. We want it to be a paper of the *volk*.'[52] This was part of the project to create an image of the Afrikaner that could transcend the particularities of geography, class and even age and gender to create a unified *volk*.

A return to the land

Key amongst the concerns of the culture-brokers, in their quest to mask factions and promote commonalities, were the poor whites. This group was feared increasingly lost to an urban culture; in 1900, 10 per cent of Afrikaners lived in urban areas, by 1926 this had risen to 41 per cent.[53] There was much concern over the breakdown of traditional rural authority structures and family life.[54] Attempts to reform the poor whites repeatedly took the form of plans to return them to the rural areas.[55] An understanding of this anxiety helps explain why articles on nature and the value of the countryside were solicited and published in the popular magazines. This phenomenon has found reflection in other communities. Morgan has observed that as the Welsh became more

---

[49] Anna Bramwell, *Ecology in the Twentieth Century* (New Haven, CT, Yale University Press, 1989) pp. 88–91.

[50] Maurice Maeterlinck, *Le Président Salazar* (Luik, Dynamo, 1969). This was intended to demonstrate his disdain for democracy, contending that individuals amount to only the honour and glory of the corporate community, whether in a termite nest or a corporate state.

[51] P.C. Schoonees, *Die Prosa van die Tweede Afrikaanse Beweging* (Pretoria, J.H. De Bussy, 1939) p.13. The insistence on antiquity is part of the ideology of many nations, see Eric Hobsbawm and Terence Ranger, *The Invention of Tradition* (London, Canto, 1983, 1997) p.14.

[52] 'Somaar gesels met ons lesers oor *Die Huisgenoot*', *Die Huisgenoot*, 15 August 1924.

[53] H. Adam and H. Giliomee, *The Rise and Crisis of Afrikaner Power* (Cape Town, David Philip, 1979) p. 147.

[54] Vincent, 'Mothers of Invention', p. 12.

[55] John Bottomley, *Public Policy and White Rural Policy* (Kingston, Queen's University, 1991); Robert Morrell (ed.), *White But Poor* (Pretoria, UNISA, 1991).

and more industrialised, so they came to cherish the image of the Welshman as 'a sturdy tough hillman, free as mountain air'.[56]

National feeling focused increasingly on the poor white question.[57] The post-South African war Relief Works Department was established to provide employment for indigent burghers and to establish irrigation projects. There was widespread feeling against entering such relief projects because it was perceived as sacrificing independent life on the land. Farming was more than merely a livelihood. A Boer's identity was wrapped up in his profession. The very semantic meaning of his label was 'farmer'. C. Louis Leipoldt, who toured the platteland extensively at the time, observed:

> what remains of the traditional conception of farming, a conception that modern civilization is rapidly blotting out. They are there for man's fundamental work, to gain from the soil a livelihood for himself and his family.[58]

The capitalisation and commercialisation of farming affected more than the livelihood of the *bywoner*; his sense of identity was challenged. Even those men who had not owned land before felt their identities under threat. Although the complete egalitarianism of Boer society was a myth, there had been a rhetoric of equality, an idea of republican *gelykheid* [equality] between white adult men, purportedly unaffected by class. The trek to the cities was a journey to the mines, railways and factories, where Afrikaners saw themselves working at unfamiliar jobs, living in squalid conditions adjacent to black shanty towns, and having to speak a foreign language – English – like a defeated race.[59] The stigma of poverty was attached to the Afrikaans family, with English social discourse portraying the Afrikaner male as the backward railway worker and the illiterate policeman.

The notion of the *agteruitgang* (regression) of the Afrikaner relative to English-speakers and blacks was variously a grim prophecy, a social evil and a routine method of drawing an angry crowd in any rural constituency. To replace this image, Afrikaners had to build a new identity, a new image of themselves. The ideology of the land wrapped up in a nostalgic motif of rural utopia was behind the nationalists' repeated attempts to restore the urban poor whites to the land right up until the 1930s. Marais's work proved particularly apposite in that it promoted the notion that Afrikaners were invested with an understanding and love of nature. On the basis of an idealised and nostalgically reinvented past, the Afrikaner was conceived as a son of the soil, with a natural affinity for nature. A favourite image was the veld as classroom. The icon of the autochthonous Boer had its success in its flexibility. The image was not static, and its power lay in its ability to be re-invented with changing times. Indeed, the iconography had a long heritage, with its roots in Marais's editorial writing in the pre-war ZAR. This dichotomous definition was now re-deployed by Marais as a definition against the English and the blacks, in securing the borders of an imagined community.

Similarly, the National Parks Act in 1926 was passed at a time of increasing

[56] Prys Morgan, 'From a Death to a View: the Hunt for the Welsh Past in the Romantic Period' in Hobsbawm and Ranger, *The Invention of Tradition,* p. 89.

[57] Keegan, *Rural Transformations*, p.20. Stanley Trapido, 'Reflections on Land, Office and Wealth in the South African Republic, 1850–1900' in Shula Marks and Anthony Atmore (eds), *Economy and Society in Pre-Industrial South Africa* (London, Longman, 1987) p. 359.

[58] C. Louis Leipoldt, *Bushveld Doctor* (Braamfontein, Lowry, 1980), p. 17.

[59] Bottomley, *Public Policy and White Rural Poverty*, p. 250.

Afrikaner Nationalist fervour – the resurgence of republican rhetoric, adoption of Afrikaans as an official language, and revival of interest in the Voortrekkers.[60] These manifestations of nationalism coincided with the entrenchment of a romantic aesthetic of nature – as part of an attempt to create a common white identity. There was a pattern of linking Afrikaner heroes with love of nature, as in the case of Gustav Preller's historical description of the Voortrekkers' 'love of nature'.[61] Denys Reitz, for example, claimed that the National Park proposal idealised Kruger's dream and insisted that it was a national duty to preserve the landscape 'just as the Voortrekkers saw it'.[62] Marais's work fits this pattern of linking the Afrikaner to a love of nature. The Afrikaans press praised the Transvaal as the first state in Africa to conserve its wildlife and affirmed that a 'volkspark' would be an apt accolade.[63] As Carruthers has argued, in attaching an Afrikaner cultural tradition to conservation, the role of poor whites in the pre-Union past was recast. No longer were the poor whites remembered as having hunted meat to supply urban markets, and, from having been a divisive issue during the ZAR, game saving was used to unite classes within Afrikaner society after the First World War.[64]

As social constructionist work on the environment has shown, landscapes are the 'symbolic environment created by a human act of conferring meaning on nature and the environment' and thus landscape reflects the self-definition of people within a particular cultural context.[65] Nature is thus 'socialized ... reorganized ... [and] made into a material manifestation of social structure'.[66] These shared and reified meanings contribute to the social network. As J.W. Bennet observes: 'Humans are constantly engaged in seizing natural phenomena, converting them into cultural objects, and reinterpreting them with cultural ideas.'[67] Marais wrote at a time when the natural world was becoming utilised as a vehicle to transmit shared ideology through the Afrikaans press. The nationalist agenda required hegemony over the anthropology of landscape, which was increasingly portrayed as inextricably part of the Afrikaans spirit. J.M. Coetzee has likened this link between land and *volk* to a theme of nineteenth-century German nationalism, like that of Wilhelm Heinrich Riehl, who thought a patriot's task was to find a natural bond between *volk* and land, to naturalise the *volk*'s possession of the land.[68]

Marais insisted on natural authenticity and criticised, for example, M. Jansen's *Die*

---

[60] Jane Carruthers, 'Creating a National Park 1910–1926', *JSAS* 15, 2 (1989).

[61] J.J. Oberholster, 'Die Neerslag van die Romantiek op ons geskiedskrywing – Gustav S. Preller' (The impact of the romantic on our historiography), *Intreerede* (Inaugural lecture), University of the Orange Free State, 6 May 1965, p.15.

[62] D. Reitz, *No Outspan* (London: Faber and Faber, 1943) p.69; D. Reitz, *Commando* (London, Faber and Faber, 1929) p.126. Cited in Carruthers 'Creating a National Park', p. 208.

[63] *Die Burger*, 14 December 1925; *Die Huisgenoot*, 8 January 1926.

[64] Stanley Trapido, 'Poachers, Proletarians and Gentry in the early twentieth century Transvaal', unpublished paper, Institute of Commonwealth Studies, University of London, 1983.

[65] Thomas Greider and Lorraine Garkovich, 'Landscapes: the social construction of nature and the environment', *Rural Sociology*, 59, 1 (1994), p.1; P.L. Berger and T. Luckmann, *The Social Construction of Reality: a treatise in the sociology of knowledge* (New York, Anchor Books, 1967).

[66] L. Busch, 'Irony, Tragedy, and Temporality in Agricultural Systems, or, values and systems are related', *Agriculture and Human Values* 6, 4 (1989), p.7.

[67] J.W. Bennett, *The Ecological Transition: cultural anthropology and human adaptation* (New York, Pergamon Press, 1976), p. 4.

[68] Coetzee, *White Writing*, p. 61.

Veldblommetje for being too Dutch and not presenting 'Die ware Afrikaanse gees' (the real Afrikaans spirit). He was particularly disparaging of mistakes like the thorn trees blooming a few months too early. Marais recalled, à propos of this, a recent literary 'fraud', who had her hero abandoned in love standing wistfully under a prickly pear and plucking a leaf – which Marais noted wryly would result in more than his heart suffering pain.[69]

Afrikaans as scientific medium

Working for the popular press, Marais had to sell his science in the same way that he had to sell his newspapers in the pre-war ZAR. It is here that his Afrikaner nationalism and science share a powerful parallel; both were complex, sophisticated conceptions that had to be reduced to journalistic newspaper style. Marais gave a South African flavour to his work, for both Nationalist and commercial reasons. This was part of a programme developed by Marais and his colleague and friend Gustav Preller. Both men realised that the use of Afrikaans would expand their constituency.[70] Revealing of the manner in which he promoted his science is the invention of the 'Oom Dirk' character, an old Boer in the Waterberg district with whom Marais claimed to be in contact, as a mechanism to 'sell' scientific ideas to the growing Afrikaner nationalist movement, and equally successfully, to the media:

> Oom Dirk had built his house at the exit of a small kloof known as Geelhoutgrag.... Never have I seen anything more beautiful in my life than the lonely little house in its natural environment... At night – it was winter and bitterly cold in the mountains – we would sit around a great stone hearth ... A flask of wild plum brandy would be kept close at hand, and then Oom Dirk would tell us all about birds and animals – everything he had had the privilege of witnessing in nature.... One could sense that everything he told one was the gospel truth. In this simple soul there was no room for lies and exaggeration.[71]

'Oom Dirk' probably never existed; oral historians could find no trace of such a figure in local memory.[72] This persona was to appeal to the Afrikaner imagination, a stock folk character, who could better capture the cadence of popular experience than his elegant urban inventor.

Marais's work has many parallels with that of Preller. A comparison between Preller and Marais is appropriate on the grounds of their close relationship, which meant almost certainly intimate discussion of their mutual narrative techniques and great familiarity with each other's work. They were also writing for the same reading public. Like Preller, Marais used personal experience and popular memory as organising principles for his work.[73] Just as Preller used popular cadences and well-known narrative forms to foster public understanding of his historical writing, Marais portrayed his science through a lens of popular idiom. Preller and Marais worked on the newspaper

---

[69] *Die Brandwag,* 25 April 1920.
[70] Hofmeyr, 'Building a Nation', p. 104.
[71] Rousseau, *Dark Stream*, p. 239.
[72] *Ibid.*, p. 239.
[73] Isabel Hofmeyr, 'Popularizing History: the case of Gustav Preller', *Journal of African History* 29 (1988), p. 523.

De Volkstem together and both incorporated journalistic devices into their serious writing. Both injected the personal and the anecdotal into the genres they created. There was emphasis on eyewitness testimony and anecdotal, 'everyday' narration. If, as Hofmeyr suggests, the secret of nationalism's success lies in its 'appropriation or re-interpretation of everyday life', then together Preller and Marais set out to capture the *lares et penates* of the platteland homes.[74] Both were aware of the *Taal* as a language of the home, a 'trusted, intimate language of the big nation-family while English is the hard commercial language of the world'.[75]

Why did Marais write in Afrikaans, thereby limiting his audience to a small South African reading public, ensuring his own obscurity, and opening himself up to plagiarism? The traditional answer has been that he wrote in Afrikaans for altruistic motives of Afrikaner nationalism. Certainly such gestures were occasionally made by scientists in public forums.[76] Marais's first biographer, F.G.M. Du Toit, notes that although Marais was more comfortable expressing himself in English, he made the sentimental decision to use Afrikaans.[77] This was certainly what he told his translator and admirer Winifred de Kok and was consistent with his personal ideology.[78] He wrote in the Afrikaans language out of *volksgevoel* (national feeling, patriotism), although he was more comfortable in English. It was much implied that his sacrifice was great; he had, after all, been a victim of plagiarism and deprived of his rightful glory because Maeterlinck won the renown denied one who published only in Afrikaans. His plagiar-ism case was supported by nationalist intellectuals, as his use of the vernacular fitted their *zeitgeist*. As Celliers noted: 'It must surely be apparent to every Afrikaner that we can only reach our goal through our own literature, nurtured in Afrikaans soil, permeated by an Afrikaans spirit and thoroughly accessible to Afrikaners in language and content.'[79]

The real answer may, however, lie in Marais's commercial sense: it was considerably easier to sell articles to the Afrikaans language press. His connections and the lower standards of these papers made them a more lucrative vehicle. It is revealing that he never resisted foreign language translations of his works, in fact he was delighted at the prospect. Popular magazines like *Die Huisgenoot* and *Brandwag* created a cult of the personality around selected literary figures.[80] Marais was able to use this phenomenon to his advantage – as *volksdigter* (people's poet) with a scientific disposition. Through science comes a language, usually the language of the metropole. From the perspective of Afrikaner nationalist development, a significant contribution was made in the medium rather than solely the message of Marais's writing. Preller claimed that Marais demonstrated the use of Afrikaans as a *scientific* as well as a *literary* language.

The superorganism and the scandal

The plagiarism scandal is not inherently important, but shows how partisan supporters of Marais ignored the available evidence and made grand claims for their hero. Marais

[74] *Ibid.*, p. 526.
[75] From a letter by Preller, TAB, A 787, V 267, F 259.
[76] Skaife, *A Naturalist Remembers*, p. 85.
[77] Robert Ardrey, *African Genesis* (London, Fontana, 1961, 1967), p. 67.
[78] Letter from De Kok to Marais in Du Toit, *Eugène Marais* , p. 170.
[79] Quoted in Hofmeyr, 'Building a Nation', p. 108.
[80] *Ibid.*, p. 109.

first wrote about termites in 1923, in *Die Burger*, New Year edition, 'Verskynsels van die dieresiel' (Phenomena of the animal soul). His book *Die Siel van die Mier* was published in 1933, and subsequently translated into English and German. In it Marais presents his own view of nature: termites, and even the higher organisms like baboons, do not act as individuals but under orders from a group soul. This, he argued, is true of the higher animals too, though their collective soul is more subtly expressed. The controversial theory of the organic unity of the termite nest is that the queen acts as a brain, controlling the organisms from her strong palace walls like a skull protecting the soft brain. Just as in an organism, food is absorbed externally and processed within the body by the workers, which act as the teeth. Ideas about co-operative relationships between organisms animated contemporary discussions of natural history. The idea of organic unity was linked to the holism promoted by Smuts and increasingly fashion-able in South Africa.[81] Antithetically to Marais, however, Smuts argued that 'the individual bee or ant lives its own life and is not lost in the joint venture of the hive or nest'.[82] In his articles Marais admitted that initially he had wanted to 'startle' the scientific world, but other naturalists had 'already become aware' of the model. [83] He inverted the work of Claude Bernard in his address to the French Academy (1869) and of Dr Durand de Gos, who, in his *Electrodynamique Vitale* (1855) and *Variétés Philosophiques* (1857), had tried to show that the vital organs of humans were separate animals.[84]

When Maeterlinck's book appeared in English translation in November 1927, he recorded in his introduction:

> So much for the facts. I have unearthed them from all kinds of places: they were confused and vague, obscure, often meaningless in their isolation.... It is only the interpretation that is more or less my own.... It would have been very easy ... to allow the text to bristle with footnotes and references.... [T]he letterpress would have been swallowed up in vast masses of comment, like one of those dreadful books we hated so much at school. There is a short bibliography at the end....[85]

No mention, however, was made of Marais. In December 1927, Marais wrote to a friend:

> I have just been greatly worried over the last book of the great Maeterlinck, *The Life of the White Ant*. He quite calmly loots a theory of mine and gives it as his own. It is the theory that the termitary is in fact a single organism in a certain stage of evolution.... He admits that he has 'borrowed' all his information but in order not to 'disfigure' his book he gives no references, – only a biography [sic] at the end in which my name does *not* figure. I am not in the least concerned about the 'honour' of priority, but I am very much afraid that I shall in the future be accused of stealing from Maeterlinck and not Maeterlinck from me.

---

[81] Dr C.F. Visser, for example, wrote an article on 'Holisme in die onderwys' (Holism in education) for *Die Huisgenoot*, 30 June 1933.

[82] J.C. Smuts, *Holism and Evolution* (London, Macmillan, 1926) p. 83. For a discussion see Thackwray Driver, 'Smuts, Ecology and Holism', Science and Society in Southern Africa (Centre for Southern African Studies, University of Sussex, September 1998).

[83] Marais, *Soul of the White Ant*, p. 80.

[84] *Ibid.*

[85] Maeterlinck, *Life of the White Ant*, pp.15–16.

There is, of course, no shadow of doubt about the plagiarism.... I am going to have to put it straight in the *Huisgenoot* and also in English in the *Star* in a fortnight's time if I get my original mss. from the Nasionale Pers before then. The theory was first described by me six years ago in a New Year Number of the *Huisgenoot*.[86] Maeterlinck's book was published a few months ago. References to my work appeared in Dutch, Flemish and Belgian-French papers from time to time and it was no doubt from one of these that Maeterlinck got his information.[87]

Marais contacted his old friends, F. Paver of *The Star* and H.G. Viljoen of *Die Huisgenoot*, both of whom had published many of his articles.[88] In an interview with the *Star* and in an article in *Die Huisgenoot*, Marais asserted his own innocence of plagiarism.[89] Viljoen made it front page news. In the latter Marais recorded aggrievedly:

I can well understand that he made use of a far-off and in Europe, unknown Afrikaans writer without citing his name. The use would not bother me in the least if he had just admitted he formulated his work from South African work. I was not slightly concerned that he mention my name. But the accusation of plagiarism against me in South Africa would be much more serious than the accusation against Maeterlinck in Europe.[90]

Marais insisted that it was 'quite clear that [Maeterlinck] had borrowed the theory' from *Die Siel van die Mier*.[91] He wove this story into the fantasy he constructed of his own sense of biography; for example, he made it part of the mythology surrounding his addiction to morphine. Ironically, however, it may be argued that the scandal actually *boosted* his own book sales and helped increase his status within South Africa. His translator noted that: 'Your foreword, giving the facts of the plagiarising, will prove magnificent publicity and will sell the book well.'[92]

The currency of science is originality of ideas, but historians of science have demonstrated repeatedly that few revolutionary ideas develop without a pedigree; most discoveries are, in the sociologist Robert K. Merton's term, 'multiples'.[93] Just as Darwin and Wallace independently discovered the principle of natural selection at very nearly the same time, Marais may conceivably have independently invented the *superorganism* notion. It is more likely, however, that both Marais and Maeterlinck were connected, directly or indirectly, to a mutual source. Afrikaner commentators Leon Rousseau and J.C. Kannemeyer accept Maeterlinck's guilt in stealing from Marais, but concede that both drew on a mutual source.[94] They contend that the articles were written in Afrikaans and were thus inaccessible to the vast majority of foreign scientists and interested amateurs. Maeterlinck, however, was Belgian and could

---

[86] Actually it appeared in *Die Burger*, New Years issue, 1923.

[87] Marais to W. Spilhaus, 10 December 1927, quoted in Du Toit, *Eugène Marais*, p. 183.

[88] Leon Rousseau, *Die Dowwe Spoor van Eugène Marais* (Cape Town, Ibis Press, 1998), p. 41.

[89] The *Star*, 24 December 1927; *Die Huisgenoot*, 6 January 1928.

[90] *Die Huisgenoot*, 6 January 1928.

[91] *Ibid.*

[92] Rousseau, *Die Dowwe Spoor*, p.43.

[93] Robert K. Merton, 'Resistance to the Systematic Study of Multiple Discoveries in Science', *European Journal of Sociology* 4 (1963): 237–82.

[94] J.C. Kannemeyer, *Geskiedenis van Die Afrikaanse Literatuur* (Cape Town, Academica, 1978), p.232; Leon Rousseau, *Die Groot Verlange* (Cape Town, Human and Rousseau, 1974), p. 393.

understand Flemish, and thus Afrikaans. Maeterlinck could certainly read Dutch, well enough to translate the medieval mystic Ruusbroec. Marais's idea first appeared in *Die Burger* in 1923, and also in *Die Huisgenoot*, 1923 to 1926, ample time for Maeterlinck to have scrutinised it.

However, the originator of the idea of the *superorganism*, and the probable source of Marais's position, was a Harvard professor of entomology, William Morton Wheeler (1865–1937). Wheeler proposed the idea of the *superorganism* in his 1911 essay 'The Ant Colony as an Organism', drawing on earlier theorists like Herbert Spencer, Ernst Haeckel and G.T. Fechner. He argued that the animal colony fulfils the criteria of an organism, behaving as a unit, being idiosyncratic in behaviour, size and structure; having a clearly adaptive growth and reproductive cycle and being differentiated into 'germ plasm' (queens and males) and 'soma' (workers).[95] From 1928, it became common to call the social insect colony a *superorganism*. Maeterlinck was quoted by Wheeler and in turn openly acknowledged his own debt to Wheeler, when he spoke of 'the spirit of the hive.... It disposes pitilessly of the wealth and the happiness, the liberty and the life, of all these winged people; and yet with discretion, as though governed itself by some great duty.' In his *The Life of the White Ant* (1927) and *The Life of the Ant* (1930), he employed Wheeler's concept more explicitly and scientifically.

Certainly, it is demonstrable that Wheeler and Maeterlinck were aware of each other's work. Both openly drew on the work of Grassi, Hegh, Bugnion and Prell. Interestingly, both Marais and Maeterlinck quote Claude Fuller who worked as an entomologist in the government Department of Agriculture.[96] Fuller wrote widely on white ants.[97] Marais refers to him as 'My friend Claude Fuller' and quotes him on peripheral technical points, while Fuller writes of sharing information with 'non-scientific friends'.[98] Maeterlinck quotes Fuller as a useful source, indicating a shared body of knowledge with Marais.[99] Marais himself certainly drew on many sources. It is also true that he had asked Preller to order recent scientific monographs on the topic of social insects from the Department of Entomology and had asked Preller not to mention his (Marais's) name.[100] It is worth noting that Marais also accused F.W.

---

[95] William Morton Wheeler, 'The Ant Colony as Organism', *Journal of Morphology* 22, 2 (1911), pp. 305–25. In addition to this article, the Transvaal Museum library contained 'Social life among the insects', *Scientific Monthly*, issues 14,15, 16, June 1922–March 1923, which contained the idea of the social organism.

[96] Claude Fuller, 'The Termites of South Africa', *South African Journal of Natural History* 3 (1922).

[97] The Transvaal Museum library contained C. Fuller's 'White ants in buildings, orchards and plantations', *Agricultural Journal* 3 (1912); 'White ants in Natal', *Agricultural Journal* .4 (1912); 'Termite economy', *South African Journal of Science* 12 (1915); 'Observations on some South African termites', *Annals of the Natal Museum* 3 (1915); 'Notes on white ants', *Bulletin of the South African Biological Society* 1, 2 (1918); 'White ant notes', *Journal of the Department of Agriculture* 2, 5 (1920) and 3, 2 (1921); 'Suid-Afrikaanse Rysmiere', *Die Landbouweekblad* 106 (1921); 'The termites of South Africa', *South African Journal of Natural History* 3, 1(1921), 2 (1922) and 'The termites of South Africa', *South African Journal of Natural History* 5 (1925).

[98] Marais, *Soul of the White Ant*, p.143 and Claude Fuller, 'Termite Economy', *South African Journal of Science* 12 (1915), p. 60.

[99] Maeterlinck, *Life of the White Ant,* p.50. For background, see Jacqueline Caenberghs, 'Marais versus Maeterlinck – De Strijd om de Ziel van de Mier', *Deus ex Machina – Tijdschrift voor literatuur en kunst* (1998), pp. 90–1.

[100] TAB A.787, Preller Collection, p. 95, Marais to Preller, 28 March 1927.

Fitzsimons of the Port Elizabeth museum of unacknowledged borrowing; perhaps he was becoming paranoid as his morphine addiction took control of him.[101]

More damning evidence shows that Marais had copied from others and had not only not acknowledged them but later maintained that their theories derived from his work. In 1933 he wrote an article for *Die Vaderland*; referring to his 1914 article on drought which appeared in the *Agricultural Journal*, he noted that 'the world famous French astronomer Flamarion had used [Marais's article] to make his predictions that the world was dessicating'. In reality, not only did Flamarion's theory predate the 1914 article, but Marais had *actually quoted him in the article*: 'In Asia and Africa ... the disappearance of water annually is so great it seems to justify the prediction of the French astronomer, Flamarion, that ... the human race will find its final eclipse in this cause.'[102] A contemporary newspaperman has commented on Marais's pathological egocentricism, which might also have been responsible for his solipsism.[103] Marais sought fame through his scientific prose. While he maintained that he was 'not concerned with publicity', even his translator and friend, Winifred De Kok, writing shortly after his death, noted that, while Marais is remembered for his poetry, it is for his scientific writing, particularly on termites, that he would wish to be remembered.[104]

Both authors had been caught in a more tangled web of ideas than previously realised. Maeterlinck probably exposes his unacknowledged use of Marais's work in his use of the word 'Nasicornic'. As Marais asserts in the *Huisgenoot* article, he derived it from the Afrikaans for *eenhoringmier*.[105] 'Nasicornic' was not a word invented by Marais, as even a cursory glance at the Oxford English Dictionary makes clear, but he revived it and coined its use in this context. This unwitting use of a neologism as though it were common scientific currency may reveal that Maeterlinck had read Marais's article of 22 January 1926. Conversely, however, it is in fact possible that Marais had looted the idea from Maeterlinck's previous book, *The Life of the Bee*, in which he writes of the 'soul of the swarm/hive' – the English translation dates back to 1901.

It is important to note that Maeterlinck's work was not unknown in South Africa. For example, Emily Hobhouse quotes him in a letter to Rachel Isabella Steyn, wife of the President of the Orange Free State.[106] Maeterlinck had used the idea of a 'group soul' two decades before Marais. It is extremely likely that both had read Wheeler – a fact Maeterlinck openly acknowledges, but Marais does not. It may be demonstrated that Wheeler's work was known in South Africa, as the reviewer in *Die Huisgenoot* refers to him, noting that in many areas Marais is in accord with him.[107] Wheeler had in any event been the first to delineate the notion of the termitary as *social organism*, drawing in turn on other forebears like Haeckel, whom Marais *had* acknowledged. The web of borrowing, acknowledged and unacknowledged, presents apposite insight into

---

[101] 'Die wêreld se mees gevreesde slang', *Die Vaderland*, 13 May 1933.
[102] 'Die wêreldberoemde French astronomer Flamarion ... het daarop ... voorspellings gegrond ... dat die gehele aarde aan die uitdroë is....'
[103] Viljoen, *'n Joernalis vertel*, p. 46.
[104] Winifred de Kok in Marais, *The Soul of the White Ant*, p. 13.
[105] *Die Huisgenoot*, 22 January 1926.
[106] Rykie van Reenen (ed.), *Emily Hobhouse Boer War Letters* (Cape Town, Human and Rousseau, 1984), p. 9.
[107] C.S. Grobbelaar, 'Die Wêreld van die Miere', *Die Huisgenoot*, 8 February 1935.

the process of science, where ideas are the result of – albeit unaccredited and often unwilling – collective effort.

Because neither Marais nor Maeterlinck made the initial breakthrough, many like the entomologist and socio-biologist E.O. Wilson relegate the scandal to the status of a 'tempest in a teapot'. [108] Not everyone deemed the theory – and hence the scandal – worthy even of a teapot. The critic C.S. Grobbelaar conceded that it offered uplifting insights into animal psychology, but maintained that it was undermined by the ludicrous mistakes of an amateur (such as asserting that a scorpion is an insect) and assaulted Marais's central thesis as old-fashioned mechanistic vitalism rather than scientific dualism. [109] Dr S.H. Skaife, writing in *Dwellers in Darkness*, dismissed the theory as 'just nonsense' and noted that 'it does not help us to understand the organisation of the termite community at all'. S.J. Du Toit reviewed *Die Siel van die Mier* in *Ons Eie Boek,* and states unequivocally that, although Maeterlinck plagiarised Marais, the work is 'not science'. He quotes a Stellenbosch University zoologist, C.A. Du Toit, who dubbed the work a 'poetic dream' rather than science. Equally, a review in the *Times Literary Supplement* of 21 July 1927 damned Maeterlinck's monograph as more poetry than biology and his central thesis of the *superorganism* as an 'arbitrary fancy'. Echoes of the scandal resonated in Britain a decade later, with the English translation of the *Soul of the White Ant* in London. It was noted that Maeterlinck had not been taken seriously by entomologists as he did not record his sources. [110]

Yet particularly in the popular Afrikaans press, rather than in either the English or the academic press, Marais's stature grew. The nationalist writer and compiler of the Afrikaans dictionary, M.S.B. Kritzinger, maintained that Marais had an amazing knowledge of the animal and insect world, of psychology and scientific developments. [111] The lesson taught by the white ants is emphasised by Kritzinger, who urged: 'Consider [Marais's] ant!' [112] Kritzinger recommends *Die Siel van die Mier* – even in his obituary of Marais. There may have been an element of self-interest, as he had collected the various articles by Marais and had compiled the book himself. In *Die Burger*, C.A. Du Toit, who admitted there were biological errors, still urged South Africa to be proud of her son, an Afrikaner researcher. [113] In a 1934 article for *Die Volksblad*, P.C. Schoonees called him an 'Afrikaner Fabre'. [114] He suggested that in a land so full of chattering politicians this book would place the young people on the right path – and quoted Proverbs, urging the youth to 'consider the ant' and ask that it be a prescribed text. By 1938, Marais's *Die Siel van die Mier* had become a set work for the Afrikaans matriculation examination. When Maeterlinck died, the Afrikaans press briefly revived the scandal, assuming Marais's innocence. [115] In 1961, the popular writer on animal behaviour, Robert Ardrey, dedicated his *African Genesis* to Marais. [116]

---

[108] E.O. Wilson, *The Insect Societies* (Cambridge, MA, Harvard University Press, 1971), p. 317.

[109] Grobbelaar, 'Die Wêreld van die Miere'.

[110] *Times Literary Supplement*, 12 June 1937.

[111] M.S.B. Kritzinger, *Volkstem*, 4 April 1936, front page news.

[112] *Proverbs,* vi, 6, *Die Volksblad*, 22 December 1934.

[113] *Die Burger*, 15 October 1934.

[114] *Die Volksblad*, 22 December 1934.

[115] *Huisgenoot*, 27 May 1949.

[116] Ardrey searched for 'the animal within man' to explain social behaviour, publishing the socio-biological *African Genesis* in 1961, *The Territorial Imperative* in 1966, *The Social Contract* in 1970, and *The Hunting Hypothesis* in 1976.

In 1999, the *Natal Mercury* commended him as one of the '100 people who made South Africa' – he was number 79 – for having 'increased the international status of Afrikaner and natural science in South Africa'.[117]

This contested idea then suffered an ignominious end. Up to about 1950 the concept of *superorganism* was dominant in the literature on social insects, but today it is seldom employed. This was part of a general trend within ethology, Wilson suggests, of the holistic becoming replaced by the experimental and reductionist.[118] The *superorganism* was championed by Alfred E. Emerson, who wrote a series of articles (1938-1962).[119] The idea was, however, already losing scientific credibility, and even he employed it only in a nominal sense, regarding the *superorganism* as a heuristic device and, from about 1950, as only analogical. Even this liberalised and adulterated use of the *superorganism* idea came under heavy criticism.[120] From the 1960s the concept was largely abandoned,; it offered no techniques or measurements suitable in the new range of ethological interests. In its day, the *superorganism* notion was the right amalgam of fact and fancy to generate a seductive mystique, a 'mirage', which served to inspire research.[121]

Conclusion

Biology as ideology has received historiographical attention recently, but too often disciplines write their histories as linear progressions in the Whig tradition, excluding dead ends and pseudo-scientific research. Science is considered 'pure', in the sense of rational and disinterested; this paper demonstrates that Marais's biological writing was not unadulterated truth, but an amalgam of individual and wider political issues, diffused within a socio-political context. It provides a window into the interaction between social forces and the creation and popularisation of scientific theories. The use of popular media to convey the new biology of Marais impacted both on Afrikaner culture and on the science itself, appearing in the everyday reading matter of Afrikaner men and women.[122] The culture-brokers sought to mask fissures within Afrikaner society by promoting a shared sense of community and culture. Marais's

---

[117] *The Natal Mercury,* 1 December 1999.

[118] Wilson, *The Insect Societies,* p. 317.

[119] See, for example, A. E. Emerson, 'Termite Nests – a study of the phylogeny of behavior', *Ecological Monographs* 8, 2 (1938), pp. 247–84. For the post-1950 sense, see his article in *Encyclopaedia Britannica* (1959), 20, pp. 871–8.

[120] See, for typical examples of the critique levelled, A.B. Novikoff, 'The Concept of Integrative Levels and Biology', *Science,* 101 (1945), pp. 209–15. T.C. Schneirla, 'Problems in the biopsychology of social organization', *Journal of Abnormal and Social Psychology* 41, 4 (1946), pp. 385–402.

[121] Wilson, *Insect Societies,* p.319. The ideas to which Marais subscribed are not dead; they live in various guises. Rupert Sheldrake, the iconoclastic physicist, uses Marais's theory. http://www.sheldrake.org/experiments/termites/ Another proponent of Marais's ideas is Richard Roll, Allstate Professor of Finance at the Anderson Graduate School of Management at the University of California. http://www.nd.edu/~mcdonald/f370/Roll.html or Richard Roll, 'What Every C.F.O. Should Know About Scientific Progress in Financial Economics: What is Known and What Remains to be Resolved', *Financial Management* 23, 2 (1994). Marais's notions have also been applied to engineering methods in a 1997 learning programme at the Gold Fields Computer Centre for Education. http://world.std.com/~lo/97.01/0610.html

[122] See, for example, *'n Paradys van Weleer* (1965), a collection of essays on animal life appearing 1926–1934 in *Die Huisgenoot* and *Die Vaderland.*

work proved particularly apposite in that it promoted the notion that Afrikaners were invested with an understanding and love of nature. On the basis of an idealised and nostalgically reinvented past, the Afrikaner was conceived as a 'son of the soil', whose 'classroom was the veld'. Yet, at the same time, the work insisted that the Afrikaner was part of a scientific modern nation, which contributed to the 'Afrikanerisation' of science and lent the academic credibility craved by a young nation. Promoted by the Afrikaner nationalist press, Marais's entomological writings in the popular media served to promote the cultural elite's creation of an Afrikaner identity. Marais's *Soul of the White Ant* offers a microcosm of the dichotomy within Afrikaner nationalism – the containment of tradition and progress within a single ideology.

It was the project of middle-class intellectuals to mask factions within the imagined community, in favour of mythologising shared cultural identity. The nationalist magazines, in which Marais was to be published, were an attempt to create a distinct Afrikaans cultural identity, to establish and then maintain standards of *Taal* purity. They were also an attempt to uplift and educate the growing underclass of poor whites. Marais did not invent a new paradigm. The termite articles were part of the socially constructed ideology for unifying purposes, promoting a shared aesthetics of Afrikanerdom, insisting on the connection between land and people.

12

Fido

Dog Tales of Colonialism in Namibia[1]

ROBERT J. GORDON

Wildlife take pride of place in discussions of animals in African environmental history; domesticated livestock loom large in debates over pastures. Yet there are other domesticated animals which open doors in the history of colonisation. That dogs are important for understanding the socio-dynamics of Namibia should be as obvious as the first sign warning visitors to 'Beware of the Dogs'. Dog stories are pervasive, although they have not been the subject of much serious analysis. A focus on dogs provides one with a convenient analytical tool to get round the problem of how cultures naturalise themselves. Moreover, it allows one to centre on the interconnections between real and symbolic issues in how humans deal with animals.

There is a scattered array of articles which deal with dogs as metaphors for understanding society and I suggest that this approach is crucial for understanding Namibian colonialism as well. As Gombrich notes, metaphors are derived from 'traditional lore' and it is this lore which defines the effectiveness of metaphor.[2] But in tracing this 'traditional lore', Namibian history and sociology have dealt almost exclusively with people or human achievements. Dogs are rarely found in Namibian historiography indexes, yet if one looks closely enough their paw-prints are everywhere. They served with distinction as hunters and guard dogs and the emergent racial attitudes towards them reflect and provide important insights into the nature of colonialism. And if one looks at more unconventional sources of history, clues to their importance are even more obvious. In Kuusi's encyclopaedic *Ovambo Proverbs* dogs are one of the most important subjects.[3] And then there are photographs. It is

---

[1] My thanks to Patricia Hayes, Udo Krautwurst, Jane Katjavivi, Werner Hillebrecht and Dag Henrichsen for advice, comments and obscure references. Hans Bothma provided useful advice on legal aspects.

[2] Cited in S. Baker, *Picturing the Beast* (Manchester, Manchester University Press, 1993), p. 87. See also A.Gottieb, 'Dog: ally or traitor? Mythology, cosmology, and society among the Beng of Ivory Coast', *American Ethnologist* 13 (1968), pp. 447–88; Elisabeth Copet-Rougier, 'Le Jeu de l'entre-deux. Le chien chez les Mkako (Est-Cameroun)', *L'Homme* XXVIII (4) (1988), pp. 108–21 and R.Ellen, 'Categories of Animality and Canine Abuse', *Anthropos* 94 (1999), pp. 57–68. An excellent recent overview is M.Mullin, 'Mirrors and Windows: Sociocultural Studies of Human-animal Relationships', *Annual Review of Anthropology* 28 (1999), pp. 201–24.

[3] Clearly a close examination of these dog proverbs would provide an important indication of the role and value of dogs in northern Namibia. See M. Kuusi, *Ovambo Proverbs* (Helsinki, 1970).

remarkable how frequently dogs seem to sneak into photographs as part of the scenery, as it were, in pictures portraying colonial life. Why dogs are ignored as a factor in African history, is a subject on which one could speculate extensively. But rather than do this, this paper shows how an examination of dogs in Namibia can help to understand the processes of colonialism by allowing the reader 'to focus our gaze on the dialectics of everyday life at the imperial frontier' as the Comaroffs put it. It is part of the epic of the ordinary which allows us to examine the netherworld of the inarticulate.[4]

How dogs are defined, used and treated, provides important insights into the nature of colonialism. Since we think of the world in the same way as we talk about it, by establishing metaphorical relations, dog stories in Namibia reflect and reinforce some of the basic tenets of a variety of colonial discourses. After first examining the 'social role' of dogs in Namibian colonial life, I discuss dogs as a specific conceptual category in the dominant culture of Namibian colonialism.

The social role of dogs

The first European explorers and hunters traversing what became Namibia were accompanied by dogs. Indeed, dogs were an indispensable part of their equipment and useful especially for hunting, as watchdogs, and as faithful companions. Outfitting his expedition in Cape Town, Francis Galton described how he acquired a pack of a half-dozen mongrels at a uniform rate of 2s.6d. each. He also chose as personal dogs a large 'attack' dog and a small 'barking' dog. In doing this he was holding to a settler practice which is still operational.[5] Africans also appreciated good dogs. Galton reports that his factotum

> Hans sold two of his curs to some of the Damara for two oxen each. I cannot conceive what could have induced them to make such a bargain. They are very keen upon dogs for they offered four oxen for another one, 'Watch'; but he was too useful to me in worrying about night marauders to be spared.[6]

Indeed, given these rates of exchange one could argue that dogs were a more profitable trade commodity than guns in Damaraland.

Dogs were an item of pride and of conversation. The books of Galton's companion, C.J. Andersson, contain numerous observations on dogs. He describes, for example, how a small dog had been ripped by a lion but managed to crawl to the campfire: 'it was a touching sight to see the faithful animal wagging its tail in recognition of its master, who was trying to replace the intestines and to stop the flow of blood'; a poignant scene this of 'the dying dog, with his wild master stooping despondently over him'. His picture is in shrill contrast to the 'starved native dogs' he found, especially among the Nama.[7]

[4] John L. and Jean Comaroff, *Of Revelation and Revolution,* Vol. 2 (Chicago, Chicago University Press, 1997), p. 29.

[5] F.Galton, *Narrative of an Explorer in Tropical Africa* (London, John Murray, 1889) p. 8. Also see C.Andersson, *Lake Ngami* (London, Hurst and Blackett, 1856), p. 27.

[6] Galton, *Narrative*, p. 148. Andersson, *Lake Ngami*, p. 228.

[7] Andersson, *Lake Ngami*, pp. 99, 278.

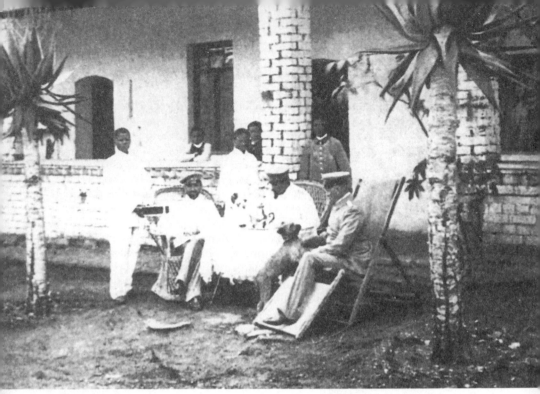

Theodore Leutwein's *Elf Jahre Governeur in Deutsch Suedwestafrika* (Berlin, 1906) is perhaps one of the most heavily consulted texts on Namibian colonialism. Of the numerous photographs illustrating this work, none are more famous than the two photo sequences illustrating life in the colonies in 1900 and then projecting into the future to the year 2000. The fantasy is fairly common: in 1900 the whites are served by African servants and in 2000 Africans are being served by Europeans. But what is important is the central position of the (fawning) dog in the 1900 picture while in 2000 the dog has completely vanished. And that is the colonial's worst nightmare. A world without dogs!

Andersson, who prided himself on being a naturalist, found it 'somewhat difficult to determine to what species of the canine race these dogs belong, or from what breed they originally descended. They bear some slight resemblance to those I have seen at the homesteads of the Swedish peasants.' He noted different breeds of local dogs and even paid a special visit to Chikongo's kraal where he 'inquired of the chief as to the breed of dogs I had seen about, which I had thought might be a cross between the native and some mongrels belonging to the Europeans; but it seems they are purely native'.[8] These observations lead to three points. First, there may have been a paucity of indigenous dogs in the nineteenth century, probably as a result of disease and predators.[9] Second, it is obvious that a process of cultural diffusion was impacting on this area long before the arrival of the first Europeans. Third, this concern with mongrel versus pure-bred dogs will be seen to be a particularly dominant trope in colonial discourse.

The unpublished reminiscences of William Chapman contain numerous observations about dogs in the period from 1880 to 1920. No hunting caravan went out without a pack of at least half a dozen dogs which served as guard dogs around camp, while in the field they were used to track wildlife and corner the more dangerous game, thus allowing the hunter to move close in for the final shot. Not only were they invaluable resources and indeed seemingly constant companions of these early European hunters, but they were used by local people as well for guarding and for hunting.

In the arid south of the country, dogs were integral to the hunting economy, and they had an additional use by local people as a form of protection for their flocks of sheep against predators such as jackals. Chapman made frequent references to the close attachment between people and their dogs. He describes the events surrounding the not insignificant murder of Will Worthington Jordan, a prominent trader and founder of the Republic of Upingtonia:

> In 1885 Jordan returned on a visit to Humpata to fetch goods he had ordered from Cape Town to Mossamedes and in Oukuanyama the Chief Nambathi insisted that Jordan should give him a small pet dog which he had but he refused and the dog was stolen. Jordan believing that the Chief had instigated one of his men to steal it for him, and a couple of days later the Chief died and there were suspicions that Jordan had procured means of poisoning him in retaliation for the loss of his pet dog!

In the Caprivi/Kavango region, Passarge also described guard and hunting dogs, noting that 'Chief Ssekumi' was an especial lover of dogs. Dogs were so prized among the Ovambo according to Moller, Chapman's contemporary, that they were used as sacrifices for various crises.[10] While Africans clearly appreciated the use of dogs, evidence for their 'dog-love' is more fragmentary and episodic.[11] I will argue that this

---

[8] Andersson, *Lake Ngami*, pp. 278, 230. C. Andersson, *Notes of Travel in South Africa* (London, L. Lloyd, 1875) p. 280. Such interest in local breeds was to continue. See, for example, the *Deutsches Kolonial Lexikon* (1920).

[9] The standard reference here would be Herbert Schneider, *Animal Health and Veterinary Medicine in Namibia* (Windhoek, 1994).

[10] National Archives of Namibia, 'Reminiscences of William Chapman' (n.d.) mimeo. P. Moller, *Journey Through Angola, Ovampoland and Damaraland* (Cape Town, Struik, 1974) p. 135. And like his compatriot, Andersson, Moller also noted different dog breeds, pp. 125, 84.

[11] See, for example, L.Wildenthal, 'Race, Gender and Citizenship in the German Colonial Empire' in F. Cooper and A. Stoler (eds), *Tensions of Empire* (Berkeley, University of California Press, 1997) p. 275.

lacuna had important ideological connotations for justifying colonialism. Dogs served another function as well – devouring the rotting carcases of rinderpest-stricken cattle. Passarge, like other German scientific travellers, seemed concerned about the possibilities of cross-breeding.[12]

As in other parts of the world, dogs were a cultural presence in colonisation.[13] Certainly settlers and officials in the German Colonial Service were highly appreciative of dogs, none perhaps more famously than Hauptmann Francke, who was seldom seen without his dog and on its death had it buried with a proper gravestone marking its burial site. Dogs were not at the forefront of colonial documentation; perhaps they were so taken for granted that discussion was deemed superfluous. Occasionally an article would appear in the settler press, such as one on the 'Bushman Question' which argued that 'the only way of following them in the thick bush is with dogs. The equipping of good Police Dogs in a suitable number would be of extra-ordinary value.' The German authorities set up a special police dog training school in Windhoek in 1911-12.[14] Police dogs in German South West Africa developed such a reputation that, when South Africa conquered the territory, one of the earliest items 'exported' back to South Africa were police dogs of the 'smouspincher' type.[15]

Taxing dogs

In the wake of the 1904–7 colonial wars many Africans found themselves stripped of their primary means of subsistence, livestock, and this meant that especially good hunting dogs became even more important instruments of survival. In 1917 the German colonial dog tax, which had focused exclusively on urban areas, was replaced by a system whereby dogs in townships were taxed at South African £1 for the first dog and 10 shillings for each subsequent dog. In the rural areas the rate was 5 shillings per dog but Europeans were allowed one watchdog tax-free and this exemption was later also extended to Nama following their urgent representations.

Shortly after taking up his position as Native Superintendent of Windhoek, Bowker complained that the reserves were 'overrun' with 'mongrel greyhounds' and suggested that 'at the same time, in the interests of sport, could the police not take steps to collect taxes and destroy dogs throughout the district generally'. Mindful of how Africans would respond to his proposal, he suggested that 'the action should be done quietly otherwise when your men arrive on the reserves there will be no dogs to be seen'. He was supported by other officials who insisted that unlicensed dogs be shot since they were swarming all over the reserves and destroying all big and small game: 'many of the Natives exist on the exertions of these dogs and should they be denied the use of such animals they would naturally be compelled to work and to go in search of

[12] S. Passarge, 'Das Okavangosumpflussland und seine Bewohner', *Zeitschrift für Ethnologie* V: (1905), pp. 649–716.

[13] J. and J.Varner, *Dogs of the Conquest* (Norman, OK, University of Oklahoma Press, 1983). M.Schwartz, *A History of Dogs in the Early Americas* (New Haven, CT, Yale University Press, 1997).

[14] *Deutsche Suedwest–Afrika Zeitung*, 28 November 1911. H. Rafalski, *Von Niemandsland bis Ordnungs-staat* (Berlin, E. Wersteitz, 1930). See Keith Shear, 'Police dogs and state rationality in early twentieth-century South Africa' in S. Dubow (ed.), *Science and Society in Southern Africa* (Manchester, Manchester University Press, 2000).

[15] The 'smouspincher' was apparently a cross between a Doberman Pincher and a Rottweiler. National Archives of Namibia (NAN) A491/1 Export and Import (Dogs).

work.'[16] Windhoek farmers complained that their livestock was being harassed by 'native dogs'. The Native Affairs Commissioner proposed that greyhounds be limited to two per person and pointed out that the tax was in line with South African and Rhodesian practice.[17] But it was not only Africans who failed to abide by existing Dog Laws. A Magistrate complained that 'the exemption from taxation of a farmer's watch dog is much abused. Why should a farmer who can well afford to pay be exempt when a native who really requires a dog to assist him to look after and guard his master's stock has to pay half of his monthly income for the privilege? I think no dogs should be exempt from taxation.'[18] Even in places where game was exceedingly rare, such as in the desert town of Luderitz, the Magistrate thought that the town was overrun with dogs and requested 100 .303 cartridges as 'the present custom of knocking them (unlicensed dogs) on the head with a stick is cruel and should be stopped'.[19]

After a tour to the South of the territory the Administrator felt that drastic action had to be taken:

> The necessity for this heavy tax was clearly demonstrated ... when I found vast numbers of dogs in (the) possession of natives and a certain class of European squatter, who profited by the employment of these animals to hunt down game and obtained a livelihood thereby instead of by honest labour.[20]

From April 1921 a uniform dog tax system 'allowing no exemptions' for urban and rural areas or for Africans and settlers was promulgated. Fees increased fourfold from 5 shillings to £1 for the first dog, to £2.10s. for two dogs, £4.10s. for three, £7 for four and £10 for five dogs. In his Report to the League of Nations for that year, the Administrator claimed:

> The law has already fulfilled its immediate object in the prevention of the pernicious evil perpetrated by certain Whites and Blacks in keeping large numbers of dogs to forage for them, ruthlessly destroying quantities of game, and affording these vagrants and loafers an easy means of livelihood, which relieves them of any need to work.[21]

But there were problems. There was a general outcry on the part of both Africans and settlers and a year later the tax rate was halved. Africans complained that there was much confusion and that it was unfair to expect a herder employed on a settler farm to forgo more than the equivalent of a month's salary for a dog licence. Strategies of resistance are clear from the complaint made by farmers that Africans refused to take out dog licences unless the Police came out to collect the taxes: 'when the Police arrive the dogs disappear'. So successful was this defiance that a few months later the Administrator had to upbraid all magistrates with a circular letter that dog taxes were not being collected.[22] Dog tax collection was piecemeal at best. One important

---

[16] 'Greyhounds' and 'Bastard Greyhounds', despite the name, were not recognised kennel-club breeds but rather categories developed by officials to confront dog diversity.

[17] NAN, A491/2 Taxation, Dogs, Bowker to Sec 25 July 1919, 14 Jan 1920.

[18] NAN, A491/2 Taxation (Dogs). Mil.Mag. Okahandja to Sec 6 Nov. 1919.

[19] NAN, A491/2 Taxation (Dogs) 1924 and June 1920.

[20] South Africa, *Report of the Administrator to the League of Nations* (Pretoria, UG 30/1922), p. 3.

[21] UG 32/1922, p. 4.

[22] *Windhoek Advertiser*, 11 June 1921. Clearly this was a major issue in a labour-strapped country. See G. Lewis, 'The Bondelswarts Rebellion', unpublished MA thesis, Rhodes University (1977) p. 49. NAN Mag.Whk to Sec 14 June 1921 and 8 November 1921.

exception was on the Bondels Reserve where between September and January 1922 there were 140 prosecutions and over a 100 fines or imprisonment.[23] Since these people could not find the money to pay either the tax or the fine, they were forced to work for settlers, who moreover could not pay cash to their labourers. In the first seven months of 1922 dog tax offences accounted for over 70 per cent of the charges laid in Warmbad.[24] This, coupled with a long legacy of systematic impoverishment, was the final factor which precipitated the Bondelswarts Rebellion in May 1922. As Captain Prinsloo, a Police Officer involved in suppressing the Rebellion, put it: 'In the absence of a rifle his dogs are his best friend and the uniformed man his worst enemy'.[25] The brutal suppression of the Bondelswarts Rebellion was a *cause célèbre* at the League of Nations.

Settlers too were dissatisfied because they were not exempt from these taxes: 'farmers complained because they had expected that the tax would be imposed upon the Natives alone in order to induce them to obtain a livelihood by honest labour'.[26] Indeed, almost before the ink on the new Dog Tax Proclamation had dried, the Outjo Farmers' Association petitioned against this 'abnormal tax', claiming that farmers needed at least two watchdogs near the house against wild animals and robbers; they sought exemptions for the first two dogs and then a tax rate of 50 pence per dog.[27] Even Superintendent Barnes of Orumbo Reserve, who had campaigned on behalf of a Native Dog tax, sought relief for two powerful dogs to destroy jackals and other pests 'free of licence'. The alternative, hunting with ammunition, was unnecessarily expensive.[28]

Farmers' Societies and municipalities continued to make representations on this issue for a number of years and the Dog Tax Proclamation probably holds the distinction of being the most amended proclamation in colonial Namibia. Proclamation 2/1924 reduced dog taxes by 50 per cent but imposed a £5 tax on 'Greyhound types' or the 'kind known as kaffir hunting dogs' which were 'approximately 70 per cent of the Native owned variety'. Greyhounds registered with the South African Kennel Club, however, were exempt from this tax. This proclamation was later suspended on the grounds that laws had to be race-blind. Exemptions were later granted to members of Vermin Hunt Clubs which were, of course, exclusively manned by settlers.[29]

Settler discourses on dogs certainly emphasised the importance of taxing hunting dogs as a means of forcing recalcitrant Africans to enter the labour market. Thus the Karibib Farmerverein resolved unanimously in 1925 that native-owned hunting dogs caused a noticeable decline in small game. Africans, they asserted, preferred owning dogs to goats: 'on the veld no kaffir is seen without several dogs, these dogs are not their property but are lent to him and then they share the pot.' They were emphatically not watchdogs because they were seldom at the kraal but continually out hunting on their own account. Nor did the society feel that they were kept to catch jackals, as the

[23] Lewis, 'Bondelswarts Rebellion', p. 50.

[24] *Ibid.*, p. 59.

[25] R. Freislich, *The Last Tribal War* (Cape Town, Struik, 1964), p. 89.

[26] South Africa (UG 16/1923) p. 11.

[27] *Windhoek Advertiser*, 18 August 1923. On settler fear and insecurity in this era see R. Gordon, 'The Vagrancy Proclamation and Internal Pacification in Namibia 1920–1945' in P. Hayes, J. Silvester, M.Wallace, W. Hartmann (eds), *Namibia Under South African Rule* (Athens, OH, Ohio University Press, 1998).

[28] *Windhoek Advertiser*, 20 April 1921.

[29] On South African vermin hunt clubs see W.Beinart, 'The Night of the Jackal: Sheep, Pastures and Predators in the Cape', *Past & Present* 158 (February 1998).

the number of jackals appeared to have increased. If jackals gave them trouble they would kill a kapater (gelded goat) and use poison. Rather, the closed season for hunting was being completely flouted. They asked the Administration to impose a £5 tax on all African-owned hunting dogs. The Verein was later joined in its concern by the *Allgemeine Zeitung* (26 May 1926) which estimated that in one district alone native-owned dogs were responsible for killing 12,000 head of game per annum. It was partially in response to issues like this that the South West Africa Wild Life Protection Society was formed later that year.[30]

At the same time, the value of dogs for settler hunting was being downplayed. Commenting on a 1935 publicity brochure being developed by the South African Railways, long-term Commissioner 'Cocky' Hahn noted that 'dogs are seldom much use because the climate is so dry. There is very little scent, the running proclivities of the birds and the lack of thick undergrowth militating against the use of setters or pointer. For recovering wounded birds a well-trained retriever would be of assistance.'[31] For lion hunting, on the other hand, dogs were indispensable.

As a means of forcing Reserve inhabitants to engage in wage labour, however, the dog tax rapidly lost its significance as other economic variables, especially grazing fees, started to have an impact. In 1928 indigenous livestock owners residing in the reserves were provided with a tax exemption for a single dog (Proclamation 5/1928), a move which raised the immediate ire of the Okahandja Farmers Association which felt this gave African farmers an unfair advantage. The Administration replied that white farmers already had exemptions for two dogs, could belong to Vermin Clubs and, moreover, had access to firearms. None of these means of vermin control were available to Africans. This exemption was swiftly taken advantage of. By 1931 99 per cent of all the dogs in the Tses reserve were tax-exempt. While locals loved their dogs, they could not afford to feed them, forcing these 'walking skeletons' to raid the railway siding consignments.[32] Eventually the Ovitoto Reserve Superintendent suggested that exemptions only be granted to well-fed dogs: 'in some cases dogs are in such a state of hunger that it is better to destroy them, than to allow them to live and suffer in hunger'.

After the Second World War the Administration set up a Commission to enquire into the Game Laws (1948). Among the factors it found leading to the 'steady diminution of game', apart from drought, wholesale slaughter by 'biltong' hunters (non-resident white hunters) and land encroachment, was 'the presence of an increasing number of kaffir dogs both in the Native Reserves as well as in the country generally'. Accordingly the Commission recommended 'that the whole matter of Dog Taxes in the Territory be taken into review, but that two dogs be allowed free to the farmer as before. It is recommended that thoroughbred dogs be licenced at £1 per head, but that mongrels or cross-bred dogs should be more highly taxed, particularly unsterilized bitches.'[33] Among the representations it received was one to make the possession of dogs by farm-workers illegal. After careful consideration it rejected this, since such legislation would infringe individual rights unduly and would also amount to class

[30] *Windhoek Advertiser*, 23 October 1926.
[31] NAN A198/2. Clearly Hahn was engaging in some class bias here. His remarks were aimed at potential overseas hunters who would favour bird hunting. On the other hand, Africans and some poor white farmers used large packs of rather undisciplined dogs to chase and corner game, actions defined by Hahn as 'unsporting'.
[32] NAN A492. 1/2 Tses Supt.letter, 14 October 1931.
[33] NAN A205/1 Commission to Enquire into Game laws.

legislation. The only solution was to increase the taxes on dogs in an effort to make the possession of such dogs uneconomical.

Until the large-scale improvement of jackal-proof fencing many herders in the south of the territory used to supplement their meagre income by using dogs to catch jackals for which they could claim a 5/- bounty per silver-tailed jackal from the Administration. It was this economic benefit which no doubt muted criticism of locally owned dogs on farms. But in the 1950s the Municipal Association of South West Africa complained that dogs were roaming the countryside doing considerable damage to stock and wildlife and that the Police were ineffective in dealing with this problem since they lacked proper equipment. Dog licensing, the Association argued, should be a municipal function. Dogs should be impounded for three days and then destroyed, while in the rural areas all unlicensed dogs should be destroyed immediately. Their recommendation that dog taxes should be doubled was implemented.[34]

Dogs as cultural category

Leach argues that pets such as dogs straddle boundaries of basic categories and thus have special ritual value.[35] They are ambiguous in our systems of classifying and ordering the world because they are mediators between binary opposites: they straddle the human and the animal, the domestic and the wild; they break and blur this distinction. Settlers saw their dogs as sharing their status and this had profound implications for their treatment of dogs and their beliefs about African treatment of dogs. Fido, the most popular dog name in the heyday of European colonialism, connotes faithfulness and loyalty.[36] Darwin believed that dogs could think as abstractly as children and 'savages' and were capable of using similar mental processes to solve problems like finding water. From such perspectives a dog which does its master's bidding and looks after its master is not only a good pet but also a well-colonised animal. Dating back to the Second Agricultural Show in Windhoek in 1914, one of the most popular events was a display of the prowess of well-trained police dogs and this pattern continued at least into the 1960s. Colonists had an almost psychopathic hatred of wild dogs.[37]

At the same time, dogs served also as mobile metaphors for understanding gradations in colonial society. To take some random examples: in describing a Portuguese official's cowardice, Chapman reports that he 'retreated as a dog would, pulling his tail between his legs'. A large concessionaire, Companhia de Mossamedes, is described as having a 'dog in the manger' attitude. One of the indignities the Angola Afrikaners suffered, Chapman claims, was that a Portuguese administrator had termed Afrikaans a dog's language. Conversely, the characteristics of dogs were also inferred from the

---

[34] NAN A491, Dogs General and Control of.

[35] E. Leach, 'Anthropological Aspects of Language: animal categories and verbal abuse' in Eric Lenneberg (ed.), *New Directions in the Study of Language* (Boston, MA, MIT Press, 1964).

[36] A. Memmi, *The Colonizer and the Colonized* (Boston, MA, Beacon Press, 1964). Galton's cousin, Charles Darwin was imposing accepted bourgeois values when he compared Fuegians to dogs in precisely these colonialist terms in *The Descent of Man*. L. M. Wendt, *Dogs: A historical journey* (New York, MacMillan, 1996), p. 130.

[37] Another important animal which straddles this boundary, Dag Henrichsen points out, is the horse. In contrast to wild dogs, in Namibia the 'wild horses of the Namib' are highly romanticised.

gender and race of the human owners. Thus dogs owned by women were seen to lack self-discipline and being less streetwise than men's dogs got killed in accidents more frequently. A Government Commission deployed racist ideas across the species divide, believing that mongrel bitches owned by Africans tended to breed indiscriminately like their owners.

The polysemic symbolic character of dogs is rarely articulated as such. Instead, one must infer it from a variety of contextual documents like folk-tales, poems, proverbs and especially photographs. It is striking how many photographs of settlers have dogs either deliberately posed, or in many cases simply wandering into the scene being photographed. This high degree of tolerance in the days when photography was a relatively expensive undertaking suggests that pet dogs were not only well fed but given extensive freedom. Posed pictures also open up intriguing questions: can posed dog love be seen as a symbolic means of compensating for hatred of people sometimes categorised as 'wild'? Or, consider the picture which H. Rafalski published entitled 'Transport of Police Dogs on a Mounted Patrol'. It consists of a dog leading a horse on a leash. The horse has two side boxes in which are seated two dogs. What does this photograph tell us about the title of the book: *Von Niemandsland bis Ordnungsstaat* (From Nomansland to Ordinance State)? And note the play on the word Ordnung which can be translated as either 'Ordinance' state or 'Ordered' state/state of order – a place where even dogs know what to do out of duty, while *Niemandsland* is synonymous with chaos. Could it be a symbolic reflection of what he considered to be the ideal settled colony, where even the dogs would take care of the means of production (the horse) and the rulers could sit back and do nothing?

Perhaps the ultimate colonial illusion was that a single well-trained dog could do the work of numerous Africans, as implied in Rafalski's photograph. It is striking how in posed photographs of Africans, dogs and whites, dogs and Africans inevitably seem to be placed at the same level. And when a group of African dignitaries were photographed and later sold as a postcard, the photographer allowed a dog to scratch itself in the foreground. A common theme in German colonial women's memoirs of life in Namibia was how Africans and dogs shared the same culinary tastes.[38] In 1927 the Farmwirtschaft Gesellschaft wrote to the Administration requesting permission to import two fully trained European sheep-dogs since flocks were decreasing due to the unsatisfactory state of 'native labour'. A year later the Karakul Breeders Association renewed the application on behalf of its Herr Held, who had brought out a professional shepherd from Germany: 'This man, at present attending to 1500 sheep, has come to the conclusion, that all dogs of this country, which he has tried up to now, have refused proper duty as there is no dog in the country to teach them their service. As the opinion of that shepherd some dogs of this country would be serviceable, if only a possibility could be found to train them by using a well trained responsible sheepdog.'[39]

Colonel Statham, author of *With My Wife Across Africa* (1922), detailing his adventures in southern Angola and northern Namibia, published a photograph of his injured dog Fita being carried in a palanquin by Africans. What type of symbolic statement is Statham trying to make by including this photograph? Most local people, both black and white, would undoubtedly have put the dog out of its misery. He clearly wishes to emphasise his role as bearer of civilisation, along with the African role in subservient servicing of the colonising man and dog.

[38] Udo Krautwurst, personal comment citing Else Sonnenberg and Clara Brockmann.
[39] NAN A491/1, Export and Import (Dogs), 27 Feb. 1928.

The treatment that masters meted out to their dogs served as a marker of fitness to rule and of civility. Harold Eedes, veteran Native Commissioner for the Kavango, claimed that local dogs were never fed in villages, kept in poor condition and subsisted mostly on human excrement.[40] Could people like that ever be competent to govern themselves? The belief in bourgeois culture that people who mistreat animals will mistreat humans is well-established.[41] Eedes certainly took this as evidence of 'low mentality and moral outlook'. So common was this belief among settlers that the maverick Peter Weidner, a long-term resident in southern Namibia, felt compelled to point out that while Nama dogs might look miserable, they were deliberately kept hungry for hunting purposes: 'in all fairness to the Hottentot, he will always allow the dog a fair share of the spoils just as the race horse trainer will also add an extra ration of oats to his horse's supper after it has won a race'.[42]

Colonial law was expressly concerned with cruelty to animals. In Namibia it was a crime, punishable by fines, imprisonment and, in gross cases, whipping, to: 'cruelly beat, kick, ill-treat, overdrive, override, over-load or torture any animal'; 'keep animals for fighting'; administer 'poison or injurious drug or substance' or 'permit, to be subjected, any animal to any operation which is performed without due care and humanity'.[43] Namibia has long had a 'Prevention of Cruelty to Animals' Proclamation (1919) and eventually, after the Second World War, a Society for the Prevention of Cruelty to Animals was formed in Windhoek. In 1948 the South African Animal Welfare Society complained to the Administration of the:

> deplorable cruelty to animals in Native Areas—neglect and semi-starvation and lack of regard for the feelings of animals, leading to deliberate maltreatment and the infliction of unnecessary pain. It may be pointed out that sympathy for the feelings of others is one of the basic principles of our civilization and that all truly civilized people extend this principle to animals.

But it wasn't just that 'civilisation' which was at stake. The memorandum went on to criticise the situation of the 'semi-starving Native dogs' which were

> too frequently kept by people who do not or cannot afford to feed them adequately, or families which might be able to feed one dog properly, keep three or four dogs in a miserable condition. This starvation of dogs too often leads to the killing of livestock by the famished animals and awkward consequences for their owners.[44]

The parallels between this argument and that for population control for blacks are so obvious as not to warrant comment.

The *Standard Encyclopedia of Southern Africa* in its entry on dogs has this to say about 'kaffir dogs': while varying considerably in terms of colours, coats and carriage, their constant characteristics include a: 'slinking gait' and a

[40] Cited in G.Gibson *et al.*, *The Kavango Peoples* (Wiesbaden, Franz Steiner Verlag, 1981) p. 45.
[41] J. Serpell, *In the Company of Animals* (Oxford, Blackwell, 1986); M. Garber, *Dog Love* (London, Hamish Hamilton, 1996), p. 16.
[42] P. Weidner, *The World Owes You Nothing* (Warmbad, n.d.), p. 29.
[43] C.H. Blaine, *Dog Law: A compilation of the law in South Africa relating to dogs* (Johannesburg, R. L. Esson, 1928) pp. 51–2.
[44] NAN SWAA A442/1 Cruelty to Animals, 20 Feb. 1948.

very suspicious nature, so that even their own masters have some difficulty in holding and handling them.... Much interbreeding.... Usually these dogs are forced by circumstances to be almost self-supporting and they live as scavengers in Bantu villages. On the hunt they help their masters to bring the game to bay, but they are wary of being embroiled in direct fights with the quarry.[45]

Without too much imagination this vocabulary could easily be used to describe how settlers saw Africans.[46] It was a common belief among settlers that African dogs were possessed of too low a discipline capacity (Dressurfähigkeit) to be trained into good hunting dogs and that indeed even the one officially recognised African breed, the Ridgeback, was of Asian origin.[47]

Not only was it believed that dogs resembled their masters, but ownership of dogs was a mark of civility. This was used by many, like Moeller, to tilt Bushmen into the category of humanity, if only just: 'There is no other domestic animal among the Bushmen than the dog but often even this, the faithful companion of man, is lacking'.[48] And even the Bushman dog was exceptional according to many early European explorers and adventurers in that it did not bark and thus was useless as a watchdog, though brilliantly resourceful as a hunter – reflecting only too clearly the colonisers' stereotype of their Bushman masters.

Finally, I would suggest that, in addition to their social functions, dogs provided for a very important psychological need of the colonisers, especially the officials who worked beyond the Police Zone where there were few white compatriots. In such a typical colonial situation, commissioners were not easily loved by their subjects. Dogs, on the other hand, loved their masters irrespective of their faults or politics. They were thus an important psychological surrogate.

One of the fundamental problems colonials faced in countries like Namibia was insecurity and dogs were perceived to play an important role in creating the semblance of control and security. As Doris Lessing pointed out for Rhodesia, large dogs were imported for two basic reasons: to terrorise possible burglars and for owners 'to surround themselves with an aura of controlled animal savagery'. All dogs were supposed to be watchdogs. It was an article of faith that Africans were by nature scared of dogs, even if everyone repeated stories about thieves poisoning fierce dogs or making friends with them.[49] Despite many such contradictions, dogs were closely entangled in the elaboration of colonial hierarchies and racial ideas.

[45] C.Marais, 'Dogs', *Standard Encyclopedia of South Africa, Vol. 2* (Cape Town, 1968), p. 55.
[46] Again such colonising strategies have a long pedigree. Andersson was renowned for his dislike of the Nama and their dogs.

> The curs are of the greatest annoyance to the traveller in Namaqualand, for since the owners rarely feed them, they greedily devour almost everything they come across. I have had my powder-flask, 'veld' shoes, and even rifle ... abstracted by them from my side during the night. A person's first impulse on making the discovery is to vow vengeance on the head of the thieves; but, on seeing the emaciated state of the poor creatures, in which every rib might be counted, anger is turned into pity (Andersson, *Lake Ngami*, p. 278).

[47] A.Fischer, 'Ueber den Jagdhund in Suedwest', *SWA Jagdkalender* (1939), pp. 163–4; H. Graf Castell-Ruedenhausen, *Jagden zwischen Namib und Kalahari* (Hamburg, Franz Steiner Verlag, 1978), pp. 160–1.
[48] Castell-Ruedenhausen, *Jagden*, p. 149.
[49] D.Lessing, *African Stories* (New York, 1966), p. 657.

Dog law cultures

Implicit in the notion of colonialism is the presumption of control. In order to understand the state's attempts to control dogs one must examine further the cultural role of dogs in Namibia, in addition to their obvious material roles. Why, if dogs were so important for African efforts to avoid having to work in the colonial labour system, did settlers not succeed in establishing a special tax for what they called 'kaffir dogs'? This was an important question, given the labour crises which plagued the settlers. Part of the answer was surely the importance that colonists attached to dogs as guard-dogs and hunting-dogs. A differential dog tax would have caused, officials believed, massive indigenous resentment. In addition, there were problems of administrative capacity to assess the tax properly and the inconvenience of collecting it. As a justification for not imposing a special 'Kafir Hunting Dog Tax' – requested by the Karib Farmerverein – a survey of magisterial districts indicated that the decimation of game by 'kafir hunting dogs' was vastly exaggerated. Finally, there were the international ramifications: the scandals of the Bondelswart and Rehoboth Rebellion were still echoing in the corridors of the League of Nations. The Administration was acutely conscious of the need not to generate another *cause célèbre*. It eventually finessed the situation by allowing every member of an officially recognized vermin extermination club or association to have tax exemptions for two dogs.[50]

Most important, though, was the problem of how exactly officials would legally differentiate African dogs from European dogs? As Magistrate Thomas put it: 'In the Union I believe the "Kaffir Hunting Dog" is a special class, but here any dog of any breed or mixed breeds after special treatment (i.e. a proper course of starvation and training) becomes a hunting dog.... Here it is by starving rather than by breeding that you produce the Kaffir hunting dog.'[51] Indeed, the only distinctive breed of African dog to be recognised as such by the South African Kennel Club was the Rhodesian Ridgeback in 1924. The other legal question befuddling dog taxes was who was being taxed: the dog or the owner; this became an issue when dogs were given away as gifts or ownership was transferred. And if ownership was crucial, could it be communal as well as individual?[52] This was not a simple question. The Stock-theft law allowed for collective culpability where the spoor of the stolen stock was traced to a kraal. So too with dogs, dog hunting packs frequently consisted of dogs belonging to several owners who might not even be aware that their dogs were out on a hunt.

Travellers, settlers and colonial authorities had particular problems with mongrels. Although the notion of a 'pure-bred' dog was highly problematic, it was frequently used as a point of contest. In 1920 Messrs Schaeffer and Lossow applied for dog licence exemptions on the grounds that they had a facility in which they were engaged in dog-breeding 'to meet the obvious wishes of the farmers who like to get dogs of pure race', and listed amongst their assets dogs specially imported from South Africa: two Greyhounds; one Bullterrier bitch; one Bullterrier male; and two pure-bred Alsatian wolf-dogs.[53]

In cases involving 'cruelty to animals' further significant pointers can also be found. Thus, in South Africa, a man who had castrated his neighbour's dogs for interfering

---

[50] Blaine, *Dog Law*, p. 227.

[51] NAN A491/2 Vol. 1.

[52] NAN A.205/1, 6 May 1949.

[53] A longer version of this paper would require a contextualising discussion of the Immorality Act.

with his bitch was found guilty of malicious injury to property and fined £25 or two months imprisonment with hard labour, yet in a similar case the person was found not guilty because his bitches were pure-bred and the dog he castrated was a 'cross-bred'.[54]

For a dog tax to be enforceable a token has to be available to distinguish taxed from untaxed dogs. The 1921 Proclamation stipulated that, in addition to a tax receipt, each dog had to wear a metal badge. Any dog without a badge could be seized by the police and destroyed. There was resistance to this strategy even before it was implemented. As the Okahandja Military Magistrate complained 'the brass badges are expensive, Native dogs do not wear collars on which to affix badges and the badges themselves are small and easily lost. They seem quite unnecessary in rural areas.'[55] But it was the unstated symbolic dimension which clearly concerned him and Africans. Dog badges resembled the brass tokens local Africans had been required to wear around their necks during the German era until replaced by pass books in 1917. At least in the earlier years of Mandate rule, Ovambo contract workers were still issued with cheap tin disks which had a small hole on one side through which a thin cord could be passed for suspension.

Conclusion

Clearly colonial dogs led charmed lives and the oft-repeated African complaint that 'Boers treated us like dogs' may not always be accurate in this context. Whose dogs and which dogs are issues of major importance and with those referents the meaning of the statement can be changed dramatically. Human-canine relationships are fascinating precisely because they are undoubtedly social. Most humans attribute human qualities to canines, and at least in colonial situations the opposite, the almost institutionalised attribution of animal qualities to humans, is equally ubiquitous. Many of the attitudes which settlers held about the relationship between Africans and dogs can be shown to be based not on empirical data but on cultural constructs. In the voluminous correspondence relating to 'Cruelty to Animals' and in examining District Level Court Records, specific cases of blacks being charged with 'cruelty to animals' are surprisingly rare.

Whites' dogs figure vividly in African cultural constructs. It is small wonder that tales of Boer dogs are a staple conversation topic in black shebeens. Indeed, local Namibians have long been concerned about the settlers' strange obsession with dogs and a rich social commentary extends to the period of German colonialism. There are Herero praise songs (*omitango*) which refer to German love of dogs: 'Germans – the people with the fox terrier. They hit you with a loaf of bread which you will eat while you are sufficient' and 'the people who like a dog and hate a person'. Both praise songs demonstrate keen sociological appreciations. These Herero singers were not alone. Writing in 1911, Tonjes reported that if a young migrant returned to Ovamboland earlier than expected they would complain that 'if the white man's dog dies, he is sad and cries; but if his black servant dies, this does not affect him and he might even push him aside with his foot'.[56]

---

[54] Blaine, *Dog Law*, pp. 50–1, 55.
[55] NAN A491/2 Taxation Dogs. Mil. Mag. Okahandja to Sec 6 Nov. 1919.
[56] H.Tonjes, *Ovamboland: Country People Mission* (Windhoek, Namibia Scientific Society, 1996) pp. 149, 111.

How dogs were treated in Ovamboland was closely tied to matters of social hierarchy. Ovambo kings kept dogs for hunting purposes and would instruct servants to

'take the dogs out and look for meat for them'. The royal dogs would sometimes attack small-stock like goats but 'Woe unto him who dares to hit or drive off the dogs: they are, after all, the king's dogs! The dogs receive only the smallest portion of the meat. Most of the meat becomes the property of their guides'.[57]

While waiting to interview a bureaucrat in Owambo, and trying to make small-talk, I politely asked what she thought was the worst Oshiwambo swear-word anyone could be called. Without a doubt, the worst insult is to call someone a dog (*ombwa*), she said, and then proceeded to proffer explanations which would have been music to any structuralist's ear: dogs don't know how to behave, they eat anything; a person has a place, a dog just wanders around; dogs do not stay in areas which are important to people like the kitchen or sleeping room; worst, dogs fornicate in public.

Brecht's poem 'A Worker Studies History' makes an elegant argument for moving beyond the 'Great Man' approach in history to include the little people, the underlings in history. This brief reconnaissance has suggested that his approach should be further extended to include 'Man's best friend'. Not only is there ample evidence to suggest that dogs played an important material role in the creation of Namibia, but in a cultural-symbolic sense they were crucial. The use of animal categories to understand human behaviour and the use of human categories to understand animal behaviour reciprocally reinforced negative stereotypes, and indeed this interplay between material and symbolic manifestations still plays itself out in aspects of contemporary Namibian society. If there is one point this essay makes, it is to show how sets of everyday practices concerning as mundane a subject as dogs can embed and entrench colonialism and bring it alive to all sectors of colonial society.

[57] Personal comm., Dag Henrichsen.

13

Past & Future Landscape Ideology

The Kalahari Gemsbok National Park[1]

JANE CARRUTHERS

The recent history of the Kalahari Gemsbok National Park provides a study of ideo-logical contestation over land and offers insights into the interface between land/place and culture/identity. As is the case in other areas of the world – Australia is a good example – national parks are currently favoured spaces for reclaiming, perhaps even reinventing, the cultures of formerly disadvantaged peoples as well as for publicising aspects of indigenous knowledge among a broader public.

South Africa has a wide variety of ecosystems and the Kalahari Gemsbok National Park (the second largest national park in the country) is the showpiece of the small arid ecology zone, although it forms part of a much larger desert area which extends into central Botswana and Namibia. The park is bounded by the Nossob and the Auob, two rivers in the Gariep system which flow strongly only once or twice a century. There are two main roads through the park which utilise these dry river beds; the rest of the protected area consists of high (10m) red parallel sand-dunes that are impossible to cross by vehicle. The national park spills over into Botswana; its status as the Kgalagadi Transfrontier Park – the first Transfrontier (Peace) Park in Africa – has recently been confirmed: in total it consists of some 40 000 sq km.[2] The national park and the Kalahari region generally is rich in wildlife and also in evidence of long

[1] I would like to thank the History Program of the Research School of Social Sciences at the Australian National University in Canberra for awarding me a Visiting Fellowship in 1999 in order to conduct this research. Many colleagues in Australia contributed to my knowledge of Aboriginal and modern Australia, particularly Tom Griffiths and Libby Robin, also Tim Bonyhady, Peter Christoff, John Dargavel, Steve Dovers, Robyn Eckersley, Guy Fitzhardinge, Richard Grove, Mandy Martin, Isabel McBryde, Peter Read, Debbie Bird Rose, Tim Rowse, George Seddon, Mike Smith, Mark Stafford-Smith, David Trigger and Christopher Vernon. Christopher Saunders helped with references and Greg Cuthbertson commented constructively on earlier drafts.
[2] *Government Gazette 19171*, 28 August 1998, Notice 1810 of 1998, Department of Environmental Affairs and Tourism, Draft Bilateral Agreement between the Republic of Botswana and the Republic of South Africa on the recognition of the Kgalagadi Transfrontier Park, pp. 51–62. According to *Peace Parks*, 3rd edition, 1999, the first transfrontier park was established in 1932: the Waterton/Glacier between the USA and Canada. In 1997 there were 136 transboundary protected area complexes involving 98 countries and they comprised some 10 per cent of the world's network of protected areas.

habitation by the San in precolonial times.[3] But there is also a more recent narrative of violent displacement and dispossession as well as assimilation and acculturation.

Many historical legacies are being played out within a modern form of land use: the national park. National parks are a Western invention, the underlying principle of which is to protects aspects of the natural environment.[4] Over time, the social dimension of national parks, once ignored, even obliterated, has become increasingly relevant, to the extent that today in addition to saving biological diversity there is strong advocacy for recognising cultural components in any national park landscape. This is demanded by international conservation agencies, and is a requirement for any World Heritage Site. The Secretary-General of ICOMOS (International Council of Monuments) has linked physical and intangible heritage directly, explaining that physical heritage only attains its true significance when 'it sheds light on its underlying values'.[5] As expressed by UNESCO, 'Our cultural and natural heritage are both irreplaceable sources of life and inspiration. They are our touchstones, our points of reference, our identity.'[6] However, neither the cultural nor the natural are unchanging but intersect with appropriate political strategies at any given time.

For many decades settlers considered the inhospitable Kalahari 'the most awful country to be found anywhere – the very last place outside the Arctic regions where man would choose to dwell'.[7] Even in the late 1920s the comment was made that 'So far the Kalahari desert has been one of the lost lands. A few white men entered it, but not all of them returned. It has been the great mystery desert of Africa ... it is one of the few places in the Dark Continent which is still dark.'[8] As for the hunter-gatherer San people who inhabited this landscape, travellers and anthropologists alike at that time regarded them disparagingly.[9] The San were thought to be related to the

[3] The use of the terms 'Bushman', 'San' and 'Khoisan' is the subject of ongoing academic and political debate. For some of the outlines of the present state of the terminology, see G. Connah (ed.), *Transformations in Africa: Essays on Africa's later past* (London, Leicester University Press, 1998) p. 24; Edwin N. Wilmsen, *Land Filled with Flies: A political economy of the Kalahari* (Chicago, Chicago University Press, 1989), pp. 26–32; John Wright, 'Sonqua, Bosjemans, Bushmen, abaThwa: Comments and queries on pre-modern identifications', *South African Historical Journal* 35 (1996), pp. 16–29; Russel Viljoen, 'Khoisan heritage and identity', *South African Historical Journal* 35 (1996), pp. 140–5 and Andrew Bank (ed.), *The Proceedings of the Khoisan Identities and Cultural Heritage Conference* (Bellville, Institute for Historical Research, University of Western Cape, South Africa, 1998). See also Richard Lee and Robert K. Hitchcock, 'African hunter-gatherers: history and the politics of ethnicity', in Connah, *Transformations in Africa*. Laurens van der Post wrote about the San in a number of popular and sentimental books, including *Venture to the Interior* (London, Chatto and Windus, 1952), *The Lost World of the Kalahari* (London, 1962), and *The Heart of the Hunter* (New York, Morrow, 1961).

[4] The historiography of national parks is substantial. See, for example, in this context, David Lawrence, 'Managing Parks/Managing "Country": joint management of Aboriginal owned protected areas in Australia', Research Paper No. 2, Parliamentary Research Service, 1996–97 as well as Roderick Nash, *Wilderness and the American Mind* (New Haven, CT, Yale University Press, 1982); Alfred Runte, *National Parks: The American experience* (Lincoln, NE, University of Nebraska Press, 1979); Jane Carruthers, *The Kruger National Park: A social and political history* (Pietermaritzburg, University of Natal Press, 1995).

[5] See Erica-Irene Daes, *Protection of the Heritage of Indigenous People*, UN Centre for Human Rights, Study Series 10 (New York, United Nations, 1997); also www.unesco.org/whc/nwhc.

[6] www.unesco.org/whc/nwhc.

[7] E.H.L. Schwartz, *The Kalahari and its Native Races: Being an account of a journey through Ngamiland and the Kalahari* (London, H.F. and G. Witherby, 1928), p. 131.

[8] W.J. Makin, *Across the Kalahari Desert* (London, Arrowsmith, 1929), pp. 16–17.

[9] See George B. Silberbauer, *Report to the Government of Bechuanaland on the Bushman Survey*

Australian Aborigines[10] and both groups were vilified in the same way. Until well after the First World War the San were described as 'the lowest form of man living', 'a relic from prehistoric times', a people content 'with a nest little better than what an animal could fashion'.They were also thought to be a 'dying race', a population incapable of assimilation, 'a race that is doomed'.[11] San were far lower on the scale of humanity than African blacks who owned livestock and had impressive technological and agricultural skills. Despite the negative image, however, aspects of the San lifestyle fascinated outsiders and in the interests of recording and conserving appropriate features of their 'culture' they were objects of study. But as the late nineteenth-century research of the Bleeks showed with relation to San traditions, stories and beliefs they recorded from /Xam informants, Westerners at that time had no intellectual tools with which to access the San set of systems which supported or nurtured their way of life.[12]

A comparison with Australia may elaborate this point. In 1985 Schrire and Gordon argued that 'it is precisely when one starts comparing policies adopted towards foragers and nomads that intriguing similarities and interesting differences [between Australia and southern Africa] which beg scholarly consideration start emerging'.[13] While the work of the late nineteenth-century anthropologists Baldwin Spencer and Francis Gillen[14] was successful in publicising aspects of central Australian Aboriginal culture, they were unable to capture the immensely strong attachment of small Aboriginal groups to 'country'. Some modern anthropologists are gaining a better understanding by analysing Aboriginal Australia as a biocentric culture whose cosmology is entirely landscape-based.[15] 'Country' brings people into existence, it is integral to their 'being'.[16] 'Country' is responsible for their conception, their 'dreaming' and their traditional law. Land is therefore 'Nourishing Terrain'[17] and there is a reciprocal duty to care for it and keep it alive.

---

[9] (cont.) (Gaborone, Government Printer, 1963), p. 131; and Makin, *Across the Kalahari Desert, passim.*

[10] Schwartz, *Kalahari*, p. 144; B.C. Cotton (ed.), *Aboriginal Man in South and Central Australia.* Part 1 (Adelaide, Govnerment Printer, 1966), p. 47. G.M. Theal, in *The Yellow and Dark-Skinned People of Africa South of the Zambezi* (London, S. Sonnenschein & Co. Ltd, 1910) stated that W.H.L. Bleek had considered the Bushmen to be related to the Aboriginal people of Australia.

[11] Schwartz, *Kalahari*, pp. 147, 149; Makin, *Across the Kalahari Desert*, p. 28.

[12] W.H.I. Bleek, *Report of Dr Bleek concerning his researches in the Bushman language and customs* (Cape Town, Government Printer, 1873); *Brief account of Bushman folklore and other texts* (London, Trübner, 1875); W.H.I, Bleek and L.C. Lloyd, *Specimens of Bushman Folklore* (London, G. Allen & Co. 1911); D.F. Bleek, *The Mantis and his Friends* (Cape Town, T.M. Miller, 1924); L.C. Lloyd, *A Short Account of Further Bushman Material Collected* (London, Nutt, 1889).

[13] C. Schrire and R. Gordon, (eds), *The Future of Former Foragers: Australia and Southern Africa* (Cambridge, MA, Cultural Survival Inc., 1985).

[14] Baldwin Spencer and F.J. Gillen, *Across Australia* (London, Macmillan and Co., 1912); *The Northern Tribes of Central Australia*, 2nd edn (Oosterhout, 1969); Sir Baldwin Spencer, *Wanderings in Wild Australia*, 2 vols (London, Macmillan & Co., 1928); S.R. Morton and D.J. Mulvaney, *Exploring Central Australia: Society, the environment and the 1894 Horn expedition* (Chipping Norton, NSW Surrey, Beatty and Sons, 1996); D.J. Mulvaney and J.H. Calaby, *"So Much that is New": Baldwin Spencer, 1860–1929, A biography* (Carlton, Vic., Melbourne University Press, 1985).

[15] Deborah Bird Rose, 'Exploring an Aboriginal Land Ethic', *Meanjin* 47, 3 (Spring 1988), p. 383.

[16] See, for example, Rose, 'Exploring an Aboriginal Land Ethic'; Deborah Bird Rose, *Nourishing Terrains: Australian Aboriginal views of landscape and wilderness* (Canberra, Australian Heritage Commission, 1996); Tim Rowse, 'Aboriginals as historical actors: evidence and inference', *Historical Studies* 22, 87 (October 1986), pp. 176–98.

[17] Rose, *Nourishing Terrains*. Also, Richard Baker, *Land is Life: From bush to town, the story of the Yanyuwa people* (St Leonards, Allen and Unwin, 1999).

Historical, anthropological and ethnographical studies are unclear on whether the southern African San have had a similar relationship to 'place'. Certainly, there are clues in comments, for example, that they use particular waterholes, that they are 'territorial',[18] or Dyer's remark that unless San indigenous biological knowledge continues to be utilised, the community will 'lose its intimate contact with nature and in the end its very identity'. Comments such as 'the land does not just belong to them ... they also belong to the land' are made, but what this really means is not elaborated in any detail[19] and no further information is forthcoming from modern general works like the *Cambridge Encyclopedia of Hunters and Gatherers.*[20] But from modern fieldwork and scholarship it seems that, while the overlap between foragers and herders is complex, the San were transhumant communities who were intimately involved with a particular home range which fed and shaped their social and economic relationships, and perhaps their spirituality as well. San studies are fraught with academic arguments, many of which owe their intensity to South Africa's racially divided past and to the part that anthropology and ethnography played in buttressing apartheid. For instance, the well known 'Great Kalahari Bushman Debate' rages still over the extent to which San should be regarded as a cultural unity or a proletarianised society.[21] However, contesting ideologies of material and ethnographic influences on the San way of life have taken on a different cast in post-apartheid South Africa because of an unexpected return of the respectability of ethnic and 'tribal' language and the equally unexpected burgeoning of Coloured identity politics together with the voluntary adoption of ethnic labelling. Much of the new discourse does not apply to San politics in Botswana or Namibia because the context is different. It is not the aim here to engage in this debate, but only to explore the relationship between the small Khomani San group and the Kalahari Gemsbok National Park in South Africa and to suggest comparisons with Uluṟu – Kata Tjuṯa National Park in central Australia. The internal politics of the Khomani San (who claim to be the only surviving indigenous San group in South Africa), as well as an analysis of the complicated 'tribal' or 'ethnic authenticity' involved, is well explained by Robins.[22]

The San of the Northern Cape (the southern San) were first studied by German philologist and theologian Wilhelm Bleek and his sister-in-law Lucy Lloyd in Cape Town. As is well known, they collected folklore and traditional beliefs from a small group of /Xam prisoner informants who were permitted to serve out their sentences in the Bleek household so that their language could be deciphered in an academic manner and committed to paper.[23] In 1911, a year after the Union of South Africa was

[18] F.C. Eloff, 'The Kalahari Ecosystem', *Koedoe* Supplement (1984), p. 18; see also Schrire and Gordon, *Future of Former Foragers*, p. 30 and H.J. Deacon and J. Deacon, *Human Beginnings in South Africa: Uncovering the secrets of the Stone Age* (London, Alta Mira Press, 1999), pp. 132, 135.

[19] R. Story, *Some Plants used by the Bushmen in Obtaining Food and Water.* Botanical Survey Memoir No. 30 (Pretoria, 1958); A. Barnard, 'Problems in the construction of Khoisan ethnicities', in Bank, *Khoisan Identities and Cultural Heritage Conference*, p. 54.

[20] R.B. Lee and R. Daly (eds), *The Cambridge Encyclopedia of Hunters and Gatherers* (Cambridge, CUP, 1999).

[21] Andrew B. Smith, 'The Kalahari Bushmen debate: Implications for archaeology in southern Africa', *South African Historical Journal* 35 (1996), pp. 1–15 is a good summary.

[22] Steven Robins, 'Land struggles and the politics and ethics of representing "Bushman" history and identity', *Kronos* (26 August 2000), pp. 56–75.

[23] Sigrid Schmidt, 'The relevance of the Bleek/Lloyd folktales to the general Khoisan traditions', in J. Deacon and T.A. Dowson (eds), *Voices from the Past: /Xam Bushmen and the Bleek and Lloyd Collection*

established, the first formal steps towards preserving San culture were taken with the passing of the Bushman Relics Protection Act.[24]

In the early years of the twentieth century no study was undertaken to establish how many San groups lived in the Northern Cape and what their community structures were. Few people visited the region and its aridity prevented economically viable settlement. Much of it had been declared a game reserve – the Namaqualand Game Reserve (102 000ha) in 1903 and the Gordonia Game Reserve in 1908 (20 725 sq km) – simply because, as was frequently the case in South Africa and elsewhere, no better use for the land could be devised.[25] The area around Kenhardt and along the Orange River had been surveyed into farms around the turn of the century but the vast majority of them remained vacant because of the lack of water. But this did not mean that there were no future prospects. On the contrary, there were schemes and dreams of transforming this landscape. With firm belief in the power of humanity to conquer nature, in 1913 Macdonald declared the area to be 'eminently suited to colonization', requiring only a 'sturdy race of British immigrants' to bring it to life. In glowing terms, MacDonald described its potential in wildlife, the likelihood of discovering diamonds, the availability of Coloured labour and the improvements in methods of 'dry farming'. He even advocated altering the climate by growing selected Australian tree species to attract rain. Anything, it seemed, was possible.[26] This way of thinking continued into the 1940s. In 1945 the South African Minister of Lands, A.M. Conroy, and a group led by L.A. Mackenzie, the South African Director of Irrigation, spent a month travelling from the Victoria Falls to Upington, cogitating on the spread of the desert and discussing ways of restoring water to the dried-up salt lakes of the Kalahari and bringing water into South Africa through a system of canals linking dry riverbeds.[27]

The Gordonia Game Reserve was no more than a name for a remote part of the Northern Cape. In the fervour of Union after 1910 national park rhetoric began to supersede 'game reserve' language and a national park in the Northern Cape was mooted in 1913.[28] However, the First World War intervened and the area was strategically important as the border between South Africa and German South West Africa. During the war there were army and police patrols and a number of boreholes were sunk along the Nossob and the Auob Rivers to water horses and camels. Once hostilities had ended and thinking that the boreholes would attract settlers, the west bank of the Nossob was divided into large farms, but whites were reluctant to settle in such a hostile environment and it was consequently reserved for Coloureds.[29]

The first National Parks Act was passed in South Africa in 1926. For political reasons that legislation was limited to the establishment of the Kruger National Park but the law did make provision for more national parks to be established at a later date.

---

[23] (cont.) (Johannesburg, Witwatersrand University Press, 1996), p. 101.

[24] A. Hall and A. Lillie, 'The National Monuments Council and a policy for providing protection for the cultural and environmental heritage', *South African Historical Journal* 29 (1993), pp. 102–17.

[25] J.A. Pringle, *The Conservationists and the Killers* (Cape Town, T.V. Bulpin, 1982), pp. 69–74.

[26] William Macdonald, *The Conquest of the Desert* (London, T.W. Laurie Ltd, 1913), pp. vii, 5, 37, 44, 77, 86, 95.

[27] L.A. Mackenzie, *Report on the Kalahari Expedition, 1945 (Being a Further Investigation into the Water Resources of the Kalahari and their Relationship to the Climate of South Africa)* (Pretoria, Government Printer, 1946).

[28] Macdonald, *Conquest of the Desert*, p. 173.

[29] A.J. Clement, *The Kalahari and its Lost City* (Cape Town, Longmans, 1967), p. 53.

This came about in 1931 when three were proclaimed, one of which was the Kalahari National Park, its name altered by a Senate amendment to the Kalahari Gemsbok National Park. According to the official account of the National Parks Board, the Kalahari park owed its existence to the enthusiasm of Piet Grobler, Minister of Lands in Hertzog's government, who had gone to the area on a hunting trip and was extremely impressed with it.[30] The 'sturdy race of British settlers' had never materialised and the area was populated by Afrikaans-speaking families with whom Grobler, as a staunch Afrikaner nationalist, had cultural and political rapport. The 1931 Kalahari Gemsbok National Park was established from parts of the old Cape provincial Gordonia Game Reserve and private farmland.[31] It was not open to visitors. Not only was it far off the beaten track from a tourist point of view, but there were no rest-camps or other facilities. A warden was appointed, one of the local landowners, Johannes le Riche. In time, the Le Riche family came to be the dynastic wardens of the Kalahari Gemsbok National Park, their efforts highly praised by the National Parks Board and the subject of a book.[32] One of the objectives of the Kalahari Gemsbok National Park had been Minister Grobler's 'explicit wish that the park should act as refuge for the Bushmen to save them from extinction'.[33] When white settlers had spurned the Nossob farms after the First World War, Coloured settlement had been encouraged, and for the new national park this 'posed a problem'. However, a land swap was carried out which moved the Coloureds further south. Initially, small groups of San continued to live in the national park and were tolerated as long as their presence was minimal.

Although park management was limited to the warden's anti-poaching efforts, and scientific wildlife studies and visitor amenities were lacking, the Kalahari Gemsbok National Park transformed the conservation landscape of the Kalahari arid zone. In 1935 the park expanded with the addition of a number of farms. Moreover, in 1938, at the request of South Africa, the Bechuanaland colonial authorities proclaimed a game reserve about 40km wide on their side of the Nossob and gave it to South Africa to administer. Little interest was taken in the San residents of the Kalahari Gemsbok National Park, and the records indicate that they were only occasionally encountered or lured with tobacco.[34] This official indifference was brought to public attention in 1936 during the Empire Exhibition when Donald Bain (a Kalahari landowner) launched a campaign to save these 'living fossils'. A number of San people were exhibited as the 'last living remnants of a fast dying race'.[35] There was no state policy regarding their welfare. Should these people be 'preserved' in reservations or assimilated? In the League of Nations in 1939, South Africa stated that assimilation into 'other tribes' was

---

[30] P. van Wyk and E.A.N. le Riche, 'The Kalahari Gemsbok National Park, 1931–1981', in G. de Graaff and D. Janse van Rensburg (eds), Supplement to *Koedoe* 1984, *Proceedings of a symposium on the Kalahari Ecosystem*, p. 22.

[31] *Debates of the House of Assembly*, 5 May 1931. See also Pringle, *Conservationists and the Killers*, pp. 69–74.

[32] The wardenship of the Kalahari Gemsbok National Park was passed down through the Le Riche family; see Hannes Kloppers, *Gee my 'n Man* (Pretoria, Afrikaner Press, 1970) and van Wyk and le Riche, 'The Kalahari Gemsbok National Park, 1931–1981'.

[33] Van Wyk and le Riche, 'The Kalahari Gemsbok National Park, 1931–1981', pp. 24–5.

[34] *Ibid.*, p. 25.

[35] *Bushmen of the Southern Kalahari* edited by J.D. Rheinallt Jones and C.M. Doke appeared in 1937 (Johannesburg, Witwatersrand University Press); also Leslie Witz, ' 'n Fees vir die oog: Looking in on the 1952 Jan van Riebeeck Tercentenary Festival Fair in Cape Town', *South African Historical Journal* 29 (1993), pp. 19–27.

being encouraged,[36] but reserves were also being discussed. Using the analogy of wildlife reserves, it was argued that while the Kruger National Park had successfully protected animals and might be a good precedent for saving the San, one could not 'ignore several major and vital differences between man and beast' which made a San reserve impossible.[37] Already they were acculturated, it was argued, many were addicted to alcohol, and criminality (particularly petty offences) was rife. Writing after his visit to the district in the mid-1930s, author Lawrence Green observed of the San that

> large areas of his desert have been cut up, surveyed, proclaimed as game reserves or ... handed over to ranchers. It was inevitable, but for the Bushman it was a tragedy. Meat he must have; yet when he trails a gemsbok bravely and brings it down within the area of a police patrol, he cannot feast in peace. The unknown horrors of prison await him – prison, where so many Bushman have languished and died like wild creatures in a zoo.[38]

In the event, in 1941 a San reserve of some 12 000ha was established next to the national park because the 'Union Government has now realised that these little humans deserve the protection already given to the animals, and a Bushman reserve has been created where they can live their own lives'. Thus, whenever a San family or group within the national park was not compliant, they were evicted into this reserve.[39] Non-compliance, for warden le Riche, included not being 'traditional', having 'mixed' rather than 'pure Bushman blood', and generally acting in a manner which indicated modernisation, arguments which resonate even today.[40] One eviction story has been told by Khomani San leader Regopstaan Kruiper, who remembered that the park warden said that the group hunted too often and with too many dogs, so the dogs were summarily shot, the people given rations and instructed to leave the park.[41]

Warden le Riche had a free hand in the Kalahari Gemsbok National Park. Ideas of ecological conservation were in their infancy and the warden's tasks were to patrol the park, prevent poaching and ensure that antelope numbers grew. Because of its size and the difficulties of transport, this was extremely difficult. After 1938, when le Riche had authority over the Bechuanaland side of the Nossob, the Coloured people who lived there were evicted and poaching apparently diminished.[42] The year 1953 was a landmark in the administration of the Kalahari Gemsbok National Park. After a general investigation into allegations of corruption and maladministration in the National Parks Board, its organisational structure was changed. With authority centralised in Pretoria and Afrikaner affirmative action under way, the development of the Kalahari Gemsbok National Park was prioritised. Rest-camps and proper roads were constructed, and the park was fenced to exclude the Coloured and San community at Mier. There was, however, no firm policy about removing all the San from the park, and some continued

---

[36] Robert Gordon, *The Bushman Myth: The making of a Namibian underclass*, (Boulder, CO, Westview Press, 1992), p. 149.

[37] Frank Debenham, *Kalahari Sand* (London, G. Bell, 1953), pp. 149–50.

[38] Lawrence G. Green, *Where Men Still Dream* (Cape Town, H. Timmins, 1945), p. 166.

[39] *Ibid.*

[40] Chasca Twyman, 'Livelihood opportunity and diversity in Kalahari wildlife management areas, Botswana: Rethinking community resource management', *Journal of Southern African Studies* 26, 4 (2000): 783–806.

[41] Nicole Basson, 'The best parts of human nature', *Keeping Track* (August/September 1997), p. 52.

[42] Van Wyk and Le Riche, 'The Kalahari Gemsbok National Park, 1931–1981', p. 26.

to live inside it. But those who remained were increasingly regarded as 'unco-operative' and their increased demands were resented. They wanted to keep dogs, to hunt, to have suitable accommodation, and they did not, apparently, want to work. Indeed, 'hulle wou 'n aardse paradys hê' [they wanted a paradise on earth]. They were their 'own worst enemies', 'interbreeding' and even losing their languages. Le Riche had wanted them to provide a tourist attraction and was incensed that they refused to wear traditional dress.[43]

For these reasons, the San were either evicted from the park or left voluntarily as their survival options diminished. Moreover, the years after the 1960s saw increased scientific studies of the arid landscape, while the role of humans in this fascinating ecosystem and the cultural heritage of people and ethnobiology were ignored.[44] While the Kalahari Gemsbok National Park became scientifically managed and visitor numbers grew, the San on the periphery became increasingly marginalised, im-poverished and alienated from the landscape that was once their total economic, social and spiritual sustenance.

As I have argued for other national parks in South Africa, they are divisive institutions and, as shown above, this is certainly true of the Kalahari Gemsbok National Park. However, in 1994 with the reconstruction of a 'new' nation it became policy that many apartheid evils would be redressed. Unlike Australia where land claims are based on traditional ownership and can apply to the earliest times of white settlement, land claims in South Africa relate to the restitution of rights in land which were lost as a result of racially based legislation after the passing of the 1913 Natives Land Act.[45] The land restitution process, however, has given publicity and a high political profile to a number of claimants and the San have used the opportunity to bolster their land claims with arguments about their status as 'indigenous people', a category set up in opposition to African blacks or settler whites.[46] Certainly for the San, land claims have a meaning wider than economic empowerment or compensation for apartheid. In their case, land claims may become a means by which 'both the dominant groups of pastoralists' can 'come to terms with their early past treatment of the San'. This has included attempts at 'ethnic cleansing'[47] and a marginalisation under apartheid which even denied the San any kind of separate group existence.[48]

While land claims in South Africa have at their legal core issues around restitution and economic empowerment, they are being creatively used by certain claimants to construct identity and cultural difference, as is being done in Australia. The Khomani San claim over two areas – one outside the national park and one within it – was submitted in September 1995. The Khomani San had an opportunity to publicise the claim and themselves in 1997 at a conference entitled 'Khoisan identities and cultural heritage' held at the University of the Western Cape. At this meeting, the land claim

---

[43] Kloppers, *Gee My 'n Man*, pp. 188–90.
[44] See the following issues of *Koedoe* 2 (1959); 8 (1965); 14 (1971); 16 (1973); 19 (1976); 20 (1977); 21 (1978); 25 (1982); 26 (1983); 27 (1984) for examples.
[45] *Restitution of Land Rights Act*, 22 of 1994 and *Land Restitution and Reform Laws Amendment Act*, 63 of 1997.
[46] C. Pietersen, 'Miscast: negotiating Khoisan history and material culture', *South African Historical Journal* 35 (1996): 135–9.
[47] *The Natal Witness*, 23 March 1999.
[48] This may, of course, change (somewhat ironically) if San political demands are subsumed within Coloured identity politics.

was linked with reviving and teaching the Khomani San language and with strategic political alliances around Coloured identity issues.[49] Negotiations around the land claims during 1997 and 1998 revitalised and cemented communities, while attracting considerable media coverage at home and abroad.[50] At first the National Parks Board resisted the land claim. Initially they disputed whether the group had indeed lived within the Kalahari Gemsbok National Park. Subsequently the group's identity was questioned and arguments were raised that an 'indigenous people' was a non-constitutional and meaningless phrase.[51] However, the claim had particular political resonance in Cape provincial politics and it received governmental support. The Khomani San were courted by politicians, who promised in 1998 that !Kabe would be taught in schools and become one of the official languages of the Northern Cape. In addition, the Khomani were promised that 11 February each year would be declared a public holiday, National Bushman Day.[52]

After some years of negotiations, in March 1999 the land claim was settled with publicity which stressed restored dignity and public apology for past wrongs. The following month the Transfrontier Park was established, having been delayed until the land claim was finalised.[53] As has been mentioned, the claim was in two parts and was settled by buying out farms south of the national park (for R15 million) and by giving the community some 25 000ha within the park itself. The national park land was immediately leased back to the state to be administered by the South African National Parks. The power of the new owners as co-managers has not yet been clarified. If they use their co-management effectively and aggressively, it may well raise the political and cultural profile of the San to an internationally significant level.[54] In this regard, they would do well to take their example from Australia, for this is what has occurred in the case of Uluru – Kata Tjuta.[55] From the outset community members there dominated the national park's Board and their traditional land utilisation practices have become part of the Plan of Management.[56] In addition, the Aboriginal stake in some of Australia's national parks has begun to impinge on Australian national consciousness more generally in terms of reverence for 'place'.

[49] Group for Environmental Monitoring, *People and Parks* 9 (Summer 1997/1998), p. 3. During the Khoisan identities conference of July 1997, speaker Petrus Vaalbooi (political rival of Dawid Kruiper for leadership of the Khomani San) apologised for giving his short address in Afrikaans and pleaded for the San dialect to be taught in schools. It is heartbreaking, he said, to be 'ontneem van ons taal, van ons identiteit en van ons grond' and he hoped that the conference would result in recapturing all three. He recounted how he had wanted to join the South African defence forces, but had been refused because he had mixed parentage and therefore a questionable identity: 'My pa is 'n hottentot en my ma is 'n boesman gebore', Bank, *Khoisan Identities and Cultural Heritage Conference*, pp. 10–11.

[50] Group for Environmental Monitoring, *People and Parks* 9 (Summer 1997/1998); *The Star*, 19 August 1997; *Sunday Independent*, 31 August 1997 and 29 March 1998; *Sunday Telegraph*, 9 November 1997. *The Citizen*, 14 January 1997 reported on how San living near Namibia's Etosha National Park, following the South African example, had demanded that Etosha be returned to them and were dispersed with teargas.

[51] *Sydney Morning Herald*, 13 February 1999.

[52] *Sunday Independent*, 15 February 1998.

[53] *Peace Parks* 1, 1999. Once the claim had been settled, San involvement was an asset to the new Peace Park because international tourists would, apparently, be particularly interested.

[54] *Sydney Morning Herald*, 13 February 1999. Report on interview with Dawid Kruiper and others.

[55] Apparently, some years ago, a group of San did pay a visit to Uluru.

[56] Department of the Environment, Sport and Territories, *Renomination of Uluru – Kata Tjuta National Park by the Government of Australia for Inscription on the World Heritage List* (Canberra, 1994).

This is entirely possible for South Africa as well, for in the northern Cape a tourist industry had developed around the Khomani San (who, in their exile from the Kalahari had been relocated to Kagga Kamma, a tourist farm in the Cederberg area), who 'paint animal figures, sing traditional songs and, when the moon is full, dance around the campfire with flaming eyes and waving limbs ... more business than pleasure, a kind of cute ethnic attraction for wide-eyed first-worlders'.[57] Such activities may well become a regular routine in the Kalahari Gemsbok National Park and may graduate from 'cute ethnic attraction' to 'traditional sacred ritual'. Plans to launch an eco-tourism venture have been announced by leader Dawid Kruiper, who at the same time denounced as fraudulent the Kagga Kamma dancers who had replaced his group.[58]

The place of ethnicity in the twenty-first-century world is hotly debated. Recapturing hidden histories is a major pursuit of historical and anthropological investigation, and it is clear that these studies almost inevitably lead to the 'birth of new ethnicities'.[59] Many multicultural polities are fracturing, but while the current politics of South Africa and Australia try to create a 'rainbow' nation – separate parts constituting a beautiful whole – it needs to be emphasised that nationality is merely an 'idea', not a discrete reality.[60] Some of the nation-building has been predicated on shared space. But there is a view that the two contrary impulses of the global village and the rebirth of regionalism, threaten nationality and demand its reconsideration.[61] In many respects recent developments in South Africa and Australia have reopened the frontier on both continents. South Africa has begun to grapple with how to homogenise disparate ethnic and class elements after a divided past. Australia is finding its past anew, giving people of Aboriginal or mixed heritage reason to pride themselves on their ancestry and giving them dignity and history. Many meetings in Australia begin with paying homage and respect to – even apologising to – the people who once inhabited the 'country' in which the gatherings occur. But San sub-nationalism worries those who aim for ethnic and national cohesion in the wake of a divided past.[62]

Successful claims against national parks create a particularly important international arena for the construction of cultural dominance because ownership of parks may enhance the power of smaller communities within the larger whole and integrate precolonial cultures as powerful voices within the larger national polity. Dispossession relates to the loss of control and use of land, but it is also linked to a deprivation of political sovereignty and consequently a loss of cultural integrity, language and cultural connections;[63] possession is an avenue to reclaiming all of these.[64] But national parks are sacred sites to other groups as well, so the issue is highly charged. Much of the

[57] Connah, *Transformations in Africa*, p. 32; *Sunday Times*, 31 May 1998. See also Sarah Nuttall and Carli Coetzee, *Negotiating the Past: The making of memory in South Africa* (Cape Town, OUP, 1998), p. 135; and Bank, *Khoisan Identities and Cultural Heritage Conference. Sunday Times*, 31 March 1991 documented the move to Kagga Kamma of Kruiper's group.

[58] *The Star*, 13 March 1997 'Regopstaan Kruiper dies at 96. Last indigenous San group surviving in South Africa'. *Sunday Independent*, 15 February 1998; *The Star*, 24 September 1998; *Natal Witness*, 23 March 1999; SABC Television, 50/50, 27 May 1999; *The Star*, 1 July 1999; *Sunday Times*, 14 May 2000.

[59] Connah, *Transformations in Africa*, pp. 35–6.

[60] W. Hudson and G. Bolton, eds, *Creating Australia: Changing Australian history*, (St Leonards, Allen and Unwin, 1997), p. 13.

[61] G. Seddon, *Landprints: Reflections on place and landscape* (Cambridge, CUP, 1998), p. 127.

[62] Robins, 'Land struggle', pp. 56–75.

[63.] For a full debate, see Susan Dodds, 'Justice and indigenous land rights', *Inquiry* 41, 2 (1998).

[64.] See Nuttall and Coetzee, *Negotiating the Past*, pp. 128–9 and p. 182.

argument as to why many national parks are sacred sites for settlers links up with the role of landscape in actively creating their national identity around their own 'place'.[65] The 'veld' is a strong evocation in the white settler culture of South Africa. A common affection for and attachment to the land bonded white South Africans, and this was nurtured by the creation of national parks which made that landscape accessible. Love of landscape or identity with it does not have to be expressed in precisely the same way. But the question here is the following: if values in places are held by discrete cultural traditions, to what extent can they be shared? Indeed, one might question, as Isabel McBryde has done, whether it is ethically desirable that they should be shared.[66] It may be inescapable that communities play out their separate destinies within a certain landscape and that there is no need for them to coalesce.

In the Western world, national parks are frequently the spearhead of landscapes of the 'nation' – 'naturalistic nationalism' as Eric Kaufmann calls it.[67] In South Africa this has certainly been the case with the Kruger National Park whose history has closely mirrored the country's political history. In terms of the restitution process, state land is easier (and often less expensive) to return to the dispossessed than is private land, and in Australia Aboriginal people are using national parks to spearhead campaigns for native title. Indeed, the very wording of the Native Title Act directly encourages Aboriginal people to make claims on parks.[68] The most widely publicised successful land claims in South Africa have also been those against national parks and the high profile these claims have received in the national and international press is directly related to the importance of national parks in the international psyche.

Until recently, national park landscapes minimised differing cultural heritage values because the built environment was absent and no resident communities were allowed. They epitomised 'nature' as national symbol and their purpose was to protect aspects of the common landscape, making it available to all. That they are now contested, and indeed *owned* by what can be regarded as ethnic communities, marks an enormous shift in national park policy. Land ownership in South Africa has been determined on a racial basis, and the interesting debate is whether national parks, once having been divisive institutions when owned by the 'white nation' as public property,[69] become more or less divisive when they have been formally parcelled out and given by the state to other population groups.[70]

[65] Thomas R. Dunlap, 'Australian nature, European culture: Anglo Settlers in Australia', *Environmental History Review* 17, 1 (1993), pp. 25–48.

[66] Isabel McBryde, '"Dream the impossible dream"? Shared heritage, shared values, or shared understanding of disparate values', Paper presented at ICOMOS Conference of Shared Heritage, Darwin, December 1993; also Isabel McBryde, '"To know the place for the first time": Consideration of diverse values for an Australian World Heritage Site', in S. Cantacuzuno (ed), *Scientific Journal Articles of Members* (Paris, ICOMOS, 1994), pp. 34–44.

[67] Eric Kaufman, '"Naturalizing the nation": The rise of naturalistic nationalism in the United States and Canada', *Comparative Studies in Society and History* 40,4 (1998), pp. 666–95.

[68] Department of the Prime Minister and the Cabinet, *The Native Title Act 1993: What it does and how it works* (Canberra, 1994).

[69] See Jane Carruthers, 'Nationhood and national parks: Comparative examples from the post-imperial experience', in Tom Griffiths and Libby Robin (eds), *Ecology and Empire: Environmental history of settler societies* (Edinburgh, Keele University Press, 1995).

[70] See, for example, B. de Villiers, *Land Claims and National Parks: The Makuleke experience* (Pretoria, Human Sciences Research Council, 1999).

In Australia, though not yet in South Africa, Aboriginal owners can close off sections of the park and prevent the public from having access to them. In this way, Aboriginal cultures are kept within communities and visitors are excluded. And yet, paradoxically, it is by making statements about the privacy of knowledge and ceremony, that Aboriginal traditional culture is being disseminated. In many respects, 'the special status of Aborigines, which whites had imposed on Aborigines as a badge of ignominy and inferiority ... [has] ... become a source of racial pride'.[71] Under apartheid, all black South Africans were made to share an undignified cultural past. But now that the common white enemy has been marginalised, as many scholars have noted, ethnic tropes are changing and it is clear that the San are 'making something of a comeback'.[72] In Australia, the 'comeback' has already taken place. Aboriginal ethnicity at Uluru is displayed as an ongoing 'traditional' lifestyle, and great pride is taken in showing the visitor how, until recently, Aboriginal communities lived in a 'state of nature', surviving off berries, roots, grubs and reptiles, living in wurleys and keeping the 'dreamtime' alive. It is not yet certain that the San would wish to embrace 'voluntary primitivism' but in the changing circumstances of South Africa they may like to do so, and the national park would be an appropriate vehicle for it.[73]

There are, however, important distinctions between the Kalahari Gemsbok National Park and Uluru – Kata Tjuta. For example, the Anangu own Uluru and live in a village inside the park, but they have little to do with the profitable tourist condominium located outside. Aboriginal people do not want to be pawns in the tourist industry, but nor do they wish Ayers Rock Resort to reap all the economic benefits. They realise that tourism owes its prosperity to Aboriginal land.[74] For the national parks of South Africa, the compelling idea is that the communities which have had ownership restored to them will benefit directly from the economic wealth generated by tourism, and they will not, as a right, live inside the park. How viable this goal is, remains to be seen.

Concerns for the direction of nature conservation in the twenty-first century feed into this debate and into those around equity and the environment. This relates to the notion raised at the start of this paper, that national parks are cultural landscapes and within this paradigm of cultural geography they need, at intervals, to be redefined.

---

[71] Schrire and Gordon, *Future of Former Foragers*, p. 14.

[72] Connah, *Transformations in Africa*, p. 31; see 'Focus: Khoisan in South African History', *South African Historical Journal* 35 (1996), pp. 1–145 and Bank, *Proceedings of the Khoisan Identities and Cultural Heritage Conference*.

[73] Gordon, *The Bushman Myth*.

[74] See David Lawrence, *Kakadu: The Making of a National Park* (Melbourne, Melbourne University Press, 1999).

Index

267